Canada – An American Nation?
Essays on Continentalism, Identity,
and the Canadian Frame of Mind

Are Canadians so influenced by the United States that they lack a distinct identity? This question has preoccupied Canadians and Canadianists for years. *Canada – An American Nation?* is a compilation of Allan Smith's essays on the influence of American society on Canadian identity. Based on the notion that Canada can best be understood if viewed in relation to the United States, Smith explores the ways in which American influences have challenged Canada's cultural independence and asks whether Canada has maintained its own identity.

Canada – An American Nation? will be of interest to scholars and students of Canadian history, Canadian studies and Canadian nationalist thought.

ALLAN SMITH is associate professor of history, University of British Columbia.

Canada –
An American Nation?

Essays on Continentalism, Identity, and the Canadian Frame of Mind

ALLAN SMITH

McGill-Queen's University Press
Montreal & Kingston • London • Buffalo

© McGill-Queen's University Press 1994
ISBN 0-7735-1229-2 (cloth)
ISBN 0-7735-1252-7 (paper)

Legal deposit fourth quarter 1994
Bibliothèque nationale du Québec

Printed in Canada on acid-free paper

This book has been published with the help of a
grant from the Pacific Coast Research Group.

Canadian Cataloguing in Publication Data

Smith, Allan, 1941–
     Canada: an American nation?: essays on
     continentalism, identity and the Canadian frame of
     mind
     Includes bibliographical references and index.
     ISBN 0-7735-1229-2 (bound)
     ISBN 0-7735-1252-7 (pbk.)
     1. Canada – Civilization – American influences.
     2. Canada – Foreign relations – United States.
     3. United States – Foreign relations – Canada.
     4. Nationalism – Canada. I. Title.
     FC97.S54 1994   303.48'271073   C94-900408-1
     F1021.S54 1994

Contents

Canada – An American Nation?

1 Introduction: The Canadian Mind in Continental Perspective

Over the years a number of factors – changing ideological fashion, altering conceptions of the community's interest, a need to accommodate new social and economic realities, the sharp and agonized thrust towards self-examination precipitated by such crises as the failure of Meech Lake – have compelled historians, politicians, and observers of Canadian life to assemble the elements which they believe constitute that life in a constantly shifting array of patterns and designs. This display has sometimes involved making those elements coalesce in the form of an essentially British community dedicated to the preservation of monarchy and Parliament on the North American continent;[1] at other times under the aspect of a northern land of hardy beings more than capable of meeting challenge and difficulty;[2] at still others in the guise of a bilingual, bicultural society offering a lesson in statecraft and justice to the world;[3] and at even others as a mosaic of cultures, races, and ethnic groups whose capacity to co-exist gives a model to all mankind.[4] Capable, apparently, of endless combination and recombination, these accommodatingly adjustable entities seem forever at the mercy of the style and influences of the moment, altogether beyond capture within the confines of a lasting conception of nationality which is able to render each of them with exactitude at the same moment that it serves the purposes and commands the assent of the citizens who make up that nationality's most elusive and difficult parts.

As important however as flux and change have certainly been, they have not governed these matters in a wholly unqualified way. One approach to the comprehension and arrangement of the country's parts – that guided by the conviction that they can be understood in a particularly useful and informative manner by examining them in terms of their situation on the North American continent – has, in fact, been much in evidence for over a century.

This, it must immediately be added, is in no sense to say that the continental approach has inspired a sense of the country which has been fixed, rigid, and absolutely unchanging. Some of those operating within its confines have developed the view that Canada's position on the North American continent has made it, in J.W. Dafoe's celebrated phrase, an "American nation," indistinguishable in all important respects from its southern neighbour.[5] Others argue the different and more complex proposition that geographical, economic, and institutional determinants operating in the Canadian half of the continent have simultaneously contained the sway of American and continental influences and made possible construction of a country with a character and existence of its own.[6] Still others – they have been increasingly prominent since the coming of the Free Trade Agreement of 1989 – take a third road, seeing the country both as a community compelled to operate within limits established by its proximity to a great power and as a state able through judicious conduct of its affairs to manage its frequently trying but essentially tractable "Life with Uncle" in ways which are far from being to its disadvantage.[7]

The very fact, however, that the offspring of the approach present themselves in a number of forms underscores that the approach itself has provided a framework for analysis and discussion which in its capacity to elicit and sustain a variety of arguments is at once uncommonly fruitful and extraordinarily enduring. Merely, indeed, to look at the range of argument which has developed is to see how constant and regular a stimulant to the production of ideas that framework has been, for that range comprehends not simply those who have sought a more or less scholarly understanding of the Canadian situation but also those whose purposes have been explicitly political. And not only anti-imperialists of the early twentieth century such as Goldwin Smith or liberal autonomists of the inter-war period like Dafoe were able to work within its limits; so also could the left-wing nationalists of the 1960s and 1970s. They, to be sure, generally avoided casting their work in anything like the clear-cut kind of Canadian-American frame employed by Smith and Dafoe; their argument that Canadian life and experience – as things relatively open to evolution towards socialism – were worth preserving against ongoing American encroachment was, nonetheless, derived from an imaginative if not always rigorous comparison of Canada and the United States.[8] And that fact made it as clear as could be that even as that argument stood divided from its predecessors by virtue of the conclusion to which it led, it was united to them thanks to its sharing of the same basic assumption: that the country was best understood by considering it in relation to its southern neighbour.

An especially clear demonstration of the continental approach's capaciousness is offered – as this last point suggests – by its ability to embrace different methodological procedures. Identified for some time with the notion that Canada could be best understood by considering the play of continental and American influences upon it, that approach has in recent years come to be associated as well with the idea that comparing the country with its southern neighbour would do much to sharpen analysis of its central features. The tendency to move in this direction is, of course, illustrated not only by the continental approach's accommodation of the work of the socialist-nationalists noted above, but also – and more importantly – in virtue of the approach's comprehension of the comparative study carried out by students of literature, social values, and political culture. By moving, in Gad Horowitz's formulation, from a concern "to explain Canadian phenomena ... by identifying them as variations on a basic North American theme" to an effort to understand them "by contrasting them with American phenomena"[9] these investigators have, in fact, been able to refine understanding of several important aspects of Canadian life. Their work on literature, certainly, helped focus attention on a Canadian literary tradition which in its relative emphasis on a harsh and inhospitable landscape differed markedly from American identification of a generally benign and welcoming environment.[10] What these analysts accomplished in relation to the understanding of social values was perhaps even more critical in its elucidation of, and explanation for, the fact that Canadians were generally more conservative and accepting of authority than Americans;[11] and their argument that Canada's political culture was in its relative tolerance of conservatism and socialism more British and European than American in character provoked a debate of fundamental importance among students of that subject.[12] As significant, however, as all of this undoubtedly is in its own right, the important point about these arguments for the purposes of this discussion remains centred on what they demonstrate concerning the breadth and capacity to sustain innovation of the overall approach under which they have taken form. Clearly capable of domiciling a wide and ever-changing variety of argument and investigation, that approach seems to have grown more expansive and fertile with each passing year.

We are now – the point is obvious – in a position to appreciate the reasons for, as well as the fact of, the approach's longevity and appeal. Nothing, indeed, reveals more fully than its quite daunting capacity to embrace a variety of ways of thinking about the country why it has survived and prospered: consistently helpful in all sorts of changing circumstances, it has simply never failed to justify faith in its utility and relevance – nor does it show signs of doing so now.[13] Given, indeed, its continuing ability to be of service to scholars and nationalists alike, its obvious compatibility with change and adaptation, and its abiding competence in the production of stimulating and informative argument, there can be little doubt that it will continue to maintain just that sort of resistance to decline which has characterized it in the past.

This book locates itself squarely within this rich and venerable tradition. Its main purpose is to use the continental perspective as a kind of heuristic device, but it also – inevitably – employs that perspective in ways relevant for the nationalist. At the core of these essays is the view that Canada cannot be understood apart from its continental context; they refine that point by insisting that the dialectic between national and continental forces is a principal structuring element in the country's history. And – like much other commentary – they draw back from any suggestion that the consequence of considering all this is some concept of an "Americanized" Canada. Where this work differs from others – and this difference defines the specificity of its approach – is in the kind of emphasis it places on ideas, attitudes, and the character of the complex which at once shapes and is made up of these several phenomena.

The essential argument can be seen from the outset: by the early years of the twentieth century, essays two and three suggest, Canadian thinking was being affected by American ideas, attitudes, and preoccupations in ways that were both significant in themselves and fundamental to the penetration of other American influences. Evident enough in respect of what happened to particular formulations such as the Canadian concept of mission (essay two), this development could be seen with special clarity in the growth of a general disposition to understand Canada as a society chiefly intelligible in North American terms (essay three). But potent though the trend in this direction undoubtedly was, it did not go completely unchallenged. Countervailing influences were very much in existence, and, as an examination of Samuel Moffett's 1907 study of the forces making for continental integration shows (essay four), those influences were in fact strong enough to nullify argument that Canada – much less the Canadian mind – was becoming "Americanized" in some absolute and final way. Canadian culture might, to be sure, need special support in its efforts to withstand the American tide (essay five). But that it got that support, and that Canadians remained determined to ensure it would continue to receive it, became in itself a much insisted-upon sign of national difference and vitality.

Consideration of the myths and symbols by means of which Canadians have tried to aid understanding of their society's character, essays six and seven argue, offers especially graphic indication of the fact that they developed and maintained a capacity to comprehend that character in terms of their own devising. Canadians had, to be sure, certain difficulty managing this transaction, for the tendency to understand their community through use of the sort of classless, egalitarian, liberal, and New World language which was prevalent in the United States remained – *pace* Dafoe – strong. They were, nonetheless, able to identify key realities in Canadian experience – linguistic duality was the most critical of them – the effect of which was a definition of Canadian society in pluralist, essentially conservative terms of a sort that allowed metaphorical representation of that society – as a mosaic – distinguishable in basic ways from the assimilationist and conformitarian concept – the melting pot – being constructed in the United States (essay six). Efforts to frame a conceptualization of the character of Canadian society which would accommodate at least some of the centripetal tendencies in it continued, moreover, down a road altogether different from the one being followed by the Americans – until the gap between the two was narrowed in consequence of *American* moves to distance the United States from the concept of the melting pot and move closer to a pluralist understanding of the American character (essay seven). The basic pattern of difference was not, however, removed, and with the emergence of race and colour as critical issues in the business of nation maintaining, that reality became transparently clear (essay eight).

The fact that Canadians, far from being overwhelmed by American ideas or consumed by a sense of their society's similarity to its neighbour, retained a capacity to address national, regional, and social issues in ways largely unmediated by such notions offers what is perhaps the most telling demonstration of the extent to which they retained a kind of ideological autonomy. Even papers original-ly written to confront these issues have relevance for the argument being made here. For in profiling the ideas with which they are directly concerned, they make the point that articulation of those ideas by those who created them did not depend upon modes of discussion framed under the influence of, or, indeed, in ways simi-lar to, American conceptualizing. This of course is not to claim that such modes were *totally* absent from argument concerned with these issues. Clearly at work in the formation of ideas concerning the place of the individual in the shaping of Canadian society (essay twelve), traces of those ideas can even be seen in the thought of so imperialist and conservative a thinker as G.M. Grant (essay thirteen). More evident, however, was the fact that efforts to explain (and usually promote) the interests and character of the regions (essays nine, ten, and eleven) and to understand the nature of the country as a whole (essay thirteen) drew their central inspira-tion from sources which, whether British, European, or – as was increasingly the case – rooted in the exigencies of the Canadian situation itself, produced a body of thought and a style of com-prehension quite capable of ordering that part of the Canadian reality with which they were concerned. Further, these efforts dealt with Canadian concerns in accordance with principles which owed very little to any sense that Canada should be seen as American – or even North American – in character. This, in the end, was critical, for Canadians' capacity to operate in terms of assumptions framed independently of American influence showed perhaps more clearly than any other circumstance the limits of that influence.

A coherent pattern, it can thus be readily seen, may easily be extracted from these papers. Drawing that pattern out, moreover, not only clarifies a complicated state of affairs; thanks to what it makes clear about the relative strength of indigenous influences, nationalists as well as analysts find themselves in the presence of much that is worth having. But while – as is by now more than evi-dent – all of this makes that construct plainly a prize to be valued, that alone does not tell the reader all there is to know about the relevance of these papers. To consider their significance in those terms alone is in fact to leave an entire dimension unexplored. While such an exercise gets to grips with the character of their contribution to a grasp of the general reality as seen by an external observer, it does little to further understanding of the manner in which that reality was experienced by those whose only view of it was from within. Fortunately, to recognize this difficulty is to see the way to removing it: let us, accordingly, shift to a different position – adopt a new perspective – and by so doing move from what these papers suggest about the objective character of the complex they delineate to a consideration of what they reveal concerning the way in which the elements of that complex presented themselves to the actors in their midst.[14]

Central to the picture this new view reveals – and in seeing this we begin to get the measure of what considering it adds to our understanding – are flux, change, and uncertainty. Where, that is to say, our earlier vantage point gave us a picture of an ideological environment which – whether the actors functioning in it were aware of the fact or not – had a certain form, order, and overall coherence, our new, more subjective view, affording us a look at things from something akin to the position of those actors themselves, presents a vision of a much more arbitrary and capricious world, the changing circumstances of living in which compel those who do so to define themselves now in "North American" terms, then in "national" ones, at some other time in ways that are "regional," and at yet another moment in none of these.

Nor – and the importance of this point can hardly be exaggerated – is this all we get in consequence of this critical change of position. In assimilating the sense it gives us of what it is to be in the presence of a welter of ways of defining oneself, any one of which might at a given moment be in play depending upon the influences or preoccupations dominant in one's mind at that moment,[15] we become conscious of the fact – again from the actor's point of view – that this confusion of alternatives is not simply an important part of the ideological environment in which that actor functions: it *is* that environment, in its entirety and with no other elements present. Where, that is to say, we can see US actors in the US community enjoying access to ideas which, by defining them and their society in terms which are at once comprehensive and easy to grasp, permit them to think about themselves in ways which transcend the immediate and particular, we see no such readily-intelligible, over-arching ideas available to Canadians.[16] To observe this fundamentally important *lacuna*, moreover, is to be involved in something quite beyond a simple repetition of the old and familiar saw that Canadians lack an identity – at least of the classically nationalist sort. Thanks to the circumstances under which the observation is made, merely to carry it out is to get a substantial bonus, for in doing so we see (though we must now abandon the subjective perspective to do so) why the state of affairs to which it refers should exist. To register, that is, the absence of a nationalizing idea in Canada at the same moment that we remark the presence of one in the United States is – if we have any curiosity at all – to look for the conditions which might explain this difference. And to do that is to see in an instant that while Americans, historically speaking, possess the principal materials – a common language, shared values, etc. – necessary to the building of such an idea, Canadians, patently do not.[17] Indeed, not only do Canadians lack what is necessary to put together a totalizing idea of the classically nationalist sort so clearly evident in the United States; they have not even been able to cobble something together from what they *do* possess. Necessarily caught up in the business of day-to-day living, unable to get perspective on the situation in which they are involved, without the capacity to stand back and view matters from "outside," Canadians have neither the disposition nor the training to see the various definitions in terms of which they do at different times think as elements which might be "added up" to give a kind of composite identity which, however obviously the work of the *bricoleur*, might provide some mark of comprehensive and overall identification.[18] Canadians stand not simply at one but at two important removes from the sort of general, consolidating, and nationalist thinking about themselves which is so much in evidence in the United States.

To look at these essays in terms of what they reveal about the actors' world as those actors experience it thus yields as much that is helpful as did our earlier, more olympian view. Indeed, in giving us a sense of what is "missing" from those actors' minds as well as of what is very much present in them, that look confers upon us not one, or even two, but three things worth having. We see – by now very clearly – the flux and variety which confronts these people; we note – with an equal lucidity – their inability to fashion overriding and general concepts of a conventionally nationalist kind; and – just because all this is so clear – we understand why they live out their lives through the agency of notions about society and nation which are pragmatic, *ad hoc*, and a response to the needs of the moment: given the absence of alternative ways of thinking, faced – as actors in society always are – with the need to rationalize, argue, persuade, and co-opt, how can they do otherwise than function within the confines of this indeterminate, provisional, quintessentially post-modern frame of mind?[19]

We can, then, learn much from an attempt to consider these essays in terms of what they suggest about the ways in which actor and observer alike see and experience the ideological complex with which they are concerned – in terms, in Collingwood's language, of what they reveal concerning the "inside" as well as the "outside" of that complex. But in thus noting what we get from this kind of reading, we must not forget that it can operate only to enhance the meaning of things which have already been singled out for attention by virtue of the fact that the overall framework of analysis and discussion has given those things significance not possessed by phenomena deemed irrelevant by that same framework to the inquiry its selection defines and regulates. As important as may be the contemplation of "insides" and "outsides," the choice of framework remains vital to the carrying out of a fruitful inquiry. For unless that choice is "right," the inquiry it shapes will not involve investigators in considering the sort of data, argument, and theory likely to yield understanding of the phenomenon they seek to comprehend.

That the framework adopted here does involve investigators in attending to just these kinds of things seems clear. No one, to be sure, would claim that examination of the issues choosing that framework leads those investigators to confront says all there is to say about the nature of the terms in which Canadians have understood themselves and their society. Looking at American influence on the structure of Canadian thought, considering the character of national metaphors in Canada and the United States, and noticing the extent to which Canadians have retained a kind of ideological autonomy *does*, however, involve persons interested in seeing those terms in ways which, at a minimum, enlarge their understanding of them and of what is involved in grappling with them. That action thus allows this discussion to join other debate stimulated by the continental framework in testifying to the fruitfulness of the device which has engendered them both. Here, then, as elsewhere, framework and argument join to affirm each other's worth. Having now seen in summary why this should be so, let us turn to the lengthier demonstration of the point in what follows.

NOTES

1 This sense of its character was particularly evident in the decades following the American Revolution; in 1912 an observer was still prepared to see in Canada's history continuing proof of the relevance of the Burkean ideal – that history, he wrote, demonstrates

"the strength of an hereditary loyalty, [and] the value of a moderate
liberty evolving through precedent into practice"; and as late as 1963
a major work could be founded upon broadly similar principles. See
S.F. Wise, "God's Peculiar Peoples," in W.L. Morton, ed., *The Shield of
Achilles* (Toronto: McClelland and Stewart, 1968), 36–59; Castell
Hopkins, *The Story of Our Country* (Toronto: The John C. Winston Co.
Ltd., 1912), "Preface," ii; W.L. Morton, *The Kingdom of Canada: A
General History from Earliest Times* (Toronto: McClelland and Stewart,
1963).

2 For the history of this notion, see Carl Berger, "The True North
Strong and Free," in Peter H. Russell, ed., *Nationalism in Canada*
(Toronto: McGraw-Hill, 1966), 3–29.

3 "The country," noted one enthusiastic supporter of this idea in 1968,
"has not only survived as a nation but has managed also to thrive
during a hundred years of Confederation. Moreover, the two cultures have not only kept their identities but have also achieved a rare
form of coexistence." Richard H. Leach, "Introduction," in Richard
H. Leach, ed., *Contemporary Canada* (Toronto: University of Toronto
Press, 1968), 5.

4 John Murray Gibbon, *Canadian Mosaic: The Making of a Northern Nation* (Toronto: McClelland and Stewart, 1938); Howard Palmer, ed.,
Immigration and the Rise of Multiculturalism (Toronto: Copp Clark,
1975); Leo Driedger, ed., *The Canadian Mosaic* (Toronto: McClelland and Stewart, 1978); Jean Leonard Elliott, ed., *Two Nations,
Many Cultures: Ethnic Groups in Canada* (Toronto: Prentice-Hall,
1983).

5 The view that environment, culture, and technology have shaped a
single North American civilization in the character of which Canada
inevitably (and for better or – as observers such as George Grant
would have it – for worse) participates has, of course, been in evidence since the late nineteenth century. Goldwin Smith first gave it
systematic form; J.W. Dafoe added his considerable weight to the
argument; many of the contributions to the Carnegie series on
Canadian-American relations invested it with a certain scholarly
force (Canada and the United States, wrote James T. Shotwell in his
introduction to one of those contributions, have created "what one
might almost call a common citizenship of English-speaking North
America, a common sense of participation in the heritage of freedom."); Frank Underhill founded his vision of the country on it; and
– in a quite different spirit – George Grant did the same. See Goldwin Smith, *Canada and the Canadian Question* (Toronto: Hunter Rose,
1891); J.W. Dafoe, *Canada: An American Nation* (New York: Columbia
University Press, 1935); J.T.S., "Introduction," in J.B. Brebner and

M.L. Hansen, *The Mingling of the Canadian and American Peoples* (New Haven and Toronto: Yale University Press and Ryerson Press, 1940), vi; Frank Underhill, *In Search of Canadian Liberalism* (Toronto: Macmillan, 1960); George Grant, *Lament for a Nation* (Toronto: McClelland and Stewart, 1965) and *Technology of Empire* (Anansi, 1969).

6 For this view see H.A. Innis, *The Fur Trade in Canada* (New Haven: Yale University Press, 1930); D.G. Creighton, *The Commercial Empire of the St Lawrence* (Toronto: Ryerson, 1937); S.D. Clark, "The Canadian Community," in George Brown, ed., *Canada* (Berkeley and Toronto: University of California, University of Toronto Presses, 1950), 375–89, reprinted as "The Canadian Community and the American Continental System," in Clark's *The Developing Canadian Community* (Toronto: University of Toronto Press, 1962), 185–98; H.G.J. Aitken, "Defensive Expansionism: The State and Economic Growth in Canada," in H.G.J. Aitken, ed., *The State and Economic Growth* (New York: Social Science Research Council, 1959), 79–114.

7 The claim that Canada, its closeness to the United States notwithstanding, has a certain independence of movement whose maintenance is a function of the skill with which it handles its relationship with the United States has, not surprisingly, been advanced mostly by diplomatic historians, political scientists, and former practitioners of the foreign policy black arts. See Kenneth M. Curtis and John E. Carroll, *Canadian-American Relations: The Promise and the Challenge* (Lexington, MA and Toronto: D.C. Heath, 1983); Charles F. Doran, *Forgotten Partnership: US–Canada Relations Today* (Baltimore: Johns Hopkins University Press, 1984); Edelgard E. Mahant and Graeme S. Mount, *An Introduction to Canadian-American Relations* (Toronto: Methuen, 1984); William T.R. Fox, *A Continent Apart: The United States and Canada in World Politics* (Toronto: University of Toronto Press, 1985); and John W. Holmes, *Life with Uncle: The Canadian-American Relationship* (Toronto: University of Toronto Press, 1981). For comment on the rise and development of the diplomatic techniques which have been found most useful in the conduct of this difficult to manage enterprise, see Allan E. Gotlieb, *"I'll Be with You in a Minute, Mr. Ambassador": The Education of a Canadian Diplomat in Washington* (Toronto: University of Toronto Press, 1991).

8 The United States, they insisted, was liberal, capitalist, imperialist, and racist while Canada, by contrast, retained enough in the way of a separate consciousness (manifest partly in its class-based politics and partly in its adherence to the political economy tradition), a different tradition of economic and social development (evident in its statism), and a disinclination to be involved in power politics (seen

in the character of its general activity at the United Nations) to distinguish it from the United States and provide a foundation on the basis of which bulwarks could be erected against further penetration of American influence. Notions of this sort underpinned most – though not all – of the work published in such collections as Trevor Lloyd and Jack McLeod, eds., *Agenda 1970: Proposals for a Creative Politics* (Toronto: University of Toronto Press, 1968); Ian Lumsden, ed., *Close the 49th Parallel, etc.: The Americanization of Canada* (Toronto: University of Toronto Press, 1970); Gary Teeple, ed., *Capitalism and the National Question in Canada* (Toronto: University of Toronto Press, 1972); and R.M. Laxer, ed., *Canada, Ltd: The Political Economy of Dependency* (Toronto: McClelland and Stewart, 1973).

9 Gad Horowitz, "Conservatism, Socialism, and Liberalism in Canada: An Interpretation," *Canadian Journal of Economic and Political Science*, 32(2), May 1966, 141.

10 Even investigators whose frame of reference was not explicitly comparative seem to have had an American foil in mind. Margaret Atwood's *Survival: A Thematic Guide to Canadian Literature* (Toronto: Anansi, 1972) appears, for example, to have been conceived in opposition to the sort of view of American literature developed in such work as Henry Nash Smith, *Virgin Land: The American West as Symbol and Myth* (New York: Vintage, 1950); R.W.B. Lewis, *The American Adam: Innocence, Tragedy and Tradition in the Nineteenth Century* (Chicago: University of Chicago Press, 1964); and Perry Miller, *Nature's Nation* (Cambridge: Harvard University Press, 1967). Be that as it may, enough explicitly comparative work exists to make clear the importance of this approach. See, for example, Marcia B. Kline, *Beyond the Land Itself: Views of Nature in Canada and the United States* (Cambridge: Harvard University Press, 1970); and Ramsay Cook, "Imagining a North American Garden: Some Parallels and Differences in Canadian and American Culture," *Canadian Literature* 103(4), Winter 1984, 10–23. Other comparative work, it is worth noting, has suggested that the treatment certain authors have given landscape and nature in the two countries has tended to run along broadly parallel rather than divergent tracks. See John Lennox, "Dark Journeys: *Kamouraska* and *Deliverance*," *Essays on Canadian Writing*, 12, Fall 1978, 84–104, and Evelyn J. Hinz, "The Masculine/Feminine Psychology of American/Canadian Primitivism: *Deliverance* and *Surfacing*," in Robin W. Winks., ed., *Other Voices, Other Visions: An International Collection of Essays from the Bicentennial* (Westport, CT: Greenwood Press, 1978), 75–96. David Stouck, "Notes on the Canadian Imagination," *Canadian Literature*, Autumn 1972, 9–26, especially 9–10, offers some comment on the utility of the Canadian-

American comparison in the study of Canadian literature, while E.D. Blodgett, "The Canadian Literatures in a Comparative Perspective," *Essays on Canadian Writing*, 15, Summer 1979, 5–24, though mainly concerned with Canada and Quebec, does the same. For some examples of the range through which work of this general sort has been operating, see Claude T. Bissell, "Haliburton, Leacock, and the American Humorist Tradition," *Canadian Literature*, 39, Winter 1969, 5–19; Fraser Sutherland, "Hemingway and Callaghan: Friends and Writers," *Canadian Literature*, 53, Summer 1972, 8–17; Clara Thomas, "New England Romanticism and Canadian Fiction," *Journal of Canadian Fiction*, 2(4), 1973, 80–6; Thomas E. Tausky, "The American Girls of William Dean Howells and Sara Jeannette Duncan," *Journal of Canadian Fiction*, 4(1), 1975, 146–58; and Catherine McLay, "Ethel Wilson's Lost Lady: *Hetty Dorval* and Willa Cather," *Journal of Canadian Fiction*, 33, Winter 1981–82, 94–106.

11 Seymour Martin Lipset has been the principal influence in the making of this case. See his "Canada and the United States: A Comparative View," *Canadian Review of Sociology and Anthropology*, 1(6), 1964, 173–89 and "Value Differences, Absolute or Relative: The English-Speaking Dominions," in his *The First New Nation: The United States in Historical and Comparative Perspective* (Garden City: Anchor, 1967), 284–312. For a critical examination of that case, see Tom Truman, "A Critique of Seymour M. Lipset's Article, 'Value Differences, Absolute or Relative: The English-Speaking Democracies,'" *Canadian Journal of Political Science*, 4(4), 1971, 497–525. Lipset's most recent and most comprehensive presentation of his argument appears in his *Continental Divide: The Values of Institutions of the United States and Canada* (New York and London: Routledge, 1990). S.F. Wise and R.C. Brown, *Canada Views the United States: Nineteenth Century Political Attitudes* (Toronto: Macmillan, 1967) also contribute to this discussion. See, as well, David M. Potter, "A Commentary: Canada's Views of the United States as a Reflex of Canadian Values," in ibid., 121–30. For a look at these issues in relation to economic elites see Wallace Clement, *Continental Corporate Power: Economic Elite Linkages Between Canada and the United States* (Toronto: McClelland and Stewart, 1977), especially chapter eight, "The Economic Elite in Canada and the United States: Corporate, Ascriptive, and Social Characteristics," 215–50.

12 A debate which, though related by its concern with views of society to the discussion of social values just noted, was made distinct from that discussion by the degree of its concentration on the character of formal, organized, and explicit political thought and action in the two countries. See Kenneth McRae, "The Structure of Canadian His-

tory," in Louis Hartz, ed., *The Founding of New Societies* (New York: Harcourt, Brace, and World, 1964), 219–74; Horowitz, "Conservatism, Socialism, and Liberalism,"; David V.J. Bell, "The Loyalist Tradition in Canada," *Journal of Canadian Studies*, 5(2), 1970, 22–33; Kenneth McNaught, "Comment on Louis Hartz 'The Liberal Tradition,'" in John H.M. Laslett and Seymour Martin Lipset, eds., *Failure of a Dream?* (Garden City: Anchor, 1974), 408–20; S.F. Wise, "Liberal Consensus or Ideological Battleground: Some Reflections on the Hartz Thesis," Canadian Historical Association *Historical Papers*, 1974, 1–14; Gad Horowitz, "Notes on 'Conservatism, Liberalism, and Socialism in Canada;'" *Canadian Journal of Political Science*, 11(2), 1978, 383–99; and H.D. Forbes, "Hartz-Horowitz at Twenty: Nationalism, Toryism, and Socialism in Canada and the United States," *Canadian Journal of Political Science*, 20(2), 1987, 287–315. For a summary statement of Lipset's views on the linked problems of values and political culture – one that saw him revise his earlier arguments and move towards a mildly pan-North American assessment of the Canadian situation – see his "Radicalism in North America: A Comparative View of the Party Systems in Canada and the United States," *Proceedings and Transactions of the Royal Society of Canada*, 1976, ser. 4, vol. 14, 19–55.

13 There are, indeed, indications that yet another approach is taking shape within its confines. Strongly revisionist – though also recalling the "continentalist" arguments of an earlier day – this approach asserts that American influences didn't simply affect the character of "liberal," "democratic," and "progressive" politics and political culture in Canada; they had an impact on the more "conservative" initiatives and thinking often considered to be at the core of what is quintessentially "Canadian." Jane Errington thus argues that the ideology of the Tory elite in Upper Canada owed no small part of its character to the fact that such figures as John Strachan, Richard Cartwright, and Christopher Hagerman were familiar with and sympathetic to the central elements of the American Federalist tradition; Paul Romney develops the view that "conservative" features – the emphasis on the positive state particularly – of Canada's political and legal culture were in part a function of what he sees as the close relationship between the thrust toward responsible government and the "legalist," "majoritarian" tradition introduced by American immigrants (which in its turn interacted with the tendency of Canadians to understand the law in the instrumentalist, "American"-like way identified in the work of American legal historian James Willard Hurst); and Tina Loo, noticing a general tendency in mid-nineteenth century British Columbia to view the law "as an instrument of eco-

nomic development," identifies the legal culture of that jurisdiction in largely Hurstian terms. This neo-continentalist vision has, of course, implications for the claim that Canadian and American society are best understood by contrasting them with each other, but even if it develops in strength, its relative lack of utility in the understanding of what has happened in other areas of importance (those involving linguistic, cultural, and racial policy, for example) make it rather more likely that this view will complement than displace work done in light of that claim. See Jane Errington, *The Lion, The Eagle, and Upper Canada: A Developing Colonial Ideology* (Montreal: McGill-Queen's University Press, 1987); Paul Romney, "Reinventing Upper Canada: American Immigrants, Upper Canadian History, English Law and the Alien Question," in Roger Hall, William Westfall, and Laurel Sefton MacDowell, eds., *Patterns of the Past: Interpreting Ontario's History* (Toronto: Dundurn, 1988), 78–107; Romney's "From the Rule of Law to Responsible Government: Ontario Political Culture and the Origins of Canadian Statism," in Canadian Historical Association *Historical Papers*, 1988, 86–119, and, for a sharp attack on those who reject the argument that a Hurstian approach can be useful in the study of Upper Canada, Romney's "Very Late Loyalist Fantasies: Nostalgic Tory 'History' and the Rule of Law in Upper Canada," in Barry Wright, ed., *Canadian Perspectives on Law and Society* (Ottawa: Carleton University Press, 1988), 119–47; and Tina Loo, "'A Delicate Game': The Meaning of Law on Grouse Creek," *BC Studies*, 96 (Winter 1992–93), 41–65.

14 The obligation of social investigators to see what they are considering from the "inside," from the point of view of the actors in the process they are considering, as well as from the "outside," in terms of the character and meaning of that process as a whole, has, of course, been a subject of discussion since philosophers and social scientists first began to distinguish the "natural" from the "human" sciences. Weber, partly concerned with this important issue, and partly reacting against Durkheim's conception of a coercive social world, certainly emphasized (as Peter Berger reminds us) "the subjective meanings, intentions, and interpretations brought into any social situation by the actors participating in it ... [arguing that] this entire subjective dimension must be taken into consideration for an adequate sociological understanding." And at least since Dilthey, philosophers of history have supposed an understanding of what has happened in the historical world to involve consideration of the human actor's activities from the subjective as well as the objective point of view. But if Collingwood made the point very forcefully indeed – by specifying in so many words the historian's obligation to

understand the "inside" as well as the "outside" of the state of affairs under investigation, as well as by defining the historical enterprise as turning on *verstehen,* that is, on the historian's ability as a thinking, imagining being to understand past reality in something like the terms in which it was viewed by those living it – it remains true that social scientists have been most prominent in emphasizing the point. Weber himself noted the need to define sociology as "a science which attempts the interpretive understanding of social action [that is, understanding from the point of view of the actor] in order thereby to arrive at a causal explanation of its cause and effects [that is, one framed from the vantage point of a distanced, 'objective,' observer]." More recently, an anthropologist has written of his discipline's stress on "an equilibrium of involvement and detachment," and more recently still, a sociologist has insisted that while a search for the whole, "a quest for connectedness [is] central to the sociologist's task" it is also true that "in studying any social figuration one is well-advised to try placing oneself within the world of experience of the various groups of people who make up the figuration." The common sense – and now commonplace – point that one must try to operate in terms of a double perspective thus reveals itself, like many such points, to be the product of an interesting history and a good deal of theoretical effort – which, it should be noted, is still very much in train. See Peter L. Berger, *Invitation to Sociology: A Humanistic Perspective* (Harmondsworth: Penguin, 1966), 146; Wilhelm Dilthey, "The Understanding of Other Persons and their Expressions of Life," in Wilhelm Dilthey, *Descriptive Psychology and Historical Understanding,* trans. Richard M. Zaner and Kenneth L. Heiges, with an introduction by Rudolf A. Makkreel (The Hague: Martinus Nijhoff, 1977), 121–44; R.G. Collingwood, *The Idea of History* (New York: Oxford University Press, 1956), 213, 266ff.; Max Weber, *The Theory of Social and Economic Organization,* rev. and ed. Talcott Parsons, trans. Talcott Parsons and A.R. Henderson (London: William Hodge and Company, 1947), 80; Clyde Kluckhohn, "Common Humanity and Diverse Cultures," in Daniel Lerner, ed., *The Human Meaning of the Social Sciences* (Cleveland and New York: Meridian Books, 1959), 254; Johan Goudsblom, *Sociology in the Balance: A Critical Essay* (New York: Columbia University Press, 1977), 4, 182; William Outhwaite, "Hans-Georg Gadamer," and Anthony Giddens, "Jurgen Habermas," in Quentin Skinner, ed., *The Return of Grand Theory in the Human Sciences* (Cambridge: Cambridge University Press, 1985), 21–39, 121–39.

15 These identities, of course, are frequently put on and taken off in a quite conscious and deliberate manner. Laurier, for example, was

able in certain circumstances and before certain audiences to play
the imperial statesman to the hilt; equally, his interest in strengthening Canadian autonomy and limiting Canadian involvement in British and European affairs not infrequently put him among those
anxious to define themselves and their country in North American,
New World terms with, as he once put it, an obligation to keep free
of "the vortex of militarism which is the curse and blight of Europe."
This kind of deliberate role-adoption, as Erving Goffman reminds us,
is also frequently found in everyday life. The daily round of most
actors, however, involves them in a process of identity-deploying
which is not the result of conscious action but simply the assuming
of various identities in an unconscious, functional way in terms of
available cultural options. "Role-playing and identity-building processes," as Berger puts it, "are generally unreflective and unplanned,
almost automatic." See O.D. Skelton, *Life and Letters of Sir Wilfrid
Laurier*, ed. D.M.L. Farr (Toronto: McClelland and Stewart, 1965),
vol. 2, 111; Erving Goffman, *The Presentation of Self in Everyday Life*
(Garden City, NY: Doubleday Anchor, 1959); Berger, *Invitation*, 127.

16 Students of the Canadian imagination, it must be conceded, claim to
have found "national" notions of a sort. Frye, however, seems to have
thought them anything but clearly definable, inhering mainly – and
rather uncertainly – in what is produced by the interaction between
a sense of region which is profoundly imaginative and a sense of
unity which does not rise above the political. "The tension," as he
put it, "between the political sense of unity and the imaginative sense
of locality is the essence of whatever the word 'Canadian' means."
Malcolm Ross is more positive. "Beneath," he asserted, "any allegiance we may owe to the political fabrication of our state as it is pre-
sently constituted, there is an almost subliminal process at work
whereby we begin to know each other as we come to know our-
selves ... Our regions retain identity. But each region, as it grows in
social culture and racial complexity, incarnates in varying degrees a
Canadian-ness, at once precarious and propitious, which is born of
the tensions that interplay and interact in the national life." But for
him too the national sense – certainly in comparison with its classically nationalist counterparts – remained vague and imprecise, something quite incapable of being brought to ground in the shape of a
neat and tidy formulation, and therefore (as he himself made clear)
something which must be understood as "an anti-nationalist nationalism to end all nationalisms." Northrop Frye, *The Bush Garden*
(Toronto: Anansi, 1971), iii; Malcolm Ross, *The Impossible Sum of Our
Traditions* (Toronto: McClelland and Stewart, 1986), 155, 123.

17 The sort of sense Will Herberg located in the widespread feeling he

found Americans to have of their common involvement in "the American Way of Life," a feeling which, he continued, gave them a sense of who they were as a people even as their awareness of themselves as members of different religious groups operated to keep points of distinction and difference among them very much alive. "The American Way of Life," as he put it, "is the symbol by which Americans define themselves and establish their unity ... As the 'common faith' of American society [it] has coexisted for some centuries with the historic faiths of the American people." Will Herberg, *Protestant, Catholic, Jew: An Essay in American Religious Sociology* (Garden City, NY: Doubleday Anchor, 1960), 78, 81. For an argument which places more stress on particularisms without denying the existence of a partly institutional, partly ideological glue binding the whole together, see Robert Wiebe, *The Segmented Society: An Introduction to the Meaning of America* (New York: Oxford University Press, 1975).

18 Some authorities consider this "adding up" of the various identities a person at different times displays to be the only way of getting an understanding of that person's overall identity. "If one," writes Berger, "wants to ask who an individual 'really' is in this kaleidoscope of roles and identities, one can answer only by enumerating the situations in which he [or she] is one thing and those in which he [or she] is another." But whether this or some other view is taken, there is agreement that if anything of a general sort is to be seen, it can be brought into view only by someone able to stand at a distance from it, and this raises the vexed question of whether anyone – the "objective" observer included – in fact is able to, or should, perform this distancing operation. While, however, opinion also divides on that score, there is again agreement that when that operation, or something like or intended to be it, does take place, this distancing doesn't simply happen. Some conscious effort to pull back and see things whole is required, and – argument continues – whatever may be the case with the objective observer the actor is usually equipped neither by training nor by disposition to make that effort. "Very few people," says Berger, "and even they only in regard to fragments of their world view, are in a position to re-evaluate what has been imposed on them." Berger, *Invitation*, 124, 136.

19 As commentators are now regularly noting, the post-modern's emphasis on multiple perspectives and on what Leszek Kolakowski terms "leaving the field of uncertainty open" seems especially relevant to an understanding of Canadian society and history. As long ago as 1969 historian J.M.S. Careless placed the absence of a Canadian orthodoxy at the centre of his definition of the country, and more recently architectural historians and literary critics alike have

been giving great weight to precisely the sort of indeterminacy he noted. They don't, to be sure, always do so in so many words – Ethel S. Goodstein's observation that "Canadian architecture is a house of many rooms with ample space for addition and alteration" rather hints at the phenomenon than confronts it directly – but when they do (the case with Robert Kroetsch and Linda Hutcheon) their message concerning the lack of a Canadian metanarrative is clear. See Leszek Kolakowski, *Modernity on Endless Trial* (Chicago: University of Chicago Press, 1990), 22; J.M.S. Careless, " 'Limited Identities' in Canada," *Canadian Historical Review*, 50(1), 1969, 1–10; Ethel S. Goodstein, "Contemporary Architecture and Canadian National Identity," *American Review of Canadian Studies*, 18(2), 1988, 127–59; Robert Kroetsch, "Disunity or Unity: A Canadian Strategy," in his *The Lovely Treachery of Words: Essays Selected and New* (Toronto: Oxford University Press, 1989), 21–33; and Linda Hutcheon, *The Canadian Postmodern: A Study of Contemporary English-Canadian Fiction* (Toronto: Oxford University Press, 1988).

Continentalism

2 American Culture and the Concept of Mission in Nineteenth-Century English Canada

A society's sense of mission rests upon the belief that it has been charged by God or history with the performance of some great task. Islamic civilization saw itself chosen by God as the instrument by which His plans for mankind, revealed to the prophet Mohammed, would be realized throughout the world. Its violent encounters with the people of Africa, Europe, and the East became triumphal stages in the great *jihad* Allah required it to prosecute. "As for their victories and their battles," wrote the writer of *Al Fakhri* in satisfied contemplation of the wonders wrought by the Prophet's followers, "verily their cavalry reached Africa and the uttermost parts of Khurasan and crossed the Oxus."[1] In time the historical process itself came to be viewed as the agency responsible for issuing the call to action. It was Lenin's conviction that history had selected the peasants and proletariat of Russia, acting in temporary alliance through their soon to be established dictatorship, to "carry the revolutionary conflagration into Europe"[2] and thereby begin the remaking of the world. The peculiar attributes held to be associated with each society's special character, in the view of their beholders admirably equipping the society possessing them for the performance of its task, became proof that that task was indeed its to fulfil. The lightning strength of the Islamic invaders itself seemed to justify their programme: it must be for them to act as they did for had they not been given the capacity? To Lenin, paradoxically,

Canadian Historical Association, *Historical Papers*, 1971, 169–82.

the very backwardness of Russia offered revolutionary socialism its initial opportunity and gave the Russian people the chance to play a great role in history.

A peoples' understanding of its special character and of the mission whose fulfilment that character validates and makes possible has frequently arisen from the manner in which meaning is attached to its location in space. From antiquity societies have supposed that climate and geography did much to make them what they were.[3] A long line of modern thinkers, beginning with Montesquieu, has similarly postulated the existence of links between environment and the character of nations.

A society's location in space may do more than inspire its sense of character and mission. It may also sharpen and refine that sense. To be located in a strange and new land may be to become more fully alive to the responsibilities one bears as the representative of a special and chosen society. In such a land, one functions on behalf of those things for which one's order stands in especially challenging and difficult circumstances.

The sense of mission and responsibility held by the Spanish and Portuguese was clearly heightened by the opening of the New World. The discovery of that place, heathenish, yet wealthy and inhabited by God's creatures, made more urgent the business of extending the sway of the culture and civilization whose leading representatives they felt themselves to be.

For three hundred years before the rise of creolism and the sense of estrangement from the Old World that accompanied it, they took it as their duty to incorporate the land in which they had been placed into the life of the land from which they had come. What was implied by the spirit in which they undertook the colonizing process, writes one observer, was not "the annexation of terra incognita, but the bringing together of what should rightfully be joined."[4] Another concurs: "The Spaniards who left Spain had not migrated initially in an act of independence; they came to America in the service of the Crown and the Church."[5]

The French of New France shared this perspective. It was theirs, they thought, to extend in the New World the French and Christian civilization whose creatures they were. "I came," wrote Champlain, "to the conclusion that I would be doing very wrong if I did not work to find some means to [introduce New France] to the knowledge of God."[6] And that knowledge was not to be drawn from some new and purer form of the old faith but from the old faith itself. Their activities controlled from the imperial metropolis, clergy, fur traders, and government officials alike functioned as its agents. They moved at the edge of the Empire, sometimes for reasons very much their own, but did not in the end feel themselves divorced from its centre.

Those English who came to live in America likewise found their sense of mission affected by their removal to a new world. What resulted in their case, however, was different than that yielded by the experience of the continental Europeans. The English in America did not consider that their position in the New World imposed upon them an obligation to hurry its incorporation into the Old. They did not see it as their divinely appointed task to function as the agents of the civilization from which they came. They moved instead to escape the confines of that civilization until they might return to it on their own terms. Their task was to create in the free and uncorrupted New World a Christian society untouched by the impure influences of the Old. Theirs would be a society which might act as an inspiration to all of mankind and even, in the course of time, regenerate the civilization whose offspring its makers were. And so, where Champlain strove to introduce the principles of French and Catholic culture into the New World, John Winthrop set himself the task of establishing a new and exemplary form of human society, one that would function, in his famous phrase, "as a city upon a hill."

More, clearly, went into the making of the view the English and the Europeans had of themselves in the New World than the stimulus offered by life in that world. However strong and powerful that stimulus might be, it did not act uniformly on those exposed to it. It could not prevent these peoples from extracting a different meaning from the signal circumstance which brought them into contact with it. What determined that this should be so was the fact that each of them was accompanied on its journey across the Atlantic by more than an undifferentiated capacity to react to a fresh new land. Each brought with it a way of seeing the world. In the end it was its highly articulated manner of viewing reality which determined the fashion in which each reacted to the lands of the western hemisphere.[7]

The Spanish and Portuguese were of the medieval world. They knew no challenge to the unity of Catholic civilization and authority. The English who crossed the Atlantic were products of a different age. With them came new modes of social organization, new economic forces, and a modern spirit. What they brought with them shaped their attitude to the world they left behind. It made them impatient with its traditions and anxious to be active. It made them knowledgeable of communities apart, for in their experience the unity of medieval Christendom was no more and men stood divided from one another. It helped, in the words of a Latin American historian, "to create a dynamic heritage contrasting with the relatively static heritage of the longer established Spanish-American."[8] In short, it distinguished the English in America from their Latin neighbours and made them feel much less closely linked to Europe.

Even more than the shape of their parent cultures was involved in the process by which these people acquired their understanding of their character and role as New World societies. Of great significance was the relationship each bore to that culture. The attitudes enjoined by the relationship themselves became primary components in the world view articulated by each of these peoples.

The English arrived alienated from their society. They had left their land in protest. Their goal, as Winthrop reminded his fellows, was to establish a society based on true Christian principle. In that sense it would be a new society, to be distinguished in the most basic of ways from that out of which it had come.[9]

The French and the *peninsulares*, by contrast, did not cross the Atlantic estranged from the culture that gave them birth. They came as the agents of a power and civilization whose values they accepted and wished to promote. Only in time, with the ideas of the Enlightenment, the example of revolutionary France and America, the rise of indigenous elites, and the collapse of the Bourbons before them did the societies of Latin America learn to reject the world from which they came.[10] Their French and Catholic neighbours to the north never did reject it. They did not think the chasm that yawned between them and their parent society after the eighteenth century to be of their making. They considered themselves to have been abandoned by a power which first gave them up and then launched itself upon the path of revolution.

At the centre of their sense of mission through the nineteenth and into the twentieth centuries was the conviction that they must keep alive in the New World the old faith of Catholic Europe. "The mission with which Providence entrusted French Canadians," wrote Mgr. L.-F.-R. Laflèche in 1866, "is basically religious in nature: it is, namely, to convert the unfortunate infidel local population to Catholicism, and to expand the Kingdom of God by developing a predominantly Catholic nationality."[11] It was of particular importance to resist the materialist perfectionism implicit in the New World ethic. Central to the ultra-montane persuasion was the notion that the New World could not be seen as a place apart. People there were not different from other people. They were not above the laws of nature, remade by their sojourn in the New World, and able to set aside the constraints which had made their compatriots on the other side of the Atlantic selfish and sinful. Their lives, accordingly, must be regulated by the same truths which had regulated them in the Old World. It was the special duty of French Canada to make clear what those truths were. This did not mean a total rejection of materialism: as Mgr. L.-A. Paquet observed in 1902, concern with material things had its place.[12] What it did indicate was a clear reluctance to commit French Canada to unqualified acceptance of the idea that the New World possessed a special and distinctive character. "We have the privilege," said Mgr. Paquet, "of being entrusted with [the] social priesthood granted only to select peoples. I cannot doubt that this religious and civilizing mission is the true vocation and the special vocation of the French race in America. ... Our mission is less to handle capital than to stimulate ideas; less to light the furnaces of factories than to maintain and spread the glowing fires of religion and thought, and to help them cast their light into the distance."[13]

English Canadians, like others in the New World, developed a conviction that they had a special mission to fulfil. Like that of their neighbours, their sense of mission owed much to the fact that those who framed it were acutely conscious of their location in space. And it too was modified by the cultural environment in which its makers operated.

The principal and overriding fact shaping the outlook of the English who first came to the northern part of North America was their reverence for continuity, tradition, and properly constituted authority. The western world was passing through a great upheaval. That upheaval had sundered the unity of the Empire and introduced dangerous principles of government on both sides of the Atlantic. Those who came to British North America, whether as Loyalists or immigrants from Britain, brought with them an outlook at the core of which was a determination that the pernicious and destructive doctrine which rested on those principles must be resisted. Their task was to erect on the North American continent a bulwark against this formidable cancer of the body politic. It was for them to recreate in this territory a society governed by modalities the very image and transcript of those at the heart of the British constitution.

Striking and incontrovertible proof that this was indeed their mission was offered, they thought, by their success in maintaining a precarious existence next to their expanding republican neighbour. British North America had been placed under a severe test in the first years of its existence. Its people had been cajoled and threatened and finally invaded. But they had not yielded nor given up the true faith. For one of them especially there was a deep lesson in British North America's demonstrated capacity to endure. To John Strachan, as S.F. Wise has pointed out, "the miraculous survival of tiny Upper Canada was a North American testimony to God's gracious dealings with those whom he designed especially to prosper."[14] It was a clear and dramatic indication that they were His agents in the New World.

Strachan's sense of his community as an outpost of British civilization and a bastion of the true faith was shared by other British North Americans. Montreal's *Canadian Review and Literary and Historical Journal* noted in 1824 that the special character of the British American provinces derived from the fact that they, "unlike most other appendages of the Empire,"[15] were almost wholly inhabited by natives of Great Britain or their descendants. They thus possessed "the same moral and political sentiments"[16] and cherished "the same domestic and national feelings as their fathers and their ancient kindred."[17] Culture in Canada, when at last it developed, would surely function as a branch "of that venerable tree of art and science which has from old spread its fruits and its shelter over so great a portion of the world."[18]

The *Canadian Magazine*, published at York, found British North America in the 1830s in process of becoming a mirror image of European society. It was, in fact,

Europe, with only one difference – means to gratify a love of reading, and intellectual acquirement – That difficulty is about to be surmounted, and then the resemblance will be complete.[19]

At mid-century the *Anglo-American Magazine* told its readers how appropriate it was

That we should rejoice over the triumph of civilization, the onward progress of our race, the extension of our language, institutions, tastes, manners, customs and feelings ... The genius of Britain presides over the destiny of her offspring – the glory of the Empire enshrouds the prosperity of its Colony – the noble courage and strength of the Lion inspires and protects the industry of the Beaver – the Oak and the Maple unite their shadow over breasts which beat in unison for the common weal.[20]

British culture and civilization was the *élan vital*. The job of those in the wilderness was to unleash its power as quickly and fully as possible. There must be no compromise between the culture of the Old World and that of the New. The one did not need purification by the clean air of the other. The culture of the Old World might indeed be altered by the atmosphere of the New. But the growth yielded by this process would be strange and abnormal. It was not therefore to be encouraged. What should be encouraged was a re-affirmation of the vitality and relevance of the Old World and its culture.

This view of British North America's character and mission, possibly only so long as the cultural milieu which shaped it retained a powerful grip on the Canadian mind, was not to endure. As American culture and ideas flowed northwards into Canada English Canadians came increasingly to form their ideas of what was signified by their location in space in terms of that variant of the New World idea which was most fully articulated in the United States. They came to view themselves not as the agent of an Old World culture charged with civilizing the New, but as beings up-lifted and restored by their New World environment whose duty it was to regenerate the Old.

No small part in this process was played by the massive and con-tinuing entry of American publications into nineteenth century Canada. With them came that vision of life's meaning which re-posed at the centre of American culture. It found itself in time positioned to do in Canada what it did in the United States: medi-ate the experience and shape the understanding of those exposed to it.

The entry of these publications was as visible as its consequences were momentous. William Lyon Mackenzie noted in the early nineteenth century that "In many parts of Canada, and New Bruns-wick, the United States journals have an extensive circulation ..."[21] In the 1850s the traveller Isabella Bishop observed the tendency of Canadians to read American literature: "Cheap American novels," she wrote, "often of a very objectionable tendency, are largely circulated among the lower classes ..."[22] At Confederation D'Arcy McGee drew attention to the manner in which Boston functioned as the cultural metropolis for Montreal. Take a thousand, he sug-gested, of our most intelligent citizens, and while you will find

Montreal unknown among them as an intellectual community, half will have been swayed by Boston books and Boston utterances.[23] Twenty years later, in an article entitled "American Influence on Canadian Thought," Sara Jeannette Duncan argued that more American than British writers were familiar to Canadians. Canadian writing displayed American characteristics. Persons born in Britain might retain an interest in British literature, but "the mass of Canadians" prefer American writing. In short, she concluded, a "great number of American books and magazines ... find ready readers here."[24]

The presence of these publications, and of the ideas contained in them, insured that Canadians would not for long see the significance of their location in terms similar to those of the Spanish and French who sought to incorporate the lands to the west into the great civilization from which they had come. They would, like Americans, come to see themselves as free of the constraints imposed by old world civilization and positioned to build a new community.

Some English Canadians adopted with enthusiasm this view of their society's experience and mission. Rebels, Reformers, and Liberals worked vigorously to have their society recognized as one in all essentials distinct from British and European. Canada's mission was to function fully as a community of the New World. It must throw off the trappings of the Old. Having done this, it might then strive to revitalize those decaying societies on the other side of the Atlantic.

William Lyon Mackenzie pronounced it essential that Canada identify itself with the struggle for liberty being waged in America in the 1830s. Nor was his vision limited to North America. Not only were the people of the New World rising up "in stern and awful majesty." It was not "to this country and continent alone, nor chiefly, [that] this revolution [is] confined. It reaches the old world."[25] The New World, free and unencumbered, was reaching out to inspire those who remained in chains across the Atlantic.

Later commentators shared Mackenzie's conviction that it was the destiny of the New World to liberate the Old by showing it what true democracy and freedom could accomplish. From the New World would radiate outwards across the Atlantic knowledge of the principles upon which society must be founded. The idea of involvement with the Old World was not, then, objectionable; indeed it was to be welcomed, for it would allow the New World to fulfil its destiny. But precisely because it was through involvement with the Old World that the New World would fulfil its destiny, that involvement had to be of the right kind. It must advance the principles which had come to be associated with life in the New. "It is," the essayist and historian J.W. Longely wrote in 1882,

the business and mission of the Western Continent to leaven the Old World with the principles of a more enlarged freedom and a juster equality, not to bend its back to the remnants of a feudalism broken but not destroyed, decaying but not extinct. A king, an hereditary aristocracy, and a State Church, would scarcely be congenial to the ideas of a free-born Canadian, who has always enjoyed a universal freedom as broad as the sky, and has imbibed from infancy a notion of equality which would be irritated and galled by closer relations with a country which still preserves privileged order and worships vested interests.[26]

If some Canadians thought it the destiny of their society to communicate to the Old World knowledge of the proper principles upon which society should rest others thought that it could best fulfil its role in the world by serving as a haven for the oppressed. William Norris of Canada First, in the words of Carl Berger, believed that "the North American environment, assisted by liberal institutions, virtually transformed ignorant Europeans into self-reliant and respectful citizens."[27] Because of this belief, he conceived "the ultimate purpose of an independent Canada to be roughly similar to the mission of the United States."[28] As Norris himself put it, independence would enable

Canada to fulfil her destiny, to be the asylum for the oppressed and downtrodden peoples of European origin where under their own vine and fig tree, they can live in the enjoyment of happiness and liberty, perpetuating British institutions down to the most recent generation.[29]

The manner in which the thought of these men paralleled that doctrine of the New World's significance articulated in the United States is impressive enough; even more illustrative of the power wielded by the American ethos was the fate met by that sense of Canada's mission held by the most imperially minded of her citizens. These were the people whose ancestors had sacrificed much to keep a united Empire. These were the people who were determined to keep the flame of British and monarchical civilization alight in the New World. These were the British North Americans whose sense of mission most closely resembled that of the

French and Spanish. These were people who knew they were in the New World but did not at the beginning agree that this fact alone made them unique and set them apart. Yet in time even they were moved to construct a vision of Canada's destiny which turned on the conception that it was indeed a fresh and vital community with qualities that clearly distinguished it.

By mid-century they had begun to suggest that the strength of Britain might after all be augmented by the peculiar vapours of the New World. The old country, suggested William Kirby in 1846, had denied itself. Its great land-based traditions had collapsed midst the smokestacks of industrialism. It no longer had the special strength necessary to sustain the principles which had made its civilization worthy and honourable. But those same principles, at the heart of which was a reverence for authority, justice, order, and a carefully regulated and hierarchically organized society, might find new life in the uncorrupted soil of the New World.[30]

This was far from an assertion that Britain and its institutions were wholly decadent and corrupt. It did not represent a total commitment to the New World idea. But it did involve a clear suggestion that the things most to be valued in British civilization might be restored by the magic of the New World. And so the idea that Canada was destined to serve as an outpost of British culture was combined with a modest and restrained version of the New World myth to produce a new conception of Canada's role and purpose in the world.

A traveller to British North America in 1849 caught the beginnings of this change. The British North American colonies, wrote James Dixon conventionally enough, "will carry out and perpetuate all that is venerable in our system."[31] But then came the new note: the suggestion that there were special and potent forces operating in the New World. England was now, in fact, Dixon asserted, being planted in "new soil," soil which "will reproduce our nation on a gigantic scale."[32]

By the 1880s G.M. Grant, stressing his country's tie with Britain, could take time to point out that it was very much a community of the New World. "We are," he wrote,

devoted to the monarchical principle, but any aristocracy, save that of genius, worth or wealth, is as utterly out of the question with us, as with [Americans].[32]

And in 1899 Colonel George Taylor Denison considered that the days of the British race itself might be numbered "unless the new blood in the Colonies, will leaven the mass."[34]

Canadians, then, found their assessment of what duties they had, and what strength they possessed, affected by a particular vision of what life in the western hemisphere entailed. They found themselves engaged in defining their place and role in the world in terms of what they increasingly held to be Canada's quintessential New World character. They found themselves, in short, subscribing to a view of their national destiny which had much in common with that expansive vision articulated so enthusiastically by the people to their south.

There were, of course, differences. Canadians, for all that they became convinced of their special power and capability as creatures of the New World, could not forget their link with the Old. They could not rest content with a role which involved them merely in acting as a model and source of inspiration for the rest of humankind. They felt themselves linked directly to the Old World. They must act directly upon it. They must use their new strength in support of that from which they had come. And so, argued the *Canadian Monthly* in 1877, Canada's

ultimate destiny is not annexation to the United States or a precarious independence ... but to be a free British dependency, at once the grateful scion and the faithful potent ally of the motherstock.[35]

Canada's tie with Britain and its heritage of British institutions made it inevitable that some of its people should conceive of their society in a manner different from that in which Americans conceived of theirs. Its tie with the Old World, they thought, had prevented it from yielding to materialism and vulgarity. Its vitality was uncorrupted by excess. yet that vitality, though channelled by Old World restraint, remained a gift of the New. It must be used to uplift and regenerate that which had kept it pure and undefiled.

Nowhere was this argument advanced with greater force than in Sara Jeannette Duncan's turn-of-the-century novel *The Imperialist.* Influenced by Henry James in both style and conceptualization, Duncan used her book to explore the tension between the Old World and the New. She examined one way in which the Empire might be revitalized and the growing American influence in Canadian and imperial affairs limited. For Murchison, the novel's protagonist, the answer lay in closer association of the Empire's different parts. Thus strengthened it might withstand American pressure. Canada, now bearing the brunt of that pressure, would certainly find its position improved.

But imperialism would not merely serve and protect Canadian independence in North America. Britain, Murchison, was convinced, was in decline. What would revitalize it was a closer association with Canada. Canada, like the United States, was a community of the New World. It was in fact potentially stronger than the United States for it had not let the potent magic of the New World go to its head. The flow of the vital New World juices through its veins had been regulated by the sense of moderation and restraint acquired from its Old World parent. But they remained the juices of the New World. Canada's destiny lay in a supreme activism directed towards allowing them to course unimpeded to the centre of the Empire.

In Murchison himself was the old made new. On the platform to make his speech to the electors of Elgin, he appeared as "a dramatic figure, standing for the youth and energy of the old blood ..."[36] He was the man of the Old World, regenerated by his sojourn in the New. Fresh and vigorous and innocent, he was prepared to use his strength and that of his society to regenerate the land from which he had come.

English Canadians, then, came to view their mission as one befitting a society not merely an extension of, but qualitatively different from, those of the Old World. How, indeed, could it have been otherwise? Their point of view was determined by the cultural matrix within which the elements composing it took form. As the character of that matrix changed, the ideas to which it gave rise changed also. English Canadians came, irresistibly, to form the fundamental myths articulating that which was supposedly basic in their national experience in terms of a vision of reality created by another people.

NOTES

1 Cited in Christopher Dawson, *The Making of Europe* (New York: Meridian Books, 1958), 134. Dawson refers to the "intense religious enthusiasm" of the Moslems which made the Holy War "a supreme act of consecration and self-sacrifice" (133).
2 Cited in Leon Trotsky, *Stalin: An Appraisal of the Man and His Influence,* ed. and trans. Charles Malamuth (New York: Harper, 1941), 424.
3 J.W. Johnson, "Of Differing Ages and Climes," *Journal of the History of Ideas,* 21, October–December 1960, 465–80.

4 Richard M. Morse, "The Heritage of Latin America," in Louis Hartz, Kenneth McRae, et al., *The Founding of New Societies: Studies in the History of the United States, Latin America, South Africa, Canada, and Australia* (New York: Harbinger Books, 1964), 152.

5 Germán Arciniegas, *Latin America: A Cultural History* (New York: Alfred A. Knopf, 1967), xxv.

6 Cited in Morris Bishop, *Champlain: The Life of Fortitude*, Carleton Library (Toronto: McClelland and Stewart, 1963), 183.

7 For a clear and concise account by a historian of the manner in which the cultural environment operates in the shaping of a society's outlook, see David M. Potter, *People of Plenty: Economic Abundance and the American Character*, 9th impression (Chicago: Phoenix, 1965) especially part one, "The Study of National Character," 3–74; for an account by two sociologists of the influence exerted by culture in the formation of ideas see Peter L. Berger and Thomas Luckmann, *The Social Construction of Reality: A Treatise in the Sociology of Knowledge* (Anchor Books edition; Garden City, NY: Doubleday, 1967); for a brief history of the concept of ideology, see George Lichtheim, "The Concept of Ideology," *History and Theory*, 4 (2), 164–95. Potter's account is straightforward and uncluttered; Berger and Luckmann argue for a new understanding of the sociology of knowledge; Lichtheim is concerned with what they would consider merely one branch of it; but all make the simple and basic point upon which the argument in this paper turns: the cultural environment in which people live shapes the manner in which they perceive the universe.

8 Irving A. Leonard, "Introduction," in Mariano Picón-Salas, *A Cultural History of Spanish America from Conquest to Independence*, trans. Irving A. Leonard (Berkeley and Los Angeles: University of California Press, 1965), x.

9 For a classic account of the manner in which Winthrop and his colleagues viewed their situation in America, see Perry Miller, "Errand into the Wilderness," in his *Errand into the Wilderness* (New York: Harper Torchbooks, 1964), 1–15. For a brief yet comprehensive examination of the American concept of mission, see Russel B. Nye, "The American Sense of Mission," in his *This Almost Chosen People: Essays in the History of American Ideas* (Toronto: Macmillan, 1966), 164–207. For a lengthier treatment of the same theme, see Albert K. Weinberg, *Manifest Destiny: A Study of National Expansion in American History* (Chicago: Quadrangle Books, 1963). For a reply to Weinberg, see Frederick Merk, *Manifest Destiny and Mission in American History* (New York: Vintage, 1966). Recent writers, without denying the proposition that Americans felt themselves apart from the Old

World, have emphasized the extent of their involvement with that world's culture. See Frank Thistlewait, *America and the Atlantic Community: Anglo American Aspects, 1790–1850* (New York: Harper Torchbooks, 1963); Howard Mumford Jones, *O Strange New World, American Culture: The Formative Years* (New York: Viking, 1967); Robert Kelley, *The Transatlantic Persuasion: The Liberal-Democratic Mind in the Age of Gladstone* (New York: Knopf, 1969); and Robert O. Mead, *The Atlantic Legacy: Essays in American-European Cultural History* (New York: New York University Press, 1969).

10 "The independence proclaimed in the *Mayflower* Compact of 1620," writes one observer, "was not formulated in Hispano-Indian America until 1810." Arciniegas, *Latin America*, xxv.

11 Mgr L.-F.-R. Laflèche, *Quelques considerations sur les rapports de la société civile avec la religion et la famille* (Trois Rivières, 1866), cited in Ramsay Cook, ed., *French Canadian Nationalism: An Anthology* (Toronto: Macmillan, 1969), 98.

12 Mgr L.-A. Paquet "Sermon sur la vocation de la race française en Amérique," cited in Cook, *French Canadian Nationalism*, 158.

13 Ibid., 154.

14 S.F. Wise, "Sermon Literature and Canadian Intellectual History," *The Bulletin of the Committee on Archives of the United Church of Canada*, 18, 1965, 15.

15 "Quebec Literary and Historical Society," *The Canadian Review and Literary and Historical Journal*, no. 1, July 1824, 3.

16 Ibid.

17 Ibid.

18 Ibid., 2.

19 *Canadian Magazine*, 1 (1), 1833, 1.

20 "The Cities of Canada: Toronto," *Anglo-American Magazine*, 1 (1), July 1852, 1.

21 "A Letter to England by Peter Russell," *Colonial Advocate*, April 1826. Cited in Margaret Fairley, ed., *The Selected Writings of William Lyon Mackenzie, 1824–1837* (Toronto: Oxford University Press, 1960) 116. "Peter Russell" was a pseudonym used by Mackenzie.

22 Isabella Bishop, *The Englishwoman in America* (London, 1856) cited in G.M. Craig, ed., *Early Travellers in the Canadas, 1791–1867* (Toronto: Macmillan, 1955), 217.

23 D'Arcy McGee, "The Mental Outfit of the New Dominion," Montreal *Gazette*, 5 November 1867.

24 Sara Jeannette Duncan, "American Influence on Canadian Thought," *The Week*, 4 (32), 1887, 518.

25 *The Constitution*, 26 July 1837, cited in Fairley, *Selected Writings*, 218–19.

26 J.W. Longely, "The Future of Canada," *Rose-Belford's Canadian Monthly*, 8 (2) February 1882, 153–4.

27 Carl Berger, "The Vision of Grandeur: Studies in the Ideas of Canadian Imperialism, 1867–1914" (Ph.D. diss., University of Toronto, 1966), 147.

28 Ibid.

29 William Norris, "The Canadian Question" (Montreal, 1875) cited in Berger, "Vision of Grandeur," 147.

30 William Kirby, *The U.E.: A Tale of Upper Canada* (Niagara, 1859).

31 James Dixon, DD., *Personal Narrative of a Tour Through a Part of the United States and Canada: With notices of the history and institutions of Methodism in America* (New York, 1849) cited in Craig, *Early Travellers*, 171.

32 Craig, *Early Travellers*, 171.

33 G.M. Grant, "Canada's Present Position and Outlook," *Rose-Belford's Canadian Monthly*, 5 (2), 1877, 198.

34 Sir Sandford Fleming Papers, Denison to Fleming, 6 May 1899, cited in Carl Berger, *The Sense of Power: Studies in the Ideas of Canadian Imperialism 1867–1914* (Toronto: University of Toronto Press, 1970), 181.

35 *Canadian Monthly*, 12 (2), 1877, 198.

36 Sara Jeannette Duncan, *The Imperialist* (Toronto: McClelland and Stewart, 1961), 229.

3 The Continental Dimension in the Evolution of the English-Canadian Mind

Of those societies which have felt the cultural, economic, and military might of the American republic over the past two hundred years, Canada was the earliest and remains the most profoundly affected. There is still, of course, a good deal of disagreement about the implications of the American economic presence in Canada. Canadians also continue to be divided over their country's capacity to devise foreign and defence policies truly independent of the United States. Government action over the past fifteen years suggests, however, the existence of a policy-makers' consensus in support of the view that the American influence on Canada's cultural life is substantial and needs to be diminished. Yet if that view, and the programs, policies, and legislation to which it has led, are clearly products of the twentieth century, the phenomenon with which they are intended to deal has a much longer history.

Societies acquire an understanding of themselves in a variety of ways. Sometimes it results from the activity of their own élites who, in the act of specifying what they view as the national character, equip their compatriots with a way of thinking about, and making sense of, their society's history and experience.[1]

Equally, however, this understanding may derive from external sources. One way in which this can happen involves the introduc-

International Journal, 31 (3), 1976, 442–69.

tion into a colonized society by its governors of a way of viewing itself – as, perhaps, inferior or backward – which is designed to legitimate the rule of those who have come to preside over its affairs.[2] While this process usually operates in societies whose majority population is non-European, Louis Hartz has suggested that the inhabitants of communities composed mainly of Europeans or their descendants may also form their ideas within the framework of a world view which is at once partial, incomplete, and of external origin. Having separated from its parent culture at some particular phase of that parent's development – when, for example, liberal ideas were in the ascendant, the case in Britain when the thirteen American colonies were founded – the new society lacks real familiarity with the entire ideological spectrum to be found in the culture from which it springs. Its people are thus quite literally incapable of conceiving the world other than in terms of the single system of ideas which accompanied them on their voyage to the new land.[3]

Occasionally, societies come to understand their world through the medium of ideas imported from beyond their frontiers neither from a conscious and deliberate program of evangelization nor from the sort of process outlined by Hartz and his followers. In these circumstances the interplay of such factors as geographical proximity, a common language, a shared tradition, similar and/or complementary economies, and the volume in which a technologically advanced and heavily populated society produces its cultural products creates a much more subtle dynamic. A similar result is, however, produced, in that one society is exposed to, and comes to form some part of its ideas in terms of, a world view developed elsewhere.[4]

In Canada's case this process assisted in the creation of a cultural environment made up to an important degree of American ideas. Canadians, exposed to this environment, evinced a clearly demonstrable tendency to assess their society's character and experience in terms of categories developed by their southern neighbours. They also, to be sure, utilized ideas imported from Britain and Europe, not to mention ones they themselves developed in the course of coming to grips with their own experience.[5] But the attention scholars have been paying to ideas of British and Canadian origin can hardly obscure the profound influence that American patterns of thought were exercising on the Canadian mind throughout the nineteenth century. Their presence powerfully assisted in the development of a mode of thinking about Canada's existence which produced a sense of identity fundamentally different from that evolving in other societies – French, Spanish, Portuguese – similarly located in the New World but more fully insulated from American ideas by their own language and culture.

This mode of thinking displayed the American influence in two main ways. Many of the basic myths in terms of which Canadians attempted to make their experience intelligible – the myths of the land, of progress, of mission, and of individualism – were cast largely in terms of ideas drawn from the south. The frequently expressed belief that Canadian society was essentially one of the New World, with a character altogether different from that of old and decaying Europe, was similarly formulated in terms drawn from the American expression of this idea. Canadians, in consequence, came to see themselves as more than the mere facts of geography allowed them to be. They were not simply joint occupants of a continental land mass. They were participants with the Americans in a way of life invested with a special, unprecedented significance.[6]

Viewing their country in this way helped make more difficult the task of conceiving of it as one whose history, literature, values, and geography entitled it to consideration as a society identifiably separate and distinct in North America. Many Canadians saw it instead as one best understood in terms of characteristics it shared with its southern neighbour. The assumption that the elements of the Canadian experience could best be understood by viewing them within a continental frame of reference thus became deeply imbedded in the English Canadian mind. By the end of the nineteenth century, the extent to which that assumption had conditioned a mode of thinking about Canada which involved conceiving it as little more than a region of North America had become a source of deep concern to observers interested in the country's cultural life and, indeed, in its very survival.

The exposure of Canadians to American news played a particularly important role in the creation of a continental frame of reference. The fact that they were so fully provided with knowledge of public controversies in the United States transformed those controversies into matters which seemed less newsworthy items from a foreign country and more vital matters which penetrated into the heart of Canada. The tendency of Canadians to view American issues as though they were their own was clearly manifest in the manner in which they approached the sectional controversy and the Civil War. Proximity combined with the plenitude of news they received to make that series of cataclysmic events as fully a part of their own experience as it was of the American.

In the 1840s and 1850s Canadians followed the sectional controversy closely. The slavery issue held a special interest for them, and, especially after the passage of the Fugitive Slave Act, they were reminded almost daily by the arrival of refugee slaves of what the conflict meant in human terms. The presence of the black refugees itself resulted in the importation of a segment of American culture and made necessary some alterations in the social institutions of Canada West.[7] The slavery controversy was made a vital issue for Canadians in other ways as well. The abolitionists included Toronto and Montreal in their speaking tours.[8] The young Wilfrid Laurier read *Uncle Tom's Cabin* and was made by it into what he later termed an out and out anti-slavery man.[9] And Canadian cultural agencies with a moral and humanitarian inclination sometimes felt compelled to take a stand on the controversy.[10]

At the same time that Canadians were being blanketed with news on these matters from American sources, their own publications were devoting considerable space to it as well. The *Globe* devoted a large amount of space to it after 1850,[11] and, just as American newspapers began to run special editions and introduce technical improvements in order to meet the increased demand for news about the controversy, so also did Canadian ones. So extensively did interest grow that occasionally new journals were established to meet the demand.[11] George Brown provided a telling part of the explanation for this phenomenal interest in American affairs when he asserted that "we, too, are Americans."[13] Canadians and the inhabitants of the United States held a kind of common citizenship and therefore, he argued, they shared the duty of preserving the honour of the continent. On the eve of the Civil War the *Globe* again emphasized the wholly natural character of Canada's interest in events to the south, "given the fact that this issue will have a most important influence on the future of this continent with which our destinies are linked."[14]

Some Canadians, then, did not have to add a continental dimension to their thinking because it was already there. They knew how tightly bound they were to the fate of the Republic. They therefore thought it wholly appropriate for them to be subjected in a massive way to news of what transpired there. Others, however, felt that it was not common concern that gave rise to the inflow of news, but rather the reverse. The flow of news, information, and people across the border brought the two societies into such close contact that, as the Montreal *Gazette* put it, "the public opinion of one country tells on the other." Those who considered *Uncle Tom's Cabin* to be "out of its latitude" in Canada were therefore in error. Canadians were as fully alive as Americans to the issues with which it dealt.[15]

The exposure of Canadians to the memoirs, biographies, and histories which were issued in such quantity after 1865 ensured that even after its termination they would continue to feel a strong sense of involvement in the Civil War. Its heroes, indeed, occasionally assumed the same status in Canada as they had attained in the United States. The sentiments which led the *British American Magazine* to characterize Stonewall Jackson "as a moral hero" who belonged "to the world as an example through all time"[16] were still in evidence thirty years later when a Canadian trade journal commented on the authorized life of Lincoln, then in preparation. The book, it said, ought to sell very well in Canada "as in no land is the name of Lincoln more revered than here."[17]

If American news and information about American public figures fostered a tendency on the part of Canadians to identify these men and events as the common property of all North Americans, the presence in their midst of American scientific literature and ideas encouraged the conviction that the elements of which the continent itself was composed, and the techniques and methods by which they could be understood, similarly knew no international boundary. In dealing with the flora and the fauna, the geography and agriculture, the geology and waterways of North America, that essentially descriptive literature did its share in heightening the sense that the natural features of Canada, the bone and sinews of the country, could be most usefully approached by viewing them in their relation to a larger, more comprehensive whole. In suggesting, therefore, that if the plants of Muskoka were to be described fully it would be necessary to consult not only the botanical works of Canadians but also "the ample text books of American botanists,"[18] G.M. Adam, writing in 1882, was reinforcing a way of viewing Canada's relationship with the rest of North America that at once grew out of and strengthened the conviction that it was best viewed in continental perspective.

In a like manner the use Canadians made of the literature and ideas of American forestry encouraged the belief that their country's characteristics could be most profitably examined by situating them in a continental context. The American experience in forest preservation was cited by Canadians in the 1870s, a process continued in popular journals in the next decade.[19] By the early twentieth century American foresters were travelling north to Canada to give Canadians access at first hand to their experience.[20] One effect of this activity was, of course, to encourage acceptance among Canadians of the idea that the forests of Canada were part of a continental resource to which common techniques of management, exploitation, and conservation could be applied.[21]

Scientific work in two areas was particularly important in strengthening the sense that Canada could best be understood as part of a continental whole. Agricultural science involved the study of conditions which were very much the same on both sides of the border. American agricultural journals were, in consequence, widely read in Canada, and many of them were written to appeal to the British North American farmer as well as to his American counterpart. Often the techniques, and sometimes even the plants, employed by Canadian farmers came from the United States. W.H. Smith noted in 1851 that Canadian fruit tree nurseries were first started in conjunction with nurseries in that country, and, by 1855, the *Anglo-American Magazine* could report that the Canadian "Horticultural Mind" had been deeply influenced by what was happening there.[22] By the 1880s agricultural science was well settled on a continental foundation. The Society for the Promotion of Agriculture was organized on a continental basis, and in 1882 it held its third annual meeting in Montreal with professors from many agricultural colleges in Canada and the United States in attendance.[23] The exchange of ideas was carried on in other ways as well, with, for example, Canadians publishing under the auspices of American agencies designed to promote agricultural activity.[24]

The situation in the field of geology was more complicated. As work proceeded, it became clear that Canada was distinguished by formations which set it off in the most fundamental way from the United States. The Precambrian shield was only the most obvious of these elemental structures. Equally, however, it was apparent that many of the continent's geological features manifested themselves independently of the boundary. Canadian geologists therefore argued that their subject could not be adequately approached without knowledge of work done by their American colleagues. As W.E. Logan put it in 1844, a knowledge of the geological structure of the United States is "indispensable to the comprehension of [Canada's] geology, and I experience much gratification in acknowledging not only the great benefits conferred by the American Surveys on the science in general, but also the essential service to be derived from them in the examination of Canada in particular."[25]

As early as the 1820s the conviction emerged that, geologically speaking, the continent was to be considered a whole. In 1824 the *Canadian Review and Literary and Historical Journal* emphasized the importance of Canadians in the field familiarizing themselves with what Americans active in it were doing.[26] By the 1840s the discovery of geological features which ran quite independently of the political boundary was a regular occurrence.[27] Logan, following his own advice, made use of the reports of the various state geological surveys and of work appearing in such publications as *Silliman's Journal of Science and Art.*[28] By the middle of the century Canadians were employing American terminology in their descriptions of geological features found in Canada.[29]

The conviction that the continent was united by its geological structure was strengthened in a variety of ways. The very fact that scholars in the field functioned independently of the border heightened the sense that the continent, in terms at least of its basic character, was a unit. As early as 1828 American geologists had begun to investigate the geology of British North America.[30] Canadians, for their part, were active in American geological circles. Logan co-operated with T.S. Hunt in the writing of an article for the *American Journal of Science and Arts* in 1863,[31] while Frank D. Adams, a leading Canadian geologist, graduated from McGill, studied at the Sheffield Scientific School (connected with Yale), and then returned to work with the Geological Survey of Canada.[32] The American-born Hunt best exemplified the continental nature of the subject. Yale-educated, Hunt spent most of his career in Canada. He functioned, however, in a frame of reference that was clearly continental. His papers generally emphasized the geological unity of the continent, and many of them were read to American audiences or appeared in American publications.[33]

The manner in which English Canadians were learning to comprehend their social and political environment, no less than the fashion in which they were acquiring knowledge of their natural circumstances, led some of them to conceive their society in ways which highlighted those elements in its character which identified it as an essentially American community. Their exposure to the American literature of politics and reform played a particularly significant role in this process, for it made them especially sensitive to factors in their experience which seemed to ally it with the American.

The tendency of the reformers in Upper and Lower Canada to draw on the ideas, policies, and rhetoric of their analogues in the

United States is, of course, well known; what should be noted is that this influence, unlike that of the British, extended beyond general principle into the area of specific reforms. When the reformers talked of general aims, it was not always possible to know whether they were most influenced by the British radicals or the Jacksonians to the south. But when it came to hard specifics – the needs of farmers, banking, education, political reforms – the American influence was unmistakable. Mackenzie's social ideal, as Lillian Gates's description of it reminds us, was clearly Jeffersonian, and occasionally American reformers provided the very words Mackenzie used in the course of his attempts to mobilize support for his aims.[34]

Canadian social and political movements of the middle of the century similarly gave evidence that American ideas were influencing the manner in which Canadians conceived of their experience. The Clear Grits continued to propose American models and to argue that the "aristocratical" forms of the British constitution were unsuited to democratic North America.[35] Much impressed with the structure of government and the character of society in Ohio and New York, they advanced those states as particularly suitable candidates for emulation by their Canadian compatriots. Then, too, campaigns mounted with respect to particular issues indicated that the presence of American ideas was playing a part in the process by which English Canadians were being led to define their society as essentially North American. If Orangeism and voluntarist notions brought from Britain helped make English Canadian Protestants deeply suspicious of any alliance between church and state, the American conviction that such arrangements were incompatible with life in a democratic community – particularly when it was a faith suffused with authoritarian and hierarchical principles which stood to benefit from them – played a part as well. "Canadians of American background," notes J.M.S. Careless, "had often expressed their own traditions of religious independence in opposing state recognition or official privileges for any church."[36]

In the last decades of the century, many Canadians, turning to the task of attempting to understand the waves of disorder breaking over Europe and North America, looked to the literature of the United States. Americans, too, were concerned with what flowed from the rise of industrialism. Their literature of upheaval and reform, concerned on the one hand with progressivism, on the other with the socialist critique, seemed to hold many of the answers for a North American society. By 1889 the *Week* could report that "sociological discussions and speculations" were having a considerable impact on "the minds of many of the younger thinkers of the United States and Canada." The leading influence, it thought, was attributable to the American reformer Henry George.[37]

Literature and ideas of this kind were indeed moving north. As American capital entered Canada in the late nineteenth and early twentieth centuries, so also did American criticism of it: "A great deal of the anti-corporate tone of the [Ontario] press," writes one historian, "was imported bodily from the United States ... Americans exported both the capital and a conscience to go with it."[38] The consequence, as a contemporary observer put it, was that "agitation for the regulation of dangerous masses of capital ... took hold of the Canadian and American mind at the same time."[39]

Learning to advocate reform in the American style sometimes meant, Canadians soon discovered, disavowal of radical strategies. To most Americans socialism was the product of a poor class-ridden society incapable of regeneration. In their view America had no need of such a prescription. Socialism would in fact destroy that in America which made it unique: free and responsible individuals. It would subject them to the very constraints whose absence had allowed them to produce the bounty with which they were surrounded. Many Canadians accepted this argument. Their contact with the work of Josiah Royce and William Graham Sumner and their exposure to the voluminous literature of laissez-faire and social Darwinism issuing from the United States familiarized them with the way in which Americans defined the responsibilities of the individual, viewed the character of life in the New World, and rejected socialism as an exotic yet potentially harmful irrelevancy. When they themselves commented on that creed it was in accents which showed clearly that they thought of themselves as members of a new and different society. One part of the Canadian critique of socialism therefore rested on the assumption that Canada, like the United States, was located in a New World to whose people the socialists had nothing to say.

"Industrial warfare," pronounced the *Week* in 1886, "is the natural offspring of the Old World." There workers were politically oppressed. But "on this continent" there was democracy. In North America "political power was in the hands of the working-class, and the workingman, if he is wronged, can do himself right in a regular way." The wealth of the New World also helped to make socialism impossible. While Europe had been filled with agitation, the *Week* pointed out, "this continent has been saved by the diffusion of wealth, or the hope of wealth ..." That wealth, moreover, was not diffused only in the cities: the rural population too had profited from the fact that ownership of property was widespread. This, in its turn, had played a part in limiting the rise of rural protest. "From Agrarian Socialism," the *Week* accordingly noted, "we on this continent have been saved by the diffusion of property in land." All of this had combined to produce a working population with a clear sense of its own interests and of what was required to serve them. When all was said and done it would be these workers themselves who, spurning the promises of unprincipled agitators, would save North America from an alien, threatening creed. "The sound-heartedness and self-reliance of Canadian and American work-men," the *Week* assured its readers, "will prevent Jacobinism from taking root on this continent; and as for pure socialism, it is but the dream of the madmen."[40]

So powerful a grip did this way of viewing Canada's character come to exercise over the Canadian mind that even some Canadian socialists felt it necessary to concede that North America was a kind of worker's paradise, unlike Europe in every way. But where the enemies of socialism argued that its introduction would destroy this paradise, the friends of that creed saw it as the perfect complement to life in the New World. In its absence, the egalitarianism of the New World would be overcome, the bourgeois idea would triumph, class distinctions would solidify, and North Americans would be Europeanized. Socialism, far from being the enemy of the special quality of life in North America, would be its saviour. It was, Canadian labour spokesman Phillips Thompson accordingly argued, against the Europeanization of North American society that social-ists had to be on their guard. His book, heavily indebted to the ideas of Henry George and Edward Bellamy, made it plain that only by resisting the ways of Europe could the special character of North American civilization be preserved.[41]

The reading of history written by Americans played no small part in fostering among Canadians the conviction that the peoples of the continent, shaped by a common historical experience in the New World, formed a single society whose members were bound together by their shared past. Even the history of European societies as it was written by Americans might heighten this belief. That history was very much the history of the Old World written by inhabitants of the New. "Believing that the American writer looked on the Past from the highest station reached in human progress," David Levin writes, "each of the romantic historians felt obligated to reflect this viewpoint in his sympathies and in his judgements."[42] While John

Lothrop Motley chronicled the triumph of the Protestant and democratic Netherlands over absolutist Spain, William Henry Prescott made plain his lack of sympathy with the Spanish autocrats of the New World. Their work, in Merle Curti's words, "... revealed some part of the nationalist sentiment; the glories of freedom and liberty, the shadows of tyranny and despotism color their pages."[43] The reputation these histories earned in Canada was high. Canadians, sharing something of the vantage point from which they were written, could respond to them with much the same enthusiasm as Americans themselves. Thus might the *Week* draw the attention of its readers to a reprint of one of Prescott's volumes with the observation that its author's great fame made it "unnecessary to sing its praises."[44]

The written history of the North American continent itself, however, served best to reinforce the sense that the experience of its people was at bottom the same. Even the history of the American Revolution became a peculiar kind of bond. Pre-eminently a shared experience, it gave Canadians and Americans something in common even as it drove them apart. English Canadians and Americans alike could look back to it as the fountainhead of their national tradition.

The tendency to think of the history of Canada and the United States as two halves of a single whole was present early in the century. Even so unremarkable a circumstance as the fact that the books concerned with Canada and the United States were shelved together in the Legislative Library of Lower Canada gave evidence of its existence.[45] When Robert Christie's history of Lower Canada was reprinted in 1865 the *Saturday Reader* described much of its contents as being "not only of Provincial, but of North American importance."[46] And when in 1884 the trade journal, *Books and Notions,* suggested that Canadian booksellers might deal in "*Americana,*" it made clear its belief that this kind of material would have as much interest for Canadians as would publications concerned specifically with Canada.[47] Prominent figures in Canadian history might be prominent in American, and when Canadians read about them it was often from the pens of American writers. The name of Tecumseh, which the *Literary Garland* thought "should be a household word in Canada," was, for example, incorporated into the Canadian tradition thanks in part to the appearance of such books as the American writer G.H. Colton's *Tecumseh, or The West Thirty Years' Since.*[48]

The work of two men was especially important in reinforcing the conviction that North Americans shared a moving dramatic past and were bound together by it. One was America's best known and most prolific nineteenth-century poet and the other one of its most skilled historians. These men, in the estimate of one Canadian journal, could even be described as "our" best writers. "Mr Parkman," noted the *Canadian Monthly*, "is our best chronicler, and Mr Longfellow, in his Evangeline, our national poet."[49] Longfellow's *Evangeline* played a role of particular importance, for the Acadians were involved in the history of New France, British North America, and the United States. Their story seemed to sum up in itself the manner in which the history of the continent and its different parts were bound up with another. Awareness of their story as Longfellow told it could not help but stimulate the tendency to regard the continent as an entity united by its historical experience. *Rose-Belford's*, accordingly, made it clear that it viewed the history through which the Acadians moved on their tragic journey as an integrated continuous whole, a romance of special and compelling interest to the entire continent.[50]

The impact of Francis Parkman's work was no less great. His books on the British and French rivalry for empire in North America emphasized, as little else could have, how closely intertwined the early histories of what would become Canada and the United States had been. Some Canadians, of course, felt a pang of regret that it was an American who had done so well by Canadian history. Even they, however, agreed that Parkman had performed a singular service. "To [him]," asserted the *Canadian Monthly*, "Canadians are deeply indebted; for he has done for us what we are almost ashamed to say no historical student here has had the courage to undertake on so complete a scale ... he has made the field of early Canadian history entirely his own." The *Week* took a similar view. "It would be difficult," that journal told its readers, "to speak or write of the history of Canada without some reference to the brilliant writings of Mr Parkman, so thoroughly has he allied his name with all that is trustworthy regarding that story."[51]

The influence of Parkman's style and judgments was, in the view of one commentator, greater than that of any other individual in the nineteenth century with whom Canadians writing history had contact.[52] It seemed wholly natural to draw upon Parkman's constructs and to apply his insights to areas of the North American experience other than those with which he himself had dealt. Alexander Morris could, as a result, be found by one critic to have followed Parkman in debunking the idea of the noble savage in his book on Indian treaties in Canada,[53] while William D. LeSueur might quote Parkman in the course of making a point about Indian superstition.[54]

By the end of the 1880s some Canadians were prepared to argue not only that the best Canadian history had been written by Americans, but that it had been written by them in the course of chronicling the history of their own society. Reading that history therefore involved examining the Canadian experience in a context which could do no other than emphasize its relationship to the American one. Justin Winsor's *Narrative and Critical History of America* could, in consequence, be identified by one reviewer not simply as the best history of the United States to have appeared, but also, if one were to exclude Parkman's work, the best written about Canada as well. It was, in fact, North American history and could not therefore be fully appreciated by those "who are not deeply versed in the history of the Continent."[55] The best Canadian history had, in sum, issued from the United States. To read that history most appreciatively required that one realize how fully integrated it was with the American. To read that history most profitably required that one possess a continental perspective.

As early as the 1820s Canadian literary figures revealed themselves aware of, and influenced by, work being done in the United States. The Philadelphia *Port Folio* was read in Montreal in the early years of that decade, and the second series of *Salamagundi*, edited by James Kirke Paulding, was known as well.[56] By the late 1830s American literary influences were affecting the character of Canada's first magazine of note, the *Literary Garland.* That magazine, Carl Klinck tells us, was not so much "Anglo-Canadian" as "Anglo-Bostonian."[57] Its English tone was supplied by Susannah Moodie, while its American cast was largely provided by the daughters of the American authoress Hannah Webster Foster. One of them, Eliza L. Cushing, published at least seventy items in it and later became its editor, while the other, Harriet V. Cheney, was a regular contributor of prose and poetry. Other American writers also involved themselves closely with the Canadian scene in these years. Perhaps the best known was Nathaniel P. Willis who provided the text which accompanied W.H. Bartlett's engravings for the 1842 volume, *Canadian Scenery.*

By the post-Confederation period, Canadian critics and writers were closely in touch with what was happening in American literary circles. American authors received critical attention in Canadian periodicals. Canadians were kept informed of the latest gossip concerning American writers. Special articles discussed the work of American authors, and might, on occasion, be brought together in book form.[58] By the 1880s Canadian literary figures accepted American writing as a legitimate cultural force. American journals came in for high and consistent praise. The *Week*, for example, found the New York *Critic* to be very good indeed. It has, the Canadian journal noted, "no superior, in our estimation, among the purely literary journals now printed in our language." *Books and Notions* thought the *Century* to be almost as worthy of praise: "Every article [in the past year]," it noted in 1885, "was readable." A year earlier, it had commented enthusiastically on the "excellence" of the better class of American periodicals.[59]

American writing did not, of course, simply commend itself to Canadians in these years: it also influenced their work.[60] Carl Klinck has in fact argued that American literary devices contributed in no small way to the growth of a Canadian poetic imagery capable of coping with the curious collection of phenomena – neo-Grecian myths and concepts of nature, Indian lore, theories of evolution, liberal theology, primitive tales – with which a North American poet was required to deal.[61] Especially significant is the circumstance that the two best known Canadian-born writers of the first half of the nineteenth century, men who would be fully exposed to the influences operating over the North American continent, moved very largely within a literary frame of reference which is best described as American.

Thomas Chandler Haliburton operated quite clearly within such a context. His familiarity with the tall tales and inflated manner of speaking common in the American West derived largely from his reading of such items as Davy Crockett's *Sketches and Eccentricities* and, as he put it himself in his *Letter-book*, "United States almanacs, road manuals, newspapers, and guide-books." He was also familiar with American popular culture as a result of the presence in Nova Scotia of American popular songs, jokes, and tales spread by word of mouth and of such institutions as the travelling American circus, all of which found a place in his writing.[62] More particularly, he probably knew the "Letters from Major Jack Downing of Downingville" which appeared in the *Daily Courier* of Portland, Maine, from 1830 to 1833. Written in a Down East dialect, they involved the kind of humour that would characterize *The Clockmaker*. "There can be little doubt," wrote R.P. Baker, "of Haliburton's indebtedness to the Maine journalist, with whose work he was unquestionably familiar."[63] Despite his clear refusal to celebrate American values or the American way of life in anything resembling an undiscriminating fashion, Haliburton's work reflected so much that was characteristic of that way of life that American humorists could draw upon it in the creation of some of their society's most memorable popular art. Artemus Ward, Josh Billings, and Mark Twain all made use of the style and technique which he made famous.[64]

John Richardson of Upper Canada was the product of a society less mature than Haliburton's. The young frontier soldier did, however, travel to Britain and Europe. There he was exposed directly to the influence of the romantic movement in both its pure and debased forms. Yet he retained his interest in the North American wilderness, of which he had first hand experience, and the appearance of James Fenimore Cooper's work inspired him to do for the forest of Upper Canada what Cooper was doing for that of the United States. Cooper, of course, was not alone in influencing him. Richardson's work was replete with Byronic gloom and romantic melodrama and owed its rather peculiar character to an amalgam of influences. One commentator has suggested that primary among them was that of Scott, whom he insists Richardson slavishly imitated.[65] But the subject of which Richardson wrote made it inevitable that it would be an American, addressing himself to substantially the same theme, who had the greatest influence. Richardson himself acknowledged the influence of Cooper in his first preface to *Wacousta*[66] and the reaction of the reviewers indicated clearly that they saw him operating in the American tradition. The *Athenaeum*, certainly, took this view.[67] A Canadian writer, wishing to treat in fiction the forests of Upper Canada, was not, after all, likely to resist the influence of American fiction concerning a similar theme. His treatment of the forest and its inhabitants did not, of course, parallel the manner in which they were discussed by his American counterparts. There were, in fact, significant differences. Richardson's forest was a place of sinister activity. It did not uplift those who moved through it in anything like the sense that Cooper's forest-dwellers were ennobled.[68] Yet the American influence on his work remained an important one.

As the century progressed American literature acquired a sophistication that marked its coming of age. Realism was not an American invention, but it had a clear and distinct American relevance.[69] It was, moreover, in its American form that it had the greatest impact in Canada. This did not, of course, mean that it arrived north of the border midst universal acclaim. One Canadian, writing on the theme of "Democracy in Literature," argued in 1889 that the writers of the romantic school not only did all that the realists claimed to do by handling common men "realistically," but that they were also able to offer work of some inspirational value.[70] Their treatment of exalted themes would ensure the remembrance of their work, while that of the realists, dealing with the common-place, would prove ephemeral. What was more, realism, specifically Howells's brand of it, would never get "general endorsement" in "conservative Canada."[71]

The Canadian novelist, Sara Jeannette Duncan, did however endorse it, and with enthusiasm. She found the passing of "senti-mental essays" dealing with "Memory," "Hope," "True Happiness," and other products of a "placidly unsophisticated imagination" an occasion for rejoicing. The work of contemporary writers, who were anxious to rise above "the purpose of charming the idle hour of that bored belle ... in her boudoir" was to be welcomed for its toughness and cynicism. Character and reality must be portrayed as they really were. Realism, moreover, was a peculiarly American mode of expression, especially to be identified with Howells and James. These two writers were engaged in "developing a school of fiction most closely and subtly related to the conditions and prog-ress of our own time." Duncan had, indeed, earlier referred with mock awe to Howells as "*The* Modern Novelist."[72]

Not only did Duncan admire the style of the realists: she used it herself. Her first book was commended by the *Illustrated London News* in a review whose writer assumed that she was an American.[73] Her finest piece of writing, *The Imperialist* (1904), revealed clearly in its attention to detail, in its concern to render a photographic likeness of life in a small Ontario town, and in its central assump-tions that she, like so many other Canadian intellectuals, had come to view her society through North American spectacles.

She remained, to be sure, a nationalist. Her concern was with the Canadian future, and she thought that future could best be rea-lized within the imperial framework. Her insistence on the strength and importance of Canada's Old World links was, however, accom-panied by a clear affirmation of her belief in Canada's character as a New World society. Possessing the vitality which flowed from its possession of that character, it would, in the proper circumstances, show itself capable of regenerating an effete and declining Britain. Its relationship with its parent society could not, then, be com-prehended exclusively in terms of harmony and a shared tradition. The sort of discontinuity and opposition which characterized deal-ings between two different social universes were, she argued, pre-sent as well.

Realism, as Henry James was showing, offered a particularly appropriate vehicle for the expression of these ideas. By focusing on that which could be minutely described, it focused on elements existing in the present. It therefore assisted in the clear articulation of the differences which existed between the dusty, tradition-laden Old World and the fresh and unencumbered New.[74] By adopting this style Duncan therefore had recourse to a method of expression which underlined the contrast between Canada's vitality and Britain's decline. Her treatment of the New World's prospects displayed, in fact, more than a little of the characteristic optimism of what R.W.B. Lewis's classic study *The American Adam* identified as the Party of Hope.[75] Canada, indeed, emerged from Duncan's pages as a more perfect representative of what the New World might produce than the United States itself. Uncorrupted by excess, it had not squandered its potential to regenerate in a surfeit of materialism and republican bad manners.

The presence of American ideas and culture augmented English-Canadian knowledge of American affairs, deepened the English-Canadian tendency to think of Canadian problems in American terms and intensified the English-Canadian conviction that Canada derived a significant part of its essential character from its participation in the life of the North American continent. It enlarged the English-Canadian frame of reference and made many English Canadians almost as fully conscious of American problems as they were of their own. Their thought acquired a continental dimension which came to equal in importance the national and imperial sense in determining the lines along which the English-Canadian outlook would be oriented. With its face turned increasingly towards another society English Canada began in the nineteenth century to move within the framework of that society's attitudes, values, and concerns. It was becoming a society characterized by a special kind of other direction.

Contemporary observers, certainly, were concerned by what they saw as a growing inability on the part of English Canadians to deal with their society in terms other than those which emphasized its character as a New World society and an integral part of the North American continent. Canadians, they argued, were bringing to their contemplation of the Canadian reality minds shaped by their contact with the ideas of another culture. They could, in consequence, acquire at best a partial and incomplete sense of what gave their society its shape and definition. Sara Jeannette Duncan, at once a critic and an exemplar of the process by which the English-Canadian mind was being affected by American influences, was particularly concerned that Canadians become aware of what an unreflective exposure to American ideas might entail. As early as 1887 she had drawn attention to the "American influence on Canadian thought." Continuing exposure to American ideas, she suggested, would produce a Canadian mind likely to "show more than cousinship for its relations over the border." The country's intellectual life would become centred in New York. Its people would lose any sense of their society as one with its own character and history.[76]

If Duncan was concerned with the assimilation of the Canadian mind to the American because of what she viewed as the serious implications this process would have for the rise of a national culture, other observers touched on what it might mean for Canada's relations with Britain and the empire. "In common with other English visitors to Canada," wrote one of them in 1907, "the writer found a scarcity of newspapers and periodicals from the United Kingdom, while, especially in the west, and at large towns like Vancouver, Winnipeg, and Toronto, there was a superabundance of American printed matter. The practical exclusion of English literature ... has had an undoubted Americanizing effect on the public mind of Canada to the detriment of the Old Country connection."[77]

Concern about the presence of American publications had, in fact, led to various proposals through the nineteenth century for the encouragement of the circulation in Canada of British and Canadian material. There was talk among printers and publishers of the manner in which copyright legislation might serve this end. Postal rates were altered to facilitate its achievement. In the 1880s, the founding of the Royal Canadian Academy and the Royal Society of Canada inaugurated the Canadian tradition of government encouragement of cultural life. Not, however, until the early years of the twentieth century were serious steps taken to affect the flow of printed material into Canada. The revision of imperial postal rates in 1907 made it easier for British publications to enter the country while the right given Canada in 1911 to control copyright within its own frontiers meant a strengthening of the Canadian publishing industry.[78]

In the 1920s concern with the character of the nation's cultural life entered a new phase. Critics, armed with what the social sciences were making clear about the manner in which a society's cultural environment was formed, began to argue that assimilation of the Canadian outlook to the American was not an inevitable, "natural" phenomenon, to be explained in terms of such factors as a like response to similar environment. It derived, instead, from the exposure of Canadians to a cultural environment largely American in its composition, in its turn the result of identifiable actions which were amenable to policy. By then, however, the conviction that Canada was best understood as a North American society integrally linked to and virtually indistinguishable from the United States had become even more firmly entrenched in the English-Canadian mind. Environmentalist modes of historical analysis derived from the work of Frederick Jackson Turner combined with the impact of new technologies of culture at the popular level to make the grip of the continental idea more powerful than ever. The decade that saw H.A. Innis and D.G. Creighton provide the first serious explanation of Canada's character and development to be cast in non-continentalist terms also, accordingly, witnessed the appearance of J.W. Dafoe's *Canada: An American Nation*, in which the continentalist version of Canada's evolution was set forth with unremitting clarity. The influence of the continentalist idea was, for the time being, to remain undiminished. Its potency, in fact, assisted the integration of the two societies. How, after all, could one treat as a foreign power the yardstick by which one measured oneself? And if one was not prepared to treat it as such, on what ground could one's involvement with it be limited?

Only in the 1960s, when America's domestic and overseas involvements offered strong evidence that that society did indeed possess a character and interests different from those of Canada, did a significant number of Canadians begin to wonder if that had not been, in some measure at least, true all along. Their growing concern to dissociate Canada from the United States was reinforced by the importance some of them attached to the making of a positive response to the nationalism of Quebec. The consequence was an intensified search for, and a strengthened appreciation of, the elements that distinguished Canada in North America. The work of Innis, Creighton, and S.D. Clark was read more widely than ever before, the character of Canadian political culture was elucidated in ways that distinguished it from that of the United States, and the argument for a distinctive Canadian literary tradition was restated.[79] This activity, moreover, received a greater measure of institutional support than in earlier years, particularly as a consequence of the strengthening of the Canadian publications industry and the creation of a more powerful agency for the regulation of broadcasting in Canada. Events of the last decade or so have, in sum, combined to produce alterations in the Canadian cultural environment which, for the first time, have begun to reduce the degree to which Canadians make sense of their world through the medium of ideas and concepts imported from the United States.

Whether the decline of the continental dimension will in the end involve a simultaneous advance towards a healthy national awareness and a true cosmopolitanism remains to be seen; the prospects, however, seem more encouraging than at any earlier period.

NOTES

1 The process by which the elements of a national tradition are defined, and the uses to which that definition can be put, have received close scrutiny. For some comments on these matters, see Frederick Hertz, *Nationality in History and Politics: A Study of the Psychology and Sociology of National Sentiment and Character* (London, 1944), especially chapter eight "Political Thought and National Ideology," 283–409.

2 Albert Memmi, *Dominated Man* (New York, 1968); Octave Mannoni, trans P. Powesland, *Prospero and Caliban: A Study of the Psychology of Colonization* (London, 1956).

3 Louis Hartz, Kenneth McRae, et al., *The Founding of New Societies: Studies in the History of the United States, Latin America, South Africa, Canada, and Australia* (New York, 1964).

4 Allan Smith, "The Imported Image: American Publications and American Ideas in the Evolution of the English Canadian Mind 1820–1900," PH.D. diss., (University of Toronto, 1971).

5 See S.F. Wise, "Sermon Literature and Canadian Intellectual History," *Bulletin of the Committee on Archives, The United Church of Canada,* 1965, 3–18; Wise, "Upper Canada and the Conservative Tradition," in Ontario Historical Society, *Profiles of a Province* (Toronto, 1967), 20–33; Wise, "Conservatism and Political Development: The Canadian Case," *South Atlantic Quarterly,* 69, Spring 1970, 226–43; Carl Berger, *The Sense of Power: Studies in the Ideas of Canadian Imperialism 1867–1914* (Toronto, 1970); Allan Smith, "Old Ontario and the Emergence of a National Frame of Mind," this volume, and "Metaphor and Nationality in North America," this volume.

6 Allan Smith, "American Culture and the English Canadian Concept of Mission in the Nineteenth Century," this volume, and "American Culture and the English Canadian Mind at the End of the Nineteenth Century," *Journal of Popular Culture,* 4, Spring 1971, 1045–51.

7 J.I. Cooper, "The Mission to the Fugitive Slaves in London," *Ontario History,* 46, Spring 1954, 133.

8 F. Landon, "When Uncle Tom's Cabin Came to Canada," *Ontario History,* 44, January 1952, 3.

9 F. Landon, "Canadian Opinion of Southern Secession 1860–61," *Canadian Historical Review*, 1, September 1920, 255.

10 In 1857, for example, the Montreal YMCA severed its connection with the American organization on the ground that southern associations rejected Negroes, and some ministers, such as J.J.E. Linton of Stratford, raised questions about the use of Sunday school papers emanating from American churches which were neutral on slavery. See W.H. Atherton, *Montreal, 1535–1914* (Montreal/Vancouver/Chicago, 1914), vol. 2, 518, and F. Landon, *Western Ontario and the American Frontier* (Toronto, 1941), 210–11.

11 Landon, "Canadian Opinion of Southern Secession," 258.

12 In 1863 the town of London in Canada West received its first evening newspaper, the *Advertiser*, in part for reasons of this kind: see Landon, *Western Ontario and the American Frontier*, 226.

13 *Globe*, 24 March 1852, cited in Fred Landon, "The Anti-Slavery Society of Canada," *Journal of Negro History*, 4, January 1919, 39.

14 *Globe*, 18 January 1861, cited in Landon, "Canadian Opinion of Southern Secession," 259.

15 *Gazette*, 3 April 1852, cited in Landon, "When Uncle Tom's Cabin Came to Canada," 2.

16 *British American Magazine*, 2, November 1863, 101.

17 *Books and Notions*, 3, September 1886, 24.

18 G.M. Adam, "Georgian Bay and the Muskoka Lakes," in G.M. Grant, ed. *Picturesque Canada: The Country as It Was and Is* (Toronto, 1882), vol. 2, 608.

19 A.N. Dawson, "The Preservation of Our Forests," *Belford's Monthly Magazine*, 1 (December 1876), 74; Carter Troop, "A Cuticular Report," *The Week*, 4, 30 June 1887, 495.

20 Bernard Fernow, a distinguished American forester, delivered a series of lectures at the Kingston School of Mines in 1903, and the head of the Yale Forest School spoke in Canada in 1906. See H.V. Nelles, "The Politics of Development: Forests, Mines and Hydro-Electric Power in Ontario 1890–1939," PH.D. diss., University of Toronto, 1969, 253–4.

21 An idea in existence as early as 1865. In that year Joseph Howe argued that "the timber trade, twisted and intertwined as it is, is a trade owned in fact by the two countries": *Speech of Joseph Howe at the Convention on the Commercial Relations of Great Britain and the United States*, 14 August 1856, 30, cited in A.R.M. Lower, *The North American Assault on the Canadian Forest* (Toronto and New Haven, 1938), 149, n 4.

22 W.H. Smith, *Canada: Past, Present and Future, Being a Historical, Geographical, Geological and Statistical Account of Canada West* (Toronto,

1851), vol. 2, 419; "Facts for the Farmer," *Anglo-American Magazine*, 6 (January 1855), 108.

23 H.J. Morgan, ed., *The Dominion Annual Register and Review, 1882* (1883), 298.

24 Ibid., 1884, 173.

25 Province of Canada, Assembly, *Journals*, 1844–45, appendix W, Report of the Geological Survey, Report of Progress for the Year 1843, dated 28 April 1844, submitted by W.E. Logan.

26 "On the Utility and Design of the Science of Geology, and the best method of acquiring a knowledge of it; with Geological Sketches of Canada," *Canadian Review and Literary and Historical Journal*, no. 2, December 1824, 384.

27 Logan, for example, reported in 1845 that the findings of American geologists at work in the northern states suggested that "a vast trough of deposits ... extends longitudinally from Alabama to some point below Quebec on the St Lawrence, and transversely from the shores of Lake Huron to the borders of the Atlantic." Province of Canada, Assembly, *Journals*, 1844–45, appendix W, Reports on the Geological Survey, presented 27 January 1845, submitted by W.E. Logan.

28 Ibid., 1849, appendix G, Geological Survey of Canada, Report of Progress for the year 1847–48, 1 May 1848.

29 W.H. Smith, for example, made use of such terminology. Writing of the shoreline of Lake Huron from the St Clair to the Saugeen, he referred to the existence of deposits of what he described as "Trenton limestone," a term taken, he noted, from the "New York nomenclature." Smith, *Canada*, vol. 1, 137.

30 Frank Dawson Adams, "The History of Geology in Canada," in H.W. Tory, ed., *A History of Science in Canada* (Toronto, 1939), 8.

31 *British American Magazine*, 2 January 1864, 334–5.

32 Morgan, *Dominion Annual Register, 1879* (1880), 286.

33 In 1879, for example, he read a paper on the Cambrian rocks of North America to the American Association for the Advancement of Science, in 1883 he published an article on the decay of rocks in the *American Journal of Science*, and in 1884 he gave a paper on "The Apatite Deposits of Canada" to a meeting of the American Institute of Mining Engineers. *Dominion Annual Register, 1879*, 283; *1883*, 220; *1884*, 173.

34 In 1837, for example, Mackenzie quoted Orestes A. Brownson on the international significance of the struggle for liberty which was taking place in the 1830s. Lillian F. Gates, "The Decided Policy of William Lyon Mackenzie," *Canadian Historical Review*, 40, September 1959, 186–7, 197.

35 J.M.S. Careless, "Mid-Victorian Liberalism in Central Canadian Newspapers, 1850–67," *Canadian Historical Review*, 31, September 1951, 224.

36 J.M.S. Careless, *Brown of the Globe* (Toronto, 1959), vol. 1, 123.

37 *The Week*, 6 (15 November 1889), 788–9.

38 Nelles, "Politics of Development," 397–8.

39 S.E. Moffett, *The Americanization of Canada* (New York, 1907), 21.

40 *The Week*, 3, 18 March, 1 April, 15 April, 11 March 1886, at 248, 281, 313, and 229 respectively.

41 T. Phillips Thompson, *The Politics of Labour*, intro. Jay Atherton (Toronto, 1975), 5. Originally published 1887.

42 David Levin, *History as a Romantic Art* (Stanford, 1959), 24.

43 Merle Curti, *The Growth of American Thought*, 3rd ed. (New York, 1964), 406.

44 *The Week*, 2, 22 January 1885, 124.

45 Lower Canada, Assembly, *Sessional Papers*, 1835, appendix D, Librarian's Report, 21 February.

46 *Saturday Reader*, 1, 2 December 1865, 194.

47 *Books and Notions*, 1, November 1884, 587.

48 Reviewed in the *Literary Garland*, 4, June 1842, 292.

49 *Canadian Monthly*, 9, May 1877, 564–5.

50 *Rose-Belford's Canadian Monthly*, 3, October 1879, 337–43.

51 *Canadian Monthly*, 6, December 1874, 567; *The Week*, 2, 29 October 1885, 764.

52 Carl C. Berger, "The Vision of Grandeur: Studies in the Ideas of Canadian Imperialism, 1867–1914," PH.D. diss., University of Toronto, 1966, 169–70.

53 William Leggo, "Canada and Her Indian Tribes," *Rose-Belford's Canadian Monthly*, 5, August 1880, 139.

54 W.D. LeSueur, "The Future of Morality," ibid., 4, January 1880, 76.

55 *The Week*, 4, 19 May 1887, 403.

56 Carl F. Klinck, "Literary Activity in the Canadas 1812–1841," in Klinck, Alfred G. Bailey, et al., eds., *The Literary History of Canada* (Toronto, 1965), 131.

57 Carl F. Klinck, "Literary Activity in Canada East and West 1841–1880," in Klinck, ibid., 146.

58 The critic and essayist George Stewart, Jr was particularly interested in American writers. His series, "Evenings in the Library," published in book form, discussed such writers as Bryant, Emerson, and Whittier. It was reviewed by the *Canadian Monthly*, 13, March 1878, 330. See also his "Longfellow in Canada," published in the *Literary World* and noted in *Rose-Belford's Canadian Monthly*, 6, May 1881, 552. The next year he read a paper on Thoreau to the Literary and Historical

Society of Quebec (Morgan, ed., *Dominion Annual Register, 1882*, 284) and, in 1887, devoted part of an article entitled "Letters in Canada" to the work of American authors, *The Week*, 4, 16 June 1887, 462. Other Canadians who wrote on American literature include Charles G.D. Roberts and J. Macdonald Oxley. See Roberts' "Notes on Some of the Younger American Poets," *The Week*, 1, 24 April 1884, 328–9, and Oxley's "Notes of a Literary Pilgrimage, part two, Boston," ibid., 4, 5 May 1887, 365.

59 *The Week*, 1, 6 December 1883, 11; *Books and Notions*, 2, October 1885, and 1, September 1884, 28.

60 One critic, for example, thought Charles G.D. Roberts' poem, "A Christmas Eve Courtin,'" to have been written "after the style of [the American poet] Carleton." Another found Gilbert Parker's "Pretty Pierre" stories to be "a poor imitation of Bret Harte." And A.G. Bailey has remarked on the frequency with which such American writers as Aldrich, Stedman, Fawcett, Bryant, and, above all, Parkman and Longfellow were taken as models by Canadian writers. See Gordon Waldron, "Canadian Poetry: A Criticism," *Canadian Magazine* 8 (2), 1896, 103; Archibald MacMechan, *Headwaters of Canadian Literature* (Toronto, 1924), 142; Bailey, "Literature and Nationalism after Confederation," *University of Toronto Quarterly*, 25, July 1956, 409–24.

61 Klinck, *Literary History of Canada*, 160.

62 V.L.O. Chittick, "Haliburton Postscript, I: Ring-tailed Yankee," *Dalhousie Review*, 36, Spring 1957, 33, and "Books and Music in Haliburton," ibid., 38, Summer 1958, 215.

63 R.P. Baker, *A History of English Canadian Literature to the Confederation* (Cambridge, MA, 1920), 82–3.

64 T.G. Marquis, "English Canadian Literature," in Adam Shortt and Arthur G. Doughty, eds., *Canada and its Provinces* (Toronto, 1914), vol. 12, part 2, 541.

65 John P. Matthews, *Tradition in Exile* (Toronto, 1962), 115.

66 Cited in Margaret L. Clark, "American Influences on the Canadian Novel," MA thesis, University of New Brunswick, 1940, 46.

67 Cited in Baker, *History of English Canadian Literature*, 130–1.

68 On this point see Marcia B. Kline, *Beyond the Land Itself: Views of Nature in Canada and the United States* (Cambridge, MA, 1970).

69 Roger B. Salomon, "Realism as Disinheritance: Twain, Howells, and James," *American Quarterly*, 16, Winter, 1964, 532–44.

70 Louisa Murray, "Democracy in Literature," *The Week*, 6, 2 August 1889, 550.

71 Ibid., 4, 21 July 1887, 549.

72 Sara Jeannette Duncan, "Outworn Literary Methods," ibid., 4, 9 June

1887, 450–1; "Literary Pabulum," 4, 24 November 1887, 831; and "W.D. Howells at Washington," 3, 22 April 1886, 327.

73 MacMechan, *Headwaters of Canadian Literature,* 137.

74 Salomon, "Realism as Disinheritance."

75 R.W.B. Lewis, *The American Adam* (Chicago, 1959), 7.

76 Duncan, "American Influence on Canadian Thought," *The Week,* 4, 7 July 1887, 518.

77 A.M. Murray, *Imperial Outposts from a Strategical and Commercial Aspect, with Special Reference to the Japanese Alliance* (London, 1907), 181–2n.

78 Smith, "The Imported Image," part 2, "The Mechanics of Culture," 102–206.

79 Harold A. Innis, *The Fur Trade in Canada* (New Haven, 1930); Donald Creighton, *The Commercial Empire of the St Lawrence, 1760– 1850* (New York and Toronto, 1937); the essays in S.D. Clark's *The Developing Canadian Community* (Toronto, 1962), especially "The Canadian Community and the American Continental System," 185–98. Also, Gad Horowitz, *Canadian Labour in Politics* (Toronto, 1968) and Margaret Atwood, *Survival: A Thematic Guide to Canadian Literature* (Toronto, 1972).

4 Samuel Moffett and the Americanization of Canada

The new world had a profound impact on the quality of European life and the shape of European thought. To some observers it was a raw and barbarous place requiring the civilizing hand of the European; others pronounced it virgin and unspoiled, a land of purity, youth, and innocence, where humans might be remade. All, however, were very nearly mesmerized by it. From the Halls of Montezuma to the Kingdom of the Saguenay it seemed a fabulous place, its treasure and potential far exceeding anything to be found in the world they knew.

In time many commentators found its incredible promise most fully realized in the United States. There liberty and abundance had combined to produce a spectacularly successful civilization, one committed to, and apparently able to sustain, a society of opportunity and freedom for all. With the making of a successful revolution, the special virtues of American society came to be viewed not simply as an emanation of place but as a function of politics, for the republican order seemed simultaneously to confirm and amplify American freedoms. American political and social principles, it was thought, would redeem Europe from the lassitude of aristocratic domination.[1]

If much of the American impact on the European world before 1900 occurred at the level of idea and inspiration, the imperialism

"Introduction," in Samuel E. Moffett, *The Americanization of Canada* (Toronto: University of Toronto Press, 1972), vii–xxxi.

of the 1890s joined with Theodore Roosevelt's aggressive foreign policy to transform America's presence in world affairs into one which was hard, tangible, and real.[2] European observers noted with concern the rise of this new constellation in the heavens of their world. "One hears," wrote the French historian Henri Hauser in 1905, "nothing spoken of in the press, at meeting, in parliament, except the American peril."[3] In 1899 the same ominous phrase had formed the title of two articles written by Octave Noel for *Le Correspondant*.[4] Italians and Germans, too, noticed the new phenomenon.[5]

The emergence of America turned, of course, on more than the war with Spain or the antics of an exuberant chief executive; its foundations rested upon America's maturing economic order, the rise of modern communications, and a mastery of technique and organization evident even then. These elements combined with the appeal of American popular culture to ensure a massive American influence abroad. In 1901 the British newspaperman W.T. Stead suggested in a volume entitled *The Americanization of the World* that it was the special flavour and energy of American civilization which powered its thrust to a kind of world domination. American business techniques, organizational principles, machinery, magazines, dress, sports, slang, capital, and values were making their way around the world. They were at once altering the style of the globe and making it tributary to the United States.

The American phenomenon had particular meaning for Britain. Especially vulnerable to Americanization, it also had the most to lose by the rise of American power. If its exposure to that power meant, Stead wrote, that it was "beginning to be energized by the electric current of American ideas and American methods," it also meant that "we can never again be the first."[6] But the United States, he continued, was not yet strong enough to become the arbiter of the world. Serious thought, therefore, should be given to an Anglo-Saxon union. Only in this way could continuing Anglo-Saxon hegemony be assured. More, only in this way could a continuing British presence at the centre of the world's affairs be guaranteed.

Americans had believed from the beginning of their history that they must be a people of moment in the world's affairs. Convinced of their society's unique and special character, they could not doubt (in John Winthrop's famous formulation) that "the eyes of

the world are upon us." And no wonder, for, as the Puritans conceived it, their task was nothing less than the undertaking of an
errand in the wilderness for the purpose of realizing God's plan for
humankind. Other societies in watching them would see how the
job was to be done. They might, then, reorder their affairs and so
build the perfect state so far as such an end was within their
means.[7]

In time, some Americans suggested a more active role for their
society. It must function as a haven for the oppressed. Its task was
to uplift the masses of the Old World by inviting them to renew
themselves in its midst.[8] As the expansionist impulse in American
life deepened, Americans began to argue that there was propriety
and justice in being yet more active in the world. The principles of
freedom were not to be served passively in the hope that other societies would of their own volition respond to the American model.
America must actively seek to enlarge the area of true democracy,
ensure the best use of available resources, and act in the interests
of less fortunate peoples. Power must be exercised in the service of
liberty. Present as a factor in American expansionism across the
North American continent in the nineteenth century, this complex
of beliefs served at its end to provide a powerful rationale for the
American thrust into the Caribbean and across the Pacific.[9]

While many Americans doubted that establishing a formal
empire was the way for America to be active in the world, few questioned the wisdom of involvement itself. Imperialism of the old and
conventional variety might be frowned upon, but what lay short of
formal empire was not. Military intervention in Latin America, the
establishing of Asian spheres of influence, the marshalling of the
fleet, and, especially, the ever-growing interest in exporting American capital and culture became features of American activity abroad.
Even reformers might support America's growing influence overseas, for it seemed plainly to involve activity in the interests of
freedom.

Imperialism was in fact closely linked to reform. It sought to do
beyond the borders of the United States what reformers wished to
do at home. Proponents of the Social Gospel like Josiah Royce
might advocate expansion, while Progressives could do the same.
They, like other Americans, believed in economic growth and national prosperity. Their tendency to take a paternal interest in
American blacks disposed them to the adoption of a similar attitude towards non-white peoples in general. Above all, they approved imperialism because they understood the United States to

be the land, indeed the home, of free and open institutions. Any extension of its domain, therefore, was *per se* an extension of freedom and democracy.[10]

No country was more fully aware of the United States, both as a symbol and an intractable reality, than Canada. Canadians had noticed for some time the impact that America was having on their society. Commentators pointed regularly to cultural invasion, close economic links, and what to them seemed the indisputable facts of geography as circumstances which would insure a large and effective American influence in Canada. Upper Canada, Sir George Arthur was informed at the end of the 1830s, must "be materially affected by the state of Politics and of the popular mind in the neighbouring Republic."[11] In the 1860s Thomas D'Arcy McGee pointed out that while American ideas had an influence on "all the populations of the New World," it had been brought most fully to bear on "those of us nearest their source."[12] By the last years of the century Sara Jeannette Duncan found Canadian cultural life rapidly being assimilated to American.[13] In 1889 a lengthy article in Canada's leading periodical, the *Week*, concluded that America's great power, reinforced by the facts of geography, made some form of union with the United States inevitable.[14] And in 1891 Goldwin Smith drew his continentalist argument together between the covers of a single book, *Canada and the Canadian Question*,[15] the burden of whose message was that Canada was a geographical, cultural, and economic absurdity – given these considerable disabilities, faced with the vitality that was America, it could not hope to survive.

Samuel E. Moffett's *The Americanization of Canada* has relevance in each of these several traditions. By examining at length and in detail the manner in which Canadian society was affected by the new industrial America of the late nineteenth century, he revealed something of the manner in which American power was making itself felt around the world. The book in that sense became a case study with a broad significance: technology, communications, and the flow of culture did not simply work to fuse the United States and Canada; they underlay the process by which the world itself was becoming Americanized.

Indirectly the book was a contribution to the literature of Anglo-American solidarity. The foundations of the special relationship between England and the United States, laid by the Treaty of Washington in 1871 and largely the result of the changing power situation which required England to take an emerging America seriously, were strengthened in the 1890s by a further alteration in the relative fortunes of the two powers coupled with a vigorous insistence on the superiority of the Anglo-Saxon peoples. The argument for Anglo-Saxon solidarity, advanced in such books as Sir Charles Dilke's *Greater Britain* (1867), J.R. Seeley's *The Expansion of England* (1883), and J.A. Froude's *Oceana* (1886), generated much enthusiasm for the notion that the Anglo-Saxon peoples of the world were a superior force and ought to act in harmony and co-operation. It was not long before Americans overcame enough of their distrust of the Old World in general and Britain in particular to argue a similar case. In the 1890s Captain Mahan's suggestions that the Anglo-American relationship should be close and firm were greeted with enthusiasm on both sides of the Atlantic,[16] while in 1903 John R. Dos Passos of New York called for "a complete and sympathetic *entente* between the Anglo-Saxon peoples." Canada occupied a vital place in all of this, for "with Canada a separate nation, as she is now, a real, lasting *entente* between the British Empire and the United States, is impossible."[17] The implication of Moffett's argument for the fact of Canada's Americanization was to suggest that one of the principal steps on the way to a reunion of the Anglo-Saxon peoples had already been taken.

Moffett – an American – was also providing a document in the literature of American expansionism. Despite his moderate and judicious tone, he was mounting an argument for the triumph of continentalism. In doing so he made clear his belief that the continental society he saw in the making was American in its contours. The process by which Canadians were being assimilated to the American way of life would eventually produce a victory, muted and not to be described in the florid language of a Benton or a Beveridge, but no less real, for manifest destiny. The American idea would at last comprehend the continent, its sway undisputed.

Moffett, of course, was a progressive expansionist. Scholarly books and articles pointing to the manner in which government and democracy had been subverted by concentrations of economic power,[18] a brand of journalism which allowed him to place his views on these matters before a wide public, and a cool and persuasive style of argument gave him impeccable progressive credentials. It was precisely his progressivism that allowed him to view with such satisfaction the obliteration of Canada. By becoming assimilated to the United States, Canada was fulfilling itself as a liberal and progressive society. Released from its bondage to the institutions of an Old World community, Canada would at last be free. The original title of Moffett's volume was, in fact, *The Emancipation of Canada.*[19] Nothing could have made clearer his conviction that Canada's well-being lay in absorption by the United States. Americanization and emancipation were synonymous and interchangeable terms.

Finally, the book had relevance to the continuing continentalist debate in Canada. That debate, near the centre of Canadian politics for twenty years, had hitherto had few serious American participants. Although politicians and journalists had called on countless occasions for the annexation of the British territories to the north, only a limited number of Americans had attempted a full and coherent case for either the desirability or the inevitability of such a development. Benjamin F. Butler, addressing the alumni of Colby College in 1889, had emphasized the great value of Canadian land and resources on the one hand and spoken of annexation as a prelude to the reunion of the Anglo-Saxton peoples on the other,[20] while Dos Passos considered the fusion of the two peoples an essential preliminary to the Anglo-American reunion. Moffett's contribution was, however, the first to be made in detailed and comprehensive terms. And, as an argument which the *Review of Historical Publications Relating to Canada* found to be written with "insight and accuracy," it was the first to be taken seriously in Canada.

While the book lacked the polemical force of Goldwin Smith's earlier text, it had considerable power, much of which derived from the capacity of its author, using his training in the social sciences, to mobilize and order quantities of information. Despite its brevity, it was in fact a more detailed and substantial argument than had yet appeared on either side of the border. All of this made it the first modern study of the processes making for continental integration.

Moffett's principal contention was that communications and the flow of trade now bound the two countries together, while a single North American civilization, founded upon the intermingling of peoples, the sharing of a democratic impulse born of life in the New World, and a common exposure to the popular culture of the United States, had already emerged. Contemplation of these phenomena led inexorably, said Moffett, to the conclusion that while "the English-speaking Canadians protest that they will never become Americans – they are already Americans without knowing it" (p. 114*). They might be politically distinct and deeply concerned to maintain their political distinctiveness, but their separate institutions contained a society in no other respect than its being thus enclosed dissimilar to its southern neighbour. Within the framework of those institutions an American society, bound to the United States in every way, had grown up.

Only recently has scholarship begun to address itself to some of the questions raised by Moffett. His concern with the manner in which Canadians viewed their collective experience, his examination of the way in which American culture had influenced the shape of the Canadian mind, his suggestion that Canadian interest in the empire grew out of nationalist motives, and his observation that investment flows as well as trade patterns were influential in the integration of the North American economy, rested upon important and early insights. In some of what he wrote, of course, he merely followed the path marked out by earlier commentators; his observation that steam and communications had operated to unify North America, for example, testified to the prescience of the New York *Herald*'s 1867 observation that the new technology would make American power as irresistible on the continent at large as it had in the American South.[21]

Even where his book followed an outline established by others, however, it made a contribution of its own. Where much of the argument for the unity of the Canadian and American peoples had come to rest on grounds of race and a shared patrimony, Moffett founded his case on arguments drawn from the new social sciences. What impelled the Americans and Canadians to move together was not a mystical bond inhering in peoples ultimately drawn from the same stock; nor was it a common language, for the process affected even the French-speaking population of North America. The impulse, instead, derived from the most solid and tangible of factors, for it was the material logic of commerce, capital, and ultimately geography which drew the two societies together.

The power of the environment, indeed, was such that it created a frame of mind in all essentials the same on both sides of the border. Canadians were not remade in the image of Americans by their reading of American news. They craved that news because they were *already* attuned to the things with which it dealt. "It is,"

---

* Page references are to the 1972 University of Toronto Press edition.

wrote Moffett, "largely a case of supply accommodating itself to demand. The newspapers print what experience has taught them their patrons wish to read" (p. 98).

Moffett's book depended for its effect not so much upon the brilliance and flash of its argument as upon the weight of its accumulated evidence. Statistics concerning population movements, railway construction, trade flows, investment patterns, and the circulation of American publications in Canada fill its pages. Quotations from Canadian, American, and British sources were deployed with effect. Evidence for old truths was found in new and uncommon places – the fact, for example, that Canadians paid streetcar fares as did Americans, at a single rate, or the presence in Canada of American fraternal associations.

The mark of the social scientist was evident, too, in the presence of theoretical concepts. By pointing to the fact that "a metropolis diffuses a potent influence on all sides" and that, therefore, "there is no city in Canada which does not have to meet the competition of a more important American city within drawing distance of its own constituency" (p. 67), he at once focused attention on a hitherto largely unappreciated circumstance making for continental integration and pressed his claim to be taken seriously as a man who knew what made society work. Finally, his argument offered testimony to the utility of the comparative method. Its validity depended upon the absence of significant distinctions between the two societies and there was but one way in which that absence could be demonstrated.

Yet, for all its interest, Moffett's book is not above criticism. Too frequently its author's pronouncements on Canada were informed by ignorance or incomprehension. A paragraph on the relationship between responsible government, the elective principle, and Durham's proposal for a British North American union defied understanding (p. 24). Another on the nature of the Canadian executive branch wrongly implied that "tacit British convention" was inferior to "formal law" (p. 31). A third misrepresented the character of *Canadien* society before the Conquest – New France contained no imitation *noblesse* "whose supremacy was humbly recognized by the mass of the people" (p. 48). On more than one occasion misunderstanding yielded to error and contradiction. If it was misleading to assert that New Brunswick "practically secured" responsible government in 1837, it was simply wrong to say that Nova Scotia got it in 1840 (p. 24). And, whereas his readers were told on page 48 that "the United Empire Loyalists were strongly predisposed to aristocratic ideas," on page 54 they were informed that, on the contrary, the Loyalists were of the egalitarian New World, "simply Americans, differing in no respect from those they had left behind in the States."

The argument itself was, in various of its stages, confused and uncertain. A number of Canadians were cited in support of Moffett's assertion that their countrymen felt only a weakening sense of attachment to Englishmen and even England; they had indeed noted the signs that the tie binding Canada to Britain was no longer what it once had been; but the tone and substance of their remarks made it clear that this was not for them a matter of indifference, much less celebration. By thus showing themselves possessed of a considerable body of imperial sentiment they deprived Moffett's point of much of its force (pp. 45–6).

Quotations from Canadian newspapers were paraded in support of the claim that the Americanization of English Canada's cultural life was well advanced (pp. 96–7). That Canadians could so argue might indeed be proof that their culture was in process of erosion, but their concern also offered undeniable testimony to the fact that the process was incomplete. Had it not been, there would have been no vantage point from which this development could be assessed, much less (as the newspapers clearly hoped it would be) halted.

If Moffett's anxiety to press his case sometimes led him in peculiar and unintended directions, the rigour of his argument was further diminished by the character of some of its principal parts. "The Silken Tie," a chapter devoted to consideration of the imperial link, was designed to expose the weak and insubstantial nature of that link, and so suggest how inevitable was the tightening of Canada's North American ties. Yet the chapter was confused in almost all of its principal assertions. It began with the observation that "at present" imperialism in Canada was no more than "effusive loyalty to the British connection" (p. 40) – an airy sentiment without foundation or depth. This was followed, consistently enough, by the solemn suggestion that Canadians on the whole, and whatever their expressed sentiments might be, were less than enthusiastic about imperial integration, a fact demonstrated by their long-standing reluctance to participate in imperial defence schemes (pp. 40–2). The final revelation, however, was only marginally supported by what had preceded it: "Canadians of all kinds are ceasing to regard themselves as the people of a British colony. They are citizens of an allied nation. Their loyalty is no longer to England, but to the British Empire, of which they consider themselves equal members, with the confident expectation that before very long they will be first" (p. 46).

Where Moffett had earlier implied, in a manner consistent with his overall argument, that Canada was only on occasion caught up in enthusiasm for empire, here he made the quite different point that Canadians were exchanging one set of attitudes to Britain and the empire for another. So, at the conclusion of a chapter whose principal aim had been to suggest the existence of a thrust away from empire, Moffett presented his readers with the portrait of a society which, far from being concerned to withdraw into a North American isolationism, hankered for involvement at the side of Britain and even aspired to become the empire's ranking power.

In finding a vital Canadian imperialism, rooted in a strong national sense, Moffett found what in fact was there. But one who gains his way by losing it does not ordinarily inspire confidence, particularly when the pathway thus uncovered leads in a direction opposite to that in which he first set out and still wished to travel.

Moffett's inability to make the Canadian nationalism he had discovered mesh with his central argument emerged with even greater force elsewhere in the book. Having inadvertently conceded the existence of a Canadian nationalism apparently capable of powering Canada to a pre-eminent position in the empire, an inevitable logic led him to assert that it would serve Canadian independence in North America as well. The tendency of Canadian unions to wish an end to their involvement with their American parents was, he wrote, "part of the workings of the growing spirit of nationality which is striving passionately to make Canada a self-sufficing entity, free from dependence either upon the old sovereign power across the sea, or the gigantic neighbor next door" (p. 94).

If Moffett's argument lacked a certain consistency, his use of the comparative method also invited criticism. He pressed his case by focusing on only those elements in Canadian life that supported his claim that the two societies were in all essentials the same. The comparison, argued in these terms, yielded results. The cost, however, came high. Minimizing the differences between the two societies to the vanishing point not only obscured reality but involved a perversion of the method itself. Canada and the United States might well be contained within a single, democratic, egalitarian, fluid New World frame. Canadians *mores* might indeed be moving to an approximation of the American. Canadians might, as Moffett claimed, be demonstrating the Americanization of their values in travelling to the United States in increasing numbers to get the divorces their law denied them at home (pp. 110–11). But was there no more to be said? Were there no questions to be raised about the quality of a social system whose conventions made necessary the adoption by Canadians of such a clumsy and awkward expedient? Here, surely, was a practice the necessity to maintain which revealed as much in the way of differences between the two societies as the willingness to have recourse to it suggested about similarities.

Often Moffett's concern to press the case for a continental society led him to pass over with the barest acknowledgment the existence of real and basic differences between Canada and the United States. The fact that the Canadian state was founded upon principles of linguistic duality, cultural diversity, and minority rights distinguished it fundamentally from the American which protected individual rather than collective liberties. The "American" features of the Union government of 1840 received lengthy analysis, but the important fact that throughout the 1840s that government was being remade to take account of the cultural duality at the centre of Canadian society received little attention (pp. 24–6). The 1848 decision to resume the printing of legislative debates in French was given the briefest of references (p. 26). The determination of the Fathers of Confederation to create a pluralist state was not mentioned at all.

Moffett lavished much attention upon the American-like character of Canadian federalism. He relentlessly exposed the democratic principles which had penetrated the heart of Canadian government (pp. 27–37). Little significance, however, was attached to the fact that maintaining the practice of responsible cabinet government and the principle of parliamentary supremacy insured that the exercise of executive power in Canada would not be circumscribed as it was in the United States, but left free and untrammelled upon the British model.

Moffett's failure properly to employ the comparative method left his case more vulnerable than it needed to be. While making much of the fact that Canadians ingested American popular culture, he neglected to point out that much the same thing was happening in Britain.[22] Britain, however, was not becoming Americanized in anything like the sense claimed for Canada. To be sure, his argument implied the critical difference: Canada was so close to the United States, the range of influences operating to Americanize it so extensive, that in its case, unlike that of Britain, no resistance was possible. But so important a point was to be made by more than implication. By failing to make it, Moffett invited the charge, which the *Review of Historical Publications Relating to Canada* did not hesitate to advance, that he had failed to make clear why the penetration of American culture into Canada should have results there it had not yielded across the Atlantic.

Occasionally, of course, Moffett saw another Canada than the one demanded by the terms of his argument. The country seemed, he had conceded, determined to survive. Its newspapers, of central importance in shaping the national outlook, might in most respects be American, but in feeling and sentiment they were "intensely Canadian" (p. 96). He even admitted (though unintentionally and on his way to another destination) the reality of an element in the Canadian experience which many Canadians had made the core of their nationalist doctrine: its northern climate and rugged topography. An eighteenth century hunter, he wrote, "might have started at the mouth of the Ohio and worked his way to the Arctic Ocean without ever noticing anything but the weather to remind him that he had passed from one country to another" (p. 8). But such fleeting glimpses of a separate Canada only enlarged the dimensions of his failure. They show him poised at the edge of a vast plain the implications of whose existence he seemed at once aware yet indisposed to investigate.

If Moffett's argument can be criticized *sui generis*, it may also be faulted for failing fully to comprehend those areas of the Canadian experience that did not conform to its central requirement. Undeniably, much had happened by 1907 to bind the two societies together. But in his haste to urge that fundamental point, Moffett failed to give others their due: he did not, in particular, explain why, in spite of all that happened to deprive Canada of a meaningfully independent existence in North America, it nonetheless continued to exist.

The assertion that the country's survival was apparent rather than real met one difficulty only to create another. What survived might be merely a shell, without substance or strength; but why, then, had *it* survived? Surely such a fragile and unsupported structure must have collapsed before 1907. The exigencies of Moffett's argument demanded that he explain this point in terms of the failures of American policy. To approach it in any other way would be to admit what it was the point of his book not to concede. The British tie, he therefore asserted, endured after the War of 1812 only because of American error. Canada's survival was owing to "a long series of American mistakes through which [the British] connection has been maintained to the present time" (p. 9). That Britain may have had a serious interest in maintaining a Canada independent in North America which more than an adept American diplomacy would have been required to overcome was a possibility his argument did not allow him to consider.

Some of Moffett's fellow Americans might have read him a lesson in what gave Canada its capacity to endure. Britain, Captain Mahan had written almost twenty years before, depended upon its premier American possession to supply a route to the East should Suez fall. Canada thus became the staff of empire, its vast railway a vital link in the imperial communications system. To insure the integrity of that system, and the survival of the nation through whose territory it ran, was a British interest of the first order. In its pursuit Britain would not hesitate to apply her seapower to America's Atlantic coast. "It is upon our Atlantic seaboard," wrote Mahan, "that the mistress of Halifax, of Bermuda, and of Jamaica will now defend Vancouver and the Canadian Pacific."[23]

Moffett's failure to see what within the country itself aided its survival on the North American continent was, however, owing to more than the limits imposed upon his argument by the nature of the case it was constructed to make; the origins of that failure were also to be traced to a vision confined by ethnocentrism and a reluctance to concede the power and worth of anything not American-like. The Americanizing process was equated with emancipation; the "progress of government," the chapter of that title made clear, was defined by the degree to which American practices had made their way to the centre of Canadian politics; and Canada was a slow and parochial society because "no Canadian government has ever had to concern itself with the maintenance of the open door in China, the construction of a Panama canal, or the conclusion of peace between Russia and Japan" (p. 20) – because, that is, no Canadian government had done the things Roosevelt's America had done.

The peculiar astigmatism which this combination induced overcame any chance there might have been that Moffett would see what any student of Canadian-American problems should have perceived: the fact that there existed potent forces in Canada making for the maintenance of a separate society.

Geography, producing an impulse to create a separate economy based on the river systems of the north, had provided a main force behind the rise of a separate Canadian society. It had given the French, and even more the English who arrived after 1760, a powerful material interest in resisting continental union. Yet of these people, or of the merchants who in rejecting involvement in the American Revolution became the initiators of a policy which still retained much of its force, or of that policy itself, Moffett had little to say. And what eluded him was more than a knowledge of the National Policy's pedigree and the sources of its strength; he failed to appreciate the degree to which, in his own day, its vitality had been maintained.[24]

Other forces, too, contributed to the maintenance of a separate Canada. The necessity to organize and administer a far-flung territory had combined with the character of French imperialism under the Old Régime, the shape of British policy after the American Revolution, and the desire to resist American expansionism to give Canada institutions more centralized and authoritarian than those which prevailed in American society. The conservatism induced by this crucial circumstance was reinforced by the coming of the Loyalists and the waves of nineteenth century British immigration. All of this conferred upon Canadians a tradition and a set of values at once the engine and the focus of their independence in North America.[25]

Moffett, then, not only failed to appreciate the strength of national feeling; more seriously, he did not see that its strength derived from the reality of a different historical experience, a fact that made it a more powerful and deeply rooted phenomenon than he had imagined.

All of this makes less than surprising his failure to take with due seriousness the search then underway in Canada for an understanding of the national character. The arguments made by those engaged in that search were impressionistic, superficial, and crude; yet social science has revealed some of them to have been constructed around more than a grain of truth. Canada has been, as some of Moffett's Canadian contemporaries claimed, a conservative society in which deference, respect for authority, and a clear tendency to think in terms of hierarchy and élites has been present.[26] This circumstance, while not altogether the happy one they thought it to be, none the less gave Canada a more than formal means of distinguishing itself from the United States. It explains, moreover, the vehemence with which many Canadians denounced the loose and egalitarian character of American society. How it had endured was a mystery; that it must collapse seemed at times a certainty.[27] The United States was, in contrast to Canada, a society without form, shape, direction, or leadership.

How wide-ranging was the discussion of whose substance and foundations Moffett seemed so wholly unaware may be gauged from the fact that, even as he wrote, its confines were enlarged to include consideration of those shifts in attitude towards the west which would prepare the way for a redefinition of the National Policy. Resolution of the problem was hardly begun; regional tension would remain a central fact of Canadian life; its contribution to the rise of continentalism would be profound; yet there was now an early awareness of the fact that maintaining the National Policy in all its orthodox simplicity would not serve the rival interests of the different Canadas. No more, wrote E.W. Thomson with an exaggeration that marked the measure of his confidence, would the west be administered "Spanish-fashion, for the benefit of eastern interests."[28] It now had its own governments. An elaborate program of railway construction was underway. The operations of grain elevators were beginning to be regulated.[29] Thomson's enthusiasm was notably premature; yet it underlined the fact that work was now in train to build a truly balanced Canada; but of that work, and of its implications for continentalism, Moffett had nothing to say.

A particularly important subtlety that altogether escaped his attention was contained in the peculiar relationship many policy-makers in Canada discerned between independence and continentalism. To them an important paradox lay at the foundation of Canadian national life: Canada could expect to survive as a separate society only by conceding the strength of the forces of continentalism. To deny wholly the continental pull would be to cause irresistible pressures to be built up in its favour. This, one of Elgin's principal arguments in pressing for the Reciprocity Treaty of 1854, had been used in the great debates over "commercial union" and "unrestricted reciprocity" before 1891; it was still clearly in evidence in Moffett's day. So long as some degree of integration between the Canadian and American transportation systems was permitted, wrote one observer, it was unlikely that the west would object to federal development policy so strongly as to weaken national unity. Canada "seems now safe from internal hurt so long as there be no federal procedure on a plausible national policy notion that traffic between West and East ought to be forced over Canadian lines."[30] A measure of continental integration might, then, meet regional grievances, reduce ill feeling among different sections of the country, and so *strengthen* Canadian unity. The forces of continentalism would be diminished and the Canadian thrust to maintain its independence in North America sustained.

There remained, of course, much truth in Moffett's principal assertions. Other observers – Smith, Stead, Dos Passos – saw the close links that existed between Canada and the United States, and even those commentators most anxious to establish the independence of Canada in North America conceded their substantial reality. In 1911 the *United Empire* reported that many Canadians opposed reciprocal trade with the United States precisely because it would draw parts of Canada, already closely attached to the adjacent parts of the republic, even nearer to it. Canadian communications, built with difficulty, "tie together many provinces which geographically, climatically, and even racially, have greater affinities with their neighbours immediately south."[31] No arrangement which might endanger those communications (and who did not know how easy it was to devise such an arrangement?) should be countenanced.

Then, too, Moffett's contention that "Greater Canada" (p. 14), the true and ample homeland of the Canadian people, was to be found in North America as a whole, owing to the heavy Canadian emigration to the United States, was an important and worthwhile point. Canadians found the United States attractive indeed. It seemed to contain within itself the entire New World's promise. And if Americans had met with fabulous success, Canadians too had made their mark in the great republic. In the last decades of the nineteenth century many of them, inspired by the good fortune of their predecessors, left to make their homes there. All of this led to a "Canadian exodus" whose causes K.L. Jones attempted to explain in 1890: "The ambitious Canadian ... reads of the Astors and the Vanderbilts, the Goulds and the Carnegies, and the immense fortunes they have rolled up in a few years. He knows they were poor boys, with no capital, and relying only on energy, pluck, and mother wit, and he believes he can follow their footsteps. His chances of success are at least as good there as they are at home. He knows of Canadians who have made their mark. The stories of Erastus Wiman and others read like fairy tales."[32] And so he determines to emigrate. Moffett's chapter on this subject dramatically reinforced Goldwin Smith's celebrated remark that if the United States was not annexing Canada it was assuredly annexing the Canadians. The point, too, was true in more than a narrow and literal sense, for many Canadians viewed their society as a community of the New World.

Yet, even among those Canadians who saw themselves as an integral part of the New World Community, there were many who did not think in terms of realizing themselves or their society's character in the continentalist mode. Canada's destiny remained one to be worked out within the empire and in terms of Canada's links to the Old World. A Canada whose people were restored by their sojourn in the New World would revitalize, and ultimately dominate the empire. The focus of sentiment, then, remained imperial. Canada was of the New World but its interest and orientation were distinct from those of the United States.

Stephen Leacock played upon these un-American and anti-American feelings when in the same year that Moffett's book appeared he urged the attractiveness and power of quite another conception of Canada's national destiny. His country, sharing fully in the abundance of the New World, must shoulder its responsibilities abroad by sharing equally fully in the responsibilities of the British Empire. Movement into the world of empire would enlarge its spirit, lead to the recognition of a wider citizenship, and, ultimately (here his turn of phrase made clear the measure of his difference with Moffett) involve "the realization of a Greater Canada."[34]

Not all Canadians shared Leacock's enthusiasm for a Canadian future so clearly the opposite of that which Moffett had conceived. For many, Canada's New World character meant that autonomy at the empire's edge, not activity at its centre, would help Canada achieve its destiny. But even they accepted the proposition that their national fate was to be worked out within the imperial system. That system must, of course, allow for the free movement of its component parts. "Canadianism," the *Canadian Liberal Monthly* told the party faithful in 1913, "is the basis of enduring Imperial Unity."[35] But once that fact was recognized, the empire might indeed endure.

The point, by now, is clear enough: Moffett failed to grasp the fact that whatever might be happening to its economy, its railways, or its divorce rate, there remained in Canada the sense of an historical experience more than marginally different from the American which fed and sustained a reservoir of national feeling the measure of whose depth he had not taken. To join the enthusiast who proclaimed in 1911 that a "distinct facial type ... is being evolved among the native-born Canadians"[36] would have been to subordinate both anthropology and good sense to a nationalism at once ludicrous, fanciful, and extreme. Yet the continuing existence of the Canadian state made it possible to argue with force and cogency that Canada did possess the resources necessary to accomplish the assimilation of immigrants to the idea that their new society should retain its independence in North America. Canada, one observer noted, "gradually makes not Britishers but Canadians," although it matters "no rap to Canada's separate political existence in America" whether immigrants become one or the other.[37] What was important was that they join in the general determination that Canada not become part of the United States. All of this meant, Lord Bryce reported in 1913, that "the temper and feelings of [the Canadian] people, and the growth of a vigourous national sentiment among them, have not been making for their union with the far larger mass of the United States."[38]

Moffett, of course, cannot be faulted for failing to foresee the results of the election of 1911. Yet it does his argument no credit that nothing in it makes those results intelligible. Nothing in it (save where consistency falters and inadvertence triumphs) suggests the existence of that core of national feeling soon to be so effectively activated by Laurier's opponents and the enemies of continentalism.

Some could claim that in 1911 Canadians merely exorcised the spectre of political and economic union while allowing the Americanization process to continue unabated; Moffett had, after all, argued at the outset that form and intent were measurably less important than substance and outcome. Yet the impulse to retain a separate political character turned, in the last analysis, on the fact that the Americanization process was incomplete. Thus might the Australian traveller H.S. Gullett write in 1911 that the Americanization of Canada was a limited phenomenon – Canadians might be American "in form" but inwardly they retained their identity and orientation. Canada, therefore, would endure. "Never," asserted Gullett, "for a moment are you oppressed by the thought that Canada is becoming Americanized in the national sense."[39]

The essential criticism of Moffett's book, then, is not that its argument was wrong, but that it lacked complexity. Where other commentators argued with care and circumspection (and in the end, more truth) Moffett, overcome with enthusiasm for an expanding America, pressed his case with a single-minded vigour uncomplicated by reflection or subtlety. In the end, the criticism made of it by the *Review of Historical Publications Relating to Canada* stands: it remains "only a partial survey of the whole question."

That said, however, one must conclude by emphasizing the book's real and lasting value. The methods Moffett employed and the data he gathered brought a new and much-needed richness to its field of inquiry. The journalistic impressionism which had characterized the work of his predecessors would, after 1907, steadily give ground to more thoroughgoing books – notably those in the Carnegie Endowment Series – which would put the study of Canadian-American relations on an entirely different footing.

The substance of his argument, moreover, provides a fresh reminder that the panoply of forces making for the Americanization of Canada are not of recent origin. If there was a golden age of Canadian independence from American influences, it cannot be located in the years at the turn of the century. Indeed, Moffett's book suggests that in times past Canada may have been more rather than less susceptible to the imperatives of continentalism. Not only have the principles of the National Policy been steadily elaborated since he wrote; they have also been applied in different areas of the national life. In their search for instruments to safeguard their country's integrity, twentieth century Canadians have come to rely upon an extensive nationalized transportation network, a complex of government-sustained cultural agencies, and a system of policies designed to eradicate regional disparity. The success of these devices has not been unqualified; nor has their range been sufficiently broad; yet their existence suggests that Canada, rather than being overcome by the circumstances to which Moffett pointed, has developed a more complete set of policies for coping with them. Paradoxically, Moffett's book commends itself in the very act of being wrong.

Finally, Moffett's work has value as a document in the history of American expansionism. By dealing in terms of inevitability with the American triumph in Canada, he revealed something of the insular self-confidence with which many Americans addressed the twentieth century. The style and character of their imperialism would differ from the British. Theirs was not an empire of direct rule. Nor did they share the habit of authority. They did, however, possess the unparalleled confidence upon which a will to power must be founded. Convinced that their case was right and their intentions just, they were beset by no thought of failure or rejection. Moffett's book captures much of this mood. Its tone of self-assurance, entirely consistent with that which imbued the nineteenth century argument for Manifest Destiny, finds it most recent analogue in the case made by George Ball, undersecretary of state in the Kennedy and Johnson administrations, for the impossibility of a separate Canada.[40] In thus epitomizing a central tendency in the American way of viewing the world it performs a useful and important function.

All of this – its pioneering of new approaches, what it reveals about the nature of the Canadian-American relationship in the early years of this century, and the contribution it makes to an understanding of the American mind – makes Moffett's book a too little known classic. It deserves a special place in the history of Canada-United States studies.

NOTES

1 For the impact of America's discovery on the European mind, see Howard Mumford Jones, *O Strange New World; American Culture: The Formative Years* (New York, 1967), especially chapters 1 and 2; J.H. Elliott, *The Old World and the New, 1492–1650* (Cambridge, 1970) especially chapter 1; and Loren Baritz, "The Idea of the West," *American Historical Review*, 66(3), 1961, 618–35. For the contribution of Americans to the emergence of a revolutionary psychology in the Atlantic world, see R.R. Palmer, *The Age of the Democratic Revolution*, 2 vols. (Princeton, 1959 and 1964). For a summary statement, see G.D. Lillibridge, "The American Impact Abroad: Past and Present," *American Scholar*, 35(1), 1965–66, 39–63.

2 For the argument that the United States became a factor in world politics because its war against Spain caused it to be perceived as a power to be taken seriously, see Ernest R. May, *Imperial Democracy: The Emergence of America as a Great Power* (New York, 1961). For Roosevelt's foreign policy, see Howard K. Beale, *Theodore Roosevelt and the Rise of America to World Power* (New York, 1962).

3 *Imperialisme américaine* (Paris, 1905), 108; cited in May, *Imperial Democracy*, 6.

4 "Péril américain," *Le Correspondant*, 194, 25 March 1899, 1083–1104; 195, 10 April 1899, 116–44.

5 Ugo Ojetti, *L'America vittoriosa* (Milan, 1899); Otto, Graf Moltke, *Nord-Amerika: Beiträge zum verständnis seiner Wirtschaft und Politik* (Berlin, 1903).

6 *The Americanization of the World: or, The Trend of the Twentieth Century* (New York and London, 1901), 356–7, 5.

7 The idea that America should function as an exemplary civilization has had a lengthy history. See Perry Miller, "Errand into the Wilderness," in his *Errand into the Wilderness* (New York, 1964), 1–15; Frederick Merk, *Manifest Destiny and Mission in American History* (New York, 1963); and Russel B. Nye, "The American Sense of Mission," in his *This Almost Chosen People: Essays in the History of American Ideas* (Toronto, 1966), 164–207.

8 By the early twentieth century, however, serious questions were being raised about the capacity of some immigrant groups to accom-

modate themselves to American society, and by 1917–24 legislation was being enacted to restrict entry to those immigrants who could successfully undergo the process of Americanization. See Oscar Handlin, "Old Immigrants and New," in his *Race and Nationality in American Life* (Garden City, NY, 1957), 74–110; and John Higham, *Strangers in the Land: Patterns of American Nativism, 1860–1925* (New Brunswick, NJ, 1955).

9 A classic account of the ideology underpinning American expansionism is to be found in Albert K. Weinberg, *Manifest Destiny: A Study of Nationalist Expansionism in American History* (Chicago, 1963). Other accounts include Richard W. Van Alstyne, *The Rising American Empire* (Chicago, 1965); Walter LaFeber, *The New Empire: An Interpretation of American Expansionism 1860–1898* (Ithaca and London, 1963); William Appleman Williams, *The Roots of the Modern American Empire* (New York, 1969); and Ernest R. May, *American Imperialism: A Speculative Essay* (New York, 1968).

10 William E. Leuchtenberg, "Progressivism and Imperialism: The Progressive Movement and American Foreign Policy, 1898–1916," *Mississippi Valley Historical Review*, 39, 1952, 483–504. Leuchtenberg's conclusions have been questioned in Barton J. Bernstein and F.A. Leib, "Progressive Republican Senators and American Imperialism, 1898–1916: A Reappraisal," *Mid-America*, 50, 1968, 163–205.

11 C.R. Sanderson, ed., *The Arthur Papers* (Toronto, 1943), vol. 1, 133, cited in G.M. Craig, "The American Impact on the Upper Canadian Reform Movement before 1837," *Canadian Historical Review*, 29, 1948, 333.

12 "A Plea for British American Nationality," *British American Magazine*, 1(4), 1863, 341.

13 "American Influence on Canadian Thought," *The Week*, 7 July 1887, 518.

14 James Bell, "The Future of Canada," *The Week*, 26 July 1889, 536–9.

15 London, New York, Toronto, 1891; reprinted in 1971 in the Social History of Canada series by the University of Toronto Press.

16 H.C. Allen, *Great Britain and the United States: A History of Anglo-American Relations 1783–1952* (New York, 1955), 562–4.

17 *The Anglo-Saxon Century and the Unification of the English-Speaking People* (New York and London, 1903), vii, 159.

18 See, for example, his *Suggestions on Government* (Chicago and New York, 1894), and his "The Railroad Commission of California: A Study in Irresponsible Government," *Annals of the American Academy of Political and Social Science*, 6, November 1895, 469–77.

19 *Review of Historical Publications Relating to Canada*, 13, 1909, 147.

20 *Should There Be a Union of the English-Speaking Peoples of the Earth? A Dissertation Delivered before the Alumni of Colby College, July 2, 1889* (Boston, 1889).

21 17 April 1867; cited in Milton Plesur, ed., *Creating an American Empire, 1865–1914* (New York, 1971), 14–15.

22 Richard Heathcote Heindel, *The American Impact on Great Britain 1898–1914* (Philadelphia, 1940).

23 A.T. Mahan, "The United States Looking Outward," *Atlantic Monthly*, 66, December 1890, 823. See also Kenneth Bourne, *Britain and the Balance of Power in North America, 1815–1908* (Berkeley, 1967).

24 For the argument that Canada's geography invited its creation, gave it its character, and underlay its survival, see Donald Creighton, *The Empire of the St Lawrence: A Study in Commerce and Politics* (Toronto, 1956). For the history of development strategies in Canada, see H.G.J. Aitken, "Defensive Expansion: The State and Economic Growth in Canada," in H.G.J. Aitken, ed., *The State and Economic Growth* (New York, 1959), 79–114. For an account which lays emphasis on the vitality of the National Policy in Moffett's own day, see Robert Craig Brown, *Canada's National Policy, 1883–1900: A Study in Canadian-American Relations* (Princeton, 1964). For an argument which, however, shows that even as Canadian governments thought in terms of a national development strategy they were thinking in terms of a continental capital market, see Michael Bliss, "Canadianizing American Business: The Roots of the Branch Plant," in Ian Lumsden, ed., *Close the 49th Parallel, Etc: The Americanization of Canada* (Toronto, 1970), 27–42.

25 For a discussion of metropolitan influences in Canadian history, see J.M.S. Careless, "Frontierism, Metropolitanism, and Canadian History," *Canadian Historical Review*, 35(1), 1954, 1–21. For the role played by institutions in creating a more conservative society in Canada, see S.D. Clark, "The Canadian Community and the American Continental System," in George W. Brown, ed., *Canada* (Berkeley and Toronto, 1950), 375–89. For the influence of the Loyalists on the shaping of Canadian political culture, see G. Horowitz, "Conservatism, Liberalism, and Socialism in Canada: An Interpretation," which forms chapter one of his *Canadian Labour in Politics* (Toronto, 1968), 3–57. For a point of view concerning the manner in which British immigration to Canada in the nineteenth century affected the country's political culture, see Gerald L. Caplan and James Laxer, "Perspectives on Un-American Traditions in Canada," in Lumsden, *Close the 49th Parallel*, 305–20.

26 See Seymour Martin Lipset, "Value Differences, Absolute or Relative: The English-Speaking Democracies," in his *The First New Nation: The*

United States in Historical and Comparative Perspective (Garden City, NY, 1967), 284–312. See also John Porter, *The Vertical Mosaic: An Analysis of Social Class and Power in Canada* (Toronto, 1965).

27 See S.F. Wise and Robert Craig Brown, *Canada Views the United States: Nineteenth Century Political Attitudes* (Toronto, 1967), and Carl Berger, *The Sense of Power: Studies in the Ideas of Canadian Imperialism 1867–1914* (Toronto, 1970), especially "Critique of the Republic," 153–76.

28 "What Will the West Do with Canada?" *University Magazine*, 6(1), 1907, 10.

29 H. Blair Neatby, "The New Century," in J.M.S. Careless and R. Craig Brown, *The Canadians, 1867–1967* (Toronto, 1967), 137–71. For a discussion of the changing character of the National Policy itself, see V.C. Fowke, "The National Policy – Old and New," *Canadian Journal of Economics and Political Science*, 18(3), 1952, 271–86.

30 Thomson, "What Will the West Do with Canada?" 11.

31 "Editorial Notes and Comments," *United Empire*, 2(3), 1911, 144.

32 "Causes of the Canadian Exodus," *The Week*, 11 April 1890, 293.

33 An examination of this theme forms the substance of Sara Jeannette Duncan's 1904 novel *The Imperialist* (Toronto: New Canadian Library, 1961).

34 Stephen Leacock, "Greater Canada – An Appeal," *University Magazine*, 6(2), 1907, 133.

35 1(1), 1913, 10.

36 Ellis T. Powell, "Industrial Development of Canada," *United Empire*, 2(3), 1911, 151.

37 Thomson, "What Will the West Do," 9–10.

38 James Bryce, *The American Commonwealth*, 2 vols. (New York, 1913), vol. 2, 585, cited in Heindel, *The American Impact on Great Britain*, 169.

39 "The Americanization of Canada: An Australian's Impressions," *United Empire*, 2(6), 1911, 418.

40 In attempting to maintain its independence, Ball wrote in 1968, Canada is fighting "a rearguard action." It must ultimately form part of a larger union, a union which, no matter what its precise form, the United States would inevitably dominate. See *The Discipline of Power: Essentials of a Modern World Structure* (Toronto, 1968), 113–14.

5 Canadian Culture, the Canadian State, and the Management of the New Continentalism

One of the most striking phenomena in contemporary North American life has been the greatly accelerated thrust toward fine-tuning and adjustment of important elements in the Canadian-American relationship. This push in the direction of a more ordered and rational continentalism, evident enough in such areas as pollution control and the handling of toxic wastes, has been most dramatic in the domain of economic affairs. The move toward regulation, procedure, and discipline so clearly manifest in the negotiation and signing of the 1989 free trade agreement has not, to be sure, yet yielded the frictionless functioning of the world's largest trade partnership which some quarters hoped it would. As recent events centred on the trade in fish, steel, pork, wood products, and other commodities show, much in that partnership continues to be disruptive and irritant-producing. Such difficulties ought not, however, to obscure the important advances in other areas. In particular, the two countries' front-line negotiators are showing a heightened awareness of the principle that negotiations become meaningful and relationships well founded only if the parties to them take each other's vital interests seriously.[1] Nothing less than the making of the free trade accord itself testifies that life has been breathed into this old and venerable notion, for it was only when officials and politicians on each side of the table recognized and moved to accommodate some of the deepest concerns of those on the other that an arrangement became possible.[2]

Canadian-American Public Policy, no. 3 (Orono: The University of Maine, 1990).

If action in conformity with this critically important principle of conduct can be clearly discerned in the way Canadian recognition of US preoccupation with energy and services helped ease the path to agreement and in the manner in which US acknowledgment of Canadian worries about dispute settlement smoothed movement along it, such positive behaviour did not characterize all parts of what went on. In the realm of cultural policy, and particularly areas in which Canada's interests are centred, no significant progress is evident. This, of course, does not mean the total absence of moves to address Canadian anxieties in the spirit called for. In some measure persuaded of the meaning government ownership, regulation, and subsidy in the cultural field has for Canadians, US officials did finally agree that "cultural industries" should not be brought within the largely free market terms of the pact. In thus making a gesture toward a vital Canadian concern, they contributed mightily to the successful outcome of the talks.[3] Little real rethinking of positions was involved, however. Although the clauses in the agreement leave Canadians the right to subsidize, regulate, and control their cultural industries, they also reserve to Americans an equally clear measure of authority to retaliate if they think action resulting from the exercise of that right affects their interests.[4] And though US pronouncements on the matter seem to confirm American acceptance of Canada's view, a glance at the language in which those pronouncements are cast makes it plain that Washington officials were in actuality little more sympathetic to, understanding of, or even knowledgeable about what Canada thinks than they ever were. Still imbued with the idea that cultural industries are economic phenomena like any others,[5] and much taken up with the fate of a major export earner,[6] the authors of the "Confidential Briefing Paper" circulated by the US government to specify the meaning of the agreement came very close to replicating the tone of the dicta earlier issued by certain of their most (it has to be said) gratuitously ill-informed colleagues. Pulling back just a bit from US Ambassador to Canada Thomas Niles' 1985 judgment ("We think that these questions should be resolved on a commercial basis and that governments shouldn't get mixed up in them")[7] and distancing itself only a little more from US Trade Representative Clayton Yeutter's 1987 expression of the free market view ("I'm prepared to have American culture on the table and have it damaged by Canadian influences after the free trade agreement. I hope Canada's prepared to run the risk too"),[8] their document did all it could to make clear that positions long considered essential had been secured in the most complete way possible. Even affirmation that "maintaining and promoting 'cultural identity' ... is of significant political importance for any Canadian government" was rather an invitation to minimize the issue's importance than the reverse, for in conveying the impression that Canada's politicians and negotiators were concerned with it mainly because of lobbying and pressure, that apparent concession functioned to encourage classification of the matter as something with little real, substantive, or lasting significance. And when the text referred to the Canadians having been compelled during negotiations "to limit [their] freedom of action ... to promote cultural development to specific industries (publishing, film, video, music, and broadcasting)," when it talked of their having been got to agree "that measures they take will not impair the benefits we would otherwise expect from the provisions of the agreement," and when it summed up by saying that "we were unable to resolve ... a few other irritants but we retained the ability to take trade remedy actions on these issues,"[9] it could not have made more plain the feeling of its authors that the neighbours to the north were to be seen as creatures in relation to whose cultural activities US interests could best be served not by a program of comprehension, generosity, and understanding, but by one of containment, limitation, and restraint.

Nor was this continuing concern to keep a close watch on Canadian cultural policy evident only in relation to fears about that policy's possible impact on US interests in the US: Canadian action continued to be scrutinized because of its bearing on US interests in Canada. Beyond the limits of a negotiation concerned with establishing conditions of access to each other's markets, this extra-territorial surveillance – and, more important, the actions to which it sometimes led – did not even get discussed. As bound and determined as they had ever been that, in any circumstances in which American cultural industries operated, those industries should face the absolute minimum of constraints, US officials thus continued in possession of most of the tools they were accustomed to using in their efforts to avoid such constraints.

That so tough and unyielding a US stance poses serious problems for Canadian policy makers has been clear for some time. Those policy makers are very much aware of American thinking and of the actions to which it can lead when US officials or legislators become unhappy with Canadian cultural initiatives[10] and have since at least the 1960s felt much pressure as they attempt to structure a cultural environment that will serve the needs of their compatriots.[11] The way in which American concern to get Canada playing by its rules can set in motion a process that complicates discussion, sours the Canadian-American atmosphere, and makes problems more difficult to solve becomes particularly evident when one considers Canadians' unwillingness to let go unchallenged what they regard as narrow, self-interested argument and behaviour (communications minister Marcel Masse's September 1989 reaction to US insistence that film distribution in Canada be kept largely in US hands is a perfect case in point[12]). Responding to that argument and behaviour in testy and exasperated terms, they on their side ensure that the relationship is anything but smooth.

Perhaps the way these well-established realities work to perturb and unsettle relations is familiar and need hardly be noted. What does require comment is the extent to which their preservation and continuance stands to perpetuate the rough functioning in the system it is at least part of the purpose of the new regime to diminish. Keeping much Canadian cultural activity and many of the programs necessary to support it in an essentially besieged, defensive, and insecure position does not simply signal maintenance of a tension-producing situation. It does not even mean merely that moves toward the more rational and well-regulated continentalism putatively in view will be more complicated and difficult than they need to be. The demonstrated determination of Canada's cultural activists to protest anything they think dangerous to what they consider a vital component of national life, and the considerable strength they possess in carrying such protests forward,[13] raise fundamental questions about the possibilities of success of those moves. Not much imagination is required to see that no more than a minimum of mutually beneficial cooperation and sound dealing is likely to emerge from a situation critical elements in the basic character of which are unsatisfactory to an important group involved in that situation, not only because those elements put in question the conditions of that group's existence but also because they raise doubts about anything more than the purely formal survival of the nation to which it belongs.

The way to deal with this potentially serious state of affairs is readily apparent – have US officials and legislators react to Canadian policy toward culture in the more informed and comprehending spirit that has not so far marked their responses to it. Knowing this solution, however, does not help much. Generating such a posture falls squarely into the category of things more easily talked of than accomplished. A look, nonetheless, at what would be involved in such a movement suggests that the prospects for success are not as bleak as at first appears. The key difficulty, of course, is that almost all the shifting of position necessary to a resolution of the problem would have to come from one side. Once, however, it is realized that what creates that reality also offers the possibility of dealing with it, the situation begins to show marked and obvious signs of a capacity to resolve itself. If Canadians see their culture as vulnerable and in need of husbanding and so allow little latitude in deciding what is necessary to preserve it,[14] the fact that Americans view theirs as strong and capable of competing bespeaks just the kind of confidence in its capacity to survive and prosper which gives them room for concession, compromise, and generosity.[15] Nor is this all that permits flexibility on the American part. Though there is not much now in US life that supports the view that culture deserves special treatment, there is something, and in the past there was more. A look by Americans at what some of their own students of culture and society – Kenneth Boulding, for example[16] – have been arguing about the issue is, then, possible, and it could work to generate a certain sympathy for the Canadian point of view. That Americans once had cultural nationalists of their own – Noah Webster, Joel Barlow, Ralph Waldo Emerson – and that those distinguished figures argued actively for exactly the sort of relationship among national vitality, self-awareness, and an indigenous culture that preoccupies Canadians provides them with a considerable body of domestically produced material, examination of which could help them comprehend why their neighbours are so concerned and anxious.[17] There is even a body of institutional and policy practice in American life the contemplation of which could provide citizens of the republic with ground for sympathy with the idea that, in certain circumstances, culture should get state support. That practice has been limited,[18] but, as use of the tax system to provide indirect public subsidies shows,[19] it has not been nonexistent, and in time it even took on the form of a measure of direct state involvement. This close association between government and culture manifested itself, moreover, not just in Cold War-driven efforts "to structure an international environment which is hospitable to American values and ideas"[20] through government participation in international broadcasting, travel abroad by American artists and performers, or circulation overseas of American published material.[21] It can be seen as well in such domestic action as the founding of the National Endowment for the Arts.[22]

That there are at least a few factors that might permit US policy makers to come to terms with the Canadian position is, of course, one thing: whether those policy makers have an interest in letting themselves be moved by these factors is quite another. Luckily, they do. A refusal generously to acknowledge Canada's concerns in the cultural field would keep the country under wholly unacceptable pressure, all but guarantee continuing tension and difficulty, and so fly in the face of everything an association working in the interest of all the parties to it should be. The point, moreover, is far from general, abstract, and theoretical. It is concrete and urgent, for even if, as the friends of the free trade agreement insist,[23] that document does not turn out to require adoption of any particular policy or program in the cultural field, a number of issues outstanding in the area at large – in broadcasting, publishing, postal rates, and film distribution – are likely soon to need work. If they are not approached in the right spirit their potential to be disruptive and tension-producing will be very great.[24] And not only can US policy makers capable of a general and overarching appreciation of the need to foster the smooth running of the Canadian-American system be said to have reason to reach out to Canadians in respect to these issues: legislators and lobbyists tied directly and closely to US cultural industries possess this too. Failure so to extend themselves is likely to result in exactly the sort of Canadian action almost certain to damage their clients' interests. As the advance of the notorious Bill C-58 (1976) against the position of American publications in Canada showed, American failure to consider Canadian requirements in the cultural area practically guarantees policy and legislative action north of the border that will be altogether at variance with what Americans would prefer.[25]

The central message contained in these pages must by now be clear. Presentation of that message, however, should include more than a sharp restatement of the fact that, in the interests of a sound and healthy Canadian-American relationship, Americans have to learn to take Canada's cultural needs seriously. Patently required is a demonstration of precisely why it is that Canadians see matters the way they do. Only if Americans appreciate the full measure of and complete reasons for the Canadian commitment to state action in the field of culture will they be able to know why the onus for change and accommodation in this critical area must rest on them. In the cause, then, of moving US policy makers away from the simple – and condescending – sense that what Senator Lloyd Bentsen once called "the cultural question"[26] is, in the words of an anonymous trade department official, an "emotional"[27] one for Canada and heading them in the direction of the much more constructive realization that many Canadians see that question as lying at the heart of their national life, being, and existence, let us now look at its origins, history, character, and meaning.

At the outset, of course, the inhabitants of what would become Canada had little consciousness of themselves or their society as anything separate, special, or distinct; they were not much concerned with building a national culture, and they felt no need for government support of cultural activity. Early British North Americans, aware of themselves in the late eighteenth and early nineteenth centuries simply as inhabitants of tiny and isolated communities in a great and extensive empire, derived such sense of self and identity as they possessed largely from their contact with the artifacts disseminated from the centre of that worldwide entity. Fur traders relied heavily on reading from home;[28] the earliest grand buildings were conceived within the confines of Old World architectural styles;[29] theatregoers saw the staples of the English stage;[30] and when attention was paid to what lay close at hand, this – as G.J. Parkyn's colour aquatints of Halifax (ca. 1800)[31] or Thomas Cary's Pope- and Goldsmith-inspired poem *Abram's Plains* (1789) show[32] – was done squarely within the framework of conventional methods, fashions, and approaches.

By the 1820s, the pattern was beginning to change. As the passage of time made British North Americans gradually more conscious of place and shared experience, they became interested in encouraging cultural undertakings by means of which this sensitivity to the near at hand could be accommodated and expressed. Montreal's *Canadian Magazine and Literary Repository* (1823–5) was one indication of the new impulse,[33] the emergence of an indigenous style of architecture in the Maritimes another,[34] and a growing concern that the school system inculcate a sense of British North America's values and history showed it being focused and formalized.[35] Writing and painting of course remained derivative in style, but there, too, a steadily developing interest in indigenous subject matter was clearly evident. By the 1840s the *Literary Garland* (1838–51) had established itself as a major vehicle for the expression of this self-consciousness;[36] John Richardson[37] and Thomas Haliburton[38] gave proof of its existence in their fictional explorations of Upper Canadian and Nova Scotian themes; and, building on romanticism's fascination with the "indigenous," "natural," and "primitive," Paul Kane displayed it in his canvases of Indian life in the west.[39]

Cultural activists were not, however, simply concerned with the production of cultural goods. Along with this early interest in direct involvement in the creative process went a desire to stimulate it through state action, something evident not just in relation to government involvement in science[40] and education[41] but in respect of the arts as well. Richardson demanded – and got – a subsidy from the Province of Canada to help him publish his history of the war of 1812,[42] and, under the influence of the publishers' lobby, an elaborate program of subsidized postal rates, tariff protection, and copyright legislation was proposed.[43]

Much of what occurred in this realm was, of course, interest-based, but that this activity had to do with more than a simple jockeying for position and advantage by a small number of colonial publishers was made clear by poet, politician, and Father of Confederation D'Arcy McGee: aware, as a nineteenth-century romantic nationalist could not help but be, of the critical role culture played in defining, building, and consolidating a community, he insisted that culture and its support were a "state and social necessity."[44] Assuredly, this pronouncement left much unsaid. There was, in particular, nothing in it to indicate that McGee was thinking of anything even approaching a full-blown alliance between government and culture for the purpose of endowing the new Canadian state with what he considered to be a principal attribute of national life. But if all this was clear, it was no less obvious that, in McGee's view at least, culture was important, was to be encouraged, and therefore had to be seen as an entirely suitable candidate for public recognition and support of the kind that would ensure that it got its ample, extensive, and necessary due.

The impulse toward cultural growth discernible in the years just considered became even more pronounced in the post-Confederation period. Essentially a consequence of the continuing increase in Canadian society's complexity – of which the steady proliferation of writers, musicians, theatre groups, artists, and, of course, readers, audiences, viewers, publishers, galleries, concert halls, theatres, and patrons was a measure – the enlargement in cultural activity was also stimulated by the seriousness with which cultural producers viewed the need to equip their new national society with what they saw as a key attribute of national life. "Now more than any other time" – journalist H.J. Morgan articulated this feeling perfectly – "ought the literary life of the New Dominion to develop itself unitedly. It becomes every patriotic subject who claims allegiance to this our new northern nation to extend a fostering care to the native plant, to guard it tenderly, to support and assist it by the warmest countenance and encouragement."[45]

Much of this "fostering care" continued to be associated with private effort. Book purchasers, magazine subscribers, theatre and concert goers, cultural entrepreneurs, patrons, and, not least, the considerable efforts of the cultural producers themselves, provided the foundation for most cultural work. But state involvement was evident too as government, enmeshed in the society over whose affairs it was presiding, became caught up in what was happening. This involvement, moreover, went beyond simply patronizing the arts – though the Dominion did commission such works as Arthur A. Clappé's masque "Canada's Welcome," performed in honour of Governor General Lord Lorne and Princess Louise at Ottawa's Grand Opera House in 1879,[46] and Robert Harris' monumental painting *The Fathers of Confederation* in 1884.[47] Responding to the concern with consciousness building spoken of by such observers as Morgan – and not a little moved by the activity of cultural lobbyists – the government found itself directly involved in promoting national self-awareness through the establishment of cultural institutions. The founding of the Dominion Archives (1872) grew out of a romantic nationalist sense of history's importance in the shaping of the nation,[48] and creation of the National Gallery (1880) was also closely linked to the nation-building enterprise. As one commentator put it, "An event such as this, in the history of Art in Canada, cannot fail to interest, not only the lover of pictures, but all who have a stake in the growing institutions and general purposes of our country."[49]

Less obvious but at least as critical was the work the government did to structure an environment favourable to cultural production through its continuing and increasingly more sophisticated manipulation of tariffs, postal rates, and copyright. The role played by those with "a stake in the growing institutions ... of our country" was particularly important as lobbyists strove to get the concessions, arrangements, and subsidies they considered the health of their businesses required.[50] It would, however, be a mistake to conclude that concern with a public presence in cultural life was interest-based in some crude, direct, and unsubtle way. Nor was it simply a function of society's natural growth and increasing complexity. More nuanced factors were at work – the romantic nationalist vision was one of them – and they began to take hold in an increasingly firm, directed, and obvious manner.

This can be clearly seen in the influence of the deepening conviction that, in an age of materialism, culture had an important role to play in society's uplift and should be given the resources it needed to do so. Alive to the arguments in Matthew Arnold's *Culture and Anarchy* (1869) and taking the view, as the *Canadian Monthly* expressed it in 1874, that one must be "devoted ... to the advancement of all that tends to elevate and refine the popular character,"[51] cultural activists sought assiduously to involve the state in their projects for uplift and regeneration. The Ontario Society of Artists, moved by this impulse to improve, got government support for its School of Arts in 1876,[52] and the governor general, mindful of art's "elevating and refining power,"[53] acted to give culture the dignity and status of state recognition by serving as patron of – and helping to organize – the Royal Canadian Academy (1879) and the Royal Society of Canada (1882).

Even more important in stimulating government support for culture and the arts was the strong feeling that, because of Canada's great size and small population (by 1880 the Dominion was slightly larger in land area than the United States – 3,665,224 versus 3,610,000 square miles – but had only a tenth of its population – 4.5 million versus 45–50 million), cultural products could have no impact – could not, indeed, even get produced and distributed – without state intervention.[54] Publishers particularly had difficulties in this domain, for the small market for Canadian books hardly justified the expense of producing them, and imperial copyright legislation (by which Canada was bound) made it easy for cheap, mass-produced British and American editions of popular British and American works to circulate in Canada and further reduced Canadian books' prospects of finding a clientele. Their call for the government to correct this situation – and the politicians' own sense that it was fundamentally inequitable – enmeshed the state in problems of publishing, regulation, and copyright until well into the twentieth century, creating a relationship that still exists.[55]

The most critical factor in generating support for the idea that the state involve itself in the community's cultural life was concern about the growing American cultural presence. As Canada's proximity to the US and, in much of the country, the absence of a language barrier, caused Canadian contact with American newspapers, books, theatrical companies, vaudeville groups, and popular music to grow, it became increasingly easy to argue that Canadians were being drawn closer and closer to the life of the republic and, perforce, losing contact with their own. As one observer put it in 1889, "American papers, magazines, books, periodicals, secular and religious, for children and for adults, fill Canadian homes ... daily intercourse popularizes the same peculiarities, slang expressions, and technical words throughout the continent. Whatever the position of the Dominion may be in detail, it is more and more recognized that its general history is necessarily bound up with that of the Great Republic, alongside of which it stretches like a fringe on a garment."[56] It was also becoming distressingly clear to some observers that even those upon whom the Dominion had to depend for a sense of itself were being subverted by the American reality. Increasingly attracted to the American market, they found themselves compelled to produce what it required. "The market for literary wares," noted an anxious Sara Jeannette Duncan in 1887, "is self-evidently New York, where the intellectual life of the continent is rapidly centralizing."[57] Some Canadians accepted the irreversibility of these trends, but to others they were a spur to action. A Canadian cultural life was very much worth preserving, they thought, and the circumstances created by America's cultural might created a clear need to ensure that it was preserved. Deliberate and conscious action was required, and, taking a leaf from the book of the economic nationalists, they set out to build that action through intervention by the state. What was done to shape what the *Canadian Magazine* described in 1902 as "a home market for Canadian writers and artists"[58] turned out – not surprisingly, given its provenance – to be renewed and more vigourous efforts in the fields of copyright, preferential postal rates, and legislated measures to slow the flow of American periodicals into Canada.[59] But even though it was absolutely consistent with the interests of the publishers, an important part of the impulse behind it came from a deeply felt concern about matters of identity and survival which fundamentally distinguished that impulse from the sometimes narrowly based, self-interested initiatives of business.

The significance of all these actions must not be exaggerated. Even taken together, governors-general, politicians, and civil servants accomplished only what one historian of them describes as "the first few hesitant and tentative steps"[60] toward using state power to build a national culture, keep United States influences at bay, and uplift and refine the people. But in supposing that a real relationship between state and culture could be – indeed, was – a reality, the performing of them signalled that a basic element in Canadian life and development was in place. So far was the legitimacy of such a tie from being questioned that when in 1907 McGill University architect Percy E. Nobbs addressed the federal minister responsible for cultural matters on the need to organize a coherent government policy on that subject, what he pronounced to be at issue in "the education of our people towards an homogeneous and distinctive taste in national architecture and design" was not state involvement – that could be taken for granted – but the level at which that involvement would occur: it was, thought Nobbs, "surely a National rather than a Provincial Matter." To him it was obvious that the state aid necessary to pull things together and give a lead to provinces and municipalities – particularly in the all-important area of establishing museums – could come only from the Dominion government.[61]

Not everyone accepted Nobbs's view of where the argument led. Quebec, in particular, refused to have the provinces so readily written out of the emerging cultural scenario. But few found much to say in opposition to its central assumption. The exigencies of shaping and maintaining a cultural life in Canada's space and under Canada's circumstances had already caused a sense of the need for and desirability and importance of state action to support culture – at whatever level, in whatever guise – to seep too deeply into Canadian consciousness for that to happen.

In the early decades of the new century, the impulse toward cultural creativity quickened substantially. Driven in part by the continuing growth in Canadian society's complexity – by 1921 the balance between the country's rural and urban populations was almost even,[62] with a concomitant growth of audiences, proliferation of galleries and museums, and development of musical groups – and in part by the new burst of nationalism stimulated by pride in Canada's accomplishments during World War I,[63] this materially strengthened thrust in the direction of painting, literature, musical endeavour, and theatre produced a body of work that, in both quality and quantity, was superior to anything that had gone before.

As in earlier years, much of what was produced was the result of private effort. Moved by a sharper sense of Canada as a northern nation, fully in touch with international influences, and operating very much in harmony with the requirements of the market, painters and their patrons developed a new view of the nation's landscape.[64] Publishers, responding to the heightened interest in things Canadian, produced and promoted work intended to demonstrate the existence of a Canadian cultural life.[65] Authors, wanting to take advantage of and promote sympathy for Canadian themes and subjects, formed a national association.[66] And composers, noting the new Stravinsky-inspired enthusiasm for the primitive and the authentic, built indigenous themes into their work.[67]

Equally, however – here, too, we see a familiar sight – the state was involved. But just as the volume and quality of what was being produced showed signs of change, so also did the character and extent of the state's presence alter. No longer manifesting itself merely at the margins and in principle, it began to play a full, active, and altogether central role.

Several factors moved it in this direction. The more complex and extensive cultural life that was coming into existence required ordering and regulation. In publishing, for example, firms were demanding resolution of the copyright question not just on the old nationalist ground but because they could not conduct business in the absence of clearly demarcated rights of ownership and control of what was being produced.[68] The new broadcasting industry was more clearly in need of intervention, as the struggles of early station owners to get access to unencumbered frequencies made clear.[69] The steadily enlarging role of government had roots, too, in an essentially nationalist concern to showcase the nation's accomplishments. That motive moved the state to involvement in the Canadian War Memorials Fund, set up by Canadian-born Lord Beaverbrook to record Canada's contribution to the Great War effort through painting and sculpture,[70] and, after 1916, it played a part in the politicians' support of Beaverbrook's War Office Cinematographic Committee.[71] Concern to show off what the nation was doing also manifested itself in the field of domestic development in the 1916 creation of a Canadian government film agency whose celebration of the nation was intended to attract tourists, investment, and immigrants.[72] By the 1930s, the state was even seeing cultural activity itself as an object to be displayed, as its moves to notice and mark theatrical accomplishment through support for the Dominion Drama Festival (1932) showed.[73]

The most important factor in the state's move toward a larger role in this period as earlier was concern about the continuing problem of American cultural penetration. New technologies were making the vulnerability to American influences which Canada's small population, large geographical size, and proximity to its great neighbour had created seem more a source of weakness than ever. The forces singled out by American journalist S.E. Moffett, when he wrote in 1907 of the way railways, steam presses, and the telegraph had knit the cultural life of the continent together,[74] were now being made effective beyond all imagining by the advent of movies and radio. As early as 1920 Archibald MacMechan added American films to his catalogue of reasons for "the subjection of the Canadian nation's mind and soul to the mind and soul of the United States,"[75] and an equally disturbed radio listener saw no less a danger in the broadcasting of the republic: "Britannia rules the waves – shall Columbia rule the wavelengths?"[76]

These worries were, of course, rooted in much the same places they always had been. There were interest-based feelings of anxiety and resentment as Canadian broadcasters and filmmakers watched American competitors enter their market.[77] There was a strong belief that the perceived shallowness and superficiality of American creations would undermine culture's moral role.[78] Members of the old elite feared that as Canadian society "Americanized," they would lose their status, prestige, and authority.[79] And there were strong convictions, based on the careful working out of the relationship between national maintenance and the retention of a Canadian sense of self, history, and tradition which McGee had begun long before, that support of culture was essential to national survival.[80] But whatever their point of origin, they all tended toward the same end: the strengthening of the already potent sense that – in Canada at least – state and culture could not be separated in any absolute, dogmatic, and unqualified way. Because it seemed so clearly to be, as one activist put it, a matter of "the state or the United States,"[81] there could be no question as to which should win out.

If effort powered by these concerns produced the Canadian Radio Broadcasting Commission in 1932, and, in 1936, the Canadian Broadcasting Corporation, similar effort based on similar anxieties yielded a similar move in relation to film. Here, to be sure, the impulse was in no small measure bureaucratic: government filmmaking, in existence since at least 1916, had by the late 1930s reached the point that it badly needed rationalizing and reorganization.[82] The sense that film was an extremely potent force for the shaping of outlook and values had, however, also grown, and there was a strong feeling that what American films were yielding in the way of close knowledge of, sympathy for, and orientation toward the United States needed qualifying. Lobbying by the National Film Society (1935) fostered interest in Canadian films,[83] and when the government established the National Film Board in 1939, its first director carefully stipulated that "it will through a national use of cinema see Canada and see it whole."[84]

By the end of the 1930s the nature of the culture-state situation had changed in important and striking ways. Earlier honoured more in principle than in practice, state action in the field of culture had now become a fixture of the national life evident in relation to the new media, plain in what happened to theatre, and to be seen as well in relation to art and even music. Whether state action's new prominence would allow it to power Canadian culture to new triumphs remained, of course, very much to be seen; that it had that prominence, however, could not be doubted.

As before, both continuity and change were evident in the years after 1940. Factors in operation for a century – the ongoing evolution of society, the steady amplification of national consciousness –

still worked to stimulate cultural activity, while imperatives present for decades – the thrust toward government regulation, the desire to display the splendours of the nation, and, above all, the concern with US penetration – persisted in fostering state involvement. In each of these areas, however, change was an unmistakable force and resulted in a range of phenomena and a set of responses to those phenomena which had an altogether new strength, vigour, and comprehensiveness.

An unprecedented vitality was certainly evident in the forces stimulating the production of culture. Social growth had, indeed, reached the point at which increased numbers of talented people and an ever larger cultural clientele were leading to two important sets of results. There was, first, more cultural accomplishment at a higher level of achievement, as the formation of the Toronto New Play Society (1946), the Royal Conservatory Opera Company (1950), and the Painters Eleven (1953) made clear. But there was also a thrust toward sophisticated organizational structures and lobbying techniques characteristic of a maturing society. As early as 1941, a militant group of activists who were convinced that the time was ripe to agitate for increased recognition met at Kingston under the leadership of painter André Bieler and sculptor Elizabeth Wyn Wood to form the Federation of Canadian Artists.[85] The momentum thus created was maintained when in 1945 sixteen arts and culture organizations came together to create the Canadian Arts Council (after 1958 the Canadian Conference of the Arts). The power and authority of the movement were augmented by the establishment of such new groups as the Society of Canadian Music (1953), the Society of Cooperative Artists (1954), the Association of Canadian Television and Radio Artists (1963), and the Writers' Union of Canada (1973).

The no less evident growth in national consciousness – spurred by a combination of changed historical circumstances and an increase in the numbers and confidence of the people expressing that consciousness – took the form of moves away from the idea – present as late as the 1930s[86] – that the country was to be understood mainly in terms of its ties to or affinities with some other country and toward the notion that its essence could best be grasped by looking at its own unique characteristics. Leading in some cases to refinement and extension of the multicultural principle which John Murray Gibbon had begun to systematize in the 1930s,[87] in others to elaboration of the northern theme after Northrop Frye gave it a new lease on life in 1943,[88] and in still others to a fleshing out of Donald Creighton's powerfully orchestrated Laurentian idea,[89] the conviction that Canada was to be understood on its own terms powerfully strengthened the confidence and certainty with which Canadians went about the task of explaining its character and meaning, a development that not unnaturally found its clearest expression in the new forcefulness and determination with which issues of identity were approached.[90]

In the domain of the forces making for a government presence in cultural life, a new strength was certainly to be seen in the part of them centred on concern that the nation's accomplishments be displayed in a way that was organized, systematic, and likely to come to the attention of people outside the country. Nor did the intensified thrust in this direction arise simply out of more determined efforts to use art for such purposes as demonstrating the nation's valour – though such efforts as the government's organization of an art program on World War II were clearly made.[91] It came as well, and, in the event, much more importantly, from a new, more subtle sense that art in itself had value and that the possession of art showed Canada to be truly a nation – cultivated, urbane, and worth taking seriously as a member of an international community of civilized states. Stimulated partly by the war-born conviction that the struggle was one of civilization against barbarity, reinforced for a time by similar Cold War notions, and powered, finally, by the policy makers' conviction that getting the country recognized as a mature and cultivated entity ought to be a principal objective of Canadian external policy, this sense underpinned the Department of External Affairs' sponsorship of the CBC's International Service (1945) and was evident in such undertakings as that ministry's later involvement with the Musicanada Festival in 1977 and the Toronto Symphony Orchestra's tour of China in 1978.[92]

The circumstances making for government involvement with culture in the form of regulation and bureaucracy showed an even more obvious strength. The proliferation of cultural activists so evident in the postwar period made it all but certain that demands for regulation and order would come with increasing frequency. Private broadcasters, for example, sought, and in 1958 got, a regulatory agency (the Board of Broadcast Governors) that would look after their concerns,[93] and the need to take in hand new realities in the broadcasting field generally – cable systems, satellite broadcasting, telecommunications – played an important role in the formation of the Canadian Radio and Television Commission (1968).[94] The enlarged number of activists in the arts fostered an enhanced role for government by demanding that it take responsibility for funding their efforts. First taking up that line during the war, maintaining it in testimony before the Royal Commission on National Development in the Arts, Letters and Sciences (the Massey Commission, 1949–51), and keeping it alive during the 1950s, they finally saw it bear fruit in the formation of the Canada Council (1957).[95] By 1969 the government's responsibilities in the area of communications had become extensive enough to justify formation of a Ministry of Communications, by 1972 the Department of the Secretary of State's work in the cultural field had grown to the point that an arts and culture branch had to be established, and by 1980 a reorganized and greatly enlarged Department of Communications was given responsibility for much of the government's work in the now greatly expanded cultural sphere.

The strongest influence making for a government presence in the cultural realm was, however – as always – that coming out of the United States. Some of what gave American culture its new reach and potency did not, of course, much affect Canada. But if the institutional apparatus set up to power American culture in its drive around the world – the United States Information Agency, Radio Free Europe, the Voice of America, the Fulbright Program – had little impact to the immediate north, the technological innovations of the period had a great deal. American popular culture, assisted by new devices – television – and improved versions of old ones – film and radio – penetrated Canada to a greater degree than ever before, and, not surprisingly, moved Canadians to update and revise the concerns they had been expressing since at least the 1880s.

If the threat was greater than ever before, the response also took on an unprecedented comprehensiveness and sweep. The better-organized, more numerous, and clearer-sighted cultural activists now in existence were able to react to this more powerful variation on an old theme with an unprecedented vigour – not to mention ingenuity and cleverness. Their pressure for a policy response to the American "threat" played a key part in the formation of the Massey Commission,[96] helped shape that body's recommendation for a funding agency for the arts, and materially affected the final decision to establish such an agency in the form of the Canada Council.[97] Nor were the new cultural nationalists concerned simply with the way the American tide might erode high culture; they were also concerned over the state of the mass media and popular culture. Formation of the Royal Commission on Publications (the O'Leary Commission, 1961),[98] the Committee on Broadcasting (the Fowler Committee, 1964–65),[99] and the Senate Committee on the Mass Media (the Davey Committee,1971)[100] clearly reflected concern with the extent to which periodicals and broadcasting were dominated by American content, and a major reworking of cultural law and policy in the 1960s and 1970s led to new instruments (the Canadian Radio and Television Commission's content regulations, 1970) and new tax provisions (Bill C-58, 1976) designed to meet that concern.[101] Film, too, got attention, with the government moving in 1968 through creation of the Canadian Film Development Corporation (CFDC) to create a Canadian feature film industry, a step it augmented in 1983 with the establishment of Telefilm Canada.[102]

Notwithstanding the great growth in the strength of the forces at work, the pattern of the events they shaped remained essentially the same as it had been for decades: American culture, entering the country, generated concern, anxiety, and a search for ways to ensure that it did not overwhelm Canadian culture. In the 1960s, however, that pattern changed. Noting the undoubted appeal of American cultural products for many Canadians and not terribly concerned with the uplift and self-definition that were mainstays of cultural nationalism, many of the new profit-oriented cultural entrepreneurs in postwar Canada, particularly in broadcasting and film, began to seek government support, not to keep American culture out but because they wanted assistance (or at least a free hand) in bringing it in. Some, indeed, reversed the trend even more dramatically by seeking that support as part of a strategy to produce, in Canada, American cultural products mainly for sale in the US market. Thus taking steps that carried them far beyond the point reached by earlier entrepreneurs (the action of those nineteenth-century Canadian publishers who had sought government intervention in the form of tariff assistance and copyright legislation, not to help them get Canadian material into the Canadian market but to aid them in delivering British and American material to that market, pales by comparison), private broadcasters and cable companies in particular worked hard to get government aid to ease the path by which they could import American material. Successful in procuring a softening of the CRTC requirement that they produce minimal amounts of Canadian programming, the cable companies got government to agree to allow them to rebroadcast American programs without payment of royalty fees to the copyright holder.[103] Film interests were busy too, lobbying to maintain the framework of legislation and subsidy that had been put in place by the CFDC and basing their action less on a concern to keep conditions conducive to the making of Canadian films than on a desire to preserve the help they needed to put out – often in close association with Hollywood – products for the American market.[104]

All of this was important. It certainly complicated the picture. And if it gave many Canadians cause to think that their cultural policies were being subverted, it also presented Americans with reason to add to the argument that Canadian government action was complicating their access to the Canadian market the claim that it was opening them up to subsidized and unfair competition in their own. One must not, however, assume that these departures from the traditional shape of things constituted an absolute and total shift in Canadian direction.[105] The CRTC might have yielded consistently to the blandishments of the private broadcasters concerning relaxation of Canadian content regulations,[106] but it also took the country's leading private network to the Supreme Court for failing to comply with its directives concerning the production of Canadian programming.[107] And the CFDC-Telefilm bureaucrats might have precipitated a situation in which, as one recent observer puts it, "a large part of [private Canadian film companies'] success relates to servicing US industry, producing programs that are competent, Canadian-made, US-conceived, and murderously banal,"[108] but they were also maintaining the skilled technical assistance and infrastructure without which there could be no hope of a Canadian film industry capable of dealing with Canadian themes and subjects.[109]

Cultural nationalists could take stock, too, in the fact that government regulation and subsidy had played a clear role in maintaining a Canadian presence in several areas of the country's cultural life. Bill C-58, it could reasonably be asserted, had made a national newsmagazine possible;[110] the CRTC's content regulations had stimulated growth of a recording industry;[111] and the CFDC had fostered production not just of feature films in Canada but of Canadian feature films.[112] There was thus ample room for the claim – and the nationalists did not hesitate to make it – that the "traditional" approach was still alive, still working, and still to be supported: far from having degenerated into a set of interest-manipulated schemes to bring American culture into Canada or enable Canadians to service the American market, Canada continued to do essentially what it always had done.

The idea of a state role in culture continued, in consequence, to attract much support. Nor did that support manifest itself only in anxiety that the free trade agreement might sweep away the cultural industries' foundations in law, policy, and subvention; polls confirmed its existence;[113] as did the action of the provinces in moving into the area of cultural support.[114] Perhaps most striking, that Canadian responses to the emergence of global systems of culture and communications have been cast in terms of familiar Canadian nostrums about state involvement makes clear the extent of their vitality. In observing that "only by making national public broadcasting strong throughout the world can cultural development continue and cultural sovereignty survive"[115] TVOntario President Bernard Ostry thus made a statement that was at once timely, apropos, and evidential of the continuing strength of a Canadian tradition.

Belief in an essentially Deutschian conception that the state is an entity held together by the ability of its people to communicate with and understand one another remains, in consequence, strong, and no less strong is the conviction that that ability must be maintained and strengthened by the activity of the state itself. When, therefore, journalist Bronwen Drainie notes that "Canada has a tradition that says artistic and cultural activity is necessary to our well-being and sense of identity," and when, further, she underscores the Canadian determination that "we will support such activity out of public funds," she is not simply making a casual reference to a minor phenomenon: she is – and the significance of the point can hardly be exaggerated – expressing a view that many Canadians consider cuts to the heart of national survival.[116]

Even a cursory glance at the country's cultural history makes it clear how deeply embedded in that history the state has been. No less fully in view – and at least as much to be noted – is the widely held feeling that that is exactly what it should be. Some of the support for that feeling – another obvious point – has been based on foundations and given for reasons that do not entitle it to be taken with great seriousness; much of it, however – this, too, is evident – rests on more substantial ground. Moved by the conviction that, in the special circumstances created by Canada's small population, large distances, and very close proximity to the United States, Canadians cannot experience a "normal" attribute of national life – contact with their own culture – in any other way than through the intervention of the state, substantial numbers of thoughtful, articulate, and informed citizens of the Dominion have, in fact, been a good deal more than merely the dupes of clever and manipulative interest groups, or the victims of a push by elites to maintain their influence, or puppets pulled along by some Weberian thrust toward bureaucracy and regulation. Directly in touch with the notion that, as a matter of principle, communities and societies have the right to contact with their own culture, that they are entitled to resist the imposition of the culture of some other community, and that they can do what they think necessary (so long as their action does not conflict with preexisting obligations and responsibilities) to secure these objectives, these people are the captives of nothing more than their own – sometimes quite acute – analysis of the situation in which they find themselves.

Underscoring the existence of this reality for the benefit of those who would change the policies and approaches it has helped foster and sustain is not, of course, necessarily to endorse maintenance of all, some, or even any of those policies and approaches. It is, however, to say that seeking to change them without a full grasp of how strongly they are rooted in a widespread conviction that state action is required for effective exercise of the Canadian community's right to know things about itself and to see the world from its point of view is to invite the most troublesome of difficulties. Moving, in particular, to raise what will inevitably be perceived as casual and thoughtless questions about the Canadian belief that Canadian culture – high and low – must be state-aided cannot help but chill and embitter the atmosphere. It will strike Canadians as at once ungenerous (the result, as they see it, of doing away with such aid would be to deny them access to what makes life in definable and self-conscious communities possible) and, given the Americans' own early concern with national culture, not a little hypocritical. Returning, then, to where it began, this paper concludes with the simple counsel offered at the outset: offense, bad feeling, and irritation ought not to be created if they can be avoided. Getting along – let this, too, reinforce an earlier message – requires understanding of each by the other and what that other perceives to be real needs. It can therefore be of no help to the process when one of the actors in it behaves in ways that have the effect of suggesting that one side sees the necessity for that understanding as being of little – even no – account. Nor – this above all is worth repeating – is this advice brought forward purely in the service of a Canadian interest. As was shown by Canada's concessions on the cable retransmission issue during the free trade talks, even the most modest American movement (in that case a shift toward the Canadian position on cultural industries sufficed) offers the prospect of American gain. There can, of course, be no guarantees. But bluster, incomprehension, and rigidity have produced not much more than half-measures, unsatisfactory compromises, and sometimes bitter stand-offs, so an approach more fully centred on acceptance of the legitimacy of Canada's position is worth trying. Certainly conducting the frequent negotiations that will be an increasingly important part of an ever more intricate relationship will require at least some adjustment in a stance that has so far bred little other than irritation, annoyance, and frustration.

NOTES

1 See, for example, K.J. Holsti, *International Politics: A Framework for Analysis*, 3rd ed. (Englewood Cliffs, NJ: Prentice-Hall, 1977), 202–3, and Howard Raiffa, *The Art and Science of Negotiation* (Cambridge, MA: Belknap Press, 1982), 126.

2 For a detailed chronicling of the process leading up to the signing and approval of the agreement, see Robert M. Campbell and Leslie A. Pal, "A Big Deal? Forging the Canada-U.S. Free Trade Agreement," in their *The Real Worlds of Canadian Politics: Cases in Process and Policy* (Toronto: Broadview Press, 1989), 315–96.

3 Though economist Richard Lipsey's generosity in suggesting that American concessions to the Canadian point of view were so ample that "when all the hype about Canadian culture is discounted, precious little was given up" is certainly excessive. "Sovereignty: Culturally, Economically, and Socially," in John Crispo, ed., *Free Trade: The Real Story* (Toronto: Gage, 1988), 155.

4 *The Canada-U.S. Free Trade Agreement* (Ottawa: Department of External Affairs, n.d.), Article 2005, clauses 1 and 2. For a spirited discussion of these and other of the agreement's clauses bearing on culture, see Susan Crean, "Reading between the Lies [*sic*]: Culture and the Free Trade Agreement," in Duncan Cameron, ed., *The Free Trade Deal* (Toronto: James Lorimer, 1988), 223–37.

5 This idea has become remarkably widespread and comprehensive. For the part of it that insists that "show-business," market-driven and market-oriented, "always [took] its cues from its audiences," see Robert C. Toll, *The Entertainment Machine: American Showbusiness in the Twentieth Century* (New York: Oxford University Press, 1982), 5. Robert Henry Stanley, *Mediavisions: The Art and Industry of Mass Communication* (New York: Praeger, 1987), 237, argues the related point that the mass media were shaped by "the logic of the market and profit maximization." Treatment of "high" culture as an economic phenomenon can be sampled in Gerald Reitlinger, *The Economics of Taste: The Rise and Fall of Picture Prices, 1760–1960* (London: Barrie and Rockliff, 1961); Mark Blaug, ed., *The Economics of The Arts* (Boulder, CO: Westview Press, 1976); and Michael P. Mokwa, William M. Dawson, and E. Arthur Prieve, eds., *Marketing the Arts* (New York: Praeger, 1980). For some critical comment on what one observer

views as the increasingly close linkages in the US between culture and what she terms "the engines of consumerism" (x), see Deborah Silverman, *Selling Culture: Bloomingdale's, Diana Vreeland, and the New Aristocracy of Taste in Reagan's America* (New York: Pantheon, 1986). The contrasting belief that the market should determine what cultural products circulate is developed in Ernest van den Haag, "Should the Government Subsidize the Arts?" *Policy Review*, 10, Fall 1979, 63–73, and Michael S. Joyce, "The National Endowments for the Humanities and the Arts," in Charles L. Heatherly, ed., *Mandate for Leadership* (Washington, DC: Heritage Foundation, 1980), 1039–56.

6 By 1988 some Washington legislators were arguing that American film companies could suffer losses of "as much as $1 billion" if movement of their product abroad were curtailed. See "Film Dispute with Canada Triggers Interest in Harsh Retaliatory Language," *Inside U.S. Trade*, 12 February 1988, 13.

7 Quoted in Jeffrey Simpson, "Sovereign Principles," *Globe and Mail*, 14 November 1985.

8 Quoted in Jennifer Lewington, "Fuzzy Words Blur Culture Debate," ibid., 5 February 1987. See also Ross Howard, "Mulroney Lashes Out at Free Trade 'Ignorance,'" ibid., and "Editorial," ibid.

9 "U.S.-Canada Free Trade Briefing Paper for Secretary Baker and Ambassador Yeutter," *Inside U.S. Trade*, 9 October 1987, 14–15.

10 For a discussion of pressures brought to bear on Canada in the course of US attempts to modify Canadian action against Canadian editions of US magazines in the mid-1960s, see Denis Smith, *Gentle Patriot: A Political Biography of Walter Gordon* (Edmonton: Hurtig, 1973), 226–32. US moves in retaliation for Canada's 1976 attempt to use its tax system to stem the flow of advertising dollars away from Canadian television broadcasters and toward operators of US channels directing programming to Canada are discussed in Stephen Clarkson, *Canada and the Reagan Challenge* (Toronto: James Lorimer, 1982), 235–6. See also the essays in *Cultures in Collision: The Interaction of Canadian and U.S. Television Broadcast Policies* (New York: Praeger, 1984), especially Theodore Hagelin and Hudson Janisch, "The Border Broadcasting Dispute in Context," 40–103.

11 In one instance pressure amounted to threats from leading American communications conglomerate Gulf and Western of a "scorched earth" policy in Canada if Canada did not modify its opposition to the takeover by that conglomerate of a publishing firm in Canada. It did, and the subsequent feeling in Canada that there had been too much yielding to American demands – business and government – became so strong that communications minister Marcel Masse was finally compelled to issue assurances that he was as determined as

ever – "the goals have not changed" – to pursue a policy of enlarging the Canadian presence in the publishing sector. See Andrew Cohen, "Book Firm Deal Will Fuel Ownership Row," *Financial Post*, 15 March 1986; Dan Westell, "Masse Reaffirms Vows to Toughen Publishing Policy," *Globe and Mail*, 11 March 1989.

12 Masse noted that "our distribution mechanisms do not give Canadian cultural products sufficient access to our own audiences" and attributed maintenance of this unpleasant reality to American lobbying against Canadian efforts to change it. His description of this "difficult situation" that has been "tolerated too long" was uncharacteristically blunt. It is quoted in Brian Milner, "Masse Promises Changes in Film, But Industry People Expected More," *Globe and Mail*, 12 September 1989. See also Chris Dafoe, "Battle Lines Drawn over Film Bill," ibid., 18 October 1989.

13 Most of the country's cultural activists were not simply unhappy about any weakening of Canadian culture's institutional and policy position in the course of the free trade talks; they actively and persistently lobbied against anything that might lead to such weakening. Representatives of the Canadian Conference of the Arts, the Writers' Union of Canada, and the Canadian publishing and broadcasting industries met with government officials; a special organization – the Cultural Industries' Alliance – was formed; large, sometimes full-page, advertisements signed by prominent actors, writers, broadcasters, and dramatists were published in daily papers; and writer Robertson Davies took the matter up with a Scottish audience and the readers of the *Times Literary Supplement*. Not all such figures held the same dark view. Writer Mordecai Richler and painters Alex Colville and Christopher Pratt favoured the initiative. But those who were displeased by the unfolding of events were noisy and vociferous in the extreme. See Richard Cleroux, "Do Not Sell Out Culture, Free Trade Meeting Told," *Globe and Mail*, 27 November 1985; John Partridge, "Cultural Sovereignty Already Destroyed, Alliance Charges," ibid., 28 July 1988; "A Foreign Power Has Control of Michelle's Mind 725 Hours a Year," ibid., 21 June 1988; "The Mulroney-Reagan Trade Deal," ibid., 19 November 1988; Robertson Davies, "Keeping the US Out of Canada," *Times Literary Supplement*, No. 4461, 6 October 1988, 1070, 1080; and John Bentley Mays, "'Untitled': An Artistic Search for Meaning in the Free Trade Debate," *Globe and Mail*, 11 June 1988.

14 In their efforts to create room for Canadian content, some Canadians are beginning to look beyond the quota system for broadcast programming that has been in existence for decades. The broadcasting bill of October 1989 proposes to stimulate Canadian program-

ming through a system of fines and penalties rather than the draconian – and therefore impractical – method of suspending licenses; but – apart from a few analysts who take a more or less explicitly "market" view of culture – most commentators remain convinced that the price of adopting a free market position for culture would be unacceptably high: there is, they think, no way to make the requirements of national survival consistent with the establishment and maintenance of laissez-faire policy in cultural products.

Indeed, they argue, as economic forces carry the country closer to the continental economic integration of which the free trade agreement is an expression, a separate Canadian culture has become a steadily more important component of a separate Canadian nation. "Independent cultural industries by Canadians for Canadian audiences," insist bodies such as the Cultural Industries' Alliance, are essential to the future of the country, and since, in those bodies' view, such industries can exist only with government support, that support is also essential. Maintaining the capacity to provide it thus becomes – here the circle of argument closes with what for most Canadians is an utterly persuasive finality – an interest that, being vital, cannot be dropped, qualified, or set aside. See Paul Koring, "Bill Widens Definition of Broadcasting," *Globe and Mail*, 13 October 1989; John Kettle, "Interview with Robert A. Russel" (a Canadian communications executive, who argues that "the difference between business and entertainment is disappearing"), *Executive*, 28, August–September 1981, 11; Stephen Brooks, *Public Policy in Canada: An Introduction* (Toronto: McClelland and Stewart, 1989), 299 ("the distinction between 'economic' and 'cultural' is largely artificial"); Steven Globerman and Aidan Vining, "Canadian Culture under Free Trade: Should Canadian-U.S. Trade Liberalization Extend to Culture?" *Canadian Business Review*, 13, Summer 1986, 18–22; statement by Cultural Industries' Alliance, quoted in Partridge, "Cultural Sovereignty."

15 Unbound by anything like the chains of position, circumstance, or reasoning that hold Canadians in thrall, Americans did not even see Sony's purchase of Columbia Pictures as an event to be reacted to in cultural rather than economic terms. Perceived, to be sure, as a shattering blow – viewed, indeed, as involving a piece of "America's Soul" – the chief significance of the sale was nonetheless held to relate to what it meant for America's waning economic power. There was simply no sense that what had happened would have an impact – negative or positive – on American culture as such. For a representative sample of that reaction, see *Newsweek* magazine's cover story, "Japan Invades Hollywood," 9 October 1989, 62–72.

16 Kenneth E. Boulding, "Placing a Value on the Arts," Keynote Address at the 1986 World Conference on the Arts, Politics, and Business, "Support for the Arts: Philanthropy or Investment?" University of British Columbia, 22 July 1986.

17 For Webster's views on an "American" language, see his *Dissertations on the English Language* (Boston, 1789). Barlow's epic poem *The Columbiad* (Philadelphia, 1808) sums up his understanding of the relationship between nationality, self-consciousness, and culture. For the classic US statement of the cultural nationalist position, see Emerson's *The American Scholar* (Boston, 1837). A still very useful discussion of these and related matters is to be found in Russel Blaine Nye, *The Cultural Life of the New Nation, 1776–1830* (New York: Harper Torchbooks, 1963), especially chapter 2, "The Foundations of an American Faith," 29–53.

18 John Quincy Adams, wrote Richard Hofstadter, "was the last nineteenth-century occupant of the White House who ... believed that fostering the arts might properly be a function of the federal government." *Anti-Intellectualism in American Life* (New York: Vintage, 1966), 158.

19 A. Field, M.O'Hare, and J.M.D. Schuster, *Patrons Despite Themselves: Taxpayers and Arts Policy* (New York: Twentieth Century Fund, 1983).

20 United States International Communications Agency, United States Embassy, Ottawa, "Highlights from an Address of Secretary of State Alexander M. Haig, Jr," 29 December 1981, 1.

21 Herbert I. Schiller, *Mass Communication and American Empire: Communication and Cultural Domination* (White Plains, NY: International Arts and Sciences Press, 1976); Donald R. Browne, *International Radio Broadcasting: The Limits of the Limitless Medium* (New York: Praeger, 1982); Kevin V. Mulcahy, "Cultural Diplomacy: Foreign Policy and the Exchange Programs," in Kevin Mulcahy and C.P. Swaim, eds., *Public Policy and the Arts* (Boulder, CO: Westview Press, 1982), 269–301; James L. Tyson, *U.S. International Broadcasting and National Security* (New York: Ramapo Press, 1983).

22 Mulcahy and Swain, eds., *Public Policy and the Arts*. See particularly D. Cheatwood, "The Private Muse in the Public World," 91–110.

23 Lipsey, "Sovereignty."

24 New broadcasting legislation proposes to give government regulatory agencies the authority to insist on Canadian content in "on-demand" television and video rental shops; the government has affirmed its intention to promote Canadian ownership in the publishing sector; new postal rates – one US official once called the postal issue "a running sore" in US-Canada relations – are likely to maintain the Canadian practice of making lower rates available to periodicals published

in Canada; and new film distribution legislation will strengthen the position of Canadian film distributors in the Canadian market. See Paul Koring, "Bill Widens Definition of Broadcasting," *Globe and Mail*, 13 October 1989; Dan Westell, "Masse Reaffirms Vows to Toughen Publishing Policy," ibid., 11 March 1989; Jennifer Lewington, "Ottawa Book Policy Target of Quiet Attack by Congress Veteran," ibid., 18 March 1989; Giles Gherson, "New Trade Feud Brews over Magazine Postage," *Financial Post*, 2 December 1987; and Chris Dafoe, "Battle Lines Drawn over Film Bill," *Globe and Mail*, 18 October 1989. For the special difficulties the province of Quebec faces in the area of film distribution, see Matthew Fraser, "Quebec Searches for Way to Battle US Film Goliath," ibid., 14 May 1988, and Stephen Godfrey, "New Quebec Film Regulations Spark Protest from US Studio," ibid., 14 April 1989. Other possible sources of difficulty concern violations by US periodicals of Canadian tariff and tax provisions governing their presence in Canada and the way the federal government's proposed Goods and Services Tax may enhance the position of US magazines in the Canadian market. See Catherine Keachie, "The Split-Run Rule," *CPPA Newsletter*, no. 128, 2, and Canadian Magazine Publishers' Association, "Canadian Magazines and the Proposed Goods and Services Tax: A Submission to the House of Commons Standing Committee on Finance," 15 September 1989. See especially 7–10, "Unfair Advantage to US Periodicals under the GST System."

25 Isaiah A. Litvak and Christopher J. Maule, "Bill C-58 and the Regulation of Periodicals in Canada," *International Journal*, 36, Winter 1980–81, 70–90.

26 Quoted in Christopher Waddell, "US Senators Support Free Trade Deal," *Globe and Mail*, 10 December 1986.

27 "Confidential Briefing Paper."

28 Jean Murray Cole, "Keeping the Mind Alive: Literary Leanings in the Fur Trade," *Journal of Canadian Studies*, 16, Summer 1981, 87–93.

29 Isaac Hildreth's Government House, Halifax, 1800, for example, was designed in the Regency manner, while John Merrick's Province House, built there after 1811, was in the Palladian tradition, which, notes Nathalie Clerk, made it attractive to British travellers, who "were naturally responsive to an architecture that reminded them of familiar models." Anthony Adamson, Alice Alison, Eric Arthur, and William Goulding, eds., *Historic Architecture of Canada* (Ottawa: Royal Architectural Institute of Canada, 1966), plate 5; Nathalie Clerk, *Palladian Style in Canadian Architecture* (Ottawa: Parks Canada, 1984), 26–7.

30 Y.S. Bains, "Shakespeare on the Canadian Stage: The First Sixty Years," *Canadian Drama*, 8 Spring 1982, 66–73.
31 Harry Piers, "Artists in Nova Scotia," *Collections of the Nova Scotian Historical Society*, 18, 1914, 110.
32 Thomas Cary, *Abram's Plains: A Poem*, ed. D.M.R. Bentley (London, ON: Canadian Poetry Press, 1986).
33 For others, see Mary Lu MacDonald, "Some Notes on the Montreal Literary Scene in the Mid-1820s," *Canadian Poetry*, 5, Fall–Winter 1979, 29–40.
34 Peter Ennals and Deryck Holdsworth, "Vernacular Architecture and the Cultural Landscape of the Maritime Provinces – a Reconnaisance," *Acadiensis*, 10, Spring 1981, 86–106.
35 Neil McDonald "Egerton Ryerson and the School as an Agent of Political Socialization," in Neil McDonald and A. Chaiton, eds., *Egerton Ryerson and His Times* (Toronto: Macmillan, 1978), 81–106; James H. Love, "Cultural Survival and Social Control: The Development of a Curriculum for Upper Canada's Common Schools in 1846," *Histoire Sociale/Social History*, 15, November 1982, 357–82; Bruce Curtis, "Schoolbooks and the Myth of Curricular Republicanism: The State and the Curriculum in Canada West, 1820–1850," ibid., 16, November 1983, 305–30.
36 For a recent discussion of the *Literary Garland*, see Carole Gerson, *A Purer Taste: The Writing and Reading of Fiction in English in Nineteenth Century Canada* (Toronto: University of Toronto Press, 1989), 45–6.
37 Catherine Sheldrick Ross, ed., *Recovering Canada's First Novelist: Proceedings from the John Richardson Conference* (Erin, ON: Porcupine's Quill, 1984).
38 R.A. Davies, ed., *On Thomas Chandler Haliburton: Selected Criticism* (Ottawa: Tecumseh Press, 1979).
39 I.S. MacLaren, "Notes towards a Reconsideration of Paul Kane's Art and Prose," *Canadian Literature*, 113–14, Summer–Fall 1987, 179–205.
40 Suzanne Zeller, *Inventing Canada: Early Victorian Science and the Idea of a Transcontinental Nation* (Toronto: University of Toronto Press, 1987).
41 Bruce Curtis, *Building the Educational State in Canada West, 1836–1871* (London, ON: Althouse Press, 1989).
42 Allan Smith, "Old Ontario and the Emergence of a National Frame of Mind," this volume.
43 For a discussion of these matters see Allan Smith, "The Imported Image: American Publications and American Ideas in the Evolution

of the English Canadian Mind, 1820–1900," PH.D. diss. University of Toronto, 1972, 133–200. See also George L. Parker, *The Beginnings of the Book Trade in Canada* (Toronto: University of Toronto Press, 1985), especially chapters 5 and 6.

44 Thomas D'Arcy McGee, "The Mental Outfit of the New Dominion," *Montreal Gazette*, 5 November 1867.

45 Henry J. Morgan, "Introduction," *Bibliotheca Canadensis: or, A Manual of Canadian Literature* (Ottawa: G.E. Desbarats, 1867), viii.

46 "Arthur Clappé," in Helmut Kallmann, Gilles Potvin, and Kenneth Winters, eds., *Encyclopedia of Music in Canada* (Toronto: University of Toronto Press, 1981), 197–8. See also Jean Southworth, "Ottawa," ibid., 718.

47 J. Russell Harper, *Painting in Canada: A History*, 2nd ed. (Toronto: University of Toronto Press, 1977), 212.

48 J.G. Bourinot, "Canadian Materials for History, Poetry, and Romance," *New Dominion Monthly*, April 1871, 193–204.

49 "A Gossip about the First Dominion Art Exhibition. By an Unlearned Visitor," *Rose-Belford's Canadian Monthly*, 4, May 1880, 545.

50 Parker, *Beginnings of the Book Trade.*

51 "The Art Union Exhibition," *Canadian Monthly and National Review*, 6, July 1874, 85.

52 Henry J. Morgan, ed., *The Dominion Annual Register and Review* (Ottawa: Maclean, Roger and Co., 1879), 302.

53 Text of Lorne's talk at the Art Institute of Montreal, 1879, in J.E. Collins, *Canada under the Administration of Lord Lorne* (Toronto: Rose Publishing, 1884), Appendix E, 425.

54 G. Mercer Adam, "Literature, Nationality, and the Tariff," *Week*, 7, 27 December 1889, 59–60.

55 For the history of these matters to 1900, see Parker, *Beginnings of the Book Trade.* For comment on a critical phase of the copyright controversy, see P.B. Waite, "Sir John Thompson and Copyright, 1889–1894: Struggling to Break Free of Imperial Law," *Bulletin of Canadian Studies*, 6, Autumn 1983, 36–49.

56 James W. Bell, "The Future of Canada," *Week*, 6, 26 July 1889, 539.

57 Sara Jeannette Duncan, "American Influence on Canadian Thought," ibid., 4, 7 July 1887, 518.

58 "The Future of Canadian Literature, No. 2," *Canadian Magazine*, 18, February 1902, 387.

59 A.D. Gilbert, "On the Road to New York: The Protective Impulse and the English Canadian Cultural Identity, 1896–1914," *Dalhousie Review*, 58, Autumn 1978, 412.

60 Ibid.

61 A copy of Nobb's statement, its reach much broader than its title

("Proposals with Regard to State Aid for Art Education in Canada") suggests, is in the Sir Edmund Walker Papers, Fisher Rare Book Room, Robarts Library, University of Toronto, Box 22, Report to Agriculture Minister Sidney Fisher, 4 May 1907, 3–4. I owe this reference to Maria Tippett. Her book *Making Culture: English Canadian Institutions and the Arts before the Massey Commission* (Toronto: University of Toronto Press, 1990) sheds light on many of the issues dealt with here.

62 M.C. Urquhart and K.A.H. Buckley, eds., *Historical Statistics of Canada* (Cambridge: Cambridge University Press, and Toronto: Macmillan, 1965), 14.

63 Margaret Prang, "The Origins of Public Broadcasting in Canada," *Canadian Historian Review*, 46, March 1965, 2–3.

64 Douglas L. Cole, "Artists, Patrons, and Public: An Inquiry into the Success of the Group of Seven," *Journal of Canadian Studies*, 13, Summer 1978, 69–78.

65 Books on painting, poetry anthologies, and, above all, histories of literature were conspicuously present in this area. See Newton McTavish, *The Fine Arts in Canada* (Toronto: Macmillan, 1925); F.B. Housser, *A Canadian Art Movement: The Story of the Group of Seven* (Toronto: Macmillan, 1926); Nathaniel A. Benson, ed., *Modern Canadian Poetry* (Ottawa: Graphic Publishers, 1930); Archibald Mac-Mechan, *Headwaters of Canadian Literature* (Toronto: McClelland and Stewart, 1924); J.D. Logan and D.G. French, *Highways of Canadian Literature* (Toronto: McClelland and Stewart, 1924); Lionel Stevenson, *Appraisals of Canadian Literature* (Toronto: Macmillan, 1926); Lorne Pierce, *Outline of Canadian Literature* (Toronto: Ryerson Press, 1927); and V.B. Rhodenizer, *Handbook of Canadian Literature* (Ottawa: Graphic Publishers, 1930).

66 M. Vipond, "The Canadian Authors' Association of the 1920s: A Case Study in Cultural Nationalism," *Journal of Canadian Studies*, 15, Spring 1980, 68–79.

67 See, in particular, Sir Ernest MacMillan's *Two Sketches for Strings Based on French-Canadian Airs* (1927), his *Six Bergerettes du Bas Canada* (1928), his *Three Indian Songs of the West Coast* (1928), and his *Three French Canadian Sea Songs* (1930). Approximately seventy of his transpositions of West Coast Indian music were published in V. Garfield, P. Wingert, and M. Barbeau, *The Tsimshian: Their Arts and Music* (New York: J.J. Augustin, 1951).

68 For the resolution of the copyright problem arrived at in 1921, see R.A. Shields, "Imperial Policy and the Canadian Copyright Act of 1889," *Dalhousie Review*, 60, Winter 1980–81, 634–58, especially 655–6.

69 "Technical limitations," notes Frank W. Peers, "on the number of available frequencies necessitated intervention by the state." See his *The Politics of Canadian Broadcasting, 1920–1951* (Toronto: University of Toronto Press, 1969), 12. The federal government first appeared on the scene in 1913 when the Radiotelegraph Act was passed. by 1922 radio broadcasting was under the authority of the Department of Marine and Fisheries, and a complex web of regulations was in existence (ibid., 15, 16).

70 Maria Tippett, *Art at the Service of War: Canada, Art, and the Great War* (Toronto: University of Toronto Press, 1984).

71 Peter Morris, *Embattled Shadows: A History of Canadian Cinema, 1895–1939* (Montreal: McGill-Queen's University Press, 1978), 59.

72 Juliet Thelma Pollard, "Government Bureaucracy in Action: A History of Cinema in Canada, 1896–1941," Master's thesis, University of British Columbia, 1979, 45–6.

73 Betty Lee, *Love and Whiskey: The Story of the Dominion Drama Festival* (Toronto: McClelland and Stewart, 1973).

74 Samuel Moffett, *The Americanization of Canada*, introduction by Allan Smith (1907; rpt. Toronto: University of Toronto Press, 1972).

75 Archibald MacMechan, "Canada as a Vassal State," *Canadian Historical Review*, 1, December 1920, 350, 347.

76 Graham Spry to Brooke Claxton, 6 October 1930, Alan Plaunt Papers, University of British Columbia Library, quoted in Prang "Origins of Public Broadcasting," 9.

77 By 1925 there were 600 stations in the US as against forty-four in Canada. "What if" – Frank W. Peers paraphrased the question in the minds of many of the forty-four – "Canadians chose to listen to the American stations, and ignore their own?" (Peers, *Politics of Canadian Broadcasting*, 13). For a look at the filmmakers' similar problems, see Morris, *Embattled Shadows*, 175–7.

78 See H.F. Angus, ed., *Canada and Her Great Neighbor: Sociological Surveys of Opinions and Attitudes in Canada Concerning the United States* (Toronto: Ryerson Press, 1938), especially 124–40.

79 Never explicitly articulated but always present in such anxious utterances as that made by *Saturday Night* editor B.K. Sandwell, when in 1928 he pronounced "the true Canadian type" to be "a small town type" whose passing from the scene would coincide with emergence of a society – urban and "American" – quite unlikely to have much sympathy for the values Sandwell preferred and in relation to which he and others like him could offer guidance. See B.K. Sandwell, "Only the Rich Should Write Novels," *Saturday Night*, 43, 6 October 1928, 2, cited in Vipond, "Canadian Authors' Association," 73.

80 "A national radio system," asserted Graham Spry, is nothing less than

"a majestic instrument of national unity and national culture." See his "A Case for Nationalized Broadcasting," *Queen's Quarterly*, 38, Winter 1931, 169.

81 Graham Spry, "Brief on Behalf of the Canadian Radio League Presented to the House of Commons' Special Committee on Radio Broadcasting in 1932," Canada, House of Commons, *Proceedings and Report of the Special Committee on Radio Broadcasting* (1932), 565, quoted in Prang, "Origins of Public Broadcasting," 28.

82 A point insisted upon by W.E. Euler, minister of trade and commerce, when he introduced the bill establishing the National Film Board. See Pollard, "Government Bureaucracy in Action," 109, n152.

83 Martyn Howe, "The Pictures," *Dalhousie Review*, 16, October 1936, 290–9, and his "Motion Picture Art," *Canadian Forum*, 16, March 1937, 12–13.

84 James Lysyshyn, *A Brief History: The National Film Board of Canada* (Ottawa: NFB Publications, 1970), 3.

85 See Claude Bissell, *The Imperial Canadian: Vincent Massey in Office* (Toronto: University of Toronto Press, 1986), 198–9.

86 Sir Robert Borden, *Canada in the Commonwealth: From Conflict to Cooperation* (Toronto: Oxford University Press, 1929); J.W. Dafoe, *Canada: An American Nation* (New York: Columbia University Press, 1935).

87 J.M. Gibbon, *Canadian Mosaic: The Making of a Northern Nation* (Toronto: McClelland and Stewart, 1938).

88 Northrop Frye, "Canada and Its Poetry," *Canadian Forum*, 23, December 1943, 207–10.

89 Donald Creighton, *The Commercial Empire of the St Lawrence*, 1760–1850 (Toronto: Ryerson Press, 1937).

90 The multicultural idea eventually got "official" recognition, the northern theme was amplified by popular historians – Pierre Berton, Peter C. Newman – as well as by commentators such as Margaret Atwood and Gaile McGregor, and Creighton himself produced a number of books – and even, toward the end of his life, a novel – intended to bring before an ever larger audience the argument that Canada, having been created not in defiance of geography but with its help, was as naturally and solidly based as any society could be. See Allan Smith, "Metaphor and Nationality in North America," this volume; Allan Smith, "National Images and National Maintenance: The Ascendancy of the Ethnic Idea in North America," also in this volume; Margaret Atwood, *Survival: A Thematic Guide to Canadian Literature* (Toronto: Anansi, 1972); Gaile McGregor, *The Wacousta Syndrome: Explorations in the Canadian Landscape* (Toronto: University

of Toronto Press, 1985); Pierre Berton, *The Mysterious North* (Toronto: McClelland and Stewart, 1956); Pierre Berton, *Klondike: The Life and Death of the Last Great Gold Rush* (Toronto: McClelland and Stewart, 1958); Pierre Berton, *Drifting Home* (Toronto: McClelland and Stewart, 1973); Peter C. Newman, *Caesars of the Wilderness* (Markham, ON: Viking, 1985); Peter C. Newman, *Company of Adventurers* (Markham, ON: Viking, 1985); Donald Creighton, *Dominion of the North* (Toronto: Macmillan, 1944); Donald Creighton, *John A. Macdonald: The Young Politician* (Toronto: Macmillan, 1951); Donald Creighton, *John A. Macdonald: The Old Chieftain* (Toronto: Macmillan, 1955); Donald Creighton, *The Road to Confederation* (Toronto: Macmillan, 1964); Donald Creighton, *Canada's First Century, 1867–1967* (Toronto: Macmillan, 1970); Donald Creighton, *The Forked Road: Canada, 1939–1957* (Toronto: McClelland and Stewart, 1976); Donald Creighton, *The Passionate Observer: Selected Writings* (Toronto: McClelland and Stewart, 1980); and the novel, Donald Creighton, *The Takeover* (Toronto: McClelland and Stewart, 1978).

91 Maria Tippett, *Lest We Forget* (London: London Regional Art and History Museums, 1989), Part I: "The Great War," 9–24; Part II: "The Second World War," 25–41.

92 For the CBC's International Service, see "Le service international de Radio-Canada," *Affaires Exterieures* 5, no. 10 (1953), 295–99, and David Ellis, *Evolution of the Canadian Broadcasting System: Objectives and Realities, 1928–1968* (Ottawa: Department of Communications, 1979). For a memoir by a staffer of how the service worked, see Dick Halhead, *Radio: The Remote Years* (Scarborough, ON: Author, 1981), 52–6. For the Musicanada Festival, see Eric McLean, "Exporting Canadian Music," *Montreal Star*, 19 November 1977. For the Toronto Symphony in China, see "Toronto Symphony" in Kallmann, Potvin, and Winters, eds., *Encyclopedia of Music in Canada*, 926.

93 Frank W. Peers, *The Public Eye: Television and the Politics of Canadian Broadcasting, 1952–1968* (Toronto: University of Toronto Press, 1979), especially 55–91.

94 Ibid., especially 283–304.

95 "The commission," observes Massey's biographer, "was overwhelmed with briefs" (Bissell, *Imperial Canadian*, 211). For the arts and culture community's continued activity during the 1950s, note the recollection of dramatist and one-time president of the Canadian Arts Council Herman Voaden: "For six more years [1951–57] we had to continue the lobbying." Frances K. Smith Papers, Box 3, File 6, Document J, Queen's University Archives, transcribed from tape recording of discussion at the Toronto Branch of the Canadian Authors' Association at the Toronto Public Library on Friday, 5 April

1968. I am grateful to Maria Tippett for supplying me with this reference.

96 The commission was certainly mindful of the threat. "American influences on Canadian life," it noted in a representative remark, "to say the least are impressive ... a vast and disproportionate amount of material coming from a single alien source may stifle rather than stimulate our own creative effort ... national independence ... would be nothing but an empty shell without a vigourous and distinctive national life." Canada, *Report of the Royal Commission on National Development in the Arts, Letters, and Sciences, 1949–51* (Ottawa: King's Printer, 1951), 18.

97 In introducing the legislation to establish the council, Prime Minister Louis St Laurent stressed its nation-consolidating, American-resisting role, making pointed reference to the way Confederation had brought entities "often inclined to the south rather than eastward and westward ... together," and associating the council's projected function in developing a national "spirit" and a national "spiritual strength" with that fundamental process of national consolidation (Canada, House of Commons *Debates*, 18 January 1957, 392).

98 Canada, *Report of the Royal Commission on Publications* (Ottawa: Queen's Printer, 1961).

99 Canada, *Report of the Committee on Broadcasting* (Ottawa: Queen's Printer, 1965).

100 Canada, Special Senate Committee on Mass Media, *Report*, 3 vols. (Ottawa: Queen's Printer, 1970).

101 Litvak and Maule, "Bill C-58"; John Meisel, "Escaping Extinction: Cultural Defence of an Undefended Border," *Canadian Journal of Political and Social Theory*, 10, Spring 1986, 248–65; Stephen Brooks, "Cultural Policy: Communications and Culture," in his *Public Policy in Canada: An Introduction* (Toronto: McClelland and Stewart, 1989), 297–323.

102 For comment on the character of the work done under the auspices of the CFDC and Telefilm, see Martin Knelman, *Home Movies: Tales from the Canadian Film World* (Toronto: Key Porter Books, 1987). See also David Clandfield, *Canadian Film* (Toronto: Oxford University Press, 1967), 87–9, 109–11.

103 For the campaign the private broadcasters mounted to bend the CRTC to their will – they were even able to get the president of their association appointed as its chairman – see the polemical but informative book by Herschel Hardin, *Closed Circuits: The Sell-Out of Canadian Television* (Vancouver: Douglas and McIntyre, 1985).

104 These, naturally, were not the terms in which the case was made. Pleas for continued support tended to rest on the ground – it had

provided the original raison d'être for the programs now in danger – that infrastructure was necessary if Canadian films dealing with Canadian subjects were to be produced, that that infrastructure, once in place, had to be preserved, and that the best way to do this was to keep it employed, even if doing so meant making American films. Film critic Martin Knelman paraphrases the case of those who argued in these terms: "Once we had a few hits under our belts, things would go better for everybody. Our actors, technicians, and writers would be employed, and there would be a market for many different kinds of movies." The claim that, as National Film Board Commissioner James de B. Domville put it in 1981, "foreign [i.e., US] markets are the solution" to the problem of creating a viable film industry in Canada that would deal with Canadian subjects was, indeed, a plausible one – if one did not look too closely at the work actually done. It certainly provided the rationale for the film companies' protests of government moves to reduce the benefits to which they had become so accustomed. See, for example, the film industry's telex to the prime minister, the minister of finance, and the minister of communications, 25 November 1981. Martin Knelman, *This is Where We Came in: The Career and Character of Canadian Film* (Toronto: McClelland and Stewart, 1977), 97; James de B. Domville, "Domestic Market Key to Dollars," *Filmworld*, 55, 15 April – 15 May 1981, 3; "Telex to the Prime Minister," *Film and TV World*, 4, 15 December 1981–15 January 1982, 1, 9.

105 Though it can be admitted that what government agencies have chosen to regard as "Canadian concerns" have increasingly reflected the fact that Canada is more of a private enterprise society than it thinks. See the article on this subject by John Meisel, "Fanning the Air: The Canadian State and Broadcasting," *Transactions of the Royal Society of Canada*, 5th ser. 4, 1989, 191–204.

106 Paul Audley, *Canada's Cultural Industries: Broadcasting, Publishing, Records, and Film* (Toronto: James Lorimer, 1983), 257.

107 Ibid., 301.

108 Salem Alaton, "A New Generation Sets the Cameras Rolling: Canada's Vigourous Commercial Film Industry Has the NFB Casting Itself in an Updated Role," *Globe and Mail*, 29 April 1989.

109 It was, thought film historian David Clandfield, particularly important to note that commercial filmmaking played a central role in providing work for "directors resting between TV assignments and more prestigious literary adaptations." Clandfield, *Canadian Film*, 109.

110 Litvak and Maule, "Bill C-58," 83.

111 Ritchie Yorke, *Axes, Chops, and Hot Licks: The Canadian Rock Music Scene,* introduction by Pierre Juneau (Edmonton: Hurtig, 1971).

112 For example, *Goin' Down the Road* (1970); *The Rowdyman* (1972); *The Hard Part Begins* (1974); *The Apprenticeship of Duddy Kravitz* (1974); *Why Shoot the Teacher* (1977); *Les Plouffe* (1981); *The Wars* (1983); *Joshua Then and Now* (1985); *I've Heard the Mermaids Singing* (1987); and *Bye Bye Blues* (1989).

113 Audley, *Canada's Cultural Industries,* 26.

114 George Woodcock, "The Provinces Become Patrons," in his *Strange Bedfellows: The State and the Arts in Canada* (Vancouver: Douglas and McIntyre, 1985), 83–90.

115 Bernard Ostry, "Can Culture Survive the Broadcast Battles?" *Globe and Mail,* 5 June 1989. See also Ostry's *The Cultural Connection: An Essay on Culture and Government Policy in Canada* (Toronto: McClelland and Stewart, 1978).

116 Bronwen Drainie, "How Truly Painful Will the Taxman's Bite Be to the Arts?" *Globe and Mail,* 22 April 1989. See also John Meisel and Jean Van Loon, "Calculating the Bush Garden: Cultural Policy in Canada," in Milton C. Cummings, Jr, and Richard S. Katz, eds., *The Patron State: Government and the Arts in Europe, North America, and Japan* (New York: Oxford University Press, 1987), especially 306–8.

Identity

6 Metaphor and Nationality
in North America

The nationalist uses language to define the nation's character and experience in a way that will provide a rationale for its continued existence. Lacking such a rationale and the mental picture of itself which that rationale helps to provide, no society can stay together. Language thus becomes an instrument to be employed in the fashioning of a nationalist ideology which itself becomes a tool designed for a particular purpose, the integrating of the human elements in a given geographical area into a coherent, self-conscious whole. In the course of fulfilling that purpose, nationalist ideology, like ideologies generally, often does violence to truth and marks reality.[1] Yet rhetoric of this sort, however much it deals in distortion, may still reflect something fundamental in the character of the society to whose mystique it attempts to give expression. Often it does this inadvertently by revealing a certain character trait in the act of focusing on something quite different. Thus nationalists, in talking about their nation's accomplishments, may reveal pride, superiority, or arrogance. In dilating upon their country's prospects for the future, they may reveal optimism, excessive self-confidence, or a will to power. In this way they may, in spite of themselves, make an unintended gesture in the direction of reality. Less inflated rhetoric may make this same gesture in other ways, intentionally, and not as a result of error or oversight. Depending on how good or conscientious they are as historians, nationalists may

Canadian Historical Review, 51 (3), 1970, 247–75.

find themselves limited in what they can make of their nation's history and character by the circumstances of that history and the nature of that character. They may try to dramatize their nation's experience by employing striking and memorable language, or by emphasizing those elements in it that make it (in their view) unique and superior. They will not, however, depart from reality entirely, they will not indulge in unlimited flights of fancy, for they know that history will not sustain them on such a journey. And so they hover only a little distance above the earth, the temptation to use forceful and dramatic language having yielded to a prosaic and even homely way of speaking about their country's experience.

Nationalist rhetoric, then, may unintentionally or by design defer to reality. Two rhetorical devices commonly employed in Canada and the United States suggest the truth of these observations. The term "melting pot," in widespread use to delineate the character of American society, does reflect something fundamental in that society, although in a manner its enthusiasts have not perhaps fully intended. The metaphor of the mosaic represents an attempt by Canadian nationalism to come to grips with a difficult, possibly intractable, fact of Canadian life.

Describing an homogeneous, coherent community, and attempting to communicate the sense and meaning of its experience, is easier than doing the same thing for a community which is not homogeneous and which lacks coherence. Canadians have known this truth for some time; Americans are beginning to discover it as they rewrite their history to take account of the role black Americans have played in its making. Generally, however, American nationalists have seen their nation as a vessel containing a single, virtually unblemished way of life, and their language has, accordingly, been confident and assured. They have known who they were and in what they believed, and their vocabulary has reflected the pride and security that this knowledge brought. Canadian nationalism, in contrast, has been less exuberant and more diffident because it recognizes how fragile and uncertain is the structure it tries to celebrate, and how delicate must be the touch of they who would work all its parts into a cohesive whole.

Canada and the United States have been peopled by immigrants. The experience that these immigrants have undergone, and the character of the society they have helped to form, has been described metaphorically in both countries. One speaks of the American melting pot and the Canadian mosaic.[2] Each of these metaphors carries a double burden. Each is supposed to symbolize the actual nature of the society to which it is applied, and each is held to represent the ideal form which that society is attempting to realize.

The melting-pot metaphor conjures up a picture of peoples of diverse origins being fused in the crucible of a new environment into a group of wholly new beings. Each of these beings has severed his ties with the Old World, and each has been regenerated by his new environment. Each has become, in Crèvecœur's classic phrase, a new man. This theme has been one of endless fascination for Americans. They have expended much time and energy elaborating the image of America as a New World, a garden, a virgin land, free from the corrupt and corrupting influences of the Old World, and capable of regenerating man.[3] The American, and all who come to America, are transformed.

In Canada the idea of creating a new being has gained nothing like the currency it has in the United States. Here the controlling metaphor has been the mosaic, a grand design consisting of many different elements, each of which retains its own character and quality while simultaneously contributing to the realization of the design as a whole. The objective is the rendering of a composite figure, not the creation of one that is wholly new. The elements of which this composite figure, this new nation, consist will be juxtaposed in such a way as to create a new nationality, one which rests not upon a common culture, but upon its capacity to serve and protect the interests, cultural and otherwise, of its component parts. The essence of this new nationality will be found in the nature of the relationship these different elements bear to one another, and not in the fact that there will cease to be different elements. There will need to be a consensus in this national state. It will, however, be a consensus which derives not so much from a shared culture or shared values as from the belief by all its peoples that their best interests are being served by continuing association in a common political framework.

Each of these metaphors idealizes the society to which it refers, and it idealizes the experience of the immigrant who has come to that society. Immigrants to the United States have often retained, and have often been encouraged to retain, some measure of their ethnic consciousness. The existence of ethnic communities, especially in the cities of the industrial northeast, is a well known fact of American life. It indicates clearly that Crèvecœur's new man has often failed to materialize, or if he has, that he has not been wholly forgetful of his transatlantic past.[4] Indeed, cultural pluralism, which is another way of talking about the mosaic, has been an important element in American social life. A classic defense of it issued from the pen of Horace Kallen, a Harvard philosopher, in 1915.[5] Kallen argued that each ethnic group had something of value to contribute to the totality of American culture, and it ought to be allowed to make that contribution. Immigrants should retain something of their Old World culture and, more than that, they should use it to enrich the life of their new homeland.

To the extent that immigrants to America have, moreover, been required to divest themselves of their ethnic identity, they have not become wholly new beings. They have not been melted down and then recast in an entirely new mould. They have become, instead, Americanized English. The dominant social type in the United States is an Anglo-Saxon type, and it is to this type that immigrants have been expected to assimilate. The American becomes, then, not a new creature, but a modification of one who is old and familiar. And so the term "anglo-conformity" has been held to describe more accurately than does the melting-pot metaphor what happens to the immigrant who comes to the United States.

Finally, while immigrants to the United States might be assimilated to the prevailing culture and value system, they are not always assimilated into the agencies and institutions that operate society. Their assimilation is behavioural, but not structural. It is not total, and here too, the melting-pot metaphor breaks down.[6]

The mosaic concept is also an idealization of reality. A greater degree of behavioural assimilation has taken place in Canada than that concept would appear to allow for. The majority of second generation German-Canadians, Icelandic-Canadians, and even Ukrainian-Canadians speak English and not their parents' native tongue. Their Old World culture, when it is retained, is regarded as something to be brought out and dusted off, rather self-consciously, on special national occasions. It does not form a central part of Canada's cultural life, and when it is brought to the attention of Canadians at large, the tendency is to regard it as an imported exotic.[7]

The mosaic further implies a social situation in which members of different ethnic communities are able to retain their ethnic identity, and yet participate to the full in the national life. Here, also, the metaphor fails to represent the reality. Positions of power, influence, and prestige have tended to go to Canadians of British descent, and continuing emphasis on ethnic origins has been judged likely to perpetuate this state of affairs.[8]

Finally, a state dedicated to the proposition that all cultural groups within it have an alienable right to flourish would be a state in which, ideally, brokerage politics would have no place. Representatives of each cultural group would know that their special interests would be looked after, and they would not, therefore, find it necessary to solicit special favours. The national interest would not demand constant adjustment of the claims of rival groups. And precisely because the interests of each group would, automatically as it were, be served, politicians would have nothing to gain by manœuvring for the support of these groups. But this clearly is not the situation. Politicians who, as André Siegfried wrote at the beginning of the century, found it necessary to "exert themselves ... to prevent the formation of homogeneous parties, divided according to creed or race or class" have noticed no changes in what is required of them. The different groups still feel it necessary to promote their interests, and those interests must still be reconciled with one another. It remains an essential part of politics in Canada to adjust the claims of different groups and interests and to insure as nearly as possible that none shall have undue influence and that the state shall not fragment along ethnic lines. The existence of the politician as broker indicates, not the presence of a fully functioning cultural mosaic, but its absence.

Notwithstanding this failure to correspond with reality, there are good historical reasons which explain why each of these terms came into use. The Puritans of New England came to see themselves as rejecting the Old World and the old ways, and their abhorrence of these things was confirmed by the American Revolution. To be an American, however, involved more than a rejection of Europe. It involved embracing a new ideal of life and society, which found expression in a peculiarly American political and social economic faith. Those who would be Americans must profess that faith. Thus John Quincy Adams could write in 1818:[9]

They (immigrants to America) come to a life of independence, but to a life of labor – and, if they cannot accommodate themselves to the character; moral, political and physical, of this country with all its compensating balances of good and evil, the Atlantic is always open to them to return to the land of their nativity and their fathers. To one thing they must make up their minds, or they will be disappointed in every expectation of happiness as Americans. They must cast off the European skin, never to resume it. They must look forward to posterity rather than backward to their ancestors; they must be sure that whatever their own feelings may be, those of their children will cling to the prejudices of this country.

It was possible for Americans to create the idea of a new man and to elaborate a national faith because America for the first two centuries of its existence was, broadly speaking, ideologically and culturally homogeneous. A consensus on fundamentals was possible, and that consensus emerged. It made the revolution and characterized American life and thought after it. At its core were the main elements of English liberal thought and the chief tendencies of enlightenment thought, elements whose impact in America was heightened by the influences of the American environment.[10] A belief in equality; a belief in progress, in individualism, in a fundamental law; and a belief that America had a special mission to show others how to order their affairs – all contained in a mind whose bent was essentially pragmatic: these were the leading elements of the American faith, and this was the quality of the mind that professed it. These liberal and egalitarian values were formalized and made part of the national identity. It was their adherence to them, their lives in a society that was shaped by its reverence for them, that defined Americans. Indeed, as Seymour Martin Lipset writes, they became part of the definition of nationhood itself.[11] Even the South, that most self-conscious of American regions, has been denied any claim to the status of a separate civilization with a faith and ritual all its own. Differences which obtained there were at most sectional variations within a common culture pattern. The South, like the North, owed its political theory more to Locke than Burke. Its economy may not have been industrial, but it was characterized by a capitalist and entrepreneurial spirit; cotton may have been king, but it went to market. And, on the other side, if the South participated in modes of thought often associated with the North, it is likewise true that the process was sometimes reversed. Even racism was not exclusively a Southern property, although slavery clearly was. D.M. Potter argues that it is necessary to recognize "how very thin the historical evidences of a separate southern culture really are," and C. Vann Woodward, who affirms the reality of a special Southern experience, asserts that the South "remains more American by far than anything else, and has all along."[12] There was, then, something that could be called an American faith, which had its being in the country as a whole. The newcomer was expected to adopt that faith as his own.

Nor was this all. Influenced by nineteenth-century racist ideas, some Americans supported their crusade for ideological purity with arguments for the exclusion of those immigrants whose racial background did not equip them with the wit or the moral fibre necessary to enable them to conform to the American Way. And so not only those who arrived with their own ideas about society, like the German socialists of the late nineteenth century, but also those whose social habits and ethnic background caused them to be deemed inferior to those who had made America found themselves treated with scorn and contempt.[13] "Americanism," however, was at root always more ideological than ethnic, more a matter of culture than of race, so that the twentieth-century overthrow of the racist assumptions upon which American nativism was based left the force of that idea, and the idea that all who came to America must be "Americanized," unimpaired. Americanism became once again what it had been in the late eighteenth and early nineteenth centuries, essentially an ideology, a set of values, a culture, which all might make their own.

Blacks, however, were to be denied the right to make it their own. They were to be denied the right to participate in this central process of American history. And to deny them this right was, perversely, to act in a manner consistent with the liberal idea itself. That idea, to which gradations in society were foreign, could provide only for each person's inclusion in society on a basis of absolute equality with all others. If they were not equal they were not truly human, and must perforce be excluded. Blacks, patently, were not equal. Their exclusion was therefore natural and inevitable. But once they became equal, the same idea required that they be incorporated into the life of the society fully and completely. They must become Americans like all other Americans. The central thrust of the civil rights movement has been, then, assimilationist. The discovery that blacks are equal has meant that they must become white Americans in all respects save the colour of their skin. They, too, must profess the national faith. They also must be brought within the Lockean consensus.[14]

Canada, by contrast, was held from the beginning to consist of two societies. Each of these two societies had its own values, traditions, life style, and language. One was French-speaking, Catholic, and, with some qualifications, agrarian and feudal; the other was English-speaking, Protestant, commercially-minded, and conservatively liberal in its view of society.[15] Agreement on fundamentals was difficult. The creation of an ideal national type in which all Canadians could see something of themselves, and which they could all strive to emulate, was impossible. The national preoccupation came to be with differences, not similarities, with creating a nation out of culturally disparate groups, not with establishing cultural uniformity. The absence of a national type (there was no Canadian Crèvecœur because there could be no Canadian new man) and the absence of a clear and specific national faith which all Canadians could profess, meant that there was nothing to which an immigrant could be required to assimilate. The only element in their experience which the two communities had in common was the link each of them retained with a transatlantic culture, that of imperial Britain in the one case, Catholic Europe in the other. Ironically, then, the one element the two shared could not result in a commitment by newcomers to a wholly new way of life. Instead it served only to encourage them to maintain their ties with their parent societies.

Confederation created a political entity which owed its birth to the concern of its people, both French-speaking and English-speaking, to preserve a British civilization in North America, one which would, in time, assume the status and dignity of a great state. There would be a consensus in this new society, as there must be in any society, but it would not derive from a particular culture or a set of values narrowly conceived. It would be a consensus which did not limit but rather encouraged diversity and freedom, and this not merely of individuals but of groups. It would be a consensus built upon what Cartier suggested were the "kindred interests and sympathies" of the British North Americans, but central to those interests and sympathies was the conviction that conformity to a national type was not possible. It would be a consensus in support of the British and monarchical system of government, as Taché made clear, but that system of government was to be supported precisely because the kind of political society it maintained in being was not monolithic. Even Macdonald, whose ideal remained a centralized state in which, ultimately, the assimilation of all laws in the provinces except Quebec would take place, thereby showing that not merely the union but the fusion of the British North American provinces had come to pass, was compelled to yield to the pluralist imperative. A legislative union, he proclaimed, was impossible, in the foreseeable future at least. It was impossible not merely because it would fail to satisfy the French-speaking Canadians, but also because it would take insufficient account of Maritime particularism. And so, irresistibly, pluralism made necessary the construction of a political system that would accommodate it.[16]

The new political nationality would embrace not simply the French and English, but the Scots and Irish as well. The Irish, Scots, or English who had emerged on the British North American shore following their voyage across the Atlantic found no particular set of values, no special way of life, which they were expected to adopt, nothing in favour of which they were expected to abandon the cultural baggage they brought with them. They were perceived as representatives of a particular Old World culture, and not as people whose principal business it was to adopt a wholly new way of life. Their way of life would of course change; they would become British North Americans; but the change would be owing to the imperatives of circumstance, not those of a national creed. The Canadian state would not, because it could not, require conformity to a single type, or even to one of two types. It was founded, in the estimation of those who made it, on diversity. In Cartier's words: "there could be no danger to the rights and privileges of either French Canadians, Scotchmen, Englishmen, or Irishmen ... no one could apprehend that anything could be enacted which would harm or do injustice to persons of any nationality."[17]

But while there was to be cultural pluralism, it was not conceived of as embracing all ethnic groups. Under the influence of nineteenth-century racist ideas, Canadians elaborated a concept of nationality that did not explicitly require assimilation to a common cultural type, but which was to be limited in other ways. Canadians like Sir John G. Bourinot concluded that the northern peoples of Europe were the first among peoples. They had developed the highest form of civilization the world had yet seen, and, of equal importance, modern self-government had evolved from their primitive tribal institutions. Canadians stood in this great tradition in two ways: Canada was itself a northern nation, and therefore its environment, like the environment of northern Europe, called into play those qualities most to be desired in humankind, those qualities which had produced the beginning of modern civilization in the German forests. Canadians were not, nor could they be, slothful Mediterranean types. Secondly, Canadians could claim descent from these same northern peoples. Even the French Canadians could be included under this dispensation, for their ancestors were the Normans, and they had been as virile, upright, and Northern a people as the world had ever seen. Indeed, the possibilities opened up by this view of things were almost unlimited. Just as the Norman French had contributed, after 1066, to the making of the modern British nation, so might their descendants in modern Canada come together with that country's Anglo-Saxon elements to form a great new Britain, a new northern Britain, which might, ultimately, replace the old Britain at the centre of the empire. In this scheme of things there was, of course, no place for the inferior races. Not only were the non-white races and the peoples of southern and eastern Europe included in this latter category, but even, occasionally, those of the United States itself. Its people, after all, lived

in a more southerly climate, one that conduced to decay and effe-
minacy. Moreover, they seemed determined to allow themselves to
be overrun with aliens who could not possibly strengthen the race.
Canada, in contrast, as Sir George Parkin emphasized, could have
no cities "like New York, St. Louis, Cincinnati, or New Orleans
which attract even the vagrant population of Italy and other countries of Southern Europe." It would not therefore slip downwards in
the scale of nations as the United States so obviously was doing.[18]
This kind of nationalism, then, allowed the French Canadians,
along with any group which could claim descent from the ancient
inhabitants of the northern forests, to be integrated into the
national character and yet retain their own special culture. It was a
clever and imaginative construction, for it seemed to satisfy both
the pressing need for a coherent nationalism and the equally
insistent demand that such a nationalism accommodate the obvious
differences within Canadian society. Yet it was able to accomplish
this feat only at the price of conceding, at one level of meaning at
least, that Canada was a pluralist society.

The anxiety aroused by the Yellow Peril revealed in a stark and
unpleasant way the limits which racism and fear could impose on
the pluralist idea; but racism in this context did not deny that idea
altogether, as it had not denied it for Bourinot and Parkin. How,
indeed, could it? For the same sanctions that required the nationalists of eastern Canada to adjust their integral nationalism if it was to
have meaning beyond English Canada prevented those who were
concerned with Oriental immigration from bolstering their arguments with appeals to a conventional cultural nationalism. The
narrow Anglo-Saxonism which pervaded the British Columbia argument for exclusion could not provide the rationale for action at
the national level. There, the argument had to be a broader and
more latitudinarian one. How else could Lemieux be got to go to
Japan? Surely he would not go in defence of a narrowly Anglo-
Saxon Canada.

The argument for restricted entry, like that for nationalist
theory, had to rest on grounds of race, not culture. For if the
nation, and not just a part thereof, was to be mobilized in its
support, that argument, like the one on which any nationally
acceptable nationalist theory would have to rest, must allow for
cultural diversity. And so Lemieux went to Tokyo, not in support of
cultural uniformity, but rather to negotiate an agreement that
would reduce racial tension. For him, the issue had to be based on
the broad ground of race. He went, as he explained upon his
return, to resolve a problem endemic wherever "the two races,

Mongolian and Caucasian, have come into contact."[19] He went, although he himself did not share the fears of those who saw it in imminent danger, to uphold the integrity of a branch of western civilization now endangered by the expanding hordes of the East. That civilization, seen from a world perspective, was homogeneous; but the broad homogeneity of a civilization is not the more narrow and restrictive homogeneity of a particular nation or culture within it. Nothing seems clearer than that it was the former and not the latter that was held to be at stake.

Two sets of events, one political and the other intellectual, worked together in the twentieth century to overthrow the assumptions upon which this racist concept of nationality was based. The fate of Germany raised questions about the validity of arguments based on the notion that one race was inherently superior, while advances in anthropology showed that there was no scientific basis for racism.[20] Colour, however, remained an obstacle. At first only a part of the message was received. The overthrow of racism might have destroyed the barriers dividing whites from each other, but those which separated white from yellow and both from black, remained. And so only some of the limits on pluralism in Canada were removed. In 1936, the governor general, Lord Tweedsmuir, was able to tell a group of Ukrainian-Canadians that by being better Ukrainians, by remaining conscious of their ethnic heritage, they would be better Canadians. But when, two years later, John Murray Gibbon published his profile of Canadian society, *Canadian Mosaic*, there was no room in it for Orientals and blacks. The book's subtitle revealed its racist heritage, for it was to be the story of "The Making of a Northern Nation." Not until after the Second World War, whose enormities made plain the consequences which might flow from racism, did the pluralist idea become inclusive. Not until then were the non-white races awarded, in principle, a full place in the fabric of Canadian society.

Bourinot had recognized that a coherent Canadian nationalist doctrine could not rest on culture, and after a fascinating and complicated search he had located its base in the nineteenth-century idea of race, and the link provided among the peoples of Canada by their common descent from the Northern peoples of Europe. There were those, however, who continued to see in cultural uniformity the key to national strength. For them, indeed, all the signs suggested that by a kind of historical necessity cultural uniformity was exactly what the future would bring, and they bent themselves to the task of hastening its arrival. The nationalism of the McCarthyites, momentarily triumphant in the Manitoba School legislation of 1890, was, however, transformed into the pluralist settlement of 1897, the necessity for which grew directly out of the absence of a nationally acceptable type to which assimilation could be urged and the reluctance of the Manitobans to accept the bicultural idea. A single culture nationalism showed itself to be impossible, for French Canadians could not accept it, and it was replaced by its opposite, the only thing acceptable to Westerners, who had by now come to regard all minorities as coequal in status. But multiculturalism, in the eyes of some bad enough, was to show itself intolerable when accompanied by multilingualism. The drive for national schools was accordingly renewed early in the twentieth century. It was successful, however, only in the limited sense that it created a population unilingual in English in most of Canada outside Quebec. It did not provide that population with a culture. That population was not "Canadianized." Ralph Connor's proposition, that in the Canadian West a nation was being created, that "out of breeds diverse in tradition, in ideals, in speech, and in manner of life, Saxon and Slav, Teuton, Celt, and Gaul, one people is being made"[21] remained essentially a prophecy unfilled. Where Crèvecœur could define his new man, Connor wrote only in vague generalities. Where Israel Zangwill in his 1908 play *The Melting-Pot* could explain clearly and in a way that could appeal to them as well as to the established members of their new society what was to happen to immigrants in America, Connor argued for a kind of domestic imperialism in which immigrants were not so much transformed by their new environment as uplifted by their contact with the Protestant Anglo-Saxons they found in it. His book demonstrates nothing more clearly than the impossibility of articulating a Canadian national type in which all elements of Canadian society could see something of themselves. His attempt to forge with his prose the device whose existence in the United States Zangwill had dramatized the year before showed itself to be a failure. What emerged in the 1920s was not a drift towards integral nationalism or in the direction of a firm idea of who and what the Canadian was (despite the persistence of arguments that this indeed ought to be the goal), but the first clear and explicit articulations of the mosaic concept. The term was first used by Victoria Hayward, who in 1922 described the Canadian West with its peculiar architecture and its polyglot population as "a mosaic of vast dimensions and great breadth."[22] The introduction to her volume took note of the way its author viewed Canadian society, and, in a gratuitous aside, contrasted that society with its neighbour to the south. The book, it said, records those

unique and beautiful racial traditions which have survived in Canada and flourished, while the passion for conformity to a provincial process of standardization has crushed them in the United States. In Canada, the Scottish Highlander, the Acadian, and the Doukhobor, for example, have not been compelled to abandon their memories. The life of their forefathers has flourished when transplanted to a new soil. That wise tolerance and appreciative catholicity which is not always found in a new land has preserved old loveliness here.[23]

Four years later Kate A. Foster of Toronto published a study of the foreign born in Canada entitled *Our Canadian Mosaic*.[24]

If Bourinot and Parkin met the difficulties created for Canadian nationalism by cultural diversity with the assertion that at the most fundamental level they disappeared, D.G. Creighton met them by asserting that at the most fundamental level they could be ignored. The Laurentian hypothesis[25] not only showed how environmentalist modes of thought, hitherto used to emphasize what was held to be Canada's essentially North American character, could be employed in the construction of an argument for the independence of Canada in North America; it also revealed how fruitless the search for the unity and cohesion of Canada was now held to be if that search was not carried beyond its people. The forces which unified the Canadian experience, it asserted, were to be found in geography. The St Lawrence River and the systems tributary to it had not only made the nation possible; they had called it into being. It was upon this great natural phenomenon that the modern Canadian state rested. It linked the regions of Canada from east to west. Its existence meant that there was nothing artificial or fragmented about that state. Canada possessed the most solid, natural, and unified of bases. More than that, the contours of Canadian history itself had been given their very shape and substance by the manifold events acted out in the course of exploiting the great transcontinental empire to which the St Lawrence system gave access.

The Laurentian hypothesis gave Canadian history a sophistication and depth it had not previously possessed. It was a dazzling achievement on other grounds as well, for it supplied strength and unity where they had not existed before. It came close to duplicating Frederick Jackson Turner's great work in American historiography. But where the frontier thesis had seemed to explain all the central questions of American history – expansion, conflict, and the special character of the American people – where it was, for its time, truly a unifying vision, the Laurentian hypothesis could explain only some of the central questions of Canadian history. It comprehended the dynamics of expansion and conflict, but the results obtained from it were less satisfactory when what it implied about the national character was examined.

It explained why Europeans had been drawn into the northern interior of North America and across its vast expanse. It explained the rise of the Canadian state. It explained the central conflicts of Canadian history. It explained why government and order preceded settlement in the west. As an historical construct, it explained much indeed. But as a nationalist vision it could do only part of the job. It explained Canadian independence in North America, and it conferred unity and cohesion on the country. But the price it required to be paid for these considerable accomplishments was high. For the hypothesis involved the clearly implied assertion that those who did not find it possible to make the proper responses to the imperatives of the great river system were to be considered Canadians only marginally and in the most formal sense. They had failed to attune themselves to the major chords of the Canadian experience. They were out of harmony with its very core and essence. They denied, or were unable to appreciate, the forces which gave their society its life and being. And so, regrettably but necessarily, they were placed beyond the pale. They had failed to discern and move within the parameters of Canadian nationhood.

The hegemony of the great river system might explain much in Canadian history, it might indeed be the central fact of Canadian history, but a nationalist theory based on it would have difficulty gaining national acceptance on other grounds as well. Such a theory could not take with great seriousness sectionalism and the genuine if not insurmountable barriers which divided the sections and gave the people in them a self-consciousness and a sense of their own interests. In its cosmology the relationship of the outlying parts to the vital centre was to be one of subordination. That relationship was to be, in fact, frankly imperial. How one would react to this arrangement, as W.L. Morton wrote, depended, like one's appreciation of a club, on the end from which one contemplated it. Those who had not contemplated it from the proper end remained unconvinced that an argument which depended on the assertion that unity and coherence were to be purchased at the price, not of subordination of the parts to the whole, but of what they regarded as the subordination of some parts to another part could ever be acceptable as the basis for a healthy nationalism.

Nine years after the Laurentian hypothesis received its first formulation, Morton questioned its adequacy as a nationalist device although he appeared to accept the main thrust of its argument as history. He found the dominance of the centre which it asserted and the cultural homogeneity it implied objectionable. "The Canadian state," he wrote, "cannot be devoted to absolute nationalism, the focus of an homogeneous popular will. The two nationalities and the four sections of Canada forbid it." Rather, he concluded, it must respond to the interests of the communities, regional and otherwise, of which it consists. "The state in Canada must promote liberty of persons and communities."[26]

In 1960 Morton, by then clearly recognizing the value of the Laurentian hypothesis for the nationalist argument yet still firmly convinced that Canadian society must be understood in pluralist terms, attempted to synthesize a modified version of that concept with the pluralist idea. His object was to articulate an idea of Canada which would on the one hand provide cohesion and on the other allow for diversity, one which would promote liberty of persons and communities without at the same time inviting fragmentation of the polity. There was, he wrote in an argument of near-metaphysical subtlety, one Canadian way of life, given its character by the northern clime. Within that broad pattern, it was true, were to be found many others. They were, however, only variants of the one. All Canadians were northerners and therefore in essence the same. But while there was above all a common response to a common northern environment, it did not enjoin a rigid and absolute conformity. Canadian society, then, was characterized, not by unity in diversity but diversity in unity. In this way Morton advanced his 1946 argument a stage and attempted to reconcile the cultural and regional diversity which so clearly characterized Canada with the homogeneity which it now seemed to him any society must have if its life were to be sustained.[27]

The fact that the Canadian state has not been the ultimate expression of a particular culture and that it is not coterminous with a single region explains much about the failure of Canadian intellectuals to articulate a classically nationalist explanation of their nation and its experience, one to which all Canadians in all parts of the country might respond. But if cultural uniformity cannot be said to exist in the country as a whole, neither has it been possible to argue that it can be found within the linguistic community with which most Canadians associate themselves. When immigrants learn English, they acquire a medium of communication, but they do not acquire a culture. This situation arose, and has been sustained, partly by design and partly by accident.

The English-speaking community was not at Confederation conceived of as culturally homogeneous. Not only the new nationality as a whole, but also the English-speaking part of it, was thought of as being culturally diverse, involving Scots and Irish as well as English elements. This concept, like so many others in Canadian history, could enter into the service both of French- and English-speaking Canadians because each of them could emphasize different elements in it. For the French, concentrating on the principle at its centre, it meant that their position in Confederation, as one nationality in a state dedicated to the service of different nationalities, was unassailable. For the English, concentrating on the reality which seemed so clear, it meant that English Canada was no less a unity than was Britain itself, for its different parts, as did those of the United Kingdom, participated in a common culture and civilization, one that was most often described as British North American. But the essential point is that the assertion of the pluralist idea not only reflected the present absence of, but also prevented the future creation of, an English-Canadian type. A commitment had been made on the level of principle not to duality but to pluralism. This did not seem so clear at the time, for the diversity which existed in English-speaking Canada in 1867 was obscured by the fact that the elements of which English-Canadian society was composed were bound together by their common language, their British heritage, and their participation in the British North American experience. The pluralist idea was thus rendered at once necessary and harmless, for while it grew naturally out of the absence of a normative type, it was not really taken, except in Cartier's rhetoric, to indicate the presence of any very meaningful degree of cultural diversity in English Canada.

The migrations of the Laurier period at last caused English-speaking Canadians to confront the implications of the pluralist idea. They were brought face to face with cultural diversity not mitigated by similarity of background and the use of a common language. The confrontation caused them to think that pluralism carried too far was undesirable, but it also revealed how powerless they were to overcome it. The absence of a normative English-speaking Canadian type to which assimilation might be urged meant that the only device which could be used to bind the society together was its British character on the one hand and its participation in the New-World experience on the other. The first of these immigrants regarded with suspicion. They missed the nationalism at the root of much of the English Canadian's attachment to the empire. For this they could not really be blamed, for many English Canadians missed it too. To immigrants, a remark like Stephen Leacock's – that if things went as they should, "pretty soon the Ukranians (*sic*) will think they won the Battle of Trafalgar" – meant only that they were being invited to submerge their ethnic identity in someone else's. It did not suggest the existence of a "Canadianism," or even an "English Canadianism," with which they could without hesitation seek to identify themselves. The monarchy, it was true, aroused the enthusiasm of some of the newcomers, but their reverence for it recalled the French-speaking Canadians' attachment to an institution that did not compel their assimilation rather than the English Canadians' celebration of an agency their allegiance to which involved them, if only vicariously, in one of the great epics of human history.

The role played by Britain in the nineteenth century was assumed by the United States in the twentieth. Canada came to be defined more by its participation in the New-World experience than its place in the imperial. The two, in fact, were now held in some quarters to be mutually exclusive. This process was intensified and made easier by Canada's absorption of American popular culture which oozed irresistibly northwards, steadily increasing in volume until it assumed the proportions of a flood. Its presence exaggerated English-speaking Canada's essentially North American character, for it suggested absolute identity where in fact there was only close similarity. And so as that part of the definition of the English-speaking Canadian character which centred upon its participation in British culture and civilization was deprived of its relevancy and receded in importance, it was replaced, not by a compact, commonly acceptable definition of Canadianism, but by the idea of Canada as an American nation. While this turn of events was agreeable to, and in fact had been partly engineered by, Canadian nationalists of the Liberal persuasion, others found it wanting.

To them this appreciation of the Canadian character seemed incomplete at the point at which it was most important to nationalists that it be complete, for by focusing on the undeniable similarities between the two societies it ignored the ways in which they differed and in consequence had little to say about that in Canada which was peculiar to it. If, therefore, the nationalism of the Canadian imperialists could be easily discredited, the nationalism of the continentalists could also, and for much the same reasons. It seemed, as Canadian imperialism had seemed to its detractors, to be a definition of the national character framed in terms of Canada's affinity to some other country. It therefore left Canada conceptually defenceless against that country.

All of this – Britain's declining relevance to a definition of the English-Canadian character, the incompleteness of a definition of that character based on its similarity to the society to the south, and the continuing impossibility of creating an English-speaking Canadian counterpart of Crèvecœur's American – left the pluralist idea exposed and alone. Of the three elements that had defined English-speaking Canada's character at Confederation, only it retained its meaning. English-speaking Canada could no longer be British, it was not merely American; the absence of an English-Canadian type meant that it was, necessarily and as before, pluralist. This resurgence of the pluralist idea in the twentieth century has been accelerated by immigrants' reaction to their new society's orientation first towards British culture and then American, for it suggested to them that English-speaking Canada was indeed other-directed, that it contained no very strong indigenous culture, and so became to them an argument for retaining their own.

It would, of course, be erroneous to deny that behavioural assimilation has taken place in English Canada. It has, and at a rapid pace. The language, the culture patterns, and the values of their new society all act upon immigrants and make of them, in some sense, "new men." But as a sociologist teaching in Canada has recently written, this process "has not removed the negative stereotypes that have identified members of different ethnic groups" in English-speaking Canada. The reason is not hard to find. Assimilation in English Canada has been open-ended. The absence of an English-speaking Canadian type has meant that there is nothing identification with which would deprive the ethnic stereotype the immigrant carried around with him of its meaning. There is nothing which cancels it out and deprives it of its potency. The persistence of ethnic identification in both a negative and positive sense has led to the argument that the Canadian mosaic be deprived of its verticality, not by obliterating it altogether (that would be impossible, since that which produced it prevents its overthrow) but by emphasizing structural assimilation on the part of those who retain their group or ethnic identification. "It would appear," Professor Isajiw writes, "that the problem of ethnic status can be dealt with ... by means of ethnic pluralism itself."[28] The creation of a society of undifferentiated atomic individuals, all of whom conform to the same type and same set of values, is not now, as it never has been, a tenable ideal, either in Canada itself or in the English-speaking part of it.

There are, of course, other factors which have played a part in the emergence of the mosaic concept. Certain ethnic groups have been motivated as much by the history of their nation or culture outside Canada as by circumstances within it to retain their ethnic consciousness. The Ukrainians, the Doukhobors, and the Hutterites have all been concerned, for reasons which lie essentially outside their Canadian experience, to retain their special character. Immigration authorities have, as a matter of policy, encouraged immigrants to retain some measure of their ethnic identity to ease the process of acculturation and reduce the intensity of culture shock. An explanation for the absence of a consensus in both culture and politics has been found in the kind of political system Canada possesses. A democratic republic requires all its citizens to share certain fundamental beliefs. The rule of citizen over citizen, the rule of a majority over a minority is not acceptable unless there is a consensus on fundamentals. A monarchy, unlike a republic, demands allegiance of its subjects, and that is all. No conformity of views is required. As Morton has said: "the society of allegiance admits of a diversity the society of compact does not, and one of the blessings of a Canadian life is that there is no Canadian way of life, much less two, but a unity under the crown, admitting of a thousand diversities."[29]

Finally, the Canadian value system, it has been suggested, encourages Canadians to see their society as one that consists of differentiated groups, rather than an homogeneous mass, all of whose members conform, or in principle ought to conform, to a single normative type:

The very strength of hierarchical status, traditional religion, and governmental authority in Canada has meant that in a variety of ways ... Canadian values fall somewhere between those of Britain and the United States ... One consequence of the relative conservatism of Canadian society has been that greater emphasis is placed on particularist group identifications, especially ethnic and regional but also to some limited degree, class and status.[30]

Not surprisingly, the French-Canadian conception of Canada has been shaped by French Canada's special and overriding concern for survival. Cartier must have seen the multinational idea as especially attractive because it provided the argument for French-Canadian rights with a force and cogency which it seemed no reasonable being could deny. If Canada were to be a state founded on the principle that no harm could be done to persons of any nationality, then clearly the French-speaking Canadians would not be alone in asking for, and receiving, special treatment. They would in fact be asking for nothing to which other groups were not only entitled, but which they were receiving. If the whole society was predicated on the assumption that the interests of different groups would be served, what could be more reasonable, more entirely in order, than that those of the French Canadians should be served as well. The pluralist idea also lent extra weight to the argument for French Canada's linguistic rights. For if these other nationalities – the English, the Irish, and the Scots – were to enjoy the right to use their language, and nothing could be clearer than that they were, then, since the French would possess the same rights in the new state, it was equally clear that they too would be secured in the use of their language. French-Canadian rights would thus become imbedded in the nature of things. If not one, or even two, but three "nationalities" were to enjoy full cultural rights in Canada, it was therefore entirely consistent with the way society was ordered, and in no sense a demand for special privileges, that the French Canadians be given the rights of their "nationality" as well. But why, then, if this explanation explains so much, why, if the pluralist idea provided so solid a base for the assertion of French Canada's collective rights, was it overshadowed and indeed re-placed in French-Canadian thinking by the bicultural idea and the principle of duality?

Cartier's pluralist argument was as much a rhetorical device as it was a description of what he took to be the realities of Canadian society. It was valuable because it allowed a forceful and convincing argument to be made in support of French-Canadian rights. If the time came when it could no longer serve that purpose, it would have lost its utility and the search would begin for something with which to replace it. By the beginning of the twentieth century it was clear that it had indeed lost whatever usefulness it may have once possessed, and so, without fanfare and almost as if it had never existed, it was laid to rest. But the matter did not quite end there, for by a strange paradox that which deprived it of its value as an argument for French-Canadian rights confirmed its worth as a description of the objective realities of Canadian society.

Cartier's argument had implied the right of each of the several cultures of which Canada was composed to its own language, a right they all in fact exercised at Confederation, and from this circumstance he deduced the right of French Canadians to their language. The pluralist idea had to involve an argument that all groups possessed language rights if it was to secure the French Canadians in theirs. Multiculturalism had to imply multilingualism. If the various cultures shared only one or, as was the case in Canada at Confederation, two languages, the multilingual implications of multiculturalism would be nullified, but – and here was the crucial point – nullified not by logic but by circumstance. Should those circumstances change, should Canada come to be composed of cultural groups which shared more than two languages, the logic of Cartier's argument would require it to be applied in support of multilingualism. And, at century's end, circumstances did change. The migrations of the Laurier years brought to Canada a substantial number of immigrants whose language was neither English nor French. If those migrations caused English Canadians to confront the implications of the pluralist idea with a vigour that made that idea's reassertion of its primacy all the more impressive, their impact on French-speaking Canada was even more dramatic. For where English Canadians ultimately found it impossible to revolutionize their conception of Canada, where they were unable to respond to the new pluralism in the way many of them would have liked, where in the end they had to concede its existence, French Canadians were able to alter fundamentally their concept of the new nationality.

For them to have followed Cartier after 1896 would have been to argue that each of these new groups was entitled to the use of its language. But multilingualism was unacceptable to the English-speaking majority. That majority was sometimes compelled to accept it, as it did in Manitoba in 1897, but it did so grudgingly. It argued consistently and with vehemence that, in the West at least, the immigrants should become fluent in the language of the majority in order to build a strong and vital nation. In so arguing, it did not trouble, as Connor had not troubled, to distinguish between recently arrived immigrants and the French-speaking Canadians whose ancestors had opened the West. In these circumstances, the argument based on pluralism could only encourage those who were already anxious to put French Canadians on an equal footing with the newcomers to do so. They would do so, however, not for the purpose of securing all of them in the use of their languages, but rather of denying them their use. The more strenuously the pluralist argument was put, the more convinced would become the majority that assimilation of all minorities, linguistic and cultural, must take place in order to prevent social and linguistic chaos. It was precisely to this identification of the French-speaking with the other minorities, undertaken for the purpose of assimilating them all, that the French took strong exception. As Armand Lavergne wrote: "In constituting the French Canadian, who has lived in the country since its discovery, the equal in rights and privileges to the Doukhobor or the Galician who has just disembarked, we have opened between the Eastern and Western sections of Canada a gulf that nothing will be able to close."[31] An argument that took them in this direction was valueless to French Canadians. It was now necessary for them to distinguish themselves from, not identify themselves with, the other minorities. In the new circumstances, then, the multicultural argument could only accelerate, not retard, the unilingual process. It would become an example of precisely the sort of particularist outlook that, in the view of the majority, must be overcome.

All of this had been obscured from Cartier's view. He could construe the new political nationality in a broad and expansive way because, far from endangering the position of the French language and the integrity of French-Canadian culture, to do so seemed to make them more secure. But after 1896 this would clearly not be the case. Multiculturalism would now resolve itself into unilingualism, and that must not be allowed to happen. For the French Canadians, language and culture were intimately related. If the rights of the one were eroded, the other would surely collapse. "The conservation of the language," wrote French Canada's leading nationalist in 1913, "is absolutely necessary for the conservation of the race, its genius, its character and its temperament."[32] What would conserve the language, what would deny unilingualism, what would distinguish the French-speaking minority from the other minorities, was a rejection of the pluralist idea in favour of a clear and unambiguous doctrine of biculturalism. The homogeneous, indeed monolithic, character of English-Canadian society had to be asserted to that the special claims of any minority within it (save of course the French) could be denied. The cultures of which Canada was composed must have the right to their respective languages, but the argument for that right must not derive from too latitudinarian a concept of Canadian nationality, or else, as the fate of Cartier's argument had plainly demonstrated, it would lose its utility.

And so, by a peculiar twist, Cartier's plan for multiculturalism had to be retired from service, owing, not to the rise of a monolithic English Canada, but to its opposite. The vigorous reaction of many English Canadians to that opposite raised the spectre of a culturally homogeneous English Canada and the reality of a unilingual one. Cartier's argument for multiculturalism provided no defence against the second of these, and therefore, in the view of the French-speaking Canadians, none against the first. It would in fact only hasten their coming, for to employ it now would be to convince the English that they must indeed act expeditiously, or Canada would become a Tower of Babel. It therefore became necessary to assert the principle of duality. That principle would not command universal assent but it seemed more susceptible of defence than the pluralist idea. The prophet of Canada as a bilingual, multicultural society became, then, the partisan of Canada as a bilingual, bicultural society. The changing character of English Canada had metamorphosed Cartier into Bourassa.

What Bourassa feared and opposed, the rise of a virtually unilingual Canada outside of Quebec, explains why the argument for biculturalism became an argument for binationalism. The refusal of the majority in English-speaking Canada to uphold the linguistic rights and therefore the cultural integrity of the minority led that minority to assert that it should have, indisputably and where it could exercise it, the political power necessary to insure its survival. If Cartier became Bourassa, Bourassa, owing in part to the fate of the bicultural idea in English Canada, became Michel Brunet. For him the history of French Canada has become the history of a people searching for a fatherland, a state which will serve and protect their peculiar traditions and culture. And with this transformation something which had been central to the thought of both Cartier and Bourassa disappeared.[33]

Some French-speaking Canadian intellectuals have tried in recent years to dissolve the equation many nationalists have been anxious to make between culture and the state. Their approach to the theory of the state in general and that of the Canadian state in particular has been functional and pragmatic. In their political theory, and especially in the political theory of Pierre Elliott Trudeau, the wisdom of and the necessity for this equation has been annihilated. In 1962 Trudeau, taking his text from Julien Benda, wrote a scathing attack on the nationalist intellectuals of French Canada. His object was to show how pernicious would be the consequences and how self-destroying in fact was the substance of their nationalism. No state, he argued, was homogeneous. Nationalism, overweening reverence for a particular way of life, therefore lead inexorably to exclusivism and ethnocentricity. This was especially true of a state like Canada, and of a province like

Quebec, where the consequences of cultural nationalism could be all too plainly seen. It produced injustice for the minorities, but more than that, it narrowed the minds of the majority and subjected them to spiritual and intellectual asphyxia. It was therefore necessary to recognize, in principle and in fact, that the state in Canada could not become the instrument of a particular culture. It was necessary to recognize that there could be no national idea in Canada, seeking like some sort of Hegelian *geist* to actualize itself in all of society. If there was, the Canadian state would collapse under a weight it could not bear. "We must," he wrote, "separate once and for all the concepts of state and nation, and make Canada a truly pluralistic and polyethnic society."[34] Three years later he made the grounds of his opposition to classical nationalism even clearer. "I believe," he wrote, "that a definition of the state that is based essentially on ethnic attributes is philosophically erroneous and would inevitably lead to intolerance."[35]

For most French Canadians, however, pluralism has yielded to dualism, which has become, in turn, the basis for some variation of the binational idea. The pluralist idea has had more currency by far in English-speaking Canada, for English-speaking Canadians have been struck not only by the country's linguistic duality but by the disparate character of that part of it in which they live. In recent years they have given renewed voice to their conviction that although Canada may be a nation in which duality figures prominently, it is replaced by pluralism beyond the level of language, and sometimes even there.[36]

Crèvecœur's new man was distinguished not only by his peculiar lineage: he was an ideologue of sorts, rendered unique by the views that he held. He was, Crèvecœur had written, not simply a new man, but a new man who acts upon new principles. He possessed a set of social, political, and economic values, and it was these, as much as the singularity of his descent and family structure, that set him apart. These principles were not, of course, entirely new. They seemed so, however, because of the degree to which they had become characteristic of the American mind. Subsequent generations of Americans made them as much their own as had those of Crèvecœur's time. The American political tradition has been almost uniformly Lockean, and a competitive individualist, entrepreneurial spirit has characterized Americans in their economic relations.[37]

Less rigorous has been Americans' emulation of their eighteenth-century prototype in other respects. They have not been universally interested in losing their ethnic consciousness. Yet it was not as if the prevailing mores of American society did not impel them in this direction. The melting pot has been the ideal; the point of a restrictive immigration policy was to get immigrants who could successfully adapt to American ways and exclude those who could not; Kallen wrote to criticize the conventional mode of thinking about what ought to happen to immigrants upon their arrival in the United States; Moynihan and Glazer found it necessary to show that assimilation was *not* occurring in New York City. The existence of cultural pluralism in the United States becomes then the measure of an ideal's failure; and the failure of that ideal should not be taken to mean that its opposite was ever part of the national ethic.

Tocqueville perceived long ago what modern social science has not found it necessary to deny, the basic impulse of American society towards conformity.[38] That impulse has not caused ethnicity to disappear; what it has produced is a large measure of social conformity and an almost irresistible tendency to conform to the essentials of the American faith, and that tendency has deprived whatever cultural diversity may exist of much of its significance. For, in the language of the social scientists, "Newcomers to America faced heavy social pressure to conform, the instruments of conformity becoming ever more efficient with the growth of industrialization, mass communication and public education. Some in-group norms and residual subcultural patterns have survived, but immigrant cultures as self-contained systemic entities began to disintegrate soon after the initial settlement." Even though they may have retained some part of their ethnic consciousness, "the ethnics internalized a loyalty to the core political symbols, values, and institutions of the American policy."[39] Their ethnic identity was thus subsumed in something larger, more inclusive, and ultimately far more influential than the diluted imperatives of a culture far from their source. "By every realistic criterion," Will Herberg writes, "the American Way of Life is the operative faith of the American people ... Sociologically, anthropologically, if one pleases, it is the characteristic American religion, undergirding American life and overarching American society despite all indubitable differences of region, section, culture, and class."[40]

Canada does not possess this basic impulse toward conformity because there has been nothing in Canada to which conformity could be urged. There is no overarching Canadian Way of Life, nor can there be an ideological Canadianism. The Canadian political tradition has no single set of transcendent values immanent in all its parts binding them to one another and to itself. The most rigid application of Hartzian categories to Canadian politics yields, as it must, a dual political tradition, a "double fragment," to use the Hartzian terminology, and even it provides only a limited insight into the nature of the Canadian political tradition. To argue that English-Canadian society is one-dimensional in the same sense that American is, to argue that it is merely a fragment of the liberal society of America, suffused by the same principles, its radical politics rendered impotent in the same way, is to miss the nuances of its political development. For while that development has been fundamentally North American, its course has been influenced by non-liberal ideologies, the ground for which was prepared by the toryism of the Loyalists. Their coming introduced a Tory "touch" into the Canadian political tradition, which not only endured itself but also equipped the Canadian mind with the capacity to respond to organic, collectivist principles and to the idea of class in the form in which they were brought to Canada by British socialists. The Canadian political tradition has, then, been ample enough to accommodate viable movements based upon conservative and socialist as well as liberal principles. It has, unlike the American, embraced political parties which range through the ideological spectrum, and in this way Canada's cultural and sectional diversity has found itself complemented by ideological diversity.[41]

If John Locke has become, in Merle Curti's phrase, "America's Philosopher,"[42] Lord Acton has become Canada's. If the American consensus was formed around Lockean principles, the circumstances contributing to the formation of the much broader Canadian consensus suggest the point at which Acton's thought has become relevant to Canadians. If the American state is the instrument of, indeed the ultimate expression of, a particular way of life, Canadians have viewed their federal state in Actonian terms, as one that ought not, and indeed cannot, identify itself with a single culture or ideology. For them necessarily, as for Acton in principle, the best state becomes that state which contains several communities, and strives to serve the interests of all of them. They have taken as theirs the ideal that Acton defined in 1861: "The coexistence of several nations under the same state is the test as well as the best security of its freedom ... we must conclude that those states are substantially the most perfect which ... include various distinct nationalities without oppressing them."[43]

The idea of Canada as a pluralist society has had, then, a lengthy history. That history, however, has been a complicated one. Circumstances have imposed the pluralist idea, and many nationalists have bitterly resented those circumstances. They have been made supremely unhappy by the fact that their nationalist conceptualizations, if they are to have meaning in all of Canada, must be framed in terms that take account, somehow, of its pluralism. They have known that nationalist imagery must not only be emotionally satisfying, but that it must also appear to be true, at least to those the essence of whose society it is supposed to represent. They have thus been caused much distress, for that imagery which is credible is not always emotionally satisfying, while that which is emotionally satisfying is not always credible. Many of them, in consequence, have wanted, not a pluralist society with its problems of identity and its lack of coherence, but a society that has a clear sense of itself and is united and strong. And so, while acknowledging the disparate character of their society on the one hand, they have tried to minimize the importance of these traits on the other. They have conceded the heterogeneous character of their society only with reluctance, or they have cleverly worked its different parts up into something meant to resemble a coherent whole. Only in the recent past has the spirit with which many Canadians have infused the pluralist view of their society undergone a change. Only recently have Canadian nationalists shown themselves willing to accept, and sometimes even celebrate, the paradox that lies at the heart of their nationalism. Two things explain why this has happened. The social sciences have shown that the life of society is to be found in its experience. The Canadian experience, as nationalists like everyone else must recognize, has had at its centre accommodation, compromise, and adjustment. An understanding of Canadian society, how it works, what is its nature, and any attempt to realize and define its character, must take these facts into account. But there is evident more than simply a new willingness to bring a functional perspective to bear on the study of Canadian society, more than a new enthusiasm for the results of emphasizing the functional method. In some quarters the absence of a monolithic Canadianism has produced positive satisfaction. It has become, in fact, the basis for a new Canadian nationalism. The reason is not hard to find. Classical nationalism, the nationalism of race, culture, unity, coherence, and strength has made itself repugnant in the twentieth century. Canadian nationalists, therefore, have had less and less difficulty adjusting to the fact that their state if it is to survive can never be nationalist in that special, impoverishing, and abhorrent way. Nowhere is this tension, and its final resolution, more obvious than in the thinking of Vincent Massey. In his panegyric *On Being*

Canadian he made it clear that he was prepared to concede the pluralist character of Canadian society only with reluctance. His acceptance of the mosaic concept was tentative and uncertain. His ideal remained a bicultural nationalism and he was at pains to show that Canada was firmly united under a common political nationality. "We may be," he wrote, "a mosaic composed of many different sizes and shapes and colours, and sometimes the cement between the bits has seemed to wear thin, but for all that the mosaic has a national pattern ... There is a continuity of principle."[44] But if in 1948 Massey's emphasis had been as much on unity as pluralism, by the early 1960s he showed himself much more willing to define the nation's character in terms of its experience and to recognize matter-of-factly and without hesitation its pluralist character. In writing of immigrants to Canada since 1945 he observed simply that "we try to fit in the new-comers much as they are, as pieces in the Canadian mosaic."[45]

The spirit informing the pluralist view of Canada has clearly altered in the recent past. In the absence of a nationally acceptable common standard, it retains, as much as any abstraction can retain, its credibility. But now, if it still is not as deeply satisfying as the primitive and emotional sense of exaltation which comes from knowledge of the unity and perfection of one's society and culture, it is at least more clearly acceptable. As Massey's work suggests, the tension that formerly existed between its credibility on the one hand and its appeal as an object of nationalist veneration on the other has shown itself to be capable of resolution.

American nationalism approximates the classical type. The American nation-state is the American people organized. It is co-extensive with a particular culture whose interest it is its primary responsibility to serve and protect. One way it has of doing this is by requiring conformity by one means or another to those values it sees as its business to preserve and strengthen. The rhetoric of the melting pot, the creation of a national faith, is but one manifestation of this impulse toward conformity.

Canadian nationalism is clearly at variance with this type. It is in fact a non-nationalism, as Canada is non-nation. American nationalism demands the assimilation of all to a common way; Canadian nationalism, because it has no choice, is predicated upon the toleration of differences. Canada cannot exalt one culture, or set of values, or way of life, over all others and require conformity to it. Canadian nationalism cannot be exclusivist or narrow; it cannot be conformist or totalitarian; if it is, the state it seeks to serve will perish. Canada must be founded on diversity, and the concept of the mosaic is one attempt to come to grips with that most fundamental of Canadian truths.

Each metaphor, then, is relevant to the national experience it is meant to represent; each has been created by the history of the country it attempts to describe, although each fails to describe with complete precision and accuracy that history; each is graphic, its meaning easily grasped; neither exalts one ethnic group over the others; each, finally, is the inevitable by-product of the kind of nationalism found in each country. The impulse towards conformity in the United States has created the melting-pot metaphor; Canada's character as a heterogeneous society has given rise to the mosaic concept; so long as each country retains these among its distinguishing characteristics, images of conformity in the one instance and diversity in the other will continue to have force and relevance as descriptions of the national character.

NOTES

1 Cf. Karl Mannheim, *Ideology and Utopia* (New York, 1936).
2 The history and meaning of the first term has been explored by Philip Gleason, "The Melting-Pot: Symbol of Fusion or Confusion?" *American Quarterly*, 16(1), 1964, 20–46. There is no comparable examination of the mosaic concept.
3 R.W.B. Lewis, *The American Adam* (Chicago, 1955); Henry Nash Smith, *Virgin Land* (Cambridge, MA, 1950); Charles L. Stanford, *The Quest for Paradise: Europe and the American Moral Imagination* (Urbana, IL, 1961).
4 Nathan Glazer and Daniel Patrick Moynihan, *Beyond the Melting Pot* (Cambridge, MA, 1963).
5 "Democracy *versus* the Melting Pot," *The Nation*, 18 and 25 February 1915.
6 Milton M. Gordon, "Assimilation in America: Theory and Reality," *Daedalus*, 90, Spring 1961, 263–85.
7 Elizabeth Wangenheim, "The Ukrainians: A Case Study of the 'Third Force,'" in Peter Russell, ed., *Nationalism in Canada* (Toronto, 1966), 85.
8 John Porter, *The Vertical Mosaic* (Toronto, 1965). See especially "Ethnicity and Social Class," 60–103.
9 *Niles' Weekly Register*, 18, 1820, 157–8, cited in Gordon, "Assimilation in America," 268.
10 For the consensus view of American history, see Louis Hartz, ed., *The Founding of New Societies* (New York, 1964), especially chapter 4,

"United States History in a New Perspective," 69–122, and also his
Liberal Tradition in America (New York, 1955); Ralph Henry Gabriel,
The Course of American Democratic Thought (New York, 1956); Daniel
Boorstin, *The Americans*, 2 vols. (New York, 1958, 1965); and D.M.
Potter, *People of Plenty: Economic Abundance and the American Character*
(Chicago, 1954). For a criticism of this important trend in American
historical writing, see John Higham, "The Cult of the 'American
Consensus': Homogenizing Our History," *Commentary*, 17, February
1959, 93–100.

11 *The First New Nation: The United States in Historical and Comparative
Perspective* (Garden City, NY, 1967), 102.

12 D.M. Potter, "The Historian's Use of Nationalism and Vice-Versa,"
American Historical Review, 67(4), 1962, 944. C. Vann Woodward,
"The Search for Southern Identity," *The Virginia Quarterly Review*, 34,
1958, 338.

13 Oscar Handlin, *Race and Nationality in American Life* (Boston, 1957);
John Higham, *Strangers in the Land: Patterns of American Nativism,
1860–1925* (New Brunswick, NJ, 1955). In an article published in
1958 Higham suggested that it is necessary to look not only to
ideology for an explanation of nativism, but also to the dynamics of
American society itself, specifically to the status rivalries that took
place within it as new groups challenged, or seemed to challenge,
the power and status of the old; see "Another Look at Nativism," *The
Catholic Historical Review*, 44(2), 1958, 147–58.

14 Hartz, ed., *The Founding of New Societies*, 16–20, 53–8; also Hartz's
article, "A Comparative Study of Fragment Cultures," in *Violence in
America: Historical and Comparative Perspectives. A Report to the National
Commission on the Causes and Prevention of Violence, June 1969* (New
York, 1969), 100–17.

15 See A.R.M. Lower, "Two Ways of Life: The Primary Antithesis of
Canadian History," Canadian Historical Association, *Report*, 1943,
5–18, and Kenneth D. McRae, "The Structure of Canadian History,"
in Hartz, ed., *The Founding of New Societies*, 219–74.

16 *Parliamentary Debates on the Confederation of the British North American
Provinces* ([Quebec City:] Queen's Printer, 1865), 60, 6, 29.

17 Ibid., 55.

18 Carl Berger, "'Race and Liberty': The Historical Ideas of Sir John
George Bourinot," Canadian Historical Association, *Report*, 1965,
87–104; Berger, "The True North Strong and Free," in Russell, ed.,
Nationalism in Canada, 3–26.

19 Canada, House of Commons, *Debates*, 1907–8, 1585.

20 See Boyd C. Shafer, "Delusions about Man and His Groupings," in
his *Nationalism: Myth and Reality* (New York, 1955), 213–37.

21 Ralph Connor [Charles William Gordon], Preface, *The Foreigner* (Toronto, 1909).
22 Victoria Hayward and Edith S. Watson, *Romantic Canada* (Toronto, 1922), 187; the introduction was by Edward J. O'Brien.
23 Ibid., xiii.
24 Mentioned in J.M. Gibbon, *Canadian Mosaic: The Making of a Northern Nation* (Toronto, 1938), Preface, ix.
25 See D.G. Creighton, *The Commercial Empire of the St Lawrence, 1760–1850* (Toronto, 1939).
26 "Clio in Canada: The Interpretation of Canadian History," *University of Toronto Quarterly*, 15(3), 1946, 227–34.
27 *The Canadian Identity* (Toronto, 1961), 89, 111–12.
28 Wsevolod W. Isajiw, "The Process of Social Integration: The Canadian Example," *Dalhousie Review*, 98(4), 1968–9, 514–15.
29 Morton, *The Canadian Identity*, 111.
30 S.M. Lipset, "Introduction," *Agrarian Socialism: The Cooperative Commonwealth Federation in Saskatchewan. A Study in Political Sociology* (Garden City, NY, 1968), xvii. For an extended treatment of this subject, see Lipset's *The First New Nation: The United States in Historical and Comparative Perspective* (Garden City, NY, 1967), especially chapter 7, "Value Differences, Absolute or Relative: The English-Speaking Democracies," 284–312; and his "Canada and the United States – a Comparative View," *Canadian Review of Sociology and Anthropology*, 1(6), 1964, 173ff.
31 *Les Ecoles du Nord-Ouest* (Montreal, 1907), 18, cited in Ramsay Cook, *Canada and the French-Canadian Question* (Toronto, 1966), 35.
32 H. Bourassa, *La Langue française et l'avenir de notre race* (Quebec, 1913), 4, cited in M. Wade, *The French Canadians* (Toronto, 1956), 622.
33 For a critical assessment of Brunet and his work, see Ramsay Cook, "The Historian and Nationalism," in Cook's *Canada and the French-Canadian Question* (Toronto, 1966), 119–42. Brunet speaks for himself in his essay "The French-Canadians' Search for a Fatherland" in Russell, ed., *Nationalism in Canada*, 47–60.
34 "La nouvelle trahison des clercs," *Cité Libre*, April 1962. Reprinted as "The New Treason of the Intellectuals" in Trudeau, *Federalism and the French Canadians* (Toronto, 1968), 177.
35 Trudeau, "Quebec and the Constitutional Problem," ibid., 29.
36 See, for example, Morton, *The Canadian Identity*; Kenneth McNaught, "The National Outlook of English-Speaking Canadians," in Russell, ed., *Nationalism in Canada*, 61–71, and J.M.S. Careless, "Limited Identities in Canada," *Canadian Historical Review*, 50(1), 1969, 1–10.
37 Besides Hartz's *The Liberal Tradition in America* and Potter's *People of*

Plenty, see Richard Hofstadter, *The American Political Tradition* (New York, 1961), especially Introduction, v–xi.

38 Tocqueville's assessment of the American character has, of course, been subjected to intensive scrutiny, and some writers have wanted to qualify certain of its central propositions. David Reisman, with Nathan Glazer and Reuel Denny, *The Lonely Crowd: A Study of the Changing American Character* (New Haven, 1950) argued that what Tocqueville called the "courtier spirit" has been more a feature of twentieth- than nineteenth-century America. Their conclusions, in turn, were sharply challenged by Carl N. Degler, "The Sociologist as Historian: Reisman's *The Lonely Crowd*," *American Quarterly*, 15(4), 1963, 483–97, who saw "other direction" as "the dominant element in our national character through most of our history" (497). Cushing Strout, "A Note on Degler, Reisman and Tocqueville," *American Quarterly*, 16(1), 1964, 100–2, defended Reisman by arguing that other direction is a subtle psychological phenomenon "quite different" from Tocqueville's tyranny of the majority, which had its effects chiefly in religion and politics. He also, however, suggested that there were no inconsistencies between the two writers. For a general discussion of this part of Tocqueville's work, see Max Lerner, "Freedom in a Mass Society," in his *Tocqueville and American Civilization* (New York, 1969), 67–79.

39 Michael Parenti, "Immigration and Political Life," in Frederic Cople Jaher, ed., *The Age of Industrialism in America: Essays in Social Structure and Cultural Values* (New York, 1968), 83, 91, 94.

40 Will Herberg, *Protestant-Catholic-Jew: An Essay in American Religious Sociology* (New York, 1955), 88, 90.

41 G. Horowitz, "Conservatism, Liberalism, and Socialism in Canada: An Interpretation," *Canadian Journal of Economics and Political Science*, 32(2), 1966, 143–92.

42 "The Great Mr. Locke, America's Philosopher, 1783–1862," in his *Probing Our Past* (New York, 1955), 69–118.

43 Lord Acton, "Nationality," in his *Essays on Freedom and Power*, selected by Gertrude Himmelfarb (London, 1956), 168.

44 Toronto, 1948, 12–13.

45 *Canadians and Their Commonwealth* (Oxford, 1961), 6.

7 National Images and National Maintenance: The Ascendancy of the Ethnic Idea in North America

As the Italian nationalist Massimo D'azeglio noted more than a century ago – "Italy is made; now we must make Italians"[1] – the formation of a state is a necessary but not a sufficient condition of nation-building. The engineers of all polities – whether they be the classical nation-states of Europe, the largely immigrant-based societies of the western hemisphere, or the new national communities of the Third World – must move beyond the business of state-structuring if they are to give the people over whose affairs the entity they are creating will preside reason for identifying themselves with it.

The task of providing what one commentator has called "inputs of support" so that there will be, in the words of another, "smooth functioning in the system"[2] has involved movement along a number of familiar pathways. Franchise extension functioned to give citizens the sense that they were involved in national decision-making;[3] the creation of national armies heightened feelings of participation in great national enterprises;[4] the emergence of secondary cleavages – those, most noticeably, following party lines – cut across primary cleavages of race, ethnicity, and religion thus fostering an orientation towards the whole;[5] and the meeting by the state of the citizens' need for such things as decent conditions of work, adequate standards of education, and an appropriate amount of leisure time gave them concrete and tangible reason to advance it their support.[6]

Canadian Journal of Political Science/Revue canadienne de science politique, 14(2), 1981, 227–57.

Some commentators insist that instruments which operated directly on the citizens' intellect and feeling played an even more vital role in the building of an orientation towards the nation.[7] The creation of symbols transcending purely local modes of identification stimulated their adoption of a national frame of reference;[8] the articulation of a set of core values, internationalization of which was made part of the process of becoming a citizen, served the same end;[9] and clearly spelled out formulations of the nation's character, containing explicit references to the role each of its parts had played in the making of the whole, did much to heighten the sense of those parts that they were involved in the life of that whole and so made their support for it more readily forthcoming.[10]

This sort of device, central to the success of any nation-building enterprise, was particularly important in the North American phase of the process. In making necessary an especially assiduous fostering of national consciousness, the existence on that continent of a large, amorphous, and steadily growing population in fact forced into play a strong emphasis on the unifying idea that, in removing oneself to so strange and distant a place, one was involved not simply in a journey of epic proportions, but in a commitment to a way of life in which the opportunities offered for personal liberty and advancement were superior to those to be found anywhere else in the world.

The achievement of ideologues in the United States in encouraging this sense of the matter was particularly notable. Their work met with so remarkable a degree of success in building national feeling that it remained essentially unchanged from the late eighteenth to the middle of the twentieth century. Nor was their concern to paint a picture of the nation that would at once square with what most citizens perceived to be the major realities in it, cement the allegiance and support of those already living there, and function as a tool which could be used to integrate newcomers more than marginally complicated by the new republic's colonial, community-oriented, particularist past. Their society's character as a community of the New World, the fact that its people were implicated as a whole in the republican experiment, and the circumstance that its elites were tutored in the precepts of English liberalism made it in the end no very difficult matter to devise a conception of it which stressed those elements in its character which could be discerned throughout its length and breadth.[11] In their emphasis on individualism and liberty, the sanctity of property, and equality of opportunity, American nationalists in fact managed to make citizenship and a sense of involvement in the whole dependent upon acceptance of a system of beliefs with which, in principle, almost everyone could be persuaded to identify. The result was to enforce national solidarity and patriotic commitment to a remarkable degree. By laying emphasis on America's power as a new world society to emancipate the individual, that system indeed acted with special force to break down people's sense of belonging to the group or society from which they had come, further emphasized what they had in common with other Americans, and gave additional meaning to their identification with them as individuals and with their new society. Americans, it became possible to argue, were uprooted from the life they had known on the other side of the Atlantic and so confronted the challenges of their new land as individuals, with nothing to aid them but their own will and initiative. As Oscar Handlin's deeply felt articulation of this theme would later have it, "in our [immigrant] flight, unattached, we discovered what it was to be an individual, a man apart from place and station."[12]

Generations of commentators, then, made clear that the United States was to be understood as the liberal society *par excellence,* a community of free and responsible individuals bound together by the commitment of each of its members to accept their fellows, and expect acceptance themselves, on the basis of what they were as beings who operated in terms of universal norms upholding the dignity and worth of each person. A community of faith and doctrine rather than race or culture, the United States gave refuge to all who were able to accept what it taught.[13] The considerable irony in all of this – that the "universal" values the immigrant was being required to adopt were in large measure the legacy of the nation's association with England, the urging of acceptance of which implied not assimilation to a wholly new system of values, but conformity to the behavioural and attitudinal norms of the anglosaxon component of American society – was generally unnoticed;[14] American nationalists remained convinced of the need to urge acceptance of their creed upon all those who came to their shores. The result was no small accomplishment: a society capable of defining itself in the most precise way and then of urging action and belief in conformity with that definition as the first test of loyalty and citizenship.[15]

Canadians, too, were able to devise a conception of the nation that could be used to assist in its consolidation. In their case, however, circumstances insured that it would be a wider and more capacious construct than that devised by their southern neighbours. Some Canadians were able, of course, to insist on a precise and narrow definition of their society which they then used to rationalize the exclusion of certain groups from participation in it. British Columbia's opponents of oriental immigration provide a case in point.[16] Such arguments could, however, have no place at the national level. In the nation at large the basic duality of French and English prevented the framing of a national idea in terms of a single creed or type. The result was an understanding of the nation which was from the beginning open-ended and imprecisely defined, so that, in the words of Cartier, "there could be no danger to the rights and privileges of either French Canadians, Scotchmen, Englishmen or Irishmen ... no one could apprehend that anything could be enacted which would harm or do injustice to persons of any nationality."[17]

Their commitment to the idea that the nation was a thing of groups having left them with no national model to which the assimilation of individuals could be urged, Canadian theorists began to give voice to the idea that what strength the Canadian state did possess – and in their view it was considerable – lay in the very fact that it was incapable of requiring assimilation to a common standard. The loyalty it received was thus, they argued, in no sense enforced but came freely, and therefore the more willingly, from those who cherished the chance which life within its confines offered to retain contact with their own language and culture. Out of this came the tendency – discernible earlier but first clearly evident in the 1920s – to define Canada as an entity the persistent attachment of whose citizens to their own cultural character did not prevent them from contributing to the maintenance of a coherent and intelligible whole; Canada, in its turn, was to take full account of the fact that it must function in a way which reflected the interests of all of the elements which composed it. Through their acquaintance with this idea, embodied in a series of picturesque if sometimes awkward metaphors – Canada as a flower garden, a stew, and most commonly a mosaic – Canadians grew used to thinking of their society as one well on the way to reconciling diversity with unity.[18] By the end of the 1960s a leading national historian could in fact define his society as "a country of relatively weak nationalizing forces [characterized by] two languages, pluralized politics, and ethnic multiplicity ... all so far contained within one distinctive frame of nation-state existence."[19] Following a century of struggle to augment its influence, the notion that Canada was to be understood as a community of particularisms seemed at last on the verge of rendering itself indispensable to the work of those who wished to conceive of the country in terms that reconciled its heterogeneous character with the maintenance of national unity.

The preservation by those who fashioned these constructs of their creatures' capacity to play a nation-consolidating role was a complicated task. Central to its successful fulfilment was the difficult business of insuring that these formulations retained their ability to get themselves accepted by the members of each society as an accurate representation of the nature of life in that society. In the absence of such acceptance, those formulations would lose their credibility and with it their effectiveness in shaping behaviour. Much effort was therefore expended striving to ensure that the image of the nation with which the citizens were presented would be taken by them to describe the way it actually worked. The interests and character of the people who composed it were defined in a way compatible with the assertion that those interests were being served and that character sustained by continuing association within its confines; the community itself was defined in a way that made credible the claim that it was reflecting and served those interests; and custodians of the national definition were constantly on the lookout for changes in any of the elements which affected the way in which citizens perceived the character of this delicate system of belief and idea, the merest appearance of which would make it necessary to determine whether *other* alterations should be made so that the whole could continue to be regarded as an object of coherence and consistency which accurately represented reality as it was seen and experienced by those to whom it had to commend itself. What was decided in consequence of these careful deliberations in its turn determined whether the national idea currently in vogue would be retained, altered, given up, or entrenched more deeply in the ideological system, with the nature of that decision – the point need hardly be spelled out – indicating whether or not real change had taken place.

In recent years – we come at last to the subject of this article – the North American phase of this ongoing struggle to keep in being a system of ideas which can be used to aid in the consolidation of the nation has become particularly taxing. Maintaining an ideological complex capable of doing what is required of it has in fact required national ideologues and policy-makers to make a series of dramatic changes in the character, substance, and position of the nation-defining ideas which compose that complex. Apparent enough in both societies, these shifts emerge with particular clarity in the United States.

Now largely abandoned is the long held view that American society is to be understood as an agglomeration of free and responsible individuals whose ancestors, having discarded the cultural baggage with which they had been outfitted on the other side of the Atlantic, soon came to be defined primarily by their commitment to the values and life patterns of their new nationality. Analysts of the United States experience currently argue that Americans derive much of what distinguishes them from their membership in groups other than the comprehensively national. Americans' association with an ethnic or racial group, they continue, is particularly important, and citizens can neither be understood nor treated equitably unless full account is taken of the fact that their relationship to American society is mediated by the fact of belonging to such a group or groups. One recent volume thus speaks of "the unmeltable ethnics";[20] another presents its readers with "a mosaic of America's ethnic minorities";[21] a third informs those who consult it that "the United States is a composite of various religious, ethnic, and racial groups."[22] All argue variations on the theme, as yet another puts it, that "the melting pot concept is far from an accurate description of American society."[23]

If the character of these and other pronouncements have made it difficult to avoid conceding that the United States has moved toward the adoption of "an ideology of cultural pluralism [with] a reduced commitment to assimilation and a greater emphasis on religious, cultural, and even linguistic pluralism,"[24] the changes which have occurred in Canada have been of a quite different, though hardly less striking, character. There the shift has come not so much with respect to the content of the idea used to epitomize the country's nature as it has in relation to the idea's status.[25] From being as late as in the 1960s the property of writers, historians, ethnic activists, and a few politicians and public servants, it moved in the 1970s to establish itself as a key element in the national unity campaign of the federal government. The subject of a major policy statement by the prime minister in 1971, its status further enhanced by the creation of various government agencies in subsequent years, by the end of the decade that idea found itself more deeply entrenched than ever before both in law and in the mentality of English and French Canadians alike.[26]

To what are these remarkable changes in the character and position of these nation-defining ideas to be attributed? Why have the thinkers of one nation, for nearly two centuries preoccupied with the task of building a national society the great majority of whose people will think of themselves as individuals defined by their acceptance of "universal" norms and values, shown a greater disposition than ever before in their past to frame a definition of their society in particularist terms? Why have the policy-makers of the other, after decades of slow and deliberate movement, suddenly accelerated the pace and moved decisively to embrace an idea to which they had earlier given little more than a tentative and partial commitment? How are these changes to be related to the business of nation-consolidating? And what can be learned from an examination of them about strategies of nation-maintenance in general?

It is evident in retrospect that a number of factors were preparing the way for a dramatically enlarged measure of acceptance by Americans of a definition of their society framed in terms of ethnic pluralism. The Cold War's encouragement of an emphasis on the United States' ethnically variegated character as a means of distinguishing that nation from what was held to be its totalitarian adversary and enforcing its claims to deal with the assorted peoples of the world was, to be sure, tentative, ambiguous, and incidental to the business of creating a rationale for the country's new global role.[27] In giving Americans reason to think that there could be virtue in an even slightly altered vision of their society, it nonetheless assisted them towards a change of attitude in respect of a phenomenon – continuing identification with the culture of one's origins – which had long seemed to them a source of weakness rather than strength. Similarly, to the extent that interest in recovering the textured, community-oriented, ethnic, dimension of American life was precipitated by the desire to avoid the flatness and anonymity of existence in the conformitarian America described at mid-century by Reisman, Whyte, and others, it may have been little more than a self-conscious and artificial reaction to a point of view about the character of American society which was in itself exaggerated; but in suggesting to Americans that a particularist identification could be therapeutic and beneficial, it also played a part in placing ethnic pluralism in a new and more favourable light.[28] Also, the fundamental shift in Western styles of organizing data to which historian John Higham drew attention in the 1970s – his reading of Philip Ariès led him to suggest that there was a distinct attenuating of Western culture's long established tendency to systematize information in closely defined categories with the result

that "*the trend towards a rigid, absolutistic definition of roles and identities, which arose in the eighteenth century, is now being reversed* [*sic*]"[29] –
might have done more to explain than cause the by then clearly
evident inclination on the part of many Americans to view their
society in a new way. But even in so acting, it helped give those who
had adopted this altered perspective a sense that what they were
doing had made them part of a broad, culture-embracing process
of change and so encouraged them to identify themselves even
more strongly with it.

More fundamental an influence than any of these in moving
Americans towards acceptance of the ethnic idea was, however, that
flowing from the crucial developments taking place in the understanding of American society as students of it, employing conceptual tools borrowed from investigators on the other side of the
Atlantic, developed a more complex appreciation of the manner in
which the individual's relations to the community as a whole were
mediated by association with the different groups of which, increasingly, that whole was held to consist. Even as the Turnerian view of
American life was moving in the opening decades of the twentieth
century towards the height of its popular and scholarly appeal,
European inspired innovations in American social science acted in
combination with the obvious persistence of ethnic attachments
among American immigrants to weaken belief in the potency of the
forces making for assimilation. Most clearly evident in the influence which Austrian sociologists Ratzenhofer and Gumplowicz
exerted on Albion W. Small's understanding of the importance of
the group in the social process, this trend can also be discerned in
the generally more nuanced view of society which such continental
thinkers as Tönnies, Simmel, Durkheim, and Weber induced American scholars to take. In thus moving observers towards an understanding of individuals as beings to be comprehended, not simply
by assessing the impact on them of their natural environment or
the values and attitudes of their society at large, but by considering
them in terms of their relationship to the various groups – class,
family, status, ethnic, racial – with which they were associated, social
scientists set the stage for a new departure in the understanding of
American life.

The sociologists' continuing concern with the cement that held
society together – not to mention the powerful forces still making
for conformity in the United States – insured, of course, that the
focus on assimilation as the ultimate outcome of the process by
which different ethnic and cultural groups interacted would not be
jettisoned completely. Investigators in the new tradition such as

W.I. Thomas, Ernest W. Burgess, and Robert E. Park were nonetheless careful to deal with the subject of ethnicity in a manner that placed emphasis on the claim that a rapid abandonment of one's culture and sense of belonging to an ethnic group had not been characteristic of America's immigrant experience. In that important way they managed to concentrate more attention on the dynamics of the ethnic experience itself than had been received before.[30] By the 1940s, R.M. MacIver's basic conviction of the importance of a commitment to universally binding principles as the source of the nation's cohesion could be partnered by his assigning of a good deal of weight to the role played by diversity in the shaping of American society.[31] In the next decade Will Herberg might build on the work of others to suggest that even if ethnic assimilation was taking place through language loss and intermarriage, the continuing importance of religious difference was preventing the formation of a society whose members had lost all sense of special group identity.[32]

With the foundations laid by these earlier investigators, commentators in the 1960s were more sympathetic to a differentiated view of American society and less hesitant in setting out their claims than they had ever been. Historian Rowland Berthoff placed emphasis on the extent to which American life was for most of those who lived it defined by their association with the groups – family, club, ethnic, religious – with which they were most closely associated,[33] while John Higham could point in 1965 to the extent to which students of American history in general were giving attention to what he called "the looseness and multitude of its many strands."[34] Other observers dealt with different principles of order and division, stressing the importance not simply of class but of class consciousness as an enduring reality in American life.[35] Studies of "community," seeking to establish the fact that American society was basically cellular, the lives of its people rooted in the small units which provided its base, became steadily more prominent features of the scholarly landscape.[36] In the field of ethnic studies itself, a major breakthrough had come as early as 1963 with the publication of Moynihan and Glazer's *Beyond the Melting Pot* with its flat assertion that "the point about the melting pot ... is that it did not happen."[37]

While these several developments adjusted the American mind to the idea that American society did not consist of a collection of undifferentiated individuals whose relation to the whole was mediated solely by a common system of belief, value, and behaviour, the emergence in the 1960s of America's black population as a major force in its national life – here finally is the crux of the matter – was crucial to the acceptance of the new idea. For some time American blacks had possessed the potential of making the American majority realize, as the Canadian majority had long since done, that the community in which it lived could not be understood simply as a collection of individuals bound together by their attachment to the same creed and values. Their delayed eruption onto the main stage of American life set in motion a process which, in forcing Americans to re-examine basic assumptions about the character of their national existence, had profound implications for traditional ways of understanding it.

That this process of re-examination had been so long in coming was owing to a variety of circumstances, the combined effect of which was to insure that the impact of the black community's presence on those who thought about the overall character of American life would be minimal. Chief among these was the fact that in attempting to incorporate the black into their vision of the national community, theorists of American nationality found themselves on the horns of an intractable dilemma. To admit that being to full status as a free and equal participant in the national life would be to act in a manner consistent with the ideas upon which they thought understanding of the nation should rest; but even if it were done only in principle, it would also be to fly in the face of what experience, anthropology, and the blacks' institutional position seemed to teach about their character and capabilities. On the other hand, to give them status as a different kind of creature might be to recognize what seemed the facts of their peculiar case, but it would also constitute a clear admission that the principles forming the bedrock of the nation were not universal and all-encompassing. In these uncomfortable circumstances, the ideologues embraced the only solution open to them: they ignored the problem altogether. American blacks were, in consequence, consigned to a kind of limbo from which they were allowed to make only the occasional foray. Theorists of the melting pot had no room for them – how could one even contemplate absolute equality with a people so clearly doomed in inferiority – while even early theorists of ethnic pluralism such as Horace Kallen felt no obligation to work them into their otherwise broad definition of American society. The black became, in consequence – Ralph Ellison's poignant and memorable phrase speaks volumes – an "invisible man,"[38] present, affecting the life of his society, yet largely unseen by those who defined its nature.

What changed all of this, and in so doing provided the impulse for an altered definition of American society, was a growing militancy on the part of the black community itself. Armed by what developments in social science had done to the racist idea, possessed of a leadership greater in strength, numbers, and capacity than at any earlier period in its history, struck by the emergence of black states in Africa, and beginning the slow process of social and economic advancement,[39] the black community gradually developed the confidence necessary to bring itself and its grievances to the attention of American society at large. As evidence of the force with which the key principles undergirding American life were able to imbed themselves in every facet of its being, the black community first founded its actions on the liberal doctrine that black Americans were, in principle, like white ones in every respect save the colour of their skins and should be treated in a manner consistent with that fact. Gradually, however, that community realized that whatever the official rhetoric of white America, it in fact thought and – more to the point – acted in terms of race. This realization, combining with the fact that blacks themselves now had a more positive attitude towards what even they had been led to see as a badge of inferiority, led to the adoption of a fundamentally different strategy. Demands now began to be made, not for an end to discrimination against blacks as individuals, but for an alteration in the way in which they were perceived as a group. Whatever it might do to foster the cohesion and solidarity of American society at large, they now saw that the national ethic's emphasis on individualism did little to meet *their* needs. On the contrary, it functioned to set up an inducement to expect that they would be judged by their capabilities or potential as individuals, which, thanks to the fact that, rhetoric notwithstanding, they were in fact judged as members of a group, was not in any sense of reality being fulfilled. They therefore began to insist on an approach to the problem of elevating their status in American life that would cut to the root of the problem. What was needed, they began to insist, was a new understanding of the group itself. The entity their membership in which had signified their inferiority for generations must now be given meaning as an emblem of equality and distinction. At its most extreme in the separatism of the black muslims, moderated in Stokely Carmichael's black power, this new emphasis on the coherence and integrity of the group soon won a more general acceptance in the black community in the form of "black pride" and the assertion that "black is beautiful."[40] But whatever form it took, it represented an attempt to give individuals a new status by virtue of, instead of in spite of, their membership in a clearly defined collectivity. By thus emphasizing the positive importance of that which stood between individual beings and the fact of their membership in American society at large, it implied – the significance of the point cannot be overemphasized – a necessity to rethink the terms in which American life had traditionally been defined.

All of this meant that what might have done no more than heighten awareness of the basic duality in American society to which W.E.B. Dubois had pointed earlier in the century was destined to bear more complex fruit. Moreover, it produced that fruit almost immediately. If white racism prevented blacks from winning acceptance as individuals and so melting into the American mainstream with the unsurprising result that their group identity was reinforced, the anglo-conformity of the dominant groups acted in much the same way to keep certain ethnic groups – principally the Catholic populations from south and east Europe – isolated from the American mainstream and so helped enforce their sense that they too were a distinct and separate entity. And just as the blacks had ultimately moved to turn this liability into an asset, so the ethnics, seeing (and in some cases resenting) their success, determined to do the same. Daniel Bell is surely right to see the ethnic revival rooted in the self-interest of the groups promoting it.[41] The result was a clear and explicit call for America to be viewed not simply as a racially dual society but also as an ethnically plural one, each of whose parts had its claims on the whole.[42] Out of this, in its turn, came a vision of America as a nation of minorities, the conciliation of which was to be seen as the *sine qua non* of a stable national existence. As early as 1968, the need to respect the minorities' capacity to disrupt the national equilibrium was substantial enough to make an appeal to minority support an explicit part of Robert F. Kennedy's presidential campaign.[43] By 1972, Richard M. Nixon could build a significant portion of his march to re-election around the need to appeal to ethnic and religious minorities in terms that related directly to their collective interests.[44] In the final analysis, then, it was the set of circumstances created by the racial and ethnic revolt of the late 1960s which got American policy-makers and moulders of opinion to engineer a change in the way the society for whose coherence and solidarity they were responsible was to be understood. With significant numbers of Americans, white as well as red, yellow, and black, no longer willing to give uncritical allegiance to a society which defined itself in terms that conveyed to them the blunt message that it was their own fault if they had not got a fair share of the national bounty, it became simply a matter of political necessity that those terms be changed. Minority Americans now had to be told – if their loyalty was to be preserved it was *essential* that they be told – that their claims on the majority *were* just, and that in so far as the way in which American society had been defined had tended to underwrite denial of those claims, it would be changed.

It was, in consequence, in the words of an American sociologist, "in order to resolve ... caste-related conflict as well as social and ideological inconsistencies [that] the United States ... attempt[ed] to eliminate caste-race categories in favour of an ideology of ethnic pluralism."[45] Reference to the need to contain the racial and ethnic revolt itself explains more than any other factor why emphasis began to be shifted away from the idea of the United States as a society which, as a matter of principle, guaranteed equality of opportunity for individuals to the idea of it as one which, as a matter of fact, made good that guarantee by enforcing equality of condition for groups. With that move, the right of a minority group to jobs, contracts, or access to the central institutions of American life in rough relation to the proportion of its numbers in the population was conceded. Here the break with the past seemed at its clearest. A quasi-corporatist definition of American society had been established.

Some Americans were plainly disturbed by the element of change they perceived in all of this. "We have [created]," an unhappy Nathan Glazer wrote in 1975, "a complex of education, culture, law, administration, and political institutions which has deflected us into a course in which we publicly establish ethnic and racial categories for differential treatment, and believe that by so doing we are establishing a just and good society."[46] Others, however, chose to emphasize the view that it represented an innovation in nothing other than means. It was, they insisted, simply a new way to accomplish a traditional end, the taking of action clearly consistent with the commitment made in the landmark legislation of 1964 to end discrimination on an individual basis. If, they argued, there were no minority group members in a given job category, educational institution, or vocational program, this was *prima facie* evidence of discrimination and justified "affirmative action" (a term first used in President Kennedy's executive order 10925) to end it. Their very preoccupation with race, culture, and ethnicity was thus, they asserted, intended to do nothing more than ensure that individuals were in fact as well as in principle free to advance themselves without fear that membership in one or the other of these categories would count against them. In their view, notes Daniel Bell, the objective was simply to "provide compensating mechanisms to allow [culturally deprived groups such as the blacks] to catch up, in order to have a 'true' equality of opportunity."[47]

Adoption by government, by the press, and by agencies of popular culture of the idea that America was a society of groups as well as individuals came, then, as part of a move to accomplish two goals. There was, first, a concern to reconcile the continued existence of the whole, to whose maintenance those who operated major national institutions were directly committed, with the potentially disruptive claims being made by some of its parts. There was, second, an interest in upholding the integrity of key principles in the American faith in the new circumstances created by the fact that groups formerly excluded from meaningful participation in the major institutions of the national life now wanted such participation. With its path of acceptance smoothed by the already occurring breakdown of the crudely individualistic concept of American society, the idea that the United States was a nation of minorities was able to carry forward its thrust to dominance on the plea that only it could maintain the unity of the nation and conserve the central elements in the country's faith.

Multiculturalism's deepening appeal in Canada was broadly based in the same sorts of circumstances as were operating in the United States. Indeed, less attracted from the outset to the liberal idea, Canadian scholars were even more inclined than their American counterparts to look with sympathy on those tendencies in North American intellectual life which lent support to the contention that national societies were something rather more complex than mere collections of essentially undifferentiated individuals. The result was a body of work which, in allowing a discussion of ethnic persistence and identity to be added to already existing arguments about regional and other cleavages, made possible the mobilizing of scholarly support for the claim that the pluralist mode of understanding Canadian society was more appropriate than it had ever been.[48] It was, as two sociologists put it in 1968, simply not very difficult to see Canada as a country characterized by "linguistic dualism," "spatial and political divisions," and "ethnic pluralism" to a degree which made it "difficult to conjure up a fixed *gestalt*, except in the geographical sense, of the social and cultural complex as a whole."[49] A heightened sensitivity towards the individual's methods of dealing with problems of *anomie*, rootlessness, and identity in modern society also brought Canadian investigators to a new, if not altogether positive, appreciation of the role ethnic identification played in modern life,[50] while the growing conviction in some scholarly circles that ethnic divisions were more fundamental and enduring that those associated with the boundaries of nation-states found a Canadian echo as well.[51]

What played the key role – here too the parallel with the American experience held – in focusing attention on ethnic pluralism was, however, changing realities in the life of Canadian society itself. The most consequential of these realities was the steadily growing militance displayed by Canada's non-French non-English ethnic groups during the 1960s. Members of the so-called "third force," concerned lest the federal government's rush to accommodate resurgent French-Canadian nationalism might raise basic questions about their own position in the national scheme of things, asserted their claims to national attention with unprecedented force and vigour. They were particularly disturbed by the creation in 1963 of the Royal Commission on Bilingualism and Biculturalism, whose emphasis on duality convinced many of them that they were in fact being perceived as an inferior element in the national life. Largely as a result of the work of the Ukrainians, who assumed much of the burden of leading the "third force,"[52] they moved first to get representation on the Commission and then began to press for parity of status among the ethnic and racial groups of which the country consisted. Undeterred by attempts to argue that their emphasis on multiculturalism tended to exacerbate rather than resolve the problems of ethnic stratification to which John Porter's 1965 study of ethnicity, class, and power in Canadian life pointed,[53] they continued to insist that the realities which had in the first instance produced ethnic consciousness still inhered in Canadian life. Moreover, they argued that this fact insured ethnic persistence, and that the proper solution to the problem of ethnic inequality was therefore to be found in structural as opposed to behavioural assimilation.

The forces compelling entrenchment of an idea of the nation that went beyond mere duality were strengthened, too, by the growing disaffection of the native population and, more importantly in political terms, of the West. Since many of that region's inhabitants were of neither French nor British origin, it soon became clear that it would consider itself even further slighted by a federal policy which seemed to ignore the "third force" in Canadian life.[54] Conciliating that part of the country therefore involved increased emphasis on the ethnic fact. The thrust in this direction was carried forward as well by changes in immigration patterns. The 1967 adoption of universalistic standards for admission greatly increased the numbers of racially distinct immigrants from non-European cultures and so, paradoxically, encouraged recourse to the multicultural idea as a device which legitimized their presence in the country without requiring of them the kind of adjustment which would be difficult, if not impossible, for many of them to make.[55] The measure of recognition contained in the 1970 publication of a special bicultural commission study of the place the ethnic groups occupied in Canadian society and the announcement on October 8, 1971 by the prime minister of a policy of "multiculturalism within a bilingual framework"[56] cannot, finally, be understood without some reference to the intellectual history of the prime minister himself. By a coincidence which, given the nature of the realities needing to be addressed, seems so extraordinary as to involve more than mere accident (would something akin to Jung's concept of synchronicity explain this remarkable concatenation of circumstance?), Pierre Elliott Trudeau had long been committed to an understanding of the state's relation to the various cultural, linguistic, ethnic, and racial groups for whose affairs it was responsible which owed much to Lord Acton's view that it could foster the integrity and serve the freedom of those groups only if it refused to become the instrument of any single one of them. Trudeau's move to imbed the multicultural idea in federal policy thus reflected a strongly held conviction that the public power could not allow itself to become identified with promoting the interests of a particular segment of society. Only if, as he had put it ten years before, we "separate once and for all the concepts of state and nation" could we "make Canada a truly pluralistic society."[57]

A complex of circumstances, some broadly similar to those obtaining in the United States, most having to do with meeting the claims of newly-militant ethnic groups, was, then, responsible for the fact that commitment to the multicultural idea grew in Canada through the 1970s. This was most obviously manifest in the action of government: for example, the creation of a federal ministry of state for multiculturalism in 1972, of the Canadian Consultative Council on Multiculturalism in 1973, and the adoption in subsequent years of multicultural policies by the provincial governments of Ontario, Manitoba, Saskatchewan, and Alberta. That commitment was also evident in the shape of the country's popular culture and the activities of its scholarly community.[58] But wherever it was to be seen, it grew at base out of the conviction, much heightened by the resurgence of regional and provincial as well as ethnic and cultural feeling in the 1970s, that the nation could be held together only by recognizing the claims of its different parts. Applauding what he saw as the close fit between the circumstances policy-makers confronted and the methods they chose to deal with them, a political scientist commented: "the strategy of a government which seeks to [consolidate the] nation ... without offending powerful interests who demand the preservation of pre-existing cultural forms and ethnic identities ... will be just the sort of multiculturalism currently being proposed."[59] New circumstances, it seemed clear, had compelled not simply an affirmation of a long-held strategy but a more pronounced determination that it play a full part in the maintaining of the nation.

If the ethnic idea was, in the view of its American proponents, to be adopted because of its utility in simultaneously preserving the loyalty of disaffected or potentially disaffected groups and allowing the affirmation of basic American principles, the essentially conservative nature of their emphasis on it was manifest in other ways as well. Some of those who advocated acceptance of that idea did, of course, do so because they thought they saw a United States fundamentally different from that observed by their predecessors, a society the character of which could be adequately represented only by what they took to be a new way of conceptualizing it.[60] The great majority of the idea's friends sought, however, to win acceptance for it, not by emphasizing the extent to which it revealed realities which had not before been seen, but by stressing the fact that it referred to ones which were both old and familiar. What, after all, had been plainer than that America, as a society of immigrants, was also a society of ethnic groups? Proceeding along this path was complicated; where the exigencies of nation-building had once made it necessary to follow references to the nation's immigrant past with the placing of a distinct emphasis on assimilation, those same needs now required that emphasis to be placed on ethnic persistence. Where, accordingly, commentators on the immigrant experience had earlier celebrated the emergence of an American type in an American society, focused on problems of adjustment, or examined the resistance immigrants faced in their efforts to join the American mainstream, they now concentrated on the extent to which the American experience was to be understood in terms of the particularist impulses in it. "Diversity in American life," argued two of them, "is an ever-recurring theme ... ethnic diversity has played and continues to play a major role in the weaving of the peculiar American social fabric."[61] Americans were even told that the *idea* that theirs was a pluralist society had a lengthy history.[62]

Locating ethnic pluralism firmly in the American tradition was, of course, an extraordinarily adroit move. In the very act of legitimizing that phenomenon by giving it roots deep in the American past, this expedient defined the limits within which it could operate by the clearly implied proviso that if ethnic pluralism departed from its traditional form it would forfeit its claim to be considered part of the American way and, by virtue of that loss, the legitimacy it had just acquired. So useful was this device that it allowed even those most critical of certain forms of the new idea to make their peace with the doctrine as a whole. Thus, concerned that its more extreme manifestations would in their emphasis on the group prejudice the traditional American belief that "America was a nation of free individuals,"[63] Nathan Glazer might seek to discredit these extravagant statements of the case by the simple expedient of suggesting that they were at odds with ethnic group theory and practice as it had evolved through the course of American history. That history made clear that immigrants were not to be compelled to give up their cultural heritage, but neither were they to be allowed to set themselves up as a state within a state or to make claims which took precedence over those which individuals were able to urge on their own behalf. Substantially the same case was made in the work of historian John Higham, long an enemy of the homogenizing of American history.[64] Acutely aware of the need to deal with the American past in ways that took full account of what he viewed as its richness and diversity,[65] his very conviction that ethnic pluralism, and an awareness of ethnic pluralism, was to be seen as an element deep in the American experience led him to encourage the rejection of forms of it inconsistent with those it had traditionally possessed, the most characteristically American of which had allowed for unity and a general response to common values. No group, Higham insisted, could become so preoccupied with its own position that it lost sight of the whole. "A multiethnic society can avoid tyranny only through a shared culture and a set of universal values which its groups accept. If integration is unacceptable because it does not allow for differences, pluralism fails to answer our need for universals."[66]

If giving ethnic pluralism status as part of the American tradition defined the bounds of the new ethnicity in ways that allowed ethnic assertiveness to be reconciled with the maintenance of American unity and American principle, that move also allowed for the containment of racial discontent. Here its utility in bringing the parts of the nation together was even more dramatically in evidence. In this area there was, of course, an obvious difficulty, for ethnicity and race seemed on the face of it wholly dissimilar phenomena, the one relative, vague, and incapable of precise definition, the other fixed, absolute, and unchanging. How, then, could a device which had relevance in the one case hope to produce results in the other? To state the problem was to see the way to solving it. One need only, insisted the friends of ethnic pluralism, to recognize blackness as a matter of culture rather than of race. What, after all, could be plainer than that what distinguished American blacks had little to do with colour and everything to do with history, culture, attitudes, and values? Even a casual comparison of American blacks with their African counterparts made this clear.[67] Commentators insisted that once the full significance of that point was grasped, the way would be open to urge blacks to advance themselves within the framework of American society in the way that other ethnic groups had done before them. They, like the Italians or the Irish, could use ethnic associations, bloc voting, and similar devices to gain a place for themselves in the central institutions of American society.

If white observers encouraged this course of action – there was, Glazer and Moynihan suggested, more than enough in the black experience to justify its characterization as ethnic, while behaviour as an ethnic group would certainly provide the best means of getting access to the key institutions in American society[68] – blacks themselves began to act in a manner consistent with it. "There is," noted a 1975 student of American race relations, "a seeking out among blacks for means of amplifying all the criteria comprising ethnicity. Definitions of their territorial origins in Africa, and territorial and economic strongholds in present American settings, old folk and religious practices, features of lifestyle, family relationships, and artistic traditions – are researched for their Afro-American flavour ... by using an ethnic definition of themselves to change their relative status, blacks are pursuing a characteristically American path."[69] That blacks were attempting to acquire status as an ethnic group seemed equally plain to another observer. Sociologist Martin Kilson suggested that in view of the fact that "the salient fact in Negro behavior is ... the historical refusal of white supremacist American society to accord Negroes a quality of ethnic characterization comparable to that accorded white ethnic groups[,] the new black ethnicity [must be seen as] an effort to redress this inferior ethnic characterization."[70]

As Talcott Parsons recognized, this blurring of the distinction between race and culture was not without its ambiguities. References to blackness as a cultural phenomenon might, as he put it, establish "symmetry ... between the definition of black Americans as an ethnic group and other white Americans" but they also "very explicitly accentuate the *racial* focus of the identity of members of the group."[71] Their role as part of a strategy which promised blacks an improvement in their position and whites a minimum amount of disruption in the *status quo* nonetheless won them a wide measure of support among both black and white leadership groups. That in its turn, insisted John Higham, made it clear that accommodating the demands of even so disaffected a minority as the blacks need not imperil the unity and coherence of the nation. The American past had made it clear how unity and diversity were to be reconciled. It was only necessary to follow a strategy of what Higham termed "pluralistic integration," an approach that admitted a real measure of cultural and ethnic diversity at the same time that it demanded a commitment to a common system of values.[72] But whether one joined Higham in talking in these terms, or preferred to follow sociologist Milton Gordon in speaking of the "liberal pluralist" model as the one most likely to encourage harmony in social life,[73] the essential point was the same: the American tradition allowed for recognition to be given to the demands of the ethnic activists, but only in so far as conferring it enforced national cohesion and fostered the maintenance of traditional institutions and principles.

Ethnic pluralism, its American partisans thus made clear, was to be seen as the handmaiden of unity. Its very existence, they argued, had found expression in agencies and forms of behaviour such as ethnic associations and bloc voting which, far from doing nothing other than functioning to preserve isolated ethnic enclaves, had encouraged the movement of ethnics towards positions of power and influence in American life. By the simple device of giving it roots in the American past, its friends were in sum not only able to legitimize it but to give it shape and definition in terms which, far from stimulating random and undirected particularist impulses, channelled and controlled them. In that sense their action did nothing so much as testify to the continuing strength of the forces making for unity, phenomena which in their turn derived from the fact that there was still much to be gained from identification with, and participation in, the institutions which defined, organized, and sustained American life.

The more obvious place the multicultural idea had occupied in the Canadian tradition meant that Canadians had relatively little difficulty in using appeals to the past in their efforts to win for it the additional measure of support they thought the changed circumstances of the late 1960s and 1970s had made necessary. The bilingualism and biculturalism commission's special study on the contribution of the ethnic groups to the national life easily drew its readers' attention to the fact that non-English, non-French elements had been present in the population as far back as the eighteenth century;[74] political scientist David Bell had no trouble locating the origins of the pluralist idea in the kind of accommodative political culture created by the Loyalists;[75] and historian J.M.S. Careless noted simply that "its roots run deep in history."[76].

When, however, it came to the task of deriving from its lengthy past a definition of it which would specify the role and place of minorities in the present, the positions of the two societies were reversed. The source of this turnabout lay in the fundamentally different positions occupied by each nation's largest minority. Where American blacks had been despised, impotent, and largely ignored through much of their history, the participation of French Canadians had been for over a century indispensable to the governance of Canada. Though their minority status had caused them to yield on many fronts, they had been able to make good their claim that they possessed, both in fact and in law, a special status in its affairs. In these circumstances the two groups would respond in very different ways to the argument – central to the multicultural case – that all the groups of which society consisted were to be seen as on a level. Where blacks in the United States took the assertion that they were on the same footing as Poles, Italians, or Irish as representing a *gain* in status, French Canadians had for decades seen anything that even appeared to be an attempt to set them on the same ground as the Ukrainians, Germans, or Hungarians as involving a *loss*. If, as a result, there was to be any hope at all that the French Canadians would accept the elevation of the multicultural idea to the eminence of a national policy, it would have to be made clear that their doing so would entail no diminution in their status. This, it was argued, could best be done by making a very careful distinction between language and culture. That action, its proponents insisted, would allow for the granting of equality of status to the nation's various cultures in a way that, thanks to the fact that nothing would be done to interfere with the already existing rights of the French language, would not deprive that language of its equality of status with English. In this way, the architects of the strategy proclaimed, pluralism and duality would be reconciled.

The program of "multiculturalism within a bilingual framework"[77] which was the institutional expression of these ideas did not, however, entirely succeed in squaring the circle. Whatever English Canada might be, French Canada, some of its leading citizens insisted, was more than a simple linguistic community. It had a culture as well as a language, and its survival depended on the maintenance of the two. They could not, in fact, be separated without grave consequences for the health of the society of whose life they were at once the base and the expression. In these circumstances a policy, the essence of which involved just such a separation, could be seen as nothing other than an attack on the integrity of francophone Canada, an initiative which, intentionally or not, would have the effect of reducing it to the status of a mere ethnic minority. A policy of duality rather than pluralism had therefore to be upheld. As Claude Ryan, then a leading Quebec journalist and later the leader of the province's Liberal party, put it in 1972, "French Canadians will never accept that their language be recognized without recognizing at the same time that they make up a community entitled to its own institutions and to its distinct habits ... [and that this community needs] a certain educational, cultural, social and sometimes even economic institution [*sic*] network without which it could not lead a normal life."[78] Without that recognition, another commentator insisted, francophone language and culture were headed for oblivion. The form of linguistic duality contained in bilingualism was in itself a sham, for in practice it functioned to strengthen the position of English in Quebec without doing anything substantial for French outside it, and now the federal government was proposing a status for francophone culture that would work even more clearly to produce the same result. Putting all cultures on the same footing would, Guy Rocher continued, lead inevitably to demands that they all be accorded the same language rights. If any of these demands were conceded, the result might well be a system of linguistic and cultural enclaves across the country of which the French would be merely one. English would become the *lingua franca*, the language recognized in fact and in principle as the medium of national communications. The ultimate result of the policy would therefore be to strengthen the position of the majority language and eventually the majority culture. In these circumstances French Canadians should have nothing to do with it.[79]

The problem of assuaging francophone doubts about multiculturalism without actually altering the substance of the policy – a move sure to alienate the people whose support it was in the first instance supposed to elicit – was solved by the expedient of lowering its profile at the same time that its range and scope was maintained and even extended. The services on which ethnic groups could draw were steadily augmented through the 1970s. However, the character of cabinet-level appointments to the ministry, and even the way the ministry itself was organized, conveyed the impression to those receptive to such a message that the matters with which it dealt were not regarded as having real priority. The treatment which the pluralist idea received in the report of the Task Force on Canadian Unity, a body established by the federal government in the wake of the November 1976 Parti Québécois victory in the province of Quebec, also suggested a diminution in the level of formal commitment to the pluralist idea on the part of those who had to be conscious of the need to tailor policy and ideas to fit all parts of the country. Ethnic pluralism, the report insisted, did indeed have a place in the hierarchy of national cleavages, but – other realities had intervened to insure – it would be one subordinate to duality and regionalism. It was, in fact, at the provincial rather than the national level that "pluralism has become a living social reality ... We recommend therefore that the provincial governments should assume primary responsibility for the support of multiculturalism in Canada."[80]

If the existence of a powerful and well-positioned minority had operated at the beginning of the country's history to open the way for the assertion of the multicultural idea, it could, then, also impose real limits on the consistency and rigour with which that idea might entrench itself at the federal level. But if all of this in its turn meant that multiculturalism as it took hold in Canada was a different and more cumbersome construct than its United States analogue, this should not be taken to mean that those differences were total. Whether the multicultural idea manifested the kind of balance and simplicity it did in the United States or whether it marked itself out as a thing of change and asymmetry as in Canada, its central purpose remained the same: to give the minorities in both societies a picture of themselves in relation to the whole from which they could take the lesson that there was a place for them in that whole with which they could, and should, be content. The very diligence and ingenuity with which the friends of Canada's survival as a cohesive society tried to cobble together a concept of the nation which could convey this message is in itself a clear measure of the seriousness with which they took the task. Only, they thought – and the fervour of their belief could hardly have been more obvious – if the whole were defined in a way that gave a place to all of its parts, could it survive as a meaningful and cohesive society. No less than their American counterparts, they thus sought not simply to contain potentially disruptive forces but to transform them into a source of strength.

Far from representing a capitulation to centrifugal forces in the national life, adoption of the ethnic idea by policy-makers and ideologues in both the United States and Canada was intended to assist in the maintenance of national unity. In directing their activities towards the attainment of this goal, commentators of course drew attention to the more sharply defined minority group sensibilities which made its achievement necessary. Paying them heed was not, however, done as an end in itself but only in so far as it was a necessary part of the process of reconciling their existence with the preservation of the society whose balance and harmony they seemed to threaten. Acceptance of the new approach was not made, in other words, contingent by most of those who urged it upon recognition of these particularisms as phenomena which made necessary the reorganization of either society in any fundamental sense. On the contrary, matters were defined in terms whose effect was to suggest that recognizing the ethnic fact in North American life involved little more than pointing to the presence in it of elements which any careful observer could see had long been active there. The concern to give ethnicity roots in the past was the clearest indicator of this. The very act of coming to a proper understanding of that phenomenon was thus made inseparable from the business of seeing that it was perfectly compatible with the national being as it had been and still was. The conciliation of the minorities and their leaders came, in consequence, to involve very little in the way of restructuring national institutions. The emphasis instead was on the manifestly less radical business of opening those organizations up to minority participation, as even a cursory examination of affirmative action programs in the United States and the strategy to make the Canadian federal civil service bilingual makes clear.

In sum, one comes away from a consideration of the ethnic idea's recent history in North America with a heightened appreciation of its nation-maintaining role, a forceful reminder of the important place beliefs and images generally occupy in community integration, and a surer sense of the complex nature of the interaction between those beliefs and images and changing realities in the societies in relation to which they function. A general line of argument about the dynamics of national maintenance having thus been rehearsed at the same moment that a ray of quite concentrated light was cast on a specific set of problems, investigators, whose receipt of so substantial a bonus deserves explicit recognition, find their yield doubled in the very act of seeing its significance clarified.

NOTES

1 Cited in C. Seton-Watson, *Italy from Liberalism to Fascism 1870–1925* (London: Methuen, 1967), 13.
2 David Easton, "Part Three: The Input of Support," in his *A Systems Analysis of Political Life* (New York: Wiley, 1965), 151–243; R.A. Schermerhorn, *Comparative Ethnic Relations: A Framework for Theory and Research* (New York: Random House, 1970), 23. For a general discussion of nation-building, see Reinhard Bendix, *Nation-Building and Citizenship: Studies of Our Changing Social Order* (New York: Wiley, 1964); K.W. Deutsch and W.J. Foltz, eds., *Nation-Building* (New York: Prentice-Hall, 1963); S.N. Eisenstadt and Stein Rokkan, eds., *Building States and Nations* (Beverley Hills: Sage, 1973); and Charles Tilly, ed., *The Formation of National States in Western Europe* (Princeton: Princeton University Press, 1975). For observations on the difficulties cultural, ethnic, and racial cleavages create for nation-builders, see Clifford Geertz, ed., *Old Societies and New States* (New York: Free Press, 1963); Cynthia H. Enloe, *Ethnic Conflict and Political Development* (Boston: Little Brown, 1973); Chester L. Hunt and Lewis Walker, *Ethnic Dynamics: Patterns of Intergroup Relations in Various Societies* (Homewood: Dorsey Press, 1974); and Wendell Bell and Walter E. Freeman, eds., *Ethnicity and Nation-Building: Comparative, International, and Historical Perspectives* (Beverley Hills: Sage, 1974). In investigating the way in which a stable liberal democratic national system was built in the United States, Seymour Martin Lipset's *The First New Nation: The United States in Historical and Comparative Perspective* (New York: Anchor Books, 1967) lays much emphasis on the role of its English-speaking, liberally minded charter group, while Kenneth D. McRae's discussion of the Canadian experience ("Empire, Language, and Nation: The Canadian Case," in Eisenstadt and Rokkan, *Building States and Nations*, vol. 2, 144–76) stresses the difficulties created for nation-builders in that country by the fact that their work had to accommodate the interests of more than one group of national importance.
3 See Bendix, *Nation-Building and Citizenship*, particularly "The Extension of Citizenship to the Lower Classes," 74–101.
4 Morris Janowitz, *The Last Half-Century: Societal Change and Politics in America* (Chicago: University of Chicago Press, 1978), 178.
5 "The available evidence," argues Seymour Martin Lipset, "suggests that the chances for stable democracy are enhanced to the extent that groups and individuals have a number of crosscutting, politically relevant affiliations." *Political Man: The Social Basis of Politics* (Garden City: Anchor, 1963), 77.

6 Indeed, notes a recent observer, national societies are to be "envisaged as systems in which societal allocations are inputs. The inputs pass through the social structure, described in terms of the degree of differentiation and the pressures towards uniformity, and result in outputs that can be assessed in terms of societal and individual goals," with these goals being determined "in terms of the basic needs of individuals." Erik Allardt, "Individual Needs, Social Structures, and Indicators of National Development," in Eisenstadt and Rokkan, *Building States and Nations*, vol. 1, 261.

7 Weber's insistence on the importance of "the feelings of the actors that they belong together" has been explicitly recalled by Easton who himself insists on the importance of "affective solidarity." Historians of nationalism, too, have consistently emphasized its character as a body of feeling which, one of them notes, "may mean whatever a given people, on the basis of their own historical experience, decide it to mean." "Nationalism," argues another, "is what the nationalists have made of it; it is not a neat, fixed concept but a varying combination of beliefs and conditions." "A nation," insists a third, "may be a configuration of meaning that transcends any concrete manifestation. On this level, a nation is a set of sentiments and myths that, like religion, is ultimately grounded only in the consciousness of the committed." See H.H. Gerth and C. Wright Mills, eds., *From Max Weber: Essays in Sociology* (New York: Oxford University Press, 1946), 183; Easton, *Systems Analysis*, 187; Louis L. Snyder, *The Meaning of Nationalism* (New Brunswick, NJ: Greenwood Press, 1954), 11; Boyd C. Shafer, *Nationalism: Myth and Reality* (New York: Harcourt, Brace, 1955), 15; and R.C. Beals, "The Rise and Decline of National Identity," *Canadian Review of Studies in Nationalism* 4(2), 1977, 148.

8 Sometimes, of course, those who deployed these constructs deliberately made them represent only a part of the whole, hoping that in gaining support for that part they would forge a national character consistent with the particular and limited values it represented. "The aim of the Argentine nationalism of [the early twentieth century]," argues one student, "was to teach the immigrant masses to revere essentially aristocratic cultural values, symbolized by the gaucho, which upper-class intellectuals claimed constituted the true Argentine character. The assumption was that the immigrants would eventually accept the hierarchical structure of Argentine society and would abandon such 'foreign' ideas as popular democracy, socialism, and anarcho-syndicalism. The public school became the vehicle that transmitted traditional creole cultural values to the immigrants and their children." Usually, however, the device chosen transcends identification with any particular part of the nation. India thus

looked back to the Buddhist emperor Asoka and took the lion-ornamented capital of one of his edict pillars as its national emblem, while Eric Williams, first prime minister of Trinidad and Tobago, used his *History of the People of Trinidad and Tobago* (Port-of-Spain: PNM Publishing, 1962) to enforce the idea that the population of those islands was linked by its common experience with slavery, plantation, and empire. As these examples make clear, the object was not necessarily to obliterate attachments to race, ethnicity, or religion but "to transform them and to raise them to a higher level of scale by shifting the focus of attention to the relationship between large sub-populations on the national stage." A system of national symbols, concludes Morris Janowitz, "offered in contrast to existing localistic and traditional boundaries thus provided a basis for collective action [which was] powerful and enduring." See Carl Solberg, *Immigration and Nationalism: Argentina and Chile, 1890–1914* (Austin: University of Texas Press, 1970), 170; McKim Marriott, "Cultural Policy in the New States," in C. Geertz, ed., *Old Societies and New States* (New York: Free Press, 1963), 35; Wendell Bell, "Ethnicity, Decisions of Nationhood, and Images of the Future," in Bell and Freeman, *Ethnicity and Nation-Building*, 295, 289; and Janowitz, *The Last Half-Century*, 182.

9 In the United States, argues Lipset, "the basic value system, as solidified in the early days of the new nation" so strongly influenced the behaviour of Americans that it "could account for the kinds of changes that have taken place in the American character and in American institutions as these faced the need to adjust to the requirements of an urban, industrial, and bureaucratic society." Lipset, *First New Nation*, 118.

10 The process is similar to that involved in maintaining what sociologists Peter L. Berger and Thomas Luckmann call "the symbolic universe," that is, the body of belief through which individuals make sense of, and acquire confidence in, the world around them and their relation to it. In telling them not only what the nature of that world is but also what place in it they occupy, it gives them information they must have if they are to lead secure and productive lives as integrated, society-supporting beings. Peter L. Berger and Thomas Luckmann, *The Social Construction of Reality: A Treatise in the Sociology of Knowledge* (Garden City: Anchor, 1967), 92–128.

11 As John Jay put it, the unity of the Americans as "a people descended from the same ancestors, speaking the same language, professing the same religion, attached to the same principles of government, very similar in their manners and customs" and occupying "one connected, fertile, wide-spreading country" provided an ample founda-

tion for a unified national existence. "The Federalist No. 2," in *The Federalist* (New York: Modern Library, 1937), 8–9.

12 Oscar Handlin, *The Uprooted* (Boston: Little, Brown, 1951), 306.

13 That American society had much success in orienting its members toward identification with the whole should not be taken to suggest that they lost sight of their relationship to the parts. "The strength of national attachments," as Morris Janowitz points out, "does not mean that local attachments became extinct." What it does mean, however, is that those local attachments become less ends in themselves and more the means of heightening the individual's sense of security. Thus, in Janowitz's terms, they allow him "to relate himself to more and more encompassing systems of authority [for] ethnicity, religion, regionalism, and the like are the intervening dimensions in a sense of nationality." Janowitz, *The Last Half-Century*, 327. For some traditional views of what composed that sense of nationality see Hans Kohn, *American Nationalism: An Interpretive Essay* (New York: Macmillan, 1957); Yehoshua Arieli, *Individualism and Nationalism in American Ideology* (Cambridge, MA: Harvard University Press, 1964); and Russel B. Nye, "The American as Nationalist," in his *This Almost Chosen People: Essays in the History of American Ideas* (Toronto: Macmillan, 1966), 43–103.

14 Even though, as Milton Gordon points out, "anglo-conformity in various guises has probably been the most prevalent ideology in assimilation in the American historical experience." "Assimilation in America: Theory and Reality," *Daedalus*, 90, 1961, 263–85, reprinted in Lawrence W. Levine and Robert Middlekauf, eds., *The National Temper: Readings in American History* (New York: Harcourt, Brace and World, 1968), 271.

15 A characteristic of American life perhaps more readily apparent to outsiders. At any rate, as Seymour Martin Lipset remarks, "From Tocqueville and Martineau in the 1830's to Gunnar Myrdal in more recent times, foreign visitors have been impressed by the extent to which the values proclaimed in the Declaration of Independence have operated to prescribe social and political behavior." Lipset, *First New Nation*, 111.

16 W. Peter Ward, *White Canada Forever: Popular Attitudes and Public Policy Toward Orientals in British Columbia* (Montreal: McGill-Queen's University Press, 1978).

17 *Parliamentary Debates on the Confederation of the British North American Provinces* ([Quebec City:] Queen's Printer, 1865), 55.

18 For a fuller treatment of this process, see Allan Smith, "Metaphor and Nationality in North America," this volume.

19 J.M.S. Careless, "'Limited Identities' in Canada," *Canadian Historical Review*, 50, 1969, 3.

20 Michael Novak, *The Rise of the Unmeltable Ethnics: Politics and Culture in the Seventies* (New York: Macmillan, 1971).

21 Donald Keith Fellows, *A Mosaic of America's Ethnic Minorities* (New York: Wiley, 1972).

22 John Slawson in collaboration with Marc Vosk, *Unequal Americans: Practices and Politics of Intergroup Relations* (Westport: Greenwood, 1979), 6.

23 Salvatore J. LaGumina and Frank J. Cavaioli, eds., *The Ethnic Dimension in American Society* (Boston: Holbrook Press, 1974), 2.

24 George De Vos, "Ethnic Pluralism: Conflict and Accommodation," in George De Vos and Lola Romanucci-Ross, eds., *Ethnic Identity: Cultural Continuities and Change* (Palo Alto: Mayfield Publishing Company, 1975), 21.

25 For a discussion of the history of the pluralist idea in Canada before 1970, see Smith, "Metaphor and Nationality."

26 For an assessment of its impact, see Jean Brunet, "The Policy of Multiculturalism within a Bilingual Framework: A Stock-Taking," *Canadian Ethnic Studies*, 10, 1978, 107–13.

27 See, for example, Francis J. Brown and Joseph S. Roucek, eds., *One America: The History, Contribution, and Present Problems of Our Racial and National Minorities* (Englewood Cliffs: Prentice Hall, 1952), 4.

28 While, however, some commentators saw the new ethnicity as playing an important role in maintaining the mental health of Americans in a bland and homogeneous society – "as America becomes increasingly depersonalized," observes one of them, "'groupism' and ethnicity serve the added important function of reducing anomie" – others viewed the form of ethnic consciousness to which these circumstances gave rise rather less generously. Oscar Handlin portrayed it as "a surrogate country" arising out of the attempt by men in motion to give themselves roots, while more recently Morris Janowitz has explained it as little more than the product of an attempt by the largely assimilated second and third generation to recover its past. "In this regard," he suggests, "ethnic concern in the 'middle class' is the equivalent of upper-class preoccupation with geneology. Accordingly, the general English-language mass media and not foreign-language press have reinforced this attenuated aspect of ethnic consciousness." The basic point – that the felt anonymity of American life helped precipitate ethnic consciousness – nonetheless stands. See Slawson, *Unequal Americans*, 6; Handlin, *The Uprooted*, 227; and Janowitz, *The Last Half-Century*, 311.

29 John Higham, *Send These to Me: Jews and Other Immigrants in Urban America* (New York: Atheneum, 1975), 243.

30 Post-World War One sociologists, Morris Janowitz writes, "empha-

sized the strength of nationality and ethnic solidarities; they did not hold the superficial view that a comprehensive 'melting pot' was rapidly developing. In fact, from a policy point of view, they opposed mechanical efforts at 'Americanization'; as pluralists they believed that ethnic solidarities and associated forms of self-help were essential for national integration." Janowitz, *The Last Half-Century*, 305. For a lengthier treatment of these matters, see Fred H. Matthews, *Quest for An American Sociology: Robert E. Park and the Chicago School* (Montreal: McGill-Queen's University Press, 1977), especially chapter 4, 84–120.

31 See Higham, *Send These to Me*, 221–2 for a discussion of this point.

32 Will Herberg, *Protestant, Catholic, Jew: An Essay in American Religious Sociology* (New York: Doubleday, 1955).

33 At the beginning of the decade, Berthoff set out some ideas about the nature of the American past which were to contribute to the conclusion, expressed in a later book-length study, that individuals had never really confronted society as isolated beings. Voluntary associations had been important agencies in their lives, and "the traditional institutions of society – the family, the community, the church – have never ceased to exist in some form throughout American history ... nor have social classes disappeared." See his "The American Social Order: A Conservative Hypothesis," *American Historical Review*, 65, 1960, 495–514, and his *An Unsettled People: Social Order and Disorder in American History* (New York: Harper and Row, 1971), 477.

34 John Higham, with Leonard Kreiger and Felix Gilbert, *History: The Development of Historical Studies in the United States* (Englewood Cliffs: Prentice Hall, 1965), 221.

35 For an influential argument in support of the contention that class existed in America, see Stephan Thernstrom, *Poverty and Progress: Social Mobility in a Nineteenth Century City* (New York: Atheneum, 1970). For an argument that a working-class sub-culture existed, see Herbert Gutman, *Work, Culture and Society in Industrializing America: Essays in American Working Class and Social History* (New York: Knopf, 1976), especially chapter 1, "Work, Society, and Culture in Industrializing America, 1815–1919," 3–78.

36 Especially in the history of colonial America. For a discussion of some of them, see Richard Beeman, "The New Social History and the Search for 'Community' in Colonial America," *American Quarterly*, 29, 1977, 422–43. For an overview of American history as a whole cast in these terms, see Robert H. Wiebe, *The Segmented Society: An Introduction to the Meaning of America* (New York: Oxford University Press, 1975).

37 Nathan Glazer and Daniel P. Moynihan, *Beyond the Melting Pot: The Negroes, Puerto Ricans, Jews, Italians and Irish of New York City* (Cambridge: MIT Press, 1963), v.

38 Ralph Ellison, *Invisible Man* (New York: Modern Library, 1952).

39 Literature exploring the emergence of the black American in the 1960s and 1970s is extensive. For a summary account of the earlier stages of the process, see Louis E. Lomax, *The Negro Revolt* (New York: Harper and Row, 1962); for a comprehensive selection of material dealing with both its earlier and later phases, see James A. Geschwender, ed., *The Black Revolt: The Civil Rights Movement, Ghetto Uprisings, and Separatism* (Englewood Cliffs: Prentice Hall, 1971). Whether blacks have made meaningful gains in terms of their socioeconomic status is a vexed question. Nathan Glazer and Robin Williams, Jr, think that, on the whole, they have; Morris Janowitz is less sure; and Glazer and Moynihan together suggest that blacks may have improved their situation both absolutely and in relation to some white ethnics, but have been prevented from fully appreciating the importance of that fact by the extent to which they have been reminded how badly off, relative to the white community at large, they still were. See Nathan Glazer, *Affirmative Discrimination: Ethnic Inequality and Public Policy* (New York: Basic Books, 1975), 40–3; Robin Williams, Jr, *Mutual Accommodation: Ethnic Conflict and Cooperation* (Minneapolis: University of Minnesota Press, 1977), 27–32; Janowitz, *The Last Half-Century*, 133; and Nathan Glazer and Daniel P. Moynihan, *Beyond the Melting Pot: The Negroes, Puerto Ricans, Jews, Italians, and Irish of New York City*, 2nd ed. (Cambridge: MIT Press, 1970), xii.

40 Margaret Mead outlined the process in these words: "The progression from integration as a principle to black power has marked a shift from the demand, on the part of both black and white, that individual black people be admitted as pupils, physicians, lawyers, etc., into the larger society, to the demand that black people *as a group* and black people as residents of particular contiguous sections of large cities or rural countries be accorded recognition as a separate people which can itself confer dignity on each of its members. Integration expressed the melting pot idea: If you will make an effort to look, act, dress, speak as much like the standard white, then though [you are] not blond like the ideal American, we will act as though you were really entirely one of us. Black power expresses the rejection of this unilateral invitation, and the demand instead for equal recognition and value based on difference." "Ethnicity and Anthropology in America," in De Vos and Romanucci-Ross, *Ethnic Identity*, 186.

41 Ethnicity, Bell writes, "is best understood *not* as a primordial phenomenon in which deeply held identities have to reemerge, but as a strategic choice by individuals who, in other circumstances, would choose other group memberships as a means of gaining some power and privilege." Daniel Bell, "Ethnicity and Social Change," in Nathan Glazer and Daniel P. Moynihan, eds., *Ethnicity: Theory and Experience* (Cambridge: Harvard University Press, 1975), 171.

42 "Neo-ethnicity among urban whites," reports one observer, "is in large part a response to the relative political success of an emergent black ethnicity ... The marginal-income city whites are especially central to neo-ethnicity, insofar as they provide the sharpest core support for a fundamental attribute of white neo-ethnicity – anti-Negro orientation." Nathan Glazer makes essentially the same point: "It turned out that the effort to make the Negro equal to the *other* Americans raised the question of who *are* the other Americans? How many of them can define their own group as being *also* deprived?" See Martin Kilson, "Blacks and Neo-Ethnicity in American Political Life," in Glazer and Moynihan, *Ethnicity*, 260, and Glazer, *Affirmative Discrimination*, 31.

43 "Above all other themes in his campaign, beyond any program, the fire that burned most hotly in him was for the underprivileged – for the minorities, for the Negroes, for the Appalachians, for the Mexican-Americans." Theodore H. White, *The Making of the President 1968* (New York: Atheneum, 1969), 173.

44 Theodore H. White, *The Making of the President 1972* (New York: Atheneum, 1973), 229–30, 344–6.

45 De Vos, "Ethnic Pluralism: Conflict and Accommodation," 21.

46 Glazer, *Affirmative Discrimination*, 219–20.

47 Bell, "Ethnicity and Social Change," 146.

48 See Paul Yuzyk, *The Ukrainians in Manitoba: A Social History* (Toronto: University of Toronto Press, 1953); John Kosa, *Land of Choice: The Hungarians in Canada* (Toronto: University of Toronto Press, 1957); Frank G. Vallee, Mildred Schwartz, and Frank Darknell, "Ethnic Assimilation and Differentiation in Canada," *Canadian Journal of Economics and Political Science*, 23, 1957, 540–9; V.J. Kaye, *Early Ukrainian Settlements in Canada, 1895–1900* (Toronto: University of Toronto Press, 1964); Elizabeth Wagenheim, "The Ukrainians: A Case Study of the Third Force," in Peter Russell, ed., *Nationalism in Canada* (Toronto: McGraw-Hill, 1966), 72–91; and Jeremy Boissevain, "The Italians of Montreal," *Special Study of the Royal Commission on Bilingualism and Biculturalism* (Ottawa: Queen's Printer, 1969).

49 See Frank G. Vallee and Donald R. Whyte, "Canadian Society:

Trends and Perspectives," in Bernard R. Blishen, Frank E. Jones, Kaspar D. Naegele, and John Porter, eds., *Canadian Society: Sociological Perspectives*, 3rd ed. (Toronto: Macmillan, 1968), 851.

50 Wsevolod W. Isajiw, for example, attributes ethnic consciousness in Canadian life in part to a concern to resist the anonymity of urban industrial society. As he puts it, "The technological culture heightens identity needs and creates identity search. Ethnic rediscoveries or 'new ethnicity' is one significant direction that this search takes." Other sociologists have argued that in Canada as elsewhere ethnic identification can in some measure be explained as an outgrowth of the concern of the third generation to define itself in terms of its past as well as its present. "A 'new ethnicity' among the third generation may," Alan B. Anderson and Daiva K. Stasiulis suggest, "assume the form of a keen interest in one's geneological and ethnic history, regardless of one's ability to speak the mother tongue or one's religious inclinations." See Wsevolod W. Isajiw, "Olga in Wonderland: Ethnicity in a Technological Society," in Leo Driedger, ed., *The Canadian Mosaic* (Toronto: McClelland and Stewart, 1978), 36, and Alan B. Anderson and Daiva K. Stasiulis, "Canadian Multiculturalism: A Critique," paper presented to the Biennial Conference of the Canadian Ethnic Studies Association, Vancouver, October 1979, 23.

51 See Dale C. Thompson, "Canadian Ethnic Pluralism in Context," paper presented to the Biennial Conference of the Canadian Ethnic Studies Association, Vancouver, October 1979, and Kenneth D. McRae, "The Plural Society and the Western Political Tradition," *Canadian Journal of Political Science*, 12, 1979, 688.

52 Wagenheim, "The Ukrainians," 73.

53 "Ethnic saliency or differentiation in social structure," Porter was still insisting in 1975, "always creates a high risk of ethnic stratification." *The Vertical Mosaic: An Analysis of Social Class and Power in Canada* (Toronto: University of Toronto Press, 1965), 558, and "Ethnic Pluralism in Canadian Perspective," in Glazer and Moynihan, *Ethnicity*, 289.

54 As early as 1963 Premier Manning of Alberta had made it clear that he would not accept a national policy that attempted to make a sharp distinction between the French-speaking and other minorities. A policy relating to those groups, he wrote the prime minister, would receive his support only if it placed all of them on the same basis. "In the matter of biculturalism," as he put it, "if the objective is to encourage citizens of all racial and ethnic origins to make their maximum contribution to the development of one overall Canadian culture embracing the best of all, we feel this would meet with endorsation and support." Otherwise, the implication was clear, there was

strong likelihood that it would not. Manning's letter is quoted in John Saywell, ed., *The Canadian Annual Review 1963* (Toronto: University of Toronto Press, 1964), 61.

55 For a discussion of the impact of the 1967 regulations, see Freda Hawkins, "The Canadian Experience," *Venture*, 23(1), 1971, 32–5. That Canada was a racially as well as a linguistically and culturally diverse society was now more obvious than ever, a fact which was underscored by and contributed to the appearance of a number of studies focusing on the history and experience of its racial minorities. See, for example, Ward, *White Canada Forever;* Ken Adachi, *The Enemy that Never Was: A History of the Japanese Canadians* (Toronto: McClelland and Stewart, 1976); and Barry Broadfoot, *Years of Sorrow, Years of Shame: The Story of the Japanese Canadians in World War Two* (Toronto: Doubleday, 1977). The history of the country's original inhabitants also received book length scrutiny – see E. Palmer Patterson, *The Canadian Indian* (Toronto: Collier-MacMillan, 1972) – while its first racial minority was examined in Robin W. Winks' comprehensive and detailed *The Blacks in Canada: A History* (New Haven: Yale University Press, 1971).

56 The phrase was used by Prime Minister Trudeau in his Commons speech announcing the policy (*House of Commons Debates*, 8 October 1971, 8545–6).

57 Pierre Elliott Trudeau, "The New Treason of the Intellectuals," in his *Federalism and the French Canadians* (Toronto: Macmillan, 1968), 177. The essay was originally published as "La nouvelle trahison des clercs," in *Cité Libre*, April 1962.

58 CBC network television, for example, emphasized the nation's multicultural character through the medium of such programs as *The Newcomers*, dealing with its indigenous as well as its immigrant population, and *King of Kensington*, situated in one of Toronto's best-known ethnic neighbourhoods. Radio and television stations such as CJBV in Vancouver and Toronto's recently licensed multilingual broadcasting channel offered programming in several languages. At the level of scholarly activity sociologists, historians, and political scientists combined to form the Canadian Ethnic Studies Association in 1971, an organization which in its turn assumed responsibility for a biannual conference exploring aspects of the ethnic experience in Canada and for the publication of the scholarly journal *Canadian Ethnic Studies*. A contribution of importance to the heightening of ethnic consciousness was made, too, by the several studies of individual ethnic groups in Canada funded during the 1970s by the Department of the Secretary of State.

59 Robert Drummond, "Nationalism and Ethnic Demands: Some Specu-

lations on a Congenial Note," *Canadian Journal of Political Science*, 10, 1977, 387.

60 W.M. Newman, for example, argues that while minorities have social mobility, they experience it not as a consequence of structural assimilation but within the framework of a parallel set of minority-group controlled institutions, a contention that prepares the way for a view of American society as in a very real sense corporatist. *American Pluralism: A Study of Minority Groups and Social Theory* (New York: Harper and Row, 1973).

61 LaGumina and Cavaioli, *The Ethnic Dimension in American Society*, 1. For a vigorous statement of the need to move from the old kind of immigrant history to the new kind of ethnic history, see Rudolph J. Vecoli, "Ethnicity: A Neglected Dimension of American History," in Herbert J. Bass, ed., *The State of American History* (Chicago: Quadrangel Books, 1970), 70–88.

62 Higham, "Ethnic Pluralism in Modern American Thought."

63 Glazer, *Affirmative Discrimination*, 5.

64 See his 1959 critique of the consensus view of American history "The Cult of the 'American Consensus': Homogenizing Our History," *Commentary*, 17, 1959, 93–100.

65 John Higham, "Hanging Together: Divergent Unities in American History," *Journal of American History*, 60, 1974, 5–28.

66 Higham, *Send These to Me*, 237.

67 "It is hardly likely," Glazer and Moynihan wrote in 1971, "that Moslem, Swahili-speaking blacks of Zanzibar would find much in common with the black institutions and culture that are now being built up in this country. They would not have any predilection for soul food, would find the styles of dress, hair, walk, and talk that are now popular as defining blackness distinctly foreign. 'Blackness' in this country is not really and simply *blackness*, it is an American Negro cultural style." Glazer and Moynihan, *Beyond the Melting Pot*, 2nd ed., xxxix.

68 "If one," they wrote, "compared [the black experience in New York] with the first fifty years of the Irish, the Italians, and the Jews, we are convinced there would be enough in that comparison to justify an ethnic rather than a racial or 'internally-colonized' self-image," a circumstance which, they continued, made it wholly realistic to suggest that blacks could improve their position in American life by following the route marked out by these earlier travellers. Ibid., xiv, xxiii–xxiv.

69 De Vos, "Ethnic Pluralism: Conflict and Accommodation," 21–2.

70 Kilson, "Blacks and New-Ethnicity in American Political Life," 237.

71 Talcott Parsons, "Some Theoretical Considerations on the Nature

50000
50000

and Trends of Change and Ethnicity," in Glazer and Moynihan, *Ethnicity*, 72.

72 Higham, *Send These to Me*, 240–3.

73 Milton M. Gordon, "Toward a General Theory of Racial and Ethnic Group Relations," in Glazer and Moynihan, *Ethnicity*, 106, 110.

74 Report of the Royal Commission on Bilingualism and Biculturalism, Book 4, *The Contribution of the Other Ethnic Groups* (Ottawa: Queen's Printer, 1970), 17–31.

75 David V.J. Bell, "The Loyalist Tradition in Canada," *Journal of Canadian Studies*, 5, 1970, especially 29–30.

76 Careless, "'Limited Identities' in Canada," 4.

77 For Prime Minister Trudeau's remarks on it, see *House of Commons Debates*, 8 October 1971, 8545–6.

78 Claude Ryan, Address to the Ontario Heritage Congress, June 1972, in Howard Palmer, ed., *Immigration and the Rise of Multiculturalism* (Toronto: Copp Clark, 1975), 148.

79 Guy Rocher, "Les ambiguités d'un Canada bilingue et multiculturel," in his *Le Québec en mutation* (Montréal: Hurtibise, 1973), 117–26; and "Multiculturalism: The Doubts of a Francophone," in *Multiculturalism as State Policy* (Ottawa: Canadian Consultative Council on Multiculturalism, 1976), 47–53.

80 The Task Force on Canadian Unity, *A Future Together: Observations and Recommendations* (Ottawa: Ministry of Supply and Services, 1979), 55–6.

8 First Nations, Race, and the Pluralist Idea: Canada and the United States in the Post-Modern Age

Much attention continues to be given to the role which management of linguistic and ethnic tension must play in the stabilization of life in the world's increasingly heterogeneous national systems.[1] Recent developments in many parts of the globe have, however, powerfully reinforced the truth that resolution and containment of racial strife is no less central to movement towards that important goal.[2] The new phase of conflict and rapprochement in South Africa,[3] growing aboriginal consciousness in Australasia[4] and Scandinavia,[5] and the stresses produced by the presence of Turkish, North African, and East Indian workers and immigrants in the classical nation states of western Europe[6] make this, indeed, obvious beyond all denying.

Difficulties of this awkward and troublesome sort are, it hardly needs to be pointed out, no less facts of Canadian and American life than they are elements in the experience of the world as a whole. Continuing unease between blacks and whites on both sides of the border, the anxiety caused in North America at large by the recent arrival of substantial numbers of Asian immigrants, and the rising militance of aboriginal peoples throughout the continent suggest, in fact, that matters are at least as complicated in these two societies as elsewhere, for in them one sees not just some but almost all the problems associated with this complex and trying phenomenon.[7]

A version of this paper was published in Stella Hryniuk, ed., *Twenty Years of Multiculturalism: Successes and Failures* (Winnipeg: St John's College Press, 1992), 233–54.

One cannot, of course, treat North America's aboriginal peoples and the immigrants from non-European societies as though they were absolutely and in all respects the same. It hardly needs stressing that important differences of history, culture, status, and position distinguish these groups from each other in a number of ways, of which the possession by one and the lack by the other of a territorial base and an ancient North American lineage are only the most evident. That said, however, it can also be noted – and, for the purposes of this paper the observation is the more important – that there are four distinct senses in which all these groups occupy common ground. Each has been the object of sustained, unrelenting, systematic, and institutionalized discrimination on the part of the continent's European-descended majority. Each has made serious efforts in the last several decades to alter its position relative to that of other groups. Each has profited from global developments, be they centred on the struggle for self-determination of native peoples, the breakdown of the racially homogeneous nation-state in Europe, or the events now unfolding in South Africa. And each has been affected in its efforts to reshape its relations with the whole by the existence of a national ideology peculiar to the larger society in which it dwells. The object of this paper is to investigate this last point.

Up to the Second World War, relations between aboriginals, blacks, and Asians on the one side and North American peoples of European origin on the other were defined and governed by theories and assumptions explicitly rooted in racist thinking. From the earliest moments of the continent's recorded history its non-European peoples were given a place distinctly inferior to that of even the least privileged Europeans. Clear enough in terms of socio-economic status – non-Europeans were almost always slaves, indentured labourers or, if "free" compelled to work at very low wages – the fact of their subordinate position was also indicated by the image of them cobbled together by their European compatriots. Sometimes, indeed, they hardly had an image of any sort. Pronounced by the racist dogma of the day to be inferior – and therefore not truly "human" at all – American blacks were certainly not to be accommodated within the framework of the liberal idea of the community which European-Americans made so very much their own in the early years of the republic's history: that idea's "community of equal individuals" simply did not leave room for full membership of those whom the verities of the age had defined as wanting and substandard.[8] And if this pushing aside in time reduced the American black to the status of what novelist Ralph Ellison would term an "invisible man,"[9] things were not necessarily much better when blacks did get "seen": the urge to keep them in their place persisted, and thus – the existence of black-face comedy, minstrel show entertainment, and the image of blacks as faithful servants and retainers makes the point – insured that they would almost always be presented as an object of condescension or amusement.[10]

In Canada the black minority's tiny size made it even easier for it to be excluded from view. As late as 1971 Robin Winks could write that "there is no historical memory in Canada of British North America's own experience with the Negro."[11] Knowledge of the presence of slaves, certainly, slipped from sight until Canadians working under the influence of the early twentieth-century American interest in the black past began to recover it.[12] Awareness of Canada's dramatic role as the terminus of the Underground Railway similarly disappeared at least until the same period.[13] And on the level of action, American blacks moving north to farm the prairies in the early twentieth century found their way all but blocked by zealous officials eager to enforce what amounted to a colour bar.[14]

On those occasions when persons of non-European origin did manage to attract and hold the attention of the majority, this was almost invariably because they were presented in what were perceived to be sinister and threatening terms. Operating under the continuing influence of racist ideas, fearing cheap labour, and disturbed by the vast cultural gap that seemed to yawn between East and West, Americans certainly saw Asians in this light. The result was a series of well-known moves to hedge them round with restrictions, deny them citizenship, limit their numbers, and eventually exclude them altogether.[15] And if, in Ronald I. Takaki's telling phrase, the republic's people viewed them as "strangers from a different shore,"[16] persons who, having come across the Pacific rather than the Atlantic, lacked the kind of legitimacy that arrivals from Europe possessed, Canadians did much the same. Their presence in the northern half of the continent channelled and contained by quotas, residential restrictions, denial of political rights, and, ultimately, internment, Asians and Asian-Canadians were made to exist at the margins of Canadian life and at the edges of the picture the country was forming of itself. Left out even of panegyrics written to celebrate Canada's diversity – John Murray Gibbon's *Canadian Mosaic* (1938) is the best example – they found space allotted to them only insofar as they could be cast in the role of threat, danger, or invading force.[17]

The image created of North America's aboriginal peoples in these years did not conform to quite this pattern. Though even more socially and economically marginalized than blacks and Asians, several factors insured aboriginals a place in the picture being created of their societies, a place which would be at once more prominent and more complex than that accorded either of the other two groups. Paradoxically, the very fact of the sad state of aboriginals as a small, overwhelmed, poverty-stricken, and disease-prone minority was one such factor: far from allowing a view of them as a menace, it compelled them to be seen as, at most, an early and temporary obstacle to the inexorable advance of white settlement. Noticing them, in consequence did not – the case, it was thought, with blacks and Asians – in any way appear to strengthen by undue recognition some sort of clear and present danger to "civilized" society's existence: it served, on the contrary, to underscore the futility of their resistance and completeness of their collapse. The feelings involved in this sort of reaction were, to be sure, often mixed: not a little guilt was discernible in the sense of many observers that what had prepared the way for the triumph of their civilization was the decimation of another. Any ambivalence of this kind could, however, be removed simply by noting that unlike one's forebears one saw the full measure of the aboriginals' tragedy. This, indeed, permitted observers to earn two sorts of psychological payoff: it allowed them to derive satisfaction from the fact that they were sympathizing with the displaced while at the same time enabling them to feel superior in their tolerance and understanding to the settlers who had been responsible for the displacing. A view of aboriginals as helpers or assistants played a particularly important part in this process. It allowed the observer to think that he or she was seeing them as figures of worth, thereby confirming his or her own capacity to take a generous and liberal view. Precisely, however, because aboriginals remained beings whose role in the execution of a project designed and promoted by whites was by definition a subordinate one, hierarchy could be maintained, and – the crowning touch – they could be presented as having at their "best" co-operated in their own subjection. And as if this were not enough, looking at the aboriginals might even yield a "modern" version of the kind of result which had earlier come from contemplation of them as the "noble savage." In thus endowing aboriginals not merely with the "old" virtues of wisdom, steadfastness, loyalty, and courage, but with the "new" kind of authenticity painters and composers – Picasso, Gauguin, Stravinsky – were by the early twentieth century discovering in the "primitive," whites were indeed acting in the clearest possible way to cast them in a role created by those whites themselves in the course of their efforts to resolve their own ambiguities and dissatisfactions with their time and place.

All these imperatives operated to keep the aboriginals close to the forefront of American consciousness. Sometimes – enthusiasm for Black Elk and his story is a case in point – the impulse to think in terms of the new noble savage, superior in sensitivity and rectitude to the displacing civilization, predominated.[18] Sometimes the thrust to show the aboriginal as the willing partner and accomplice of the white man was most in evidence, as the examples of Little Beaver and Tonto make clear.[19] Most often, however, the sense of aboriginals as beings bound to disappear triumphed: even, then, as Americans acknowledged the aboriginal role in the nation's history they were able, in the end, to relegate the aboriginals themselves to a much less than central position in what had transpired. And whether they did this through the subtle, complex, ambivalent forms and thinking explored in Brian Dippie's *The Vanishing American*[20] or through the crude and simple images of the western movie,[21] the message was in essence the same: here in all its nobility or pathos, courage or venality, strength or subordination, was a people destined for marginality.

The Canadian image of the aboriginals had much in common with the picture developed in the United States. But if Canadians shared the belief that Natives were fated to decline – a conviction evident in government policy and among anthropologists alike[22] – and if the Canadian exposure to American popular culture did much to shape Canadians' general sense of how they were to be seen,[23] it is also true that the Canadian sense of them and their meaning differed in important ways from that developed to the south. From early in the eighteenth century there had in fact been a distinction between British and American attitudes to the native population, with Americans tending to view it as an obstacle to settlement and expansion while the British saw it – in at least some manifestations – as an ally in imperial efforts to maintain and extend the British position on the continent.[24] With the American Revolution and the War of 1812 this difference in view sharpened, and aboriginals became associated with what by the early nineteenth century had begun to be seen as the British North American struggle to survive against American pressure. Figures such as Joseph Brant and Tecumseh emerged as Canadian national heroes,[25] and the willingness to grant a public role to aboriginals carried over into other realms as well. Pauline Johnson was thus able to perform her poetry readings in her ancestral Mohawk dress, the 1908 tercentenary celebrations of Quebec's founding featured active participation by Iroquois chiefs speaking their own language, and in 1927 the governor-general attended Juliette Gaultier's concert of northern Alaskan, Copper Indian, Inuit, Ojibway, and West Coast aboriginal songs.[26]

Much of what went on was, to be sure, as tawdry and exploitative as anything happening in the United States. The appearance of Blackfoot and other aboriginals at the Calgary Stampede was a particularly pathetic sight.[27] Even when cheapness and an absence of dignity didn't determine its contours, the picture presented was in its carefully contrived presentation of the aboriginals as figures who had played a key role in the building of the white person's nation very much a white person's construct. Not only, indeed, were aboriginals almost always presented in terms altogether acceptable to – and usually defined by – their conquerors, they might even, as the celebrated case of Grey Owl made clear, be white themselves.[28] But whatever its defects, this imaging of aboriginals – here was the central difference between the Canadian and the American renderings – kept very much in the foreground the idea that they had played a positive role in the history of Canadian nation-building and that they and their ideology might – *pace* Grey Owl – even be said to have a role in the present. If, in consequence, the aboriginals of the north joined their American counterparts in occupying a space rather different from that assigned to blacks and Asians, it was not exactly the same space as the one filled by those counterparts: the product of a different historical experience, its limits and boundaries were different as well and the area it enclosed offered possibilities and prospects duplicated nowhere else in North America.

If it is clear that essentially racist categories of thinking defined the place assigned to North America's visible minorities before the Second World War, it is equally obvious that those categories began to lose their force and legitimacy during and after that great conflict. And if it is plain that many factors of widely varying sorts – the need to placate an Asian ally, moral revulsion at Nazi excess, the Boasian-inspired shift towards a relativist anthropology, the new socio-economic status of the visible minorities – acted together to produce this result, it is also evident that one – the simple need to find a way to live together as transportation, technology, and integrated economies drove the world's peoples closer to each other – gradually became more prominent.[29]

These realities, obvious enough in their general manifestation, were also plainly operating on this continent. What needs to be noted in the context of any discussion of them in North America, however, is not the fact of their existence on these shores but the peculiar character of the arguments used to relate them to the taking of practical action here. This, indeed, is critical, for the North American forms of those arguments not only gave Canadians and Americans their sense of why what was being advocated ought to be done: those forms emerged out of a long and complicated experience of the adjustment of many different kinds of groups to life within the framework of the same general community. In thus deriving their shape and character from an extensive involvement with the managing of relations among different sorts of entities the arguments in question take on a more than ordinary interest: in them may lay clues for the handling of such phenomena on a broader and more comprehensive front.

The way in which "national tradition" shaped the doing of what got done during and after the Second World War was not, of course, always and everywhere in evidence. The result of the Americans' beginning in 1943 to modify their view of how Asians might be understood in relation to the national whole was shaped almost entirely by the exigencies of their war-time alliance with Chiang Kai-shek's China: ending Chinese exclusion, wrote President Roosevelt, would at once "correct an historic mistake and silence the distorted Japanese propaganda ... [and recognize China's] great contribution to the cause of decency and freedom."[30] For its part, the immediate post-war period's decision to broaden the modification of restrictions on immigration to include Filipinos and East Indians was produced mainly by concern to remove the ground for charges of racism. So far were proponents of this measure from talking in "traditional" American terms about admitting the oppressed and downtrodden to the land of opportunity that such advocates as Congresswoman Clare Booth Luce made a point of linking their support to the fact that, in limiting admissions from the places to 100 a year, what was being proposed would not "lower our living standards and weaken our culture."[31]

By 1952, however, the Walter-McCarran Immigration and Nationality Act was signalling the existence of a sense that Asians could now be brought to the US through an approach that involved seeing them as much as individuals to be judged in terms of their capacity and merit as it did as members of a racial group their association with which was assumed to be the key determinant of their worth – with the result that the number of Chinese admitted to the United States from 1952 to 1960 shot up from virtually nothing to 27,502.[32] The 1965 Immigration Act carried that process forward to the point where its absolute abandonment of racial criteria could be proclaimed in a presidential ceremony at the Statue of Liberty which was clearly intended to associate the new immigrants of colour not only with their predecessors from Europe but also with those predecessors' experience in fitting in, adjusting, and becoming good Americans. As President Johnson put it in remarks linking the initiative to America's traditional interest in the independent, upwardly mobile, autonomous individual, the act "repairs a deep and painful flaw in the fabric of American justice ... those who come [now] will come because of what they are – not because of the land from which they spring."[33]

By the 1970s the thrust toward the new American ethnicity[34] was complicating the task of arguing that what the individual brought by way of cultural or racial baggage ought to count as nothing as that individual moved to adopt American values, profess the American faith, and distinguish him- or self through personal effort and striving. The fact, however, that that thrust, for all its emphasis on heritage and background, never involved abandonment of the idea that Americans were defined essentially by their possession of those values and that faith insured that concern to demonstrate proprietorship of these things would remain much in evidence. Asian-Americans, certainly, felt no diminution in the need to show how "American" they had become. Sometimes, indeed, they made their case in terms that demonstrated a quite extraordinary anxiety that their efforts in this direction be seen and appreciated. "America," ran Harry H.L. Kitano's remarkable 1969 effusion, "likes success stories – the bigger the better. Therefore, America should enjoy the story of the Japanese in the United States ... for it is a story of success Japanese-American style ... [of a] hero [who] pulls himself up by the bootstraps."[35] Theirs – another commentator struck the same note – was "the great American success story writ large – a Horatio Alger tale on an ethnic scale."[36] And a third writer, claiming to be in possession of all the American virtues in spite of his Asian appearance, followed suit by proclaiming himself nothing more or less than an "American in Disguise."[37] Nor was there any slackening of the effort to present Asian-Americans as having objectively accommodated themselves to what they found around them. One study identified them as having "on the whole ... acculturated more rapidly to this country than several European ethnic groups."[38] Another stressed the fact that "like the immigrants from Europe, many Asians saw America as a place for a fresh start."[39] And in a celebrated 1990 meditation on the decline of the white majority in the United States, *Time* Magazine defined the Asian-American communities as ones which "bustle with the pride and promise of middle class America."[40] Whether, in sum, one looked at what Asian-Americans were saying or at what others were saying about them, one saw the same message: Asian-Americans were to be seen as a people whose American experience, like the American experience of others before them, had brought fully into play the individualist virtues so clearly definitive of life in the great republic: caught up and involved in the American way, they related to that way, to each other, and to the community as a whole, not as members of a group to be understood in terms of its own traditions and culture but as exemplars of the general manner of being and existence.

If it took some time for the impact of the national faith on the new view of Asians to become evident, that faith's involvement in the changing sense of blackness and its meaning was obvious from the outset. The grounding of the 1954 Supreme Court decision in Brown *vs* The Board of Education of Topeka on the principle that one's position before the law was no longer to be viewed as something mediated by race certainly made that decision a triumph for the idea that society was to be seen as composed of free and equal individuals. And the fact that major national publications (*Time, Newsweek, US News and World Report*), anxious to contain "leftist" challenges from those who saw society as group or class based, encouraged sympathy for the mainstream Civil Rights movement by presenting it – in contrast with its "radical" competitors – as a force committed to "American" values ensured that those values would be seen as having a close association with that movement.[41]

This, of course, did not mean that all went smoothly. As the persistence of prejudice and discrimination attest, not a few whites continued to operate in terms of the "old" racist ideas. And blacks as well still saw race as something more than a mere irrelevance. In their case, however, this complicated matters, not so much because it involved adherence to old patterns of thought and behaviour, but because it lead to something quite new. Where, that is to say, their sense of themselves as members of a racially defined group had once led to adoption of a defensive posture – which usually meant seeking to ease relations with the white majority by behaving in ways consistent with that majority's image of them[42] – it now pushed them into a much more aggressive stance. Taking up ideas ultimately grounded in the notions of *négritude* and identity developed by such thinkers as Frantz Fanon, blacks urged celebration of blackness as a badge of distinction and even superiority. And not only, some of them asserted, was blackness to be seen as beautiful; it might even be viewed as the foundation on which separate, self-contained, racially defined communities could stand.[43]

But though all this played a central role in the emergence of the new American ethnicity,[44] its significance ought not to be exaggerated. Notwithstanding the vocal and obvious performance of those who took up these arguments, most discussion of blackness and its meaning was informed, not by the notion that status and membership in the community were to be viewed as in some way related to race, but by the idea that these things should be seen as a function of individual worth and accomplishment. Blackness, advocates of this position argued, was certainly not to be disregarded as an element in one's identity. What needed to be noted, however, was that it was a component of that identity in much the same sense that being Polish or Italian or Norwegian helped make up the *personae* of those Americans involved with the ethnic groups those terms designated. And just as a person's membership in such a group had not stood in the way of incorporation into the American mainstream, so also the fact of being what was increasingly referred to as Afro-American need not present insurmountable obstacles to those characterized by that reality as, in typically American fashion, they moved toward the same destination. As one black American would eventually put it, "Hard work, education, individual initiative, stable family life, property ownership – these have always been the means by which ethnic groups have moved ahead in America ... these 'laws' of advancement apply absolutely to black Americans also."[45]

This encouraging fact, some partisans of the argument were quick to point out, didn't at all mean that Afro-Americans were exactly like other immigrant groups. Plainly, as any examination of income, education, and employment statistics would make clear, Afro-Americans in fact stood in a different, inferior position. But, those partisans also insisted – and here the measure of their agreement with the others came obviously into view – this had little to do with race. Historical experience was the critical factor. Afro-Americans were "behind" because of the debilitating effects produced by centuries of involuntary immigration and slavery. And if, as seemed so clear, the problem were socio-economic, and the causes of it the same, it followed that its resolution would also be socio-economic. To the considerable extent, then, that affirmative action programs came to bear on blacks they were defended not on the ground that they offered special assistance to a racially defined group but in terms of the way they helped individual members of that group overcome the disadvantages of their background so that they might compete with others on a footing of genuine equality and fairness. On no account, its friends argued, were such programs to be seen as validating any sort of permanent or special status for a group of people defined in racial terms. Race, to be sure, was a prerequisite for assistance, but that was so only because of its link with social and economic deprivation. Once that had been eliminated, *prima facie* evidence that the United States had become – the term is McGeorge Bundy's – a "racially neutral"[46] society would exist, and individuals would be able to compete freely and equally. Colour would be no more a badge of identity – or a ground for either reverse or regular discrimination – than one's tie to the culture of Ireland, Czechoslovakia, or Finland.

The national ethic's intervention in the understanding of aboriginals was hardly less complicated than its presence in the debate about Asians and blacks. There, too, however, there was little doubt about the character of the final outcome. Initially, indeed, it seemed as though there would hardly be complications at all. Postwar ideas about the importance of seeing "through" racially based stereotypes to the individual "behind" them seemed very clearly to be combining with long-standing notions about moving aboriginals into mainstream society by undermining the supports of their collective identity in ways that were producing a strengthened thrust in that assimilationist direction. The 1950s certainly saw a revival of the kind of thinking behind the Dawes Act (1887), with legislators such as Utah Senator Arthur Watkins spearheading moves to undo the work of the Roosevelt Administration's Indian Reorganization Act (1934) by returning to the notion that the Indians' relationship to the land be allowed to evolve in ways consistent with individual property ownership.[47]

That this "Indian Freedom Program" ran afoul of the revived aboriginal consciousness of the 1960s and 1970s – this was yet another dimension of the new emphasis on ethnicity to which reference has already several times been made – was a difficulty, but the formation of the American Indian Movement (1968), Indian achievement of favourable land settlements in Alaska, Maine, and Massachusetts, and the uprisings of Alcatraz, Mount Rushmore, Fort Sheridan, and above all Wounded Knee (1973) did not by any means succeed in replacing "American" modes of thinking about the "aboriginal problem" with ones based on a strong and clear sense of aboriginals as a group – or groups – to be dealt with as such. To be sure, the Nixon Administration abandoned the "Indian Freedom Program" in 1970, schooling was sometimes altered in ways that allowed native teachers to deal with native culture, and in 1975 Congress committed itself to a policy of Indian self-determination designed to allow those willing and able to sustain it a share in running their own affairs.[48] An assertion that "the Indian world may really have been a genuine, influential civilization worth taking seriously in American history" could also be made.[49] But a tendency to see aboriginals as members of an ethnic minority destined, like all the others, to accommodate itself to the mainstream was much in evidence too. One commentator's observation that "their situation is in come ways singular" was thus followed up by the observation that they "have confronted the complete range of dilemmas familiar to other American minorities" and the even more telling assertion that "modern Pan-Indianism is the crucible in which elements in the larger society combine with elements in Indian life to produce new definitions of identity within the American social order."[50] Another observer presented "the first Americans ... as people who are an integral part of modern American life." "American Indians are vital, integral parts of American society and indeed are important currents in the American mainstream."[51] A third was more circumspect – he was careful to stress aboriginal concern with at least a measure of autonomy – but even he ended by emphasizing the fact that their relationship was to the whole and that it would be worked out in the whole's terms: the aboriginals might want "greater control over their own lives and futures," but they were also to be seen as moving "into more active engagement with the larger society."[52] And use of the term "first Americans" itself spoke volumes, for nothing could have made clearer than its steady and regular deployment the existence of a deep conviction that for all that might set the aboriginals apart, they were, when all was said and done, to be understood as part of the national whole, different from their fellow Americans to be sure, but set apart from them chiefly in terms of the time of their arrival on the American shore.[53] Even the aboriginals themselves might occasionally get caught up in this way of seeing things. Their spokespersons certainly suggested on more than one occasion that what they wanted for themselves and their fellows was perfectly intelligible in terms of familiar and accepted American ways of understanding human aspirations and meeting human needs. Not hesitating, even at the height of agitation in 1969, to identify itself as "American," one group – the American Indian

Task Force – in fact made it plain that, in asking for "the right to pursue our sacred dream" it was seeking nothing more or less than movement towards an objective that was definitively American: a quest of the kind, as it put the matter, "Is the American way. We claim our birthright."[54]

That the matter of defining the terms upon which people of colour could be brought within the American polity as fully functioning members of it should have been resolved in ways altogether consistent with the individualist, egalitarian, and homogenizing elements of the American tradition is not surprising: the idea that Americans were individuals united to each other and to the whole by the bonds of a common faith in equality, individualism, and the American way of life was so deeply entrenched that, once race lost its legitimacy as a tool for the hierarchical ordering of human beings, that idea was bound to come to the forefront.

This did not mean that all traces of a pluralistic view of the nation disappeared completely from view. President Reagan himself could pronounce his ideal to be an "orderly, compassionate, pluralistic society – an archipelago of prospering communities and divergent institutions."[55] And by 1989 sociologist Daniel Bell might classify the United States as "a modern civil society ... one that is heterogeneous and often multiracial," and one in which the problem of order and government turned on recognition of "the principle of toleration and the need for plural communities to agree on rules governing procedures within the frame of constitutionalism."[56]

For the most part, however, rhetoric of this kind yielded to description and imaging of a much more conventional American sort. Reagan's most consistently sounded note, shaped by his concern to avoid any sense that he was underwriting the kind of balkanization of American society such commentators as Kevin Philips feared,[57] simultaneously signalled his view that there was an overarching American faith to which Americans responded as individuals and his sense that this truth needed to be consistently, forcefully, and regularly underscored. And if the re-articulation of traditional values in what one observer called Reagan's "culture of national pride" was intended to reinforce the fact that all citizens were bound together by virtue of their common participation in an overarching system of values,[58] the same was true of the extraordinary image President Bush presented in talking of American society as an ostensibly plural one, the components of which stood out like a "thousand points of light in a broad and peaceful sky." Quite apart from the fact that Bush's exegesis of these words' meaning rendered race invisible by referring to many sorts of groups – church, neighbourhood, educational – without mentioning ones defined by colour, the image itself invited seeing an America whose different parts were to be understood as essentially the same. Not only, indeed, did that image represent the nation as a thing made up of elements distinguishable from each other only in terms of their brightness and intensity; by seeing those elements as anchored and stabilized by their setting in the "broad and peaceful sky," it made them bound to move in a kind of heavenly lockstep, incapable of any independent motion and thrust.[59]

Even presidential candidate Jesse Jackson's compelling metaphor of the Rainbow Coalition yielded to the power of belief in the American way. Increasingly concerned, like most national figures, to emphasize elements of unity rather than division, Jackson first moved away from the image of the rainbow to that of the quilt – something, as he told the Democratic National Convention in 1984, which was, in spite of its variegated pattern, "held together by a common thread."[60] Then, as his campaign developed, it became ever clearer that while the existence of racially defined groups might have been his starting place, it was not where he intended to finish. He began to argue that what was important about groups was the way membership in them operated to keep people out of the mainstream. It then followed that the way to remedy that situation was not to confirm and entrench the existence of those groups – that could only worsen the problem it was intended to resolve – but to make them disappear as things controlling the fate of those belonging to them. Just as the state of being of Italian or Greek descent had ceased to operate as a phenomenon denying full participation in American life to those characterized by it, so also must the same happen in regard to "blackness," "yellowness," and "redness." The need was to create an effective citizenship for visible minorities, to give "a united voice to those blacks, browns, Native Americans, Asian Americans, Arab Americans, Jewish Americans, and Caribbean Americans and the poor who lack *power*,"[61] something that could only by done by diminishing the importance of what set them apart in favour of what would unite them with each other and with Americans in general. For Jackson, in short, the only problem with the existing model of American society was that too few Americans were represented in it. Excluded Americans lacked power, effective citizenship; the way to resolve their difficulty lay not in recognizing and empowering the groups to which they belonged but in rendering their groupness "invisible" in the way European-based ethnicities had been rendered invisible. Those people could then be dealt with, and act, as what the American creed insisted they were: citizens entitled to their share of involvement in and control over how their society was run.

Once again, then, the enduring strength of the quintessential American idea was evidenced: Americans were, in the end, to be defined, not by membership in whatever sub-group to which they might belong, but by their common orientation toward a set of values and the behaviour those values enjoined. Far from having developed into something conceived of as a community of communities, Americans' society remained what it had always been held to be: a comity of principle, commitment, and idea, acceptance of membership in which united individual Americans to each other and to the whole they combined to make up. As Everett Carll Ladd argued in 1987, "The United States is a nation founded on an ideology ... [which] is given force and coherence by a far-reaching commitment to the individual." It was, in consequence, to this "expression of a nation-defining consensus on political values," to the Constitution embodying it, and to the individual American's acceptance of it, that one must look in order to grasp and comprehend the character of the whole.[62]

Canadians no less than Americans viewed the problem of race in the postwar period through their own sense of society as well as by means of the prism made available by the new notions about that phenomenon itself. But where the putting of these two things together had had one consequence south of the border, it would produce quite a different outcome north of it. At the root of this development was the fact that Canadians had learned to see the national whole quite differently than Americans had come to view theirs. Rendered by their history quite incapable of dismissing the importance of certain group affiliations – linguistic, ethnic – as factors of consequence in the definition of the individual's identity and relationship to the whole, Canadians came to terms with the new non-racist thinking not by viewing race as something to be discounted in principle but by granting it status as a constituent of identity and a mediator of one's relations with the whole which was no more or less worthy of recognition than other constituents.[63]

This did not mean that this sort of recognition of race always dominated the Canadian approach. Citizenship and immigration minister Ellen Fairclough certainly defended her department's 1962 moves to end racially based quotas on immigration by focusing in no small part on the recognition this would give to the individual: the proposed changes, she insisted, would permit "any suitably qualified person" to be considered for immigration "entirely on his [sic] own merits."[64] Similarly the federal government's 1969 White Paper proposing the abolition of aboriginal status was, in its view of aboriginals as candidates for assimilation into the white mainstream, built on the notion that group characteristics associated with race and visible difference were to be treated as of virtually no consequence.[65] And even in the very course of stressing the country's racial and cultural diversity, the 1988 Multiculturalism Act could be used as a vehicle for projecting the idea that Canada, "a family of individuals," must never lose sight of the integrity of the person.[66]

If, however, the Canadian recognition of race and colour was by no means universal, unqualified, and omnipresent it was enough in evidence to warrant the claim that Canadians did indeed see these things as realities still having to be recognized rather than as matters which might now be ignored. Certainly, immediate post-war supporters of enfranchising Asian-Canadians assembled their case not by treating race as something to be set aside but by drawing new conclusions from the fact of its existence. Race remained, they insisted, a reality, but where it had once been viewed as the ground for a hierarchical and exclusionary understanding of society, it must now be seen simply as an instrument for the categorization of certain groups of accepted and accommodated citizens. As the Vancouver *News-Herald* put it in 1946, "In a new world, drawn from all races," maintaining a policy of discrimination based on colour made no sense.[67]

A tendency to assess claims to just treatment by considering the status and posture of the group on whose behalf those claims were being made was particularly evident in the part of the suffrage argument relating specifically to Chinese-Canadians. Supporters of their right to vote argued that these people had been given the franchise not on the ground that proper and just treatment of the individual required it, but because the Chinese-Canadian community had as a collective entity earned the right to have it. Generally loyal and patriotic during the war, that community's contribution of personnel to the armed forces was particularly noteworthy. So striking a display of civic and military virtue on the part of one of society's components clearly deserved the obvious and appropriate response from society at large and it was to ensure that that group got that response that the vote had been conferred. That was why – British Columbia MP George Pearkes drew explicit attention to the notions of obligation and responsibility in the decision – "the

Government of BC has given the franchise not only to these young [service] men but to all Canadian-born Chinese."[68]

Supporters of the restoration of the right of Japanese-Canadians to live and travel anywhere in Canada similarly founded their case on arguments that turned on a sense of society as an agglomeration of groups – racial as well as other kinds – though in this case emphasis was on the relationship between treating each of those groups fairly and the smooth and harmonious functioning of the whole. Canada, proclaimed the Winnipeg *Free Press*, is "a nation of minorities." Maintaining any one of them in a position of inferiority was fraught with great danger, for "if this precedent is once established for one minority it can be applied to any minority" – a situation that would lead not only to unimaginable injustice but complete social breakdown.[69]

The sense that racial, like other groups, existed, and that law and policy was to operate on them as such, might even extend to collectivities not yet a part of Canadian society. Fairclough herself, for all her emphasis on using immigration reform to open the way for the triumph of individual merit, made it clear that those mainly to profit from the 1962 changes would all be groups of people defined in racial terms: "The chief beneficiaries," as she told the House of Commons, "will be the Asians, Africans, and nationals of Middle Eastern countries."[70]

As time passed, the emerging Canadian sense of race as a reality to be accommodated became particularly evident in arguments about its relevance to the nation's character as a political society. The tendency in the United States – the comparison, in this domain as in others, is instructive – was to move away from the notion that race was a factor of consequence. The result was a clear departure from the idea that politicians identifiable as members of visible minorities should be seen as nothing other than representatives of their groups and a shift toward the notion that they were to be viewed as the agents of racially mixed constituencies to whose voters they could relate as if race had ceased to be a factor. The assumption that if one was black one's voters would be too as in the classic case of Harlem Congressman Adam Clayton Powell thus yielded to the idea, epitomized by the new black mayors of the 1960s, that this need not at all be the case.[71] The "disappearance" of race was even more clearly evident in the 1976 election of S.I. Hayakawa to the United States Senate. Attributed almost entirely to his defence of "American" values while president of San Francisco

State College (as one commentator put it, his "defiance of radicals ... propelled him into the United States' Senate"), his victory perfectly embodied the idea that voter and candidate should deal with each other in terms of their interests as citizens and Americans, with any sort of sub-group affiliation relegated firmly to the sidelines.[72] Racial awareness and identification did not as a practical matter vanish altogether – black Congressmen, for example, caucused as a group – but the principle was clear: members of racial minorities in politics were to be seen not as representatives of their communities but as proof that racism was ceasing to impede the citizen as he or she sought status and advancement within a polity of free, autonomous, and equal individuals. Even as Jesse Jackson's emergence as a national political figure was held to signal the decline – perhaps the end – of racism, it could also be seen as exemplifying the kind of mobility and achievement long thought to be at the heart of the American idea. As *Time* magazine put it in 1988, Jackson had not only "taught white America that a black person is ... somebody," he has taught it that "he [or she] can be anybody. Even President of the United States."[73]

In this area as in others the contrast with Canada is striking. Here, the sense that the political process had in some formal way to recognize and allow for the existence of the racially defined groups that helped make up the society over whose affairs it was presiding became steadily stronger. This, to be sure, did not completely define the understanding of all members of visible minorities who occupied elective office. New Democrats Rosemary Brown and Howard McCurdy have been as concerned with cleavages of class and gender as with those of race,[74] while even Lincoln Alexander's sojourn in the House of Commons as a member of so non-ideological a party as the Conservative saw him function, and identify himself, as more than simply a black MP.[75] But if these elected politicians haven't especially wanted to see themselves – or to be seen – as giving a kind of virtual representation to the racial group of which they are members, others have willingly conformed to the view of society as composed of various sorts of groups to the reality of which their presence in public life offers testimony. Douglas Jung certainly did not hide what he felt to be the relationship between his election as the first Chinese-Canadian MP and what he viewed this to mean for the way Canadian society as a whole was to be understood.[76] Moe Sihota's maintenance of his close ties with the Indo-Canadian community following his 1986 election to the British Columbia Legislature was altogether consistent with the early identification of him as in some sense a representative of one of the many groups of which the country consisted.[77] And the fact that Manitoba Legislature member Elijah Harper moved to dispatch the Meech Lake Accord in the name of the nation's aboriginal peoples makes plain the way he viewed himself and his responsibilities.[78]

That members of racially definable groups who hold public office have come increasingly to play a part in validating and giving expression to the idea that Canada is a society of racially based as well as other sorts of particularisms is plainest in relation to appointees to public office. Almost without exception, these people have received what they have not just as a recognition of their individual ability and distinction but also as a sign that the groups to which they belong have status as component parts of the Canadian community. Certainly the Diefenbaker government's strong orientation toward an understanding of Canada as a class-, race-, and even gender-differentiated society[79] led it to use the Senate to encourage that view of matters. And if the 1960 appointment of James Gladstone as the first aboriginal senator was the earliest outcome of this determination,[80] the Trudeau government's 1984 selection of Anne Cools as the first black member of that body showed it retaining its vitality.[81] By 1990 the use of appointees to signal the fact that Canada was a nation of many sorts of particularism was established enough to ensure that the Citizens' Forum on National Unity, organized to provide a vehicle for the expression of public opinion on national unity and constitutional reform, would include a black and an aboriginal as well as French speakers, representatives of the regions, ethnics, and women.[82]

At the provincial level the same point was made in exactly the same way. When, in consequence, British Columbia Premier W.A.C. Bennett included Kamloops mayor Peter Wing in his delegation to the 1968 constitutional conference, his action did not simply underline the fact that Canada was a nation of particularisms or even the reality that those particularisms varied from region to region: it drove home the point that some of them were racially based.[83] Ontario Premier David Peterson's choice of a black and a Chinese for his cabinet was intended to underscore the racially heterogeneous character of his province.[84] Lincoln Alexander's 1985 appointment as the first black lieutenant-governor of Ontario was, as federal cabinet minister David Crombie put it, meant to be "a symbol to this province, that in this province there is a place in the Ontario sun for everybody."[85] And when in 1988 David Lam became British Columbia's first lieutenant-governor of Chinese origin, the message was equally clear: given the fact that, as Lam

himself said, "My role through life has been that of a bridge builder, offering help to those of different cultures," it was altogether
appropriate that he should be the Crown's representative in a
jurisdiction where racial diversity was especially evident.[86]

If public figures of colour in Canada convey a quite different message about the relationship of race to society than do their American counterparts, the same is true of the signal sent by Canadian
films and television programs. Here too an explicit comparison is
worth making. What appeared on American screens dealt very
heavily in the idea that it was the integrity of the individual rather
than the character or influence of the group which had to be
brought into view.

The tendency to operate in terms of the old stereotypes did
linger on – Hollywood's "rehabilitation" of the Japanese saw Mar-
lon Brando case in the role of the amiable but childlike interpreter
in *Teahouse of the August Moon* (1956), Mickey Rooney's Japanese
character in *Breakfast at Tiffany's* (1961) was even more retrogres-
sively stereotypical, and the television version of *Amos 'n' Andy*
endured into the 1960s.[87] But even more than Burt Lancaster's
Indian in *Apache* (1954), Sidney Poitier's black in *Guess Who's
Coming to Dinner* (1967) clearly displayed a marked tendency to
expose racist thinking as a barrier to the getting of a "good" view of
the individual "hidden" by skin colour. By the time the Poitier film
appeared, the thrust in this direction was very obvious – and no less
plain was the even more critical reality that "seeing" that individual
was coming to mean getting a picture of him or her as altogether
indistinguishable (save in terms of the now unimportant fact of
skin colour) from the characteristically "American" types who made
up America's white majority. The fact, indeed, that the larger
number of blacks who began to appear on American television in
the mid-1960s were almost always given roles that could have gone
to whites[88] made it clear that the impulse was very much to show
that race didn't "matter." And if supporting roles – teachers,
students, secretaries, an astronaut – sent this message, the same was
even more obviously the case when blacks became principals. Bill
Cosby's portrayal of secret agent Alexander Scott in *I Spy* (1965–8)
could, in the view of one commentator, "have been played by a
white man."[89] Diahann Carroll's character Julia Baker in *Julia*
(1968–71) was, as Carroll herself put it, a "white Negro."[90] And
Ron Glass's Detective Ron Harris on *Barney Miller* (1975–83), "was
an ambitious and upwardly mobile black professional ... Like
Cosby's Alexander Scott, he was also a convert to the values of a

white, middle class America and his character did not pose a physical or sexual threat to common sensibilities."[91]

Television programs and films that featured a variety of racial groups were also informed by the idea that what lay behind visible difference were essentially undifferentiated individuals attuned to the values of mainstream America. Of the black, Asian, and several types of ethnic members of the starship Enterprise's polyglot crew on *Star Trek* (1966–9), the only one portrayed as genuinely different – physically, temperamentally, and culturally – was the Vulcan Mr Spock: a being literally not from this world. The aboriginal component in the character of Will Sampson's asylum inmate "the Chief" in *One Flew Over the Cuckoo's Nest* (1975) was developed only insofar as was necessary to make the point that all people, irrespective of background, are in the common predicament created by authority and an irrational world. And in putting "chinks" as well as "spooks" into the category of persons whom the bigoted Archie Bunker found wanting, the script writers of *All in the Family* (1971–82) associated them with the larger number of persons whose character, personality, and individual worth Bunker's racism prevented him from acknowledging.[92]

Even efforts, when they finally came, to consider members of racial groups as such suggested that "American mass culture continued to operate as an ... assimilative force, seeking to maintain social stability while gradually merging people of different backgrounds into the cultural mainstream."[93] Black shows that were too "black" either failed to find a sufficiently large audience on prime time television – the case with the *Richard Pryor Show* (1977)[94] – or were laundered to gain the white following necessary in the competition for ratings – as happened with Richard Roundtree's character John Shaft in the early 1970s.[95] *Roots* (1977) and *Roots: The Next Generation* (1979) managed to capture something of the black Americans' slave heritage, but they also told their tale as a kind of immigrant epic, "a bourgeois success story," the recounting of which situated blacks in a major national myth in just the same way as immigrants of all sorts were located there.[96] The appearance of Mr T., on one level a figure of threatening ghetto blackness, was a gesture in the direction of defining some of the links that might exist among race, culture, and identity, but in the end that interesting figure too became a protagonist of the idea that differences among individuals really were matters of appearance only: B.A. Baracus, Mr T.'s character on *The A Team* (1983–4), was mechanically adept and a man of daunting native intelligence, while the public persona Mr T. himself adopted involved him in espousing the values – education, self-help, hard work – of middle-class America.[97]

In Canada the prevailing ethic helped to insure that the visual media would not only attempt to assert the integrity of the individual but also move to explore, or at least acknowledge, whatever relationships might exist among racial characteristics, identity formation, and group consciousness. The move in that direction, to be sure, was not always straightforward. Canadian feature films – *Act of the Heart* (1970), *Outrageous!* (1977) – showed black faces mixed in undifferentiatedly with white ones, while television's concern to present members of visible minority groups in terms of their personal competence and identities put even less emphasis on subgroup affiliation. Broadcast journalists of Chinese, East Indian, and Japanese origin have, in consequence, become steadily more prominent with no significance being attached to their racial background, while dramatic vehicles such as *Street Legal* (1987–94) and *De Grassi High* (1988–92) featured characters of colour who were distinguished from their colleagues, friends, and schoolmates by nothing more than the traits of personality and behaviour rooted in their differing individual temperaments.[98]

But the central trend is clear. That trend, moreover, is exemplified not only in such documentaries as the National Film Board's *Circle of the Sun* (1961), the first film to record the Blood Indian Sun Dance, which acknowledged that members of racially distinct groups could find at least part of their identity in the rituals of the group to which they belonged.[99] The trend can be seen revealing itself in feature film making and television programming as well. The treatment given the history of southwestern Ontario's black community in the four-part series from the mid-1960s, *The Road*, certainly made the point that that community's relation to slavery, abolition, and the underground railway gave it a unique and special character.[100] The television version of Pierre Berton's *The National Dream* (1974) acknowledged the essential role of Chinese labourers in the construction of the Canadian Pacific Railway and even attempted to portray something of their working conditions and culture.[101] Several episodes of the *Beachcombers* (1972–90) depicted Japanese, East Indians, and Middle Easterners as at one and the same time participants in their own community rhythms and actively involved in the general life of the British Columbia coast.[102] And *King of Kensington* (1974–80) presented an urban community made plural and diversified not simply by the ethnic presence in it but because of the role in its life of blacks and Asians as well.[103]

The aboriginals continued to hold the most prominent place on the nation's television and cinema screens, a fact which is a measure of the native peoples' continuing involvement in white Canadians' efforts to define and comprehend the country. This, moreover, was true in more than the sense that larger numbers of aboriginal characters were to be seen, and in more than the fact that those characters began increasingly to be played by aboriginal actors. It showed itself as well in the critically important respect that efforts were consistently made to portray individual aboriginals as beings shaped by and related to their culture, a phenomenon which was itself explored on no small number of occasions.

This was sometimes done through efforts to deal with native cultures on their own terms. Initial attempts smacked very much of tokenism – the "Indian" on *The Forest Ranger* (1964–6) was played by a white – but even here there was an attempt to present the character as the exemplar of forest lore and a way of life.[104] *Cariboo Country* (1960–7) didn't simply feature aboriginal characters (with Chief Dan George playing one of them): it attempted to treat some of the realities of aboriginal life and culture. Two 1966 shows in particular – "All Indian" and "Sarah's Copper" – did this, managing in the process to make something of the values and world view of the Chilcotins intelligible to the larger community beyond.[105] And the very popular *Beachcombers* used the character of Jesse (played by Patrick John) to project its audiences into coastal aboriginal life. For example, in one episode ("Steelhead," 1977) Jesse undergoes the ritual process of purification through the four-day fast that would bring him a vision confirming his life path and identity.[106]

More, however, than the aboriginal in some kind of communal isolation was brought into view. Jesse himself functioned not just to introduce "the distinctive motif of Salish values and customs" but to show "the conflicts and synthesis of those conflicts with modern life."[107] As early as 1961 the dramatic production *Riel* could present "both sides of the issue" in at least one phase of the confrontation of white, aboriginal, and Metis values.[108] A particularly poignant indication of what might be at work in the clash of cultures was given in the 1964 made for television film, *The Education of Phyllistine*, which used fine performances by Dan George and Nancy Sandy to convey something of the experience of an aboriginal girl in a white school.[109] And at the end of the 1980s the program *Spirit Bay*, in its depiction of life in a fictional northern Ontario Ojibway community, presented something of what it meant to be concerned with the preservation of one culture and set of values in the face of relentless pressures from another culture. "The residents of Spirit Bay [are thus presented as having] adapted to white society while retaining traditional links to the land through trapping, fishing, and hunting. The episodes ... focus on the spiritual kinship be-

tween Spirit Bay families, nature, and modern life on the reserve."[110]

Not only producers and writers attempted to deal in the conviction that identity in the world they portrayed could never be
understood unless attention was given to groups as well as the
individuals composing them. Actors and other cultural activists
pressed the point too. In their case, though, the issue was rather
different: preoccupied with their own circumstances as job seekers
and citizens, they focused not on how best to depict worlds imagined for film and television but on how the one in which they
actually lived was to be understood and confronted. Here too,
however, the national ethic intervened, ensuring that that "real"
world would be made sense of in much the same manner as the
"created" one. Far, then, from basing their claims to work and be
seen on an appeal exclusively to the principles of individual rights
and equality of opportunity, these actors argued their case in quite
different terms. As members of a society asserting its character as a
community of equally important groups, each of which has the
same right to be "seen" as the others, they put forward their right
to insist that their group – and they as members of it – be seen too.
As the black actor Richardo Keens-Douglas put it, there could be
no doubting the fact that the country's character as a community of
groups each of which had the right to be seen validated the appearance of visible minority actors on stage and even justified their
playing "white" roles. "Canada ... is a mosaic, and we have to help
each other."[111]

The same sort of argument, the core of which was the idea that
Canada consisted of groups among which various sorts of obligation and responsibility subsisted, was also at the root of the black
community's impatience with what it saw as the racist character of
the Royal Ontario Museum's (ROM) exhibit *Into the Heart of Africa*
and the irresponsibility of the Canadian Radio and Television
Commission's (CRTC) decision to reject an application for a black
music station in Toronto. Irritation at the fact that the ROM was
"not really seeking assistance or wanting input"[112] from that community certainly grew out of a feeling that some sort of prescriptive
right to be consulted was being ignored, while the reaction of
Milestone Communications president Denham Jolly to the CRTC
judgment (which would, he said, make the black community ask
where it "fits into the mosaic of Canada"[113]) expressed even more
clearly the feeling that the position and entitlements of a group
were being disregarded. In these cases, to be sure, the anxiety for
action was as important as the view of society which validated it.

And with reason, too, for, as Chinese-Canadian broadcaster Adrienne Clarkson had once put it, no matter how attractive the Canadian idea of society might be to persons of colour, it was by no means enough simply to proclaim it: "We are in the process of creating something unique in Canada" but the world must be able to "see" what it is.[114] This shift in emphasis ought not, however, to obscure the fact that the same basic point remained at issue: cultural activists of colour, like script writers dealing with matters of race on the screen, saw the nation's people as divided into (among other things) racially distinguishable groups, the individual members of which derived at least some of their rights and sense of identity from the fact of that membership. On that central sense of things activists stood united.

Perhaps the clearest indication of the fact that the Canadian sense of nation conditioned a response to race and community quite different from that of Americans is to be seen in the realm of ritual and symbolism. Ceremony, sign, and rite of course function in both societies in broadly the same way – their Durkheimian role in enforcing social solidarity hardly needs to be noted[115] – but their fulfilment of that function is not at all similar. In the United States the fixed and homogeneous character of the nation which symbol represents and membership in which public ritual affirms assures that those symbols and rituals will be stable and unchanging: embodiments of a nation and a national faith always and everywhere the same, they must themselves not vary or alter. When, therefore, the moment came to show that, like the nation itself, ritual and symbol could have as much meaning for persons of colour as they did for white Americans, this was done not by changing them but by demonstrating that they could accommodate and embrace (sometimes quite literally) those different sorts of person. So strongly did this imperative operate that when the organizers of the great Civil Rights March of 1963 decided to go to the nation's capital, they were moved to make the very monuments of the country's commitment to democracy and freedom their focus. Concentrating particularly on the Washington Monument and the Lincoln Memorial, the marchers' occupancy of the space between and around those grand edifices functioned to show that what they were seeking simply had to be seen as entirely consistent with the spirit of nation with which those fixed, stable, and constant structures had always resonated.[116] And when official America reached out to show that race was now not to be perceived as an obstacle to involvement in the public life, it too moved to use symbol and ceremony to make the point, not through changes in that symbol and ceremony, but by bringing blacks publicly and clearly into contact with them very much as they stood. The fact that race was now held at the highest levels not to matter could, as a result, be indicated by a widely circulated photograph showing Martin Luther King in the Oval Office with President Johnson,[117] while the same message might be sent by inviting Leontyne Price to sing "America the Beautiful" at the inauguration ceremonies of 1965.[118]

By the 1980s the thrust to show that existing symbol and ritual could epitomize the involvement of all sorts of people in the national life had broadened considerably. Not only was King given a national holiday, an act associating him with "an honour granted to only one other US citizen, George Washington";[119] others besides blacks were being explicitly linked to the sacred mysteries, rites, and texts of the republic. The cover of *Time* magazine's special issue marking the two hundredth anniversary of the Constitution thus featured the opening words of that document superimposed on a background of white, yellow, black, brown, and red faces,[120] while – as a striking colour photograph of two elderly Chinese-American women against the backdrop provided by a wall-painting of the American flag made clear[121] – proximity to Old Glory itself could be used to suggest full and complete participation in the life of the nation.

Nowhere was the concern to associate minorities with the stable and unchanging symbols of American life clearer than in the way those minorities were brought into contact with military dress. Sometimes, of course, that dress did vary. General MacArthur himself wore nonregulation clothing during the early period of America's involvement in World War Two, and "in Vietnam uniforms were drastically modified by love beads and peace slogans." That departures from the norm in physical appearance might be tolerated was demonstrated by black soldiers' winning of the right to wear Afros.[122] All of this, however, was done on an *ad hoc* basis. What counted remained, in principle, "a standardized uniform to symbolize the nation": as "a symbolic declaration that an individual will adhere to group norms and standardized roles" that garment simply couldn't be allowed to lose its character as a thing always and everywhere the same. The American armed forces therefore issued no clerical collars for Christian chaplains, no yarmulkes for Jews, and "efforts by military personnel to use turbans have also met with failure."[123] Far too suggestive of a subgroup affiliation which might in some way diminish loyalty to the army and the state it served, these adornments made way for a style of dress which reinforced the sense that the whole – whether army or society – was made up of essentially undifferentiated individuals linked directly to it. So deeply entrenched was the idea that in putting on a recognized sort of uniform one was, as it were, taking on the outward and visible sign of an inward and common identity that that idea even influenced the significance indicated by non-military dress. Thus when the South African black leader Nelson Mandela appeared on the streets of New York in June 1990 wearing a New York Yankees jacket and cap, the message was clear: worthy, as his American admirers thought, of identification with the fundamental values and assumptions of American society, he could quite appropriately be costumed in clothing whose long-standing association with a central element in American civilization made it the perfect way to symbolize that identification.[124]

In Canada, the relation between national symbol and the new view of race was rather different. Far from signalling their recognition of the racial minorities' altered status by associating the members of those minorities with the fixed and unchanging things of the nation, Canadians set out to accomplish that all-important goal by modifying the configuration, set, and design of those very things. In this, as in other areas, Canadians were conforming with national tradition, for the early emergence of strong particularisms had made it nothing short of mandatory that symbol, song, and ritual be framed in terms reflective of diversity and pattern. Even in the days of Canada's strong British orientation the devices used to represent the nation stressed the variegated character of its people – as the *Maple Leaf Forever*'s (1871) reference to the "lily, thistle, shamrock, [and] rose" makes clear.[125] The national anthem itself defined the country's unity in terms of its inhabitants' occupancy of a shared geographical space ("the True North") rather than of unifying creed or common ethnicity, the song's lyrics were written in two languages, and the meanings conveyed in each of these were so dissimilar as to have virtually nothing in common.[126]

In time, as awareness of ethnic pluralism as well as linguistic duality deepened, symbols changed to reflect the fact: by the 1960s the "old" national flag could be retired from service and a new one, more fully capable of embodying what was now perceived to be the country's character, sought. Prime Minister Pearson's preferred design of three maple leaves – one for Canadians of English-speaking background, one for those of French, and one for all the others – indicated just how far the move to change symbol to accord with "reality" might go. It manifested an obvious and complete acceptance of the idea that tradition and continuity were acceptable only insofar as they might be compatible with the ever greater variety time's passage seemed to be bringing.[127] Even the final design sent the same sort of message: representing the idea that the only acceptable symbol was one proclaiming the unity of the nation a thing inhering in its (diverse) peoples' sharing of a common landscape and environment, the single maple leaf's origin in a concern that openness and accommodation be allowed for could not have been clearer.[128] And when, finally, the new flag was flown in public, the circumstances of its appearing there almost always reflected the fact of diversity too: generally raised – save at purely federal functions – in company with the flags the provinces had selected to express and embody their several senses of identity, it snapped and waved in ways that could not help but underscore the central place of particularisms in the national life.[129]

Given all this, it is hardly surprising that once race presented itself in its post-war guise, it too became a reality to be accommodated by change and alteration. Various sorts of symbolic form accordingly found themselves caught up in a kind of flux and movement. The thrust in that direction certainly became evident in public architecture. Already in marked contrast to the American approach (the formidably consistent neo-classicism of Washington's public buildings stood in its uniform "republican" character at the opposite pole from the mixing of styles evident in such things as Ottawa's gothic Parliament buildings and its "chateauesque" Supreme Court[130]), the tendency literally to build an acknowledgment of heterogeneity into the nation's physical representation of itself had by the 1980s produced the extraordinary Museum of Civilization designed by Metis architect Douglas Cardinal. Not only, then, did that building's long, low, curved, and flowing lines root it firmly in the Metis tradition of involvement with the Canadian prairie landscape (Cardinal had wanted a structure "inspired by the land and people here");[131] seen in association with all that lay around it, the building perfectly embodied the point that Canada had to be understood in terms of the presence in it of several different types of group, racial as well as cultural and linguistic.

Willingness to adapt and modify symbolic displays in order that racially based heterogeneity be "seen" is particularly evident in relation to the vexed question of military and para-military dress. Canada is linked to a tradition which, since the Eighteenth century days of the kilt's acceptance, has not viewed uniforms as in some way bound to avoid acknowledgment of the cultural and racial spe-

cificity of their wearers.[132] Because of this authorities in both the
Canadian armed and police forces have been moving to alter dress
codes in ways consistent with the new awareness of racial heterogeneity. Both the Canadian Forces[133] and the RCMP[134] now permit
the wearing of turbans, and various city policy forces have made it
clear that aboriginal officers will be permitted to wear braids.[135]

Even the Canadian Constitution has evolved a symbolic as well as
legal import consistent with the general pattern. Once by virtue of
its language provisions a "sign" that Canada was to be viewed as
linguistically dual, it has gradually come to stand for (as well as
institutionalize) the fact that the country has also to be seen as a
collection of groups differentiated by gender, ethnicity, and race.
The changes made in its character by the Diefenbaker Bill of Rights
(1960) were certainly seen as conveying this message. Those
changes indicated, proclaimed one of their staunchest supporters,
that the position of racial as well as other minorities was now
recognized, a fact that, had it been a reality twenty years earlier,
would have had a decisive relevance for "the relocated Japanese of
World War II"[136] More clearly still, the 1982 Charter of Rights was
taken as a quite unambiguous sign of the country's character as
(among other things) a society of groups, each of which had rights
and some of which were racial in nature. The kind of "segmental
accommodation" evident in the new document's according of
recognition to aboriginal peoples clearly indicated, thought one
observer, that the country was very much to be seen in this way.[137]
What had been done to provide for gender, race, and the disabled,
observed another, made it at least as obvious that the nation should
be understood in terms of "concepts of community based on
shared characteristics such as race, sex, or handicap, that transcend
provincial boundaries."[138] And, said a third, the fact that "the
Charter ... hand[s] out particular constitutional niches to particular
categories of Canadians, such as women, aboriginals, etc.,"[139] very
clearly reinforced a view of the country as something to be understood as a congeries of groups some of which were racially defined.

That one can see important differences in the manner in which the
Canadian and American understandings of nation and society has
led inhabitants of the two countries to respond to the issue of race
is clear: thanks to quite dissimilar views concerning whether, to
what extent, and in what ways the individual's identity and relation
to the whole is mediated by subgroup affiliations the two societies
have, in fact, followed pathways that could hardly be more separate.

To note this truth, let it immediately be added, is not necessarily to say that one of these routes has up to now been in some clear way superior to the other. The American effort to end discrimination by insisting that the citizen be seen and judged as an individual has been, at best, a qualified success,[140] while the Canadian approach to the matter also leaves much to be desired.[141] But if honours are not to be awarded on the basis of the relationship these approaches bear to what has so far happened, perhaps they can be conferred on the ground of their consistency – or lack of it – with what appears likely to come. In this respect, the Canadian approach has a clear and definable edge. Altogether in harmony with the emerging sense that society is to be seen in more complex ways than the liberal, homogenizing, conformitarian model allows, its utility as a guide to action and understanding in the future seems, in fact, all but guaranteed.

It is certainly hard to deny that approach's congruence with the developing notion – articulated by William H. McNeill and others – that homogeneous societies of essentially undifferentiated individuals are, in the sweep of history, anything but "normal." Resting on the view that this sense of things emerged only in the quite special conditions in western Europe during the eighteenth century, and turning even more centrally on the claim that whatever realities may once have validated it are now disappearing, McNeill's case for the way the world should be seen (in which he asserts that "marginality and pluralism were and are the norm of civilized existence") offers, in fact, nothing short of a rendering on the global scale of the sense of things in terms of which Canadians have for some time been tending to think.[142]

It is equally difficult to dispute the harmony between the Canadian idea and what theorists are beginning to posit concerning the relationship among race, identity, and culture. Following the anti-racist revolution of the 1940s to its logical conclusion; developing the view that there is no more sense in dismissing all awareness of race as involving inevitably racist "socially-imagined"[143] categories than there is in rejecting the idea that feelings of identity may be based on a sense of things shared with members of the same racial group; and asserting that one can notice that awareness, those feelings, and the culture they help produce without being obliged to view them hierarchically in relation to others, those theorists have done much to show just how consistent with the Canadian sense of things the emerging understanding of the relationship is. Herder himself, they point out, insisted that race as well as language and ethnicity helped define the different cultures whose variety and equality he wished to celebrate. He thus rebuked Kant for his belief in the inferiority of blacks to Europeans,[144] and put the essential conviction contained in that gesture even more clearly into play in his observation that "the shapeless rocks with which the Chinese ornaments his garden" were no less evidence of "the plan of reflective understanding [which] is everywhere observable" than was "the ideal beauty of Greece."[145] The thrust to establish the claim that the culture which emerges from the activity of a racially definable group is to be treated as a cultural "fact," no more or less worthy of note, study, and appreciation than any other such reality, is even more obvious in what contemporary theorists have been saying on their own behalf. John Rex has been very much at pains to insist on the importance of examining what emerges from the circumstance that "individuals may value physical characteristics similar to their own, identify with them, and pursue actions with them so that they come to share not merely physical but cultural characteristics."[146] M. Michael Rosenberg has similarly stressed the legitimacy of looking at the consequences of race's functioning "as a symbolic marker used by individuals to characterize themselves and others."[147] And Janet Helms' concern to bring under review what is produced by the "sense of group or collective identity based on one's *perception* [sic] that he or she shares a common racial heritage with a particular racial group" is no less clearly evident.[148]

Perhaps hardest of all to question is the Canadian approach's consistency with what has been establishing itself as the conventional, post-modern wisdom of the age. Many-dimensioned, but based essentially on the notion that the nature of the relationship between language and the reality it purports to describe precludes any grappling with essences, absolutes, or the real, that wisdom invites us to deal with the world in terms of the tentative, indeterminate, contingent, and provisional, valuing all that we come into contact with in terms of its potential not to bring us to a sense of what is right, authoritative, or final, but to enrich our understanding of the problem, situation, or reality we confront. And if, in the words of Jean-François Lyotard, it is clear that "postmodern knowledge ... refines our sensitivity to differences and reinforces our ability to tolerate the incommensurable,"[149] it is no less obvious that the Canadian sense of society – resting as it does and must on the idea that there *is* no idea, no orthodoxy, no universalizing discourse in terms of which an *imperium* of language, ethnicity, culture, or race can be imposed – is characterized by just the sort of demanding but liberating thrust toward the open, accommodative, and essentially indefinable which is at the heart of that way of seeing the world.

There is, then, much of a general and wide-ranging sort to be said in support of the proposition that Canadian activities in the domain of multiracial management mesh perfectly with what the contemporary sense of society and the world suggests ought to be done. Perhaps, however, the most dramatic indication of these actions' consistency with developing ideas is something much more focused, specific, and, it has to be said, surprising: the fact that Americans themselves are showing signs of movement in the direction it indicates. Finally forced by the sheer intractability of race and racial consciousness to confront the realities those phenomena represent and help shape, not a few Americans are turning away from the liberal-individualist idea of society and moving toward one framed in terms which concede a much larger community-making role to various sorts of groups not the least important of which are those racial formations themselves. Going, in consequence, far beyond the quite limited pluralism of the 1960s and 1970s, Americans have been starting to think and act in terms of a sense of the sort of real and substantial diversity that simultaneously (1) allows a link between race, culture, and identity and (2) demonstrates acceptance of the idea that the individual's involvement in the whole may after all be mediated by more enduring and substantial factors than those associated with simple ethnicity. This, moreover, is manifest in more than the fact that minorities are becoming more self-conscious, assertive, and forthright: US society at large is shifting toward an altered sense of how these groups' place in the whole is to be understood. One sees, in consequence, the sort of heightened Chinese-American consciousness embodied in the fiction of Maxine Hong Kingston accompanied by a greater disposition on the part of the majority of the population to understand the Chinese-American experience not simply in terms of the adoption of American values but as something shaped by things – strong family structure, for example – rooted in the imperatives of Chinese life and culture itself.[150] Evident, too, is the way the intensified aboriginal awareness noticeable in the new push to have land claims met or in the concern to use film as a vehicle for self-expression has been matched by indications – the making and the commercial success of the movie *Dances With Wolves* (1990) is the clearest of them – that non-native Americans are willing to entertain the idea that aboriginal American society had an integrity, coherence, and character of its own.[151] And so plainly in view as to be absolutely unavoidable is the manner in which the kind of driving, insistent, raw sense of blackness articulated in rap – "Are you proud of what you are?" asks one song – has been paralleled by

227 First Nations, Race, and Pluralism

an acceptance of black culture on the part of the non-black community – viewers, listeners, cassette buyers – which in its enthusiasm, extent, and amplitude goes far beyond anything discernible in the days when "black is beautiful" was the rallying cry.[152]

Were, in sum, the Canadian approach to be seen simply as a kind of harbinger of the way world history is beginning to be viewed, theories of race and culture articulated, and the universe of thought and action understood, this would be quite enough to reveal it as offering prospects not made available by the traditionally American outlook. When, however, one adds to all this the fact that that approach can now also be regarded as having anticipated the direction in which Americans themselves are beginning to move, the case for its pre-eminence strengthens considerably indeed. That Canadians' history has enabled them to know something of what it is to deal with various sorts of pluralism and diversity does not, of course, offer absolute and conclusive proof that their path is in some general and comprehensive way the "right" one. That, however, much contemporary movement seems to be in the direction of approaches consistent with that course of action suggests that it possesses, at a minimum, a certain congruence with what large – and growing – numbers of observers think appropriate and workable. Certainly and above all the compatibility between the Canadian approach and the post-modern idea is clear. And in resting on the sense of indeterminacy and the contingent already much noted in these pages, Canada's national experience has not only in a manner of speaking prefigured that idea: it has also managed to point – as current American practice suggests – to what might have to be the mode of proceeding adopted by other "nations" in the future. In, then, eschewing the notion of the absolute, refusing to privilege particular ways of linguistic, cultural, and racial being, and making no single mode of existence the measure against which all others should be judged, the Canadian approach has established its credentials not merely as the product of one country's idiosyncratic past but as a guide to action quite in harmony with the non-metaphysic of our time.[153]

NOTES

1 For some of what has resulted, see Frederick S. Shiels, ed., *Ethnic Separatism and World Politics* (Lanham, MD: University Press of American, 1984); Paul Brass, ed., *Ethnic Groups and the State* (London: Croom Helm, 1985); Donald L. Horowitz, *Ethnic Groups in Conflict*

(Berkeley: University of California Press, 1985); Neil Nevitte and Charles H. Kennedy, eds., *Ethnic Preference and Public Policy in Developing States* (Boulder, CO: Lynne Rienner, 1986); John F. Slack, Jr, ed., *The Primordial Challenge: Ethnicity in the Contemporary World* (New York: Greenwood, 1986); Anthony D. Smith, *The Ethnic Origins of Nations* (New York: Oxford University Press, 1987); Nancie L. Gonzalez and Carolyn S. McCommon, eds., *Conflict, Migration and the Expression of Ethnicity* (Boulder, CO: Westview Press, 1989); Manning Nash, *The Cauldron of Ethnicity in the Modern World* (Chicago: University of Chicago Press, 1989); and Werner Sollors, ed., *The Invention of Ethnicity* (New York: Oxford University Press, 1989).

2 Whether "ethnicity" and "race" can be distinguished from each other and if so on what grounds are vexed questions. There is general agreement that both are constructs, given their meaning at least as much by the experience, psychology, and convictions of the agent thinking and acting in terms of them as they are by "realities" of language difference, physical appearance, and other such characteristics. But there is also argument that the markers which precipitate that thinking and acting tend to be more stable, enduring, and involuntary in the one case than the other, a circumstance that can link those markers to that thought and action in at least three senses. A distinct physical appearance can give the "marked" people a sharper sense of being bound to others similarly configured, reinforce their feelings of shared tradition and experience, and so – the case with Asian or aboriginal North Americans – play a part in maintaining attachment to the "common" culture and identity. In an instance where the culture of a "marked" group does not endure – the case with the Africans brought to this continent in slavery – a feeling that one shares physical attributes with others can help to "replace" what has gone missing or been taken away: it can provide elements whose contemplation reinforces the sense of things-held-in-common necessary to emergence of the group self-consciousness without which little in the way of culture-building can be accomplished. And – a quite different matter – being "marked" physically can affect the thought, action, and culture of the persons "outside" the boundaries defined by those markers in two ways. Those persons' contemplation of these indicators can (in certain circumstances) trigger a sense that the society in which the markers exist is to be viewed as socially rich and textured. But it can also activate (at a minimum) stereotypical responses of a distinctly unsettling sort – as the Canadian sociologist K. Victor Ujimoto noted following his encountering (at a scholarly conference!) a widespread assumption that he was Japanese. For some recent comment on these and re-

lated issues, see Michael Banton, *The Idea of Races* (London: Tavistock, 1977); Michael Banton, "Analytical and Folk Concepts of Race and Ethnicity," *Ethnic and Racial Studies*, 2(2), April 1979, 127–38; John Rex, *Race Relations in Sociological Theory*, 2nd ed. (London: Routledge and Kegan Paul, 1983); E.E. Cashmore, ed., *Dictionary of Race and Ethnic Relations* (London: Routledge and Kegan Paul, 1984); John Rex and David Mason, eds., *Theories of Race and Ethnic Relations* (Cambridge: Cambridge University Press, 1986); E. Ellis Cashmore, *The Logic of Racism* (London: Allen and Unwin, 1987); and Michael Banton, *Racial Consciousness* (New York and London: Longman, 1988). See also Gordon W. Allport's classic *The Nature of Prejudice* (Reading, MA: Addison-Woley, 1989). For Ujimoto's experience, see his "Visible Minorities and Multiculturalism: Planned Social Change Strategies for the Next Decade," *Journal of Canadian Studies*, 17(1), 1982, 111–21.

3 For its general contours, see Pamela Reynolds and Sandra Bowman, eds., *Growing Up in a Divided Society: The Contexts of Childhood in South Africa* (Evanston, IL: Northwestern University Press, 1986); Heribert Adam and Kogila Moodley, *South Africa Without Apartheid: Dismantling Racial Domination* (Berkeley: University of California Press, 1986); Brian Lapping, *Apartheid: A History* (New York: George Braziller, 1987); Fatima Meer, *Higher Than Hope: The Authorized Biography of Nelson Mandela* (London: Hamish Hamilton, 1988); *South Africa: The Sanctions Report*. Prepared for the Commonwealth Committee of Foreign Ministers on Southern Africa. Foreword by Shridath Ramphal, Commonwealth Secretary-General (London: Penguin, 1989); and Anthony Hazlitt Heard, *The Cape of Storms: A Personal History of the Crisis in South Africa* (Fayetteville: University of Arkansas Press, 1990).

4 Richard Broome, *Aboriginal Australians: Black Response to White Dominance* (Sydney: Allen and Unwin, 1982); Jeremy R. Beckett, ed., *Past and Present: the Construction of Aboriginality* (Canberra: Aboriginal Studies Press, 1988); Ian Keen, ed., *Being Black: Aboriginal Culture in "Settled" Australia* (Canberra: Aboriginal Studies Press, 1988); Gillian Cowlishaw, *Black, White, or Brindle: Race in Rural Australia* (Cambridge: Cambridge University Press, 1988); S. Bennett, *Aborigines and Political Power* (Sydney: Allen and Unwin, 1989); and H. Reynolds, *Dispossession: Black Australians and White Invaders* (Sydney: Allen and Unwin, 1989).

5 Harald Eidheim, *Aspects of the Lappish Minority Situation* (Oslo: Universitetsforlaget, 1971); Peter Jull, "Greenland: Lessons of Self-Government and Development," *Northern Perspectives*, 7(8), 1979, 1–8; Ole Oleson, *Home Rule for Greenland* (Ottawa: Department of

Indian and Northern Affairs, 1979); Hans Christian Gullov, "Home
Rule In Greenland," *Inuit Studies*, 3(1), 1979, 131–42; Peter Jull,
"Aboriginal Peoples and Political Change in the North Atlantic
Area," *Journal of Canadian Studies*, 16(2), 1981, 41–52; Jens Brosted,
ed., *Native Power: The Quest for Autonomy and Nationhood of Indigenous
Peoples* (Oslo: Universitetsforlaget, 1985); and Noel Dyck, ed., *Indi-
genous Peoples and the Nation-State: Fourth World Politics in Canada,
Australia, and Norway* (St John's: Institute of Social and Economic
Research, Memorial University, 1985).
6 M.M. Kritz, Charles B. Keely, et al., eds., *Global Trends in Migration:
Theory of Research on International Population Movements* (New York:
Center for Migration Studies, 1981); M.J. Miller, "The Political
Impact of Foreign Labour: A Re-evaluation of the Western European
Experience," *International Migration Review*, 16(1), 1981, 27–60;
Stephen Castles, Heather Booth, and Tina Wallace, *Here For Good:
Western Europe's New Ethnic Minorities* (London: Pluto Press, 1984);
and Stephen Castles and G. Kosack, *Immigrant Workers and Class
Structure in Western Europe*, 2nd ed. (Oxford: Oxford University Press,
1985).
7 North American scholars and policymakers alike have been trans-
fixed by these issues. To begin grasping what they consider to be at
stake, see Peter S. Li, "Race and Ethnicity," in Peter S. Li, ed., *Race
and Ethnic Relations in Canada* (Toronto: Oxford University Press,
1990), 3–17, and Vic Satzewich, "The Political Economy of Race and
Ethnicity," in ibid., 251–68. For background to the situation in the
United States, Gary B. Nash and Richard Weiss, eds., *The Great Fear:
Race in the Mind of America* (New York: Holt, Rinehart and Winston,
1970), and Gary B. Nash, *Red, White and Black: The Peoples of Early
America* (Englewood Cliffs: Prentice-Hall, 1974) can still be read with
profit. Alden T. Vaughan's excellent "From White Man to Redskin:
Changing Anglo-American Perceptions of the American Indians,"
American Historical Review, 87(4), 1982, 917–53, similarly concerned
with the period before 1800, is broader in scope than its title suggests. For the current state of discussion, see Andrew Hacker, "Trans-
national America," *New York Review of Books*, 22 November 1990,
19–24, and the books reviewed therein.
8 For recent refinements of and some attempts to qualify the view that
American society was founded on a commitment to Lockean liberal
orthodoxy, see John Murrin, "The Great Inversion, or Court versus
Country: A Comparison of the Revolution Settlement in England
(1688–1721) and America (1776–1816)," in J.G.A. Pocock, ed.,
Three British Revolutions: 1641, 1688, 1776 (Princeton: Princeton

231 First Nations, Race, and Pluralism

University Press, 1980), 368–453; Joyce Appleby, "Republicanism in the History and Historiography of the United States," *American Quarterly*, 37(4), 1985, 461–598; Lance Banning, "Jeffersonian Ideology Revisited: Liberal and Classical Ideas in the New American Republic," *William and Mary Quarterly*, 43(1), 1986, 3–19; Joyce Appleby, "Republicanism in Old and New Contexts," ibid., 20–34; and J.G.A. Pocock, "Between Gog and Magog: The Republican Thesis and *Ideologoia Americana*," *Journal of the History of Ideas*, 48(1), 1987, 325–46. None of this, however, touches the basic point being urged here: even had Americans understood their society in terms drawn from the classical republican tradition, blacks would still have been excluded from effective involvement in its affairs on the ground that they lacked, as a matter of racial endowment, the civic virtue necessary for participation.

9 Ralph Ellison, *Invisible Man* (New York: Modern Library, 1952). For additional comment on the dynamic at work here, see Allan Smith, "National Images and National Maintenance: The Ascendancy of the Ethnic Idea in North America," this volume, especially 168–9 above.

10 For the development of these and related images, see Robert Blake and Wayne Dennis, "Development of Stereotypes Concerning the Negro," *Journal of Abnormal and Social Psychology*, 38(4), 1943, 525–31; Arnold Shankman, "Black Pride and Protest: The Amos n' Andy Crusake," *Journal of Popular Culture*, 12(2), 1979, 236–52; J. Fred MacDonald, *Don't Touch That Dial! Radio Programming in American Life, 1920–1960* (Chicago: Nelson-Hall, 1979), 327–70; Thomas Cripps, "The Myth of the Southern Box-Office: A Factor in Racial Stereotyping in American Movies, 1920–1940," in James C. Curtis and Lewis L. Gould, eds., *The Black Experience in America* (Austin: University of Texas Press, 1970), 116–44; and Thomas Cripps, *Slow Fade to Black: The Negro in American Film, 1900–1942* (New York: Oxford University Press, 1977). For two general examinations of white America's images of blacks, see Winthrop Jordan, *White Over Black: American Attitudes Towards the Negro, 1550–1812* (New York: Norton, 1977), and George M. Frederickson, *The Black Image in the White Mind: The Debate on Afro-American Character and Destiny, 1817–1914* (New York: Harper and Row, 1977).

11 Robin W. Winks, *The Blacks in Canada: A History* (New Haven and Montreal: Yale and McGill-Queen's University Presses, 1971), 472.

12 For the revival of interest in Canada's slave past, see William Renwick Riddell, "The Slave in Upper Canada," *Journal of Negro History*, 4(4), 1919, 372–86; William Renwick Riddell, "An Official Record of Slavery in Upper Canada," *Ontario Historical Society Papers and*

Records, 25, 1929, 393–7; and William Renwick Riddell, "Additional Notes on Slavery," *Journal of Negro History*, 17(3), 1932, 368–77.

13 The refocusing of attention on refugee American slaves was carried out in W.H. Withrow, "The Underground Railway," Royal Society of Canada, *Proceedings and Transactions*, 2nd ser., 8, 1902, 49–77; Fred Landon, "Canada's Part in Freeing the Slave," Ontario Historical Society *Papers and Records*, 17, 1919, 74–84; Fred Landon, "The Negro Migration to Canada After the Passage of the Fugitive Slave Act," *Journal of Negro History*, 5(2), 1920, 22–36; Fred Landon, "Negro Colonization Schemes in Upper Canada Before 1820," Royal Society of Canada, *Proceedings and Transactions*, 3rd ser., 23, 1929, 73–80; F.H. Howay, "The Negro Immigration into Vancouver Island in 1858," Royal Society of Canada, *Proceedings and Transactions*, 3rd ser., 29, 1935, 145–56; Fred Landon, "Agriculture Among the Negro Refugees in Upper Canada," *Journal of Negro History*, 21(3), 1936, 304–12; and Fred Landon, "When Uncle Tom's Cabin Came to Canada," *Ontario History*, 44(1), 1952, 1–5.

14 Harold Troper, "The Creek Negroes of Oklahoma and Canadian Immigration, 1909–11," *Canadian Historical Review*, 53(3), 1972, 272–88.

15 The Asian presence generally in the United States is discussed in Roger Daniels and Harry H.L. Kitano, *American Racism: Exploration of the Nature of Prejudice* (Englewood Cliffs: Prentice Hall, 1970); Stanford M. Lyman, *The Asian in North America* (Santa Barbara: ABC-Clio, 1977); John Dower, *War Without Mercy: Race and Power in the Pacific War* (New York: Pantheon, 1986); and Roger Daniels, *Asian America: Chinese and Japanese in the United States Since 1850* (Seattle: University of Washington Press, 1988). For a look at East Indians in the United States, see Joan M. Jensen, *Passage From India: Asia Indian Immigrants in North America* (New Haven: Yale University Press, 1988). Much of the discussion of the American experience with persons of Japanese origin is centred on the internment issue of the Second World War. For the classic liberal account of that issue, see Carey McWilliams, *Prejudice: Japanese-Americans: Symbols of Racial Intolerance* (New York: Little, Brown, 1944; 2nd ed., New York: Archon Books, 1971), along with Roger Daniels, *Concentration Camps USA: Japanese Americans and World War II* (New York: Holt, Rinehart and Winston, 1971), and Kevin Allen Leonard, "'Is That What We Fought For?' Japanese Americans and Racism in California, The Impact of World War II," *Western Historical Quarterly*, 21(4), 1990, 463–82. For a general view of the Japanese experience in North America written from the point of view of a Japanese immigrant, see *Kazuo Ito Issei: A History of Japanese Immigrants in North America*, trans. Shinichiro Nakamura and

Jean S. Gerard (Seattle: Japanese Community Service, 1973). Not surprisingly, given the weight of their numbers, the American experience of persons of Chinese origin has been looked at more extensively than that of other Asians. See, in particular, Gunther Barth, *A History of the Chinese in the United States, 1850–1870* (Cambridge, MA: Harvard University Press, 1974); Jack Chen, *The Chinese of America* (San Francisco: Harper and Row, 1980); Stuart Creighton Miller, *The Unwelcome Immigrant: The American Image of the Chinese, 1785– 1882* (Berkeley: University of California Press, 1969); Rose Hum Lee, *The Chinese in the United States of America* (Hong Kong: Hong Kong University Press, 1960); Sanford M. Lyman, *Chinese Americans* (New York: Random House, 1974); S.W. Kung, *Chinese in American Life: Some Aspects of their History, Status, Problems, and Contributions* (Seattle: University of Washington Press, 1962); Calvin Lee, *Chinatown, U.S.A.* (Garden City, NY: Doubleday, 1965); and Roger Daniels, ed., *Anti-Chinese Violence in North America* (New York: Arno, 1978). By the 1930s, the American popular image of Asians was developing in interesting ways. Still very much seen as figures to be kept at a certain physical and psychological distance, some of them could nonetheless be presented in terms of their possession of distinctly positive qualities. J.P. Marquand's fictional character Mr Moto, the hero of five books (*No Hero, Thank You Mr Moto, Think Fast, Mr Moto, Mr Moto Is So Sorry, Last Laugh, Mr Moto*) produced between 1935 and 1940, thus appeared as "the representation of Eastern subtlety combined with Western efficiency ... a gentleman of wit and charm. Up to 1939 it must have seemed possible to some that Japan would be moderate and reasonable in its expansion in the Far East – that the Mr Motos would defeat the Japanese military fanatics." Consult Millicent Bell, *Marquand: An American Life* (Boston: Little, Brown, 1979), 219, 221. And while the decade's very popular Charlie Chan movies presented their Chinese-American protagonist in stereotypical terms – impassive demeanour, accent – they also showed him to be consistently more intelligent than the caucasian American police with whom he frequently worked. On balance, however, the image of Asians and Asian-Americans remained negative and condescending.

16 Ronald I. Takaki, *Strangers From a Different Shore: A History of Asian Americans* (New York: Penguin, 1989).

17 As in Hilda Glynn-Ward's lurid and sensational *The Writing on the Wall*, introduction by Patricia Roy, which was originally published in 1921 (Toronto: University of Toronto Press, 1974). For the state of mind which produced this sort of work, see Patricia E. Roy, "British Columbia's Fears of Asians, 1900–1950," *Histoire Sociale/Social History*, 13(25), 1980, 161–72, and W. Peter Ward, *White Canada Forever:*

Popular Attitudes and Public Policy Toward Orientals in British Columbia (Montreal: McGill-Queen's University Press, 1978, 1990). For the Asian experience in Canada generally, see Ken Adachi, *The Enemy That Never Was: A History of the Japanese Canadians* (Toronto: McClelland and Stewart, 1978); Edgar Wickberg, *From China to Canada: A History of the Chinese Communities in Canada* (Toronto: McClelland and Stewart, 1982); Patricia Roy, *A White Man's Province: British Columbia Politicians and Chinese and Japanese Immigrants 1853–1914* (Vancouver: University of British Columbia Press, 1989); Patricia Roy, J.L. Granatstein, Masako Iino, Hirako Takamura, *Mutual Hostages: Canadians and Japanese During the Second World War* (Toronto: University of Toronto Press, 1990); Norman Buchignani and Doreen M. Indra, with Ram Srivastiva, *Continuous Journey: A Social History of South Asians in Canada* (Toronto: McClelland and Stewart, 1985); and Hugh Johnston, *The Voyage of the Komagata Maru: The Sikh Challenge to Canada's Colour Bar* (New Delhi: Oxford University Press, 1979; Vancouver: University of British Columbia Press, 1989).

18 *Black Elk Speaks: Being the Life Story of a Holy Man of the Oglala Sioux as told to John G. Neihardt* (New York: William Morrow, 1932).

19 For the emerging popular stereotype of the Indian in post-Civil War America, see Charles R. Wilson, "Racial Reservations: Indians and Blacks in American Magazines, 1865–1900," *Journal of Popular Culture*, 10(1), 1976, 70–80. The manner in which the understanding of the aboriginal as Little Beaver or Tonto – a friendly and helpful, but also childlike and subservient, creature – was perpetuated is examined in Maurice Horn, ed., *The World Encyclopedia of Comics* (New York: Chelsea House, 1976), vol. 2, 577–8, and Andre S. Horton, "Ken Kesey, John Updike, and The Lone Ranger," *Journal of Popular Culture*, 8(3), 1974, 571, 572.

20 Brian Dipple, *The Vanishing American: White Attitudes and US Indian Policy* (Middletown: Wesleyan University Press, 1982).

21 For the case in support of the view that "Hollywood's adherence to the demonic stereotype of the Indian in pre-fifties films is, by now, a generally recognized scandal," see Ralph Willett, "The American Western: Myth and Anti-Myth," *Journal of Popular Culture*, 4(2), 1970, 456.

22 For the assumptions underlying federal government policy, see John L. Tobias, "Protection, Civilization, Assimilation: An Outline History of Canada's Indian Policy," in Ian A.L. Getty and Antoine S. Lussier, eds., *As Long As the Sun Shines and the Water Flows* (Vancouver: University of British Columbia Press, 1983), 39–55. For a more detailed view of the first decades of the twentieth century see E. Brian Titley, *A Narrow Vision: Duncan Campbell Scott and the Administration of Indian*

Affairs in Canada (Vancouver: University of British Columbia Press, 1986). Among the anthropologists, Diamond Jenness' 1932 representation of the coastal tribes of British Columbia as "tossed at the mercy of the tide [of white settlement], unable to gain a secure foothold" was typical. "The survivors today," he continued, "with few exceptions, feel that their race is ruined and calmly, rather mournfully, await the end." Diamond Jenness, *The Indians of Canada* (Ottawa: National Museum of Canada, [1932]), 261.

23 For a general assessment of the impact of American movies in Canada, see H.F. Angus, ed., *Canada and her Great Neighbour: Sociological Surveys of Opinions and Attitudes in Canada concerning the United States* (Toronto: Ryerson, 1938), especially chapter five, "Motion Pictures," 124–40.

24 For late seventeenth- and early eighteenth-century efforts (largely inspired by the colonial governors) to find aboriginal allies against the French, see Richard R. Johnson, "The Search for a Usuable Indian: An Aspect of the Defence of Colonial New England," *Journal of American History*, 64(3), 1977, 623–51. For comment on the way in which what Wilbur R. Jacobs calls "Britain's increasing concern for the Indian" had by 1763 produced the division between colonial American and official British attitudes so evident in the Royal Proclamation of that year, see Jacobs' *Dispossessing the American Indian: Indians and Whites of the Colonial Frontier* (New York: Scribner, 1972), 109. For American and British attitudes to the aboriginal "threat" generally, see John E. Ferling, *A Wilderness of Miseries: War and Warriors in Early America* (Westport: Greenwood Press, 1980), especially chapter two, "The Indian Wars," 29–56.

25 Brant, "the distinguished Chief of the Mohawks," first got a little book to himself in 1872, by 1903 had, as "the friend of the English from First to last," won inclusion in T.G. Marquis' pantheon of national heroes, and in 1929 was being memorialized in these terms: "It is perhaps due as much to Joseph Brant as to anyone else that the Union Jack still floats over the northern half of this continent." See [William E. Palmer], *Memoir of the Distinguished Mohawk Indian chief, sachem, and warrior, Capt. Joseph Brant; compiled from the most reliable and authentic records. Including a brief history of the principal events of his life, with an appendix.* (Brantford: Stewart, 1872), 5; T.G. Marquis, "Joseph Brant," in his *Builders of Canada From Cartier to Laurier* (Toronto: J.L. Nicholls, 1903), 193; and W.J. Karr, "Joseph Brant: The Mohawk Ally of Britain," in his *The History of Canada Through Biography[.] Explorers, Soldiers, and Statesmen: Canadian Pacific History* (Toronto: J.M. Dent and Sons, 1929), 124. Tecumseh came to public attention in John Richardson's *Tecumseh: The Warrior of the*

West (London, 1828), was made the central figure in Charles Mair's
Tecumseh: A Drama (Toronto: Hunter, Rose, 1886), appeared in
Marquis' work as "the Friend of the British" ("Tecumseh," 212), and
as "the last great Indian ally of the British" (171) received a chapter
("Tecumseh: The War Chief of the Shawnees," 166–71) to himself in
Karr's book. For an overview of the treatment given aboriginals'
place in national history, see James W.St.G. Walker, "The Indian in
Canadian Historical Writing," Canadian Historical Association
Historical Papers, 1971, 21–51; Walker's "The Indian in Canadian
Historical Writing, 1972–1982," in Getty and Lussier, eds., *As Long
As the Sun Shines and the Water Flows*, 340–57; and Bruce C. Trigger,
"The Historian's Indian: Native Americans in Canadian Historical
Writing From Charlevoix to the Present," *Canadian Historical Review*,
57(3), 1986, 315–42.
26 Maria Tippett, *Making Culture: English-Canadian Institutions and the
Arts Before the Massey Commission* (Toronto: University of Toronto
Press, 1990), 137, 66, 68.
27 The trophy-like display of aboriginals as exotics from another age is
captured perfectly in two photographs in James Gray, *A Brand of its
Own: The 100 Year History of the Calgary Exhibition and Stampede* (Saskatoon: Western Producer Prairie Books, 1985), 26, 62. The first,
taken in 1908, shows a file of aboriginals with travois and Hudson's
Bay Company blankets moving stolidly past a row of houses on a
residential street. The other dates from the early 1920s and depicts a
group of fringed, buckskinned, and beaded Stoney, Sarcee, and
Blackfoot Chiefs against the background of the downtown Calgary
cityscape.
28 For a recent look at Grey Owl's extraordinary career, see Donald B.
Smith, *From the Lake of Shadows: The Making of Grey Owl* (Saskatoon:
Western Producer Prairie Books, 1989).
29 The contact-created thrust to conceptualize encounters between and
among racial groups in ways which did not, in principle, place any at
a disadvantage in relation to the others was seen as early as 1952 in
Everett and Helen Hughes' pronouncement that "both sociology
and anthropology are in fact sciences of the contact of peoples." By
the 1980s it had produced several frank admissions that the impulse
behind what was taking place was a quite fundamental concern to
see group relations adjusted in ways that would establish social
balance and equilibrium. Even, in consequence, as Robert Miles'
marxist-grounded theory led him to argue that "the concepts 'race'
and 'race relations' have no analytical value" he could concede that
what made the whole matter an issue in Britain had been the arrival
of "physically distinctive" immigrants in the 1950s. Other observers

simply noted the role the new realities were playing in the inten-
sification of the problem. "Historical evidence," wrote Michael
Banton, "suggests that the attitudes and behaviours which today are
called racist have changed and developed over time to become more
complicated in our own generation." Others still stressed the need to
comprehend the situation in order that effective policy might be
framed in relation to it: "How [otherwise] shall we seek ... to understand the world, to predict the sequence of events, and to achieve
some control over them?" Observers, then, agreed on the fundamental point: the issue of race was an urgent, practical one and had to be
addressed for the most pressing of policy reasons. See Everett C.
Hughes and Helen C. Hughes, *When Peoples Meet: Racial and Ethnic
Frontiers* (Glencoe: The Free Press, 1952), 17; Robert Miles, *Racism
and Migrant Labour* (London: Routledge and Kegan Paul, 1982), 3,
1; Michael Banton, *Racial and Ethnic Competition* (Cambridge: Cambridge University Press, 1983), 4–5; and George Eaton Simpson and
J. Milton Yinger, *Racial and Cultural Minorities: An Analysis of Prejudice
and Discrimination*, 5th ed. (New York: Plenum Press, 1985), 3.

30 "Message from the President of the United States Favoring Repeal of
the Chinese Exclusion Laws," *House Document* 333, 78th Cong. 1st
sess. (Washington, DC, 1943), Serial 10793, 1–2. Cited in Shih-Shan
Henry Tsai, *The Chinese Experience in America* (Bloomington: Indiana
University Press, 1985), 115. See also Jack Chen, *The Chinese of
America* (San Francisco: Harper and Row, 1980), 206, and, for an
early, detailed study, Fred W. Riggs, *Pressures on Congress: A Study of
the Repeal of Chinese Exclusion* (New York: King's Crown Press, 1950).

31 *Congressional Record*, 10 October 1945, 9529–30. Cited in David
Reimers, *Still the Golden Door: The Third World Comes to America* (New
York: Columbia University Press, 1985), 15.

32 Tsai, *Chinese Experience*, 139.

33 New York *Times*, 4 October 1965. Cited in Reimers, *Still the Golden
Door*, 86.

34 For discussion of that thrust, and of the way in which its emphasis on
"roots" and "tradition" was made consistent with a continuing stress
on the American way of life, see Allan Smith, "National Images and
National Maintenance," 165–72, 175–8 above.

35 Harry H.L. Kitano, *Japanese-Americans: The Evolution of a Subculture*
(Englewood Cliffs: Prentice Hall, 1969), xi.

36 Edwin O. Reischauer, "Foreword," in Bill Hosokawa, *Nisei: The Quiet
Americans* (New York: William Morrow and Company, 1969), xi.

37 Daniel I. Okimoto, *American in Disguise* (New York and Tokyo: Wal-
ker/Wetherhill, 1971).

38 Hilary Conroy and T. Scott Miyakawa, eds., *East Across the Pacific:*

Historical and Sociological Studies of Japanese Immigration and Assimilation (Santa Barbara: Clio Press, 1972), xi.

39 Takaki, *Strangers From a Different Shore*, 18.

40 Howard G. Chua-Eoan, "Strangers in Paradise," *Time*, 135(15), 9 April 1990, 32–3. For studies commenting on the structural and behavioural assimilation of Asians, see H. Brett Melendy, *Asians in America: Filipinos, Koreans, and East Indians* (Boston: Twayne Publishers, 1977); Parmatma Saran and Edwin Eames, eds., *The New Ethnics: Asian Indians in the United States* (New York: Praeger, 1980); and Darrel Montero, *Japanese Americans: Changing Patterns of Ethnic Affiliation Over Three Generations* (Boulder: Westview Press, 1980).

41 Richard Lentz, *Symbols, the News Magazines, and Martin Luther King* (Baton Rouge: Louisiana State University Press, 1990). For a memoir of King, which similarly views him as wanting to move blacks towards the centre of American life, see Flip Schulke and Penelope Ortner McPherr, *King Remembered* (New York: Norton, 1986). The more radical phase of the 1960s movement is investigated in Clayborn Carson, *In Struggle: SNCC and the Black Awakening of the 1960s* (Cambridge: Harvard University Press, 1981), while Reynolds Farley, *Blacks and Whites: Narrowing the Gap?* (Cambridge: Harvard University Press, 1984) assesses the Civil Rights movement in terms of its concrete accomplishments in the areas of political rights, income, education, and family structure. Three recent studies, each focusing on a particular area or problem, and all of them emphasizing the integrationist, liberal, and assimilationist approach of the movement, are Stephen F. Lawson, *In Pursuit of Power: Southern Blacks and Electoral Politics 1965–1982* (New York: Columbia University Press, 1985); Minion K.C. Morrison, *Black Political Mobilization: Leadership, Power, and Mass Behavior* (Albany: State University of New York Press, 1987); and James W. Button, *Blacks and Social Change: Impact of the Civil Rights Movement in Southern Communities* (Princeton: Princeton University Press, 1989).

42 "In order," notes Daniel C. Thompson, "to facilitate their own survival under various conditions and degrees of servitude, discrimination, and individual and institutionalized hostility, [blacks] have invented, refined, and borrowed intact a variety of survival techniques and strategies." Daniel C. Thompson, *Sociology of the Black Experience* (Westport: Greenwood Press, 1974), 39.

43 Raymond L. Hall, *Black Separatism in the United States* (Hanover: University Press of New England, 1978).

44 The character of the relationship is spelled out in Allan Smith, "National Images and National Maintenance," this volume.

45 Shelby Steel, "On Being Black and Middle Class," *Commentary*, 85(1), January 1988, 47. The classic black statement of this position is Thomas Sowell, *Ethnic America: A History* (New York: Basic Books, 1981).

46 McGeorge Bundy, "The Issues Before the Court: Who Gets ahead in America?" in William H. Chaffe and Harvard Sitkoff, eds., *A History of Our Time*, 2nd ed. (New York: Oxford University Press, 1987), 409. For a slightly different statement of this position, see Bundy's "Beyond Bakke: What Future for Affirmative Action?" *Atlantic Monthly*, 242(5), November 1978, 69–73.

47 For a general discussion of the Dawes Act, see Wilcomb E. Washburn, *The Indian in America* (New York: Harper and Row, 1975), 242–9. For a look at what Watkins attempted, and at its fruits among the Menominee of Wisconsin and the Klamath in Oregon, see William Hodge, *The First Americans: Then and Now* (New York: Holt, Rinehart and Winston, 1981), 164–6 and 388–91. John Collier, Roosevelt's Commissioner for Indian Affairs, the official responsible for drafting the Indian Reorganization Act of 1934, and a man in favour of a genuine pluralism in the United States, described the Watkins approach as concerned to create "a dead manipulable flatness of human life in the United States ... the individual isolate, 'freed' from grouphood, culture, and home, an atomized 'go-getter.'" For these and other comments, see John Collier, "Divergent Views on 'Pluralism and the American Indian,'" in Robert C. Owen, J.J.F. Deetz, et al., eds., *The North American Indians: A Sourcebook* (New York: Macmillan, 1967), 682–6.

48 Stephen Cornell, "American Indians: Asserting their Rights," *Dialogue* 74(4), 1986, 36–9.

49 William Brandon, *The Last Americans: The Indian in American Culture* (New York: McGraw-Hill, 1974), 22.

50 Hazel W. Hertzberg, *The Search for an American Identity: Modern Pan Indian Movements* (Syracuse: Syracuse University Press, 1972), vii, viii.

51 Hodge, *First Americans*, vii, 504.

52 Cornell, "American Indians," 39.

53 Even when they were considered to be a disappearing people, efforts were made – as the sobriquet "vanishing American" indicates – to use the designation "American" to give them some kind of status in, and identification with, the society which had come to prevail. See Dippie, *Vanishing American.*

54 "Press Statement to Congress Made by American Indian Task Force, November 12, 1969." Cited in Alvin M. Josephy, ed., *Red Power: The American Indians Fight for Freedom* (Lincoln: University of Nebraska Press, 1971), 141.

55 William A. Schambra, "Progressive Liberalism and American 'Community,'" *The Public Interest*, no. 80, 1985, 47.

56 Daniel Bell, "'American Exceptionalism' Revisited: The Role of Civil Society," *The Public Interest*, no. 95, 1989, 56.

57 Kevin Philips, "The Balkanization of America," *Harper's*, 256(1536), May 1978, 37–47.

58 William H. Chaffe, *The Unfinished Journey: America Since World War II* (New York: Oxford University Press, 1986), 483. For a study of Reagan's rhetoric, see Paul D. Erickson, *Reagan Speaks: The Making of an American Myth* (New York: New York University Press, 1985).

59 "President Bush's Address to Congress, February 9, 1989," in *President Bush: The Challenge Ahead* (Washington: Congressional Quarterly, 1989), 123, 122–3.

60 Quoted in Roger D. Hatch and Frank E. Watkins, eds., *Reverend Jesse L. Jackson: Straight From the Heart* (Philadelphia: Fortress Press, 1987), xvii.

61 Ibid., xiii.

62 Everett Carll Ladd, "The Constitution as Ideology," *Dialogue*, 79(1), 1988, 31.

63 For a view of the process by which Canadians came to see linguistic and ethnic cleavage as a central element in their society's character, see Allan Smith, "Metaphor and Nationality in North America," 127–58 above.

64 Canada. House of Commons. *Debates*, 19 January 1962, 9.

65 *Statement of the Government of Canada on Indian Policy, 1969* [the "White Paper"] (Ottawa, 1969).

66 Hon. Gerry Weiner, Minister of State (Multiculturalism), in Canada. House of Commons. *Debates*, 11 July 1988, 17428.

67 July 19. Cited in Carol F. Lee, "The Road to Enfranchisement: Chinese and Japanese in British Columbia," *BC Studies*, 30, 1976, 61.

68 Canada. House of Commons. *Debates*, 2 May 1947, 2715. That Pearkes now saw Asian-Canadians as capable of patriotic thought and action was, of course, an indication of the extent to which thinking about race had changed. Until and even during the Second World War, there had been strong doubts, held on racist grounds, concerning the capacity of members of visible minority groups to function in terms of these attributes. See Patricia Roy, "The Soldiers Canada Didn't Want: Her Chinese and Japanese Citizens," *Canadian Historical Review*, 59(3), 1978, 341–58, and James St G. Walker, "Race and Recruitment in World War I: Enlistment of Visible Minorities in the Canadian Expeditionary Force," *Canadian Historical Review*, 70(1), 1989, 1–26. For discussion of the relationship between racism and military service in the United States, see A.E. Barbeau and F. Henri,

The Unknown Soldiers: Black American Troops in World War I (Philadelphia: Temple University Press, 1974), and Jack D. Foner, *Blacks and the Military in American History: A New Perspective* (New York: Praeger, 1974).

69 Quoted by Angus MacInnis in Canada. House of Commons. *Debates*, 15 March 1948, 2227.

70 Ibid., 19 January 1962, 10.

71 The shift away from what Louis E. Lomax described as the kind of "ghetto politician" epitomized by Powell, a man fearful of having his "district integrated right out from under him," to the sort of figure who could draw support from all racial groups and so claim "full-fledged participation in the benefits of the American way of life" was embodied not just in the election of black mayors in Los Angeles, Detroit, Cleveland, Birmingham, Oakland, and Atlanta but also, as William H. Chaffe points out, in the increase in the number of blacks in Congress. This went from four in 1959 to ten a decade later to eighteen by 1980. Louis E. Lomax, *The Negro Revolt* (New York: Harper and Row, 1962), 196; Chaffe, *Unfinished Journey*, 438.

72 Robert Lekachman, *Visions and Nightmares: America After Reagan* (New York: Macmillan, 1987), 7.

73 "Taking Jesse Seriously," *Time* Magazine, 135(5), 11 April 1988, 22.

74 Brown's attachment to feminism was particularly noticeable. If the play of words in the title of her autobiography drew attention both to her individuality and her identity as a person of colour, the dedication of the book to "women everywhere who strive to change their world" made plain her commitment to the women's movement. Rosemary Brown, *Being Brown: A Very Public Life* (Toronto: Random House, 1989).

75 As he continued to do upon his elevation to cabinet rank in the Clark government of 1979–80, for if his attainment of that distinction in some sense involved "using" him to give status and recognition to the group of which he was a part, it also made him the responsible minister of all Canadians concerned with the affairs of his department.

76 That society was, he suggested, very much a composite of different groups, a reality that gave the representatives of those groups special duties as they became active in the life of the whole. While, then, he told the Commons in his first speech, he wanted to acknowledge the fact that his constituents "have thought at all times of me only as a Canadian," he was also "aware of the responsibilities which rest upon me ... as the first member of my race to sit in this house." Canada. House of Commons. *Debates*, 11 November 1958, 968.

77 He was, as one of the journalists covering his victory celebration noted, "the first Indo-Canadian in Canada to be elected." Judith Lavoie, "NDP's Victory Chant at Esquimault Centre – 'We Want Moe,'" Victoria *Times-Colonist*, 23 October 1986.

78 Harper was, of course, also seen by them as their representative – as, indeed, a kind of consolidating force. As Bernard Ominiyak, chief of the Lubicon Band, put it, "Elijah Harper means much to the aboriginal people ... There is greater unity among us since Meech Lake." Cited in John Howse, "New Native Hero: Elijah Harper Dominates a Post-Meech Summit," *Maclean's*, 103(29), July 1990, 13.

79 Manifest in such effusions as MP Arthur Maloney's 1957 exultation in the fact that his was "a truly national party" because its support "knew no boundaries of race, or class, or creed" and in such pronouncements as Diefenbaker's assertion that "the women of Canada deserved and had the right to expect representation in cabinet." Canada. House of Commons. *Debates*, 31 October 1957, 203; John Diefenbaker, *One Canada: Memoirs of the Right Honourable John G. Diefenbaker: The Years of Achievement 1957–1962* (Toronto: Macmillan, 1976), vol. 2, 47.

80 For Gladstone's career, see Hugh Dempsey, *The Gentle Persuader: A Biography of James Gladstone, Indian Senator* (Saskatoon: Western Producer Prairie Books, 1980).

81 The relationship between her appointment and its role in recognizing the black community was certainly emphasized in newspaper and other comment. The *Globe and Mail* captioned its story "First Black among Five Named to Senate," while the *Canadian Annual Review* similarly stressed the fact that her elevation made her "the first black to be appointed to the Senate." *Globe and Mail*, 14 January 1984; R.B. Byers, ed., *The Canadian Annual Review of Politics and Public Affairs* (Toronto: University of Toronto Press, 1987), xi.

82 Susan Delacourt, "National Unity Panel Unveiled," *Globe and Mail*, 2 November 1990.

83 David J. Mitchell, *W.A.C. Bennett and the Rise of British Columbia* (Vancouver: Douglas and McIntyre, 1983), 397.

84 Bernard Simon, "The Good Life Gets Better," *Financial Times*, 22 May 1990.

85 Quoted in Darcy Henton, "Lt-Gov 'Linc' Pledges He'll Work for All Ontarians," Toronto *Star*, 21 September 1985. Crombie's concern to have appointments of this kind seen as conveying the message that the groups the appointees came from were by virtue of those appointments getting status and recognition was even clearer in what he had to say concerning the federal government's reasons for involving itself in the creation of a Chair of Sikh and Punjabi Studies

at the University of British Columbia: this was, he told the House of Commons in 1988, part of "a message to the Sikh community that clearly we wanted to make sure that they were not alienated from either this Government or this Parliament." Canada. House of Commons. *Debates*, 15 March 1988, 13747.

86 Quoted in Keith Baldrey, "BC's 25th Lt-Gov Calls Post Milestone," Vancouver *Sun*, 10 September 1988.

87 *Amos n' Andy* was the focus of particular concern. For the effort to get it off the air, see Kathryn C. Montgomery, *Target: Prime Time; Advocacy Groups and the Struggle Over Entertainment Television* (New York: Oxford University Press, 1989), 14–15.

88 Ibid., 22.

89 J. Fred MacDonald, *Blacks and White TV: Afro-Americans in Television Since 1948* (Chicago: Nelson-Hall, 1983), 100.

90 Ibid., 116.

91 Jimmie Reeves, "Television Stars: The Case of Mr. T.," in Harold Newcomb, ed., *Television: The Critical View* 4th ed. (New York: Oxford University Press, 1987), 447.

92 Montgomery, *Target*, 28.

93 MacDonald, *Blacks and White TV*, 127.

94 Ibid., 189–91.

95 Ibid., 202.

96 Ibid., 221.

97 Reeves, "Television Stars," 447, 452–3.

98 For this point in relation to these films, See Maria Topalovich, *A Pictorial History of the Canadian Film Awards* (Toronto: Stoddart, 1984), 89, 117. So far as television is concerned, Adrienne Clarkson's Chinese ancestry was treated as incidental from the moment of her appearance on CBC, and by the late 1980s the same was true of the approach taken to the backgrounds of journalists Der-Hoy Yin, Susan Harada, and Ian Hanomansing. *Street Legal*'s black actor Anthony Sherwood played a lawyer with no particular involvement in a culture or racial community, while *De Grassi High*'s B.L.T. and Yik were sometimes set apart by high spirits and certain prankishness but hardly ever by their membership in a racial group.

99 Topalovich, *Pictorial History*, 56.

100 Paul Rutherford, *When Television Was Young: Primetime Canada 1952–1967* (Toronto: University of Toronto Press, 1990), 381.

101 It also attempted to depict aboriginals – on the prairies – as a people of dignity with whom the newcomers were at least morally obliged to treat.

102 Mary Jane Miller, *Turn Up the Contrast: CBC Television Drama Since 1952* (Vancouver: University of British Columbia Press, 1987), 102.

103 Ibid., 136.
104 Sandy Stewart, *Here's Looking at Us: A Personal History of Television in Canada* (Toronto: CBC Enterprises, 1986), 245.
105 Miller, *Turn Up the Contrast*, 77. For additional comment on "Sarah's Copper," see Rutherford, *When Television Was Young*, 381, 382, 513.
106 Miller, *Turn Up the Contrast*, 106.
107 Ibid., 105.
108 Ibid., 214.
109 Topalovich, *Pictorial History*, 64.
110 F.B. Rainsberry, *A History of Children's Television in English Canada, 1952–1986* (Metuchen and London: Scarecrow, 1988), 131.
111 Quoted in Ray Conlogue, "Great Expectations," *Globe and Mail*, 18 August 1990.
112 Hazel A. Da Breo, "Royal Spoils: Imperialists, Missionaries, and the Royal Ontario Museum's African Collections," *Fuse Magazine*, 13(3), 1989–90, 33.
113 Quoted in Lawrence Surtees, "CRTC Dissension: Rejection of Black Music Station and Approval of Country Rock Splits Agency," *Globe and Mail*, 9 August 1990.
114 Quoted in Urjo Kareda, "The Daughter Also Rises," *Saturday Night*, 101(6), June 1986, 38.
115 For discussion of that role, see Raymond Firth, *Symbols: Public and Private* (London: Allen and Unwin, 1973); and David Kertzer, *Ritual, Politics, and Power* (New Haven: Yale University Press, 1988).
116 A photograph of the scene, taken from the Lincoln Memorial, looking towards the monument, and showing the vast crowd of marchers occupying the mall, perfectly communicates this sense of the meaning of what was happening. See "The Washington March," *Time* Magazine, 83(1), 3 January 1964, 25.
117 Ibid., 13.
118 "The Inauguration," ibid., 85(5), 29 January 1965, 19.
119 Jacob V. Lamar, Jr, "Honoring Justice's Drum Major," ibid., 127(4), 27 January 1986, 16.
120 "The Constitution at 200," ibid., 130(1), 6 July 1987. Special issue, cover.
121 Ibid., 135(15), 9 April 1990, 32. The same point was made in a history text's use of a colour photograph of Boy Scouts of Asian (and other) descent together with an American flag. The photograph's caption drove the message home: "The decade of the 1970s saw the mass immigration to the United States of people of color ... As evidenced by these smiling Boy Scouts, younger Asian-Americans took quickly to the ways of their new country." Mary Beth Norton, David M. Katzman, et al., *A People and a Nation: A History of the United*

States; Vol II; Since 1865 3rd ed. (Boston: Houghton Mifflin, 1990), 985.

122 Nathan Joseph, *Uniforms and Nonuniforms: Communication Through Clothing* (New York: Greenwood, 1986), 27, 87, 88.

123 Ibid., 36, 67, 88.

124 "Morning Stroll," *Globe and Mail,* 27 June 1990. Front page photograph.

125 Alexander Muir, "The Maple Leaf Forever," in Sir Ernest Macmillan, *A Canadian Song Book* (Toronto: Dent, 1938), 6.

126 Adolphe-Basile Routhier's original version, written in 1880, had a distinctly militant, even martial, tone, referring at one point to the country's *"bras [qui] sait porter l'épee ... [et] la croix."* Robert S. Weir's 1908 English rendering focused more consistently on the landscape, representing the country as the "true north ... where pines and maples grow." For both, see Macmillan, *Canadian Song Book,* 3–4.

127 John A. Munro and Alex I. Inglis, *Mike: The Memoirs of the Rt Hon. Lester B. Pearson* (Scarborough: New American Library of Canada, 1976), vol. 2, 295.

128 For the story of the flag's adoption, see J.L. Granatstein, *Canada 1957–1967: The Years of Uncertainty and Innovation* (Toronto: McClelland and Stewart, 1986), 201–5.

129 The provinces moved to select their own flags almost immediately upon completion of the process at the federal level, with Quebec, Ontario, Newfoundland, and Manitoba particularly quick off the mark. For a look at their actions, see J.R. Matheson, *Canada's Flag: A Search for a Country* (Belleville: Mika Publishing, 1986), 231. For a discussion of the manner in which a strong sense of identity led a national sub-unit of a different sort to adopt its own flag, see Percy Biddiscombe, *"'Le Tricolore et l'étoilé';* The Origin of the Acadian National Flag, 1867–1912," *Acadiensis,* 20(1), 1990, 120–47.

130 The individual buildings themselves might also offer a certain mixture of styles to the observer's eye. While, notes Alan Gowans, Pearson and Marchand's Parliament Buildings of 1916 really were Gothic, their predecessors designed by Fuller and Stent (1859) borrowed so extensively from other traditions that they were best seen as representing "Picturesque Eclecticism." And if, propose two other commentators, the piers of Ernest Cormier's Supreme Court (1938–9) "suggest classical columns," that building was also characterized by its "steep châteauesque copper roofs." Alan Gowans, *Building Canada: An Architectural History of Canadian Life* (Toronto: Oxford University Press, 1966), 142, 119; Harold Kalman and John Roaf, *Exploring Ottawa: An Architectural Guide to the Nation's Capital* (Toronto: University of Toronto Press, 1983), A3.

131 Quoted in "Showcasing Canada," *Maclean's*, 102(28), 10 July 1989, 39.

132 Joseph, *Uniforms and Nonuniforms*, 53. See also Cynthia Enloe, *Ethnic Soldiers: State Security in Divided Societies* (Athens: University of Georgia Press, 1980), 35.

133 Michael Valpy, "Dress Code Stance Hardly Multicultural," *Globe and Mail*, 6 March 1990.

134 Ross Howard, "Cadieux Gives Sikh Mounties Right to Wear Turbans on Duty," *Globe and Mail*, 16 March 1990.

135 Fiorella Grossi, "Braids Now Allowed for Native Officers," *Globe and Mail*, 18 June 1990.

136 J.R. Taylor, Vancouver Burrard. Canada. House of Commons. *Debates*, 4 July 1960, 5699.

137 Michael Asch, *Home and Native Land: Aboriginal Rights and the Canadian Constitution* (Toronto: Methuen, 1984), 86.

138 Katherine Swinton, "Competing Visions of Constitutionalism: Of Federalism and Rights," in K.E. Swinton and C.J. Rogerson, eds., *Competing Constitutional Visions: The Meech Lake Accord* (Toronto: Carswell, 1988), 283.

139 Alan C. Cairns, "Ritual, Taboo and Bias in Constitutional Controversies in Canada," *The Timlin Lecture*, 13 November 1989, University of Saskatchewan, 7. Cairns had written the year before that the Charter's granting of "specific constitutional recognition to women, aboriginals, official language minority populations, [and racial and] ethnic groups through the vehicle of multiculturalism" made it obvious beyond doubt the sort of country to which its existence pointed. Cairns, "Citizens (Outsiders) and Governments (Insiders) in Constitution-Making: The Case of Meech Lake," *Canadian Public Policy*, 14 Supplement, September 1988, 122. See also T.C. Christopher, "The 1982 Canadian Charter of Rights and Freedoms and Multiculturalism," *Canadian Review of Studies in Nationalism*, 14(2), 1987, 341.

140 One observer found old stereotypes of the black re-appearing in the 1980s under the guise of what he called "the new minstrelsy." Another noted in 1985 that "native Americans ... continued to suffer more severely from poverty and disease than any other cultural group in the United States, a situation largely unrecognized by the federal government." And in 1982 two sociologists could enumerate the "multiple oppressions" – poor housing, low incomes, racism, sexism – experienced by significant numbers of Chinese-American women. See MacDonald, *Blacks and White TV*, 149–237; Bernard Bailyn, Robert Dallek, et al., *The Great Republic: A History of the American People* (Lexington, Toronto: D.C. Heath and Company, 1985), 846; and

Chalsa Loo and Paul Ong, "Slaying Demons with a Sewing Needle: Feminist Issues for Chinatown's Women," *Berkeley Journal of Sociology*, 27, 1982, 77–88.

141 Studies and polls indicate that prejudice continues to exist, while members of visible minority groups report experiences that confirm its presence. One even suggests that the official policy of cultural and racial diversity is itself racist and manipulative, functioning "to mobilize the various non-Anglo and non-White minority groups on behalf of the hegemonic ethnic group." Peter S. Li, "Prejudice Against Asians in a Canadian City," *Canadian Ethnic Studies*, 11(2), 1979, 70–7; James W. St G. Walker, *Racial Discrimination in Canada: The Black Experience* (Ottawa: Canadian Historical Association, 1985); "A Black View of Canada," *Maclean's*, 99(3), 20 January 1986, 24–6; Fil Fraser, "Black Like Me," *Saturday Night*, 102(1), January 1987, 180–4; Ann Walmsley, "Uneasy Over Newcomers," *Maclean's*, 102(1), 2 January 1989, 28–9; "An Angry Racial Backlash," *Maclean's*, 102(28), 10 July 1989, 14–24; Aminur Rahin, "Multiculturalism or Ethnic Hegemony: A Critique of Multicultural Education in Toronto," *Journal of Ethnic Studies*, 18(3), 1990, 29–46.

142 William H. McNeill, *Polyethnicity and National Unity in World History* (Toronto: University of Toronto Press, 1986), 6.

143 Robert Miles, *Racism* (London: Routledge, 1989), 71.

144 Perry Anderson, "England's Isaiah," *London Review of Books*, 12(24), 20 December 1990, 7.

145 J.G. Herder, *Reflections on the Philosophy of the History of Mankind* [1784–1791], trans. and intro. F.E. Manuel (London, 1968), 98. Cited in Brian J. Whitton, "Herder's Critique of the Enlightenment: Cultural Community versus Cosmopolitan Rationalism," *History and Theory*, 27(2), 1988, 153.

146 John Rex, *Race and Ethnicity* (Milton Keynes: Open University Press, 1986), 15.

147 M. Michael Rosenberg, William B. Shaffir, et al., eds., *An Introduction to Sociology* 2nd ed., (Toronto: Methuen, 1987), 544.

148 Janet Helms, *Black and White Racial Identity: Theory, Research, and Practice* (New York: Greenwood, 1990), 3.

149 Jean-François Lyotard, *The Postmodern Condition: A Report on Knowledge*, trans. G. Bennington and B. Massumi (Minneapolis: University of Minnesota Press, 1984), xxv. Two historians have recently debated the meaning of the post-modern phenomenon in ways that have relevance far beyond the confines of their discipline. See F.R. Ankersmit, "Historiography and Postmodernism," *History and Theory*, 28(2), 1989, 137–53; Perez Zagorin, "Historiography and Postmodernism: Reconsiderations," ibid., 29(3), 1990, 263–74; and Ankersmit,

"Reply to Professor Zagorin," ibid., 275–96. Ankersmit's claim that "the essence of post modernism is precisely that we should avoid pointing out essentialist patterns" virtually replicates that of Lyotard. See "Historiography and Postmodernism," 151.

150 Maxine Hong Kingston, *Tripmaster Monkey: His Fake Book* (New York: Random House, 1987). George F. Will's emphasis on "cohesive families" is one manifestation of that disposition. See his "The Liberal's Racism," in his *Suddenly: The American Idea at Home and Abroad 1986–1990* (New York: The Free Press, 1990), 322. The 1991 decision by Penguin Books of New York to republish Shawn Wong's *Homebase*, originally issued in 1979 on a very small scale by Afro-American novelist Ishmael Reed, is another.

151 For comment on a recent land claims issue, see Nicholas Hentoff, "Sacred Land," *The Nation*, 250(1), 1 January 1990, 5–6. The American Indian Film Festival and its director Mike Smith are discussed in Jay Scott, "The Western's Last Frontier," *Globe and Mail*, 24 November 1990. What, exactly, the making of *Dances With Wolves* suggests about white attitudes to "Indianness" and its nature remains ambiguous. The hero and heroine are whites who "become" aboriginals, a development which leaves (and seems intended to leave) the distinct impression that being "Indian" is to be viewed as a state of mind. Equally, however, great pains were taken to insure that Indian characters were played by native Indians, a step indicating a belief on the part of those taking it that as recent theory suggests there is a connection (though not a necessary one) among and between race, culture, and identity.

152 These words are from the song of the same name by the rap group KRS-ONE. The new black sense that race and culture are in some real sense co-extensive is perfectly articulated by black feminist bell hooks: "Black Americans have every political reason to recognize our place in the African diaspora, [and] our solidarity and cultural connections with people of African descent globally." See her *Yearning: Race, Gender, and Cultural Politics* (Toronto: Between the Lines, 1990), 133. White American acceptance of what this new self-consciousness has produced is indicated by the popularity of such network television shows as *Arsenio Hall* and *In Living Color*, while even *The Economist* has noted the widespread appeal of rap: "Commercial rap," it suggests, "cuts across race and class as the music – and culture – of young America." "Are You Proud of Who You Are?" *Economist*, 317(7684), 1990, 25.

153 One must not, however, leave the impression that the contrast between Canadian and American views of multiculturalism and multiracialism has been totally erased: while two recent commen-

tators – one Canadian, the other American – both urge accommodation of these phenomena, the spirit and measure in which they do so are quite different. For Charles Taylor's subtle but uncompromising argument that affirming equality means recognizing particularisms, see his *Multiculturalism and "The Politics of Recognition"* (Princeton: Princeton University Press, 1992). For David A. Hollinger's concern that acknowledgment of pluralism be consistent with maintenance of a common basis for citizenship, consult his "How Wide the Circle of the 'We'? American Intellectuals and the Problem of the Ethnos Since World War II," *American Historical Review*, 98(2), 1993, 317–37.

The Canadian Frame of Mind

9 Old Ontario and
the Emergence of a
National Frame of Mind

That Ontario played a leading role in promoting the national idea in post-Confederation Canada is well known. Canada First drew most of its members from that province, much of the literature which attempted to delineate the character of the new nation was produced there, and the principal Canadian support for such agencies as the Royal Society of Canada and the Royal Canadian Academy was provided by its inhabitants. If, however, the fact that the national idea after 1867 was largely Ontario-created is hardly new, less widely broadcast has been the circumstance that as early as the 1820s Upper Canadians had begun to think of their province, and the larger British North American society of which it was a part, as potentially a great nation within the empire. Upper Canada, they thought, was to be understood not simply as an extension of British civilization in an imperial province but as a community with a character and experience of its own. It was this conviction which, within forty years, matured into a belief that the territory Upper Canadians inhabited might function as the centre of a British North American civilization ripe for union into one political framework.

Through the first half of the century Upper Canadians became steadily more preoccupied with the business of creating cultural

F.H. Armstrong, H.A. Stevenson, et al., eds., *Aspects of Nineteenth Century Ontario* (Toronto: University of Toronto Press, 1974), 194–217 agencies that would expand their knowledge of themselves. Imported culture, many of them felt, could not do the whole job involved in educating Canadians. If they were to learn from, and about, those things close at hand, only a local culture, generated within the framework of local agencies, would suffice.

The important role to be played by educational institutions in acquainting people with their society and training them to function in it was early realized. By 1818 Robert Gourlay could notice the concern of "gentlemen of competent means" to have their children educated "without sending them abroad for the purpose."[1] It was true, of course, that much of the concern felt by Upper Canadians in the 1820s and 1830s over the presence of American teachers and American texts in their schools grew out of anxiety that it would weaken the imperial orientation of their pupils. By the 1840s, however, there was a growing conviction that the schools should be used to encourage a sense of local patriotism as well. As that decade began the first edition of Alexander Davidson's *The Canadian Spelling Book* took note of the peculiar importance spelling-books had in heightening their users' awareness of the objects to which the words in them referred, an attribute which allowed them to play an important role in the formation of community consciousness. The great variety of books in use in Upper Canada prevented them from playing that role, nor was the situation helped by the fact that most of those books came from Britain or the United States. All of this, Davidson asserted, must be a cause of concern to "every individual possessed of any degree of *true* patriotism."[2] It was the object of his spelling-book to change it, and in so doing to help make the schools agencies of assimilation to a way of life rooted in the community of which they were a part. Egerton Ryerson, sharing this concern, argued in 1841 that the school system of Canada West must be "not only *British*, but *Canadian*."[3] Four years later, Alexander Macnab, assistant superintendent of education for Canada West, could lament the fact that the books used in Canadian schools were not suited to the circumstances of Canadian youth.[4] And in 1849 Thomas Higginson, superintendent of common schools for the Ottawa District, similarly insisted upon the importance of textbooks which focused on the peculiarities of the community which would make use of them:

It may be proper to urge upon the Board of Education the necessity of preparing a Geography and a History of Canada for the use of the Schools. It is a matter of regret, that while we can learn from our Text-books something of almost every other country, we can learn nothing of our own; and it is deeply to be regretted that some person of talent has not, ere this, prepared such a work, – pointing out our country's advantages, natural, social, and political. Such a work would be a secure basis whereon our young people could and would rest their loyalty and patriotism; such a work would develope [sic] events and circumstances around which the associations of heart and memory might cluster, as around a common centre, making us what we should be, what we require to be, and what we have never yet been, – a united, a prosperous, and a contented people.[5]

The important role locally produced texts might play in the educational system was fully appreciated by the officials charged with the responsibility of passing judgment on Egerton Ryerson's recommendation that the Irish National Series of textbooks be introduced into the schools of Canada West. In accepting that recommendation they made clear their conviction that there should be no interference with the "few isolated School-Books ... published in the Province."[6] These reflected its character in a way no imported material could, and must not be deprived of their place. By the 1850s this concern with the bias and content of textbooks and the curriculum had clearly shown results. Normal School students in Toronto, for example, were examined in Canadian history and geography,[7] and, at the end of the decade, J.G. Hodgins' *The Geography and History of British America and of the Other Colonies of the Empire* was in use in the city's schools.[8] In 1866 it was joined by Hodgins's *A History of Canada; and of the other Provinces in British North America*, and in 1865 the Toronto publisher James Campbell issued the first of a projected series of volumes for use throughout the provinces. A geography text, its national character came in for special mention. No longer, noted the publisher, should British North Americans have to rely on books published beyond their borders, which invariably reflected the interests and character of the country in which they were produced. What was needed was a book "intended especially for the use of Schools [sic] in the British North American Provinces."[9] It was now available.

If the manner in which Upper Canadian educational authorities viewed their educational system revealed them to be thinking of their community as one which possessed characteristics of its own, the way in which some of their fellow citizens approached the problem of periodical literature showed them to possess similar convictions. *Barker's Canadian Magazine*, founded in 1846 for the avowed purpose of informing Canadians about their community, professed itself especially concerned with the encouragement of Canadian writing.[10] *The Maple Leaf or Canadian Annual* of Toronto, appearing in 1847, 1848, and 1849, similarly set itself the task of acquainting Canadians with their country. Only Canadians, it announced, would be permitted to contribute to its columns.[11] By the 1860s *The Canadian Quarterly Review and Family Magazine* could be founded at Hamilton, in the words of its prospectus, to enhance understanding of "national politics and interesting family literature. It will review and advocate, aside from party interests, those leading questions that affect the moral, political and mutual well-being of Canadians; and afford original and selected prose and poetry of a choice and useful character."[12] The *British American Magazine*, published at Toronto in 1863–4, was very much concerned to enlarge its readers' frame of reference by acquainting them with the affairs of British North America as a whole. A three-part article appearing in 1863 urged Canadians to seize the Northwest before Manifest Destiny triumphed there.[13] Others attempted to acquaint them with the Maritimes[14] or to introduce them to important figures in their past.[15]

Newspapers played an even more central role in developing a Canadian frame of reference. As the University of Toronto's Daniel Wilson noted in 1860, they had a "great influence" in shaping the outlook of those exposed to them.[16] That influence was especially evident in certain areas. So concerned were they with politics, an observer reported, that "the smallest farmer" was able to have a newspaper suitable to his political views.[17] That fact made them invaluable in heightening awareness on the part of Canadians that they lived in a separate political jurisdiction. Nor was the influence of the newspaper confined to reinforcing the sense that Canadians lived in an emerging polity with characteristics uniquely its own. As Henry Morgan observed in 1867, reading newspapers played a role in the rise of literary sensibility as well. "The morning journal," he noted, "may be said to be as much a literary as it is a political organ ..."[18]

By the late 1850s Upper Canadian journalists were sufficiently cognizant of their role in creating a sense of community and self-consciousness to form an association for the purpose of helping overcome the tendencies towards division which seemed so clearly to threaten the future of their province. This special anxiety was hardly inhibited by the fact that those tendencies were in some ways most pronounced in the world of Canadian journalism itself. Many leading journalists were in politics, and factionalism was rife among the others. The desire to overcome these internal divisions was one of the considerations motivating the founders of the Canadian Press Association. When, therefore, the association was formed at Kingston in September 1859, it was highly conscious of its role as a unifying agent and anxious to make itself effective as such.[19] Five years after its formation, it took note of the movement towards British North American union in a manner which, if jocular and light-hearted, also indicated clearly that it appreciated the significance of what was taking place. The people of the five provinces, noted the association's president at its 1864 meeting in Belleville, should be encouraged in their efforts to unite:

> Dreaming we could be a nation,
> By a great confederation ...
> Urging that a five-fold mingle
> Stouter far than is a single;
> That one foot on the Pacific
> Should excite no thought terrific,
> And the other on th'Atlantic,
> Ought to drive no neighbour frantic.[20]

By 1867 a number of resolutions had been introduced calling for members of the Quebec and Maritime press to join the association, and in that year David Wylie, a former president, suggested changing its name from the Canadian to the British North American Press Association.[21] That it might spread outwards from Ontario into the whole of British North America was a prospect welcomed by D'Arcy McGee. Such a move, he thought, would not only raise standards and professionalize the business of running a newspaper but also aid in the distribution of news and therefore heighten the national sense.[22]

While journalism and the treatment given contemporary events assumed for some Canadians a role of importance in the making of a Canadian sensibility, others worked towards the same end by offering encouragement to the idea that theirs was a society bound together by a common and meaningful past. In 1823 Charles Fothergill of York projected a "Canadian Annual Register" which, besides examining recent events, would include material on the early history of Canada.[23] Before many years had passed, the War of 1812 had become a staple of Canadian historical writing. Canadians, much of it argued, had been compelled to resist a common threat and as a consequence had become a self-conscious people determined to preserve its collective existence. Given equal emphasis with the necessity of maintaining the link with Britain was the role Canadians themselves had played in securing their land from invasion. David Thompson's *History of the Late War between Great Britain and the United States* (1832), John Richardson's *War of 1812* (1842), and G. Auchinleck's *A History of the War between Great*

Britain and the United States (1855) argued that the bulk of the fighting had been done by the locally-raised militia valiantly rising to the defence of their homeland. Canadians, then, were fully capable of uniting in support of a common cause. That, in fact, was one of the principal points Montreal's *Literary Garland* thought Richardson's book to contain.[24]

That the impulse behind the writing of Canadian history should be a nationalist one was a point made explicitly by the *Anglo-American Magazine* in 1852. Discussing a proposal for yet another history of the War of 1812, it suggested that its purpose should be "the setting before Canadians, in a modest though spirited manner, the achievements of their fathers ... and the awakening the memory of their own past struggle in defense of the loved land of their adoption ... such a review will, nay must, tend to foster in our day the same national feeling which at that time impelled every colonist to fly to arms to repel the hated invasion of their republican neighbours ... the real object of our undertaking [must be] the exposition of the loyalty, courage and energies of the brave yeomanry of Canada."[25]

In the 1860s Upper Canadians sought especially to contribute their share of heroes to the nationalist pantheon. Charles Lindsey's *The Life and Times of William Lyon Mackenzie,* published at Toronto in 1862, only marginally met this criterion, for Lindsey was critical of Mackenzie's tendency towards precipitate action and thought the justified grievances of the farmers might have been met without the necessity for rebellion, but Henry J. Morgan's *Sketches of Celebrated Canadians and Persons Connected with Canada* (1862) was clearly intended to mark out the manner in which Canadians had worked together to create a common tradition. Morgan's object, he explained, was to show that "we have had and do possess men as truly great, talented and devotedly loyal as any other kingdom, not excepting the mother country herself. We may also be able to convince the youth of this rising nation, that their sires, grandsires, and great grandsires, had names associated with great deeds and glorious efforts in the cause of freedom and loyalty ... A just pride, an intense love of our native country, and an ardent hope and desire for its future greatness, have alone enabled and prevailed on us to go through a task of great mental labor, yet to us one of love."[26] Four years later he expanded his work in order to intensify the pride and sense of accomplishment British North Americans as a whole must feel in their society. *The Place British Americans Have Won in History* (1866) rested upon the earlier volume but included the great men of all the provinces.

Few of those concerned to encourage the development of a national frame of reference failed to appreciate the role literature might play in their enterprise. In conformity with the dictates of romanticism, Upper Canadians regularly pointed to their past as the repository of material that would illuminate the Canadian experience and provide an abundance of material for Canadian writers. War, primitive peoples, and the tribulations of the pioneer combined to produce a mine of readily exploitable material. "The sufferings of the United Empire Loyalists," proclaimed York's *Canadian Literary Magazine* in 1833, "– the privations of those who sank beneath the gnawings of Famine in Hungry Bay, – the adventures of the Hunter, especially if he possessed the romantic spirit of Lord Edward Fitzgerald, – the Guerilla-like achievements of the late War, – the past and present condition of the aborigines, – are subjects equally interesting to the Canadians and to him who has adopted Canada for his country."[27] The *Canadian Literary Magazine* took the exploration of these themes as its central task, hoping throughout that in so doing it would "receive the support of every individual who feels a desire that Canada should possess a literature of its own ..."[28] Another journal, based in the same city, thought much had already been accomplished. *The Roseharp*, in fact, professed to see Upper Canada's cultural life on the threshold of a great breakthrough: "This Province has now arrived at such a state of improvement in population and wealth, that we already see the dawning of the Arts and Sciences; but genius in a young country requires the fostering care of the community at large to bring it forward to the world ... The object ... is to encourage and diffuse sentiments of loyal patriotism – a taste for literature and the fine arts; and by exciting emulation, give energy, and rouse into action, the dormant seeds of genius."[29]

By the middle of the century, calls for a native literature were frequently made. A resident of Williamstown, Canada West, writing in 1848 on "Our literature, Present and Prospective," recommended greater devotion to native historical writing and national songs.[30] The year following, Egerton Ryerson looked forward "to the day when [school] libraries will be increased and enriched by Canadian contributions and publications."[31] In 1855 Daniel Wilson called for a Canadian literature "which shall embrace independent representatives in each department of knowledge."[32] The *Wesleyan Repository and Literary Record* argued in 1860 that "even if unexceptionable literature could be obtained from other lands, it is nevertheless, highly desirable that we should cultivate a national literature of our own."[33] And in 1863 Hamilton's *Canadian Illustrated*

News pronounced poetry to be "as much an element of healthy national life as commerce or manufactures."[34]

Poets, responding to these pleas, continued in the 1860s to write with their accustomed vigour of the virtue and importance of dealing in verse with their own society. "Let me hear the tales, and stories," wrote George Washington Johnson, unabashed by the echoes of Longfellow which resounded throughout his 1864 poem "Manitoulin,"

> Ballads, songs, and wild traditions,
> And Canadian, Indian legends,
> That are woven with our history ...
> Let it not appear a puzzle
> That the song that first I sing you
> Is about my native country.[35]

A new and significant note was struck in that decade by the fact that Canadian poetry began to be anthologized. This operation was designed to show by bringing it together in one place that a body of Canadian literature existed. In that sense it was artificial and lacked spontaneity. The attempt, moreover, was clearly designed to stimulate an all too obviously weak interest in Canadian literature. Yet the fact that it could be made at all indicates, as its makers intended it should, that there was now in existence a body of literature reflective of, and based upon, the Canadian experience.

For E.H. Dewart, the very act of bringing this material together was a nationalist undertaking. It confirmed the existence of a separate and distinct Canadian national life. "A national literature," he wrote, introducing the anthology to which many Upper Canadians had contributed, "is an essential element in the formation of national character. It is not merely the record of a country's mental progress: it is the expression of its intellectual life, the bond of national unity, and the guide of national energy."[36]

This idealist vision of the role literature might play in reflecting, integrating, and directing the national experience formed the core of H.J. Morgan's *Bibliotheca Canadensis*, published in 1867. A catalogue of his country's literature, its avowed purpose was to demonstrate that Canadians had for some time possessed a sense of their country as a distinct and special place, one to the comprehension of whose character they had devoted much energy.

The existence of a body of national literature provided critics with the opportunity to assess not only the success with which Canadians had articulated their national tradition but also the depth and richness of the tradition itself. The development of a Canadian tradition, and of a literature embodying it, had been retarded, thought one, by Canada's lack of a mythic and heroic past. Much progress had, however, been made in the land since its discovery. The journey Canadians had undertaken through time was a kind of odyssey of the human spirit, demonstrating the great works of which humans were capable. A substantial literature might be built around the exploration of that epic theme. Canadians, then, could overlook the fact that the mists of antiquity had not yet cast "their picturesque and mystic spells"[37] over the land. The materials for a national literature might be drawn from other sources. Canada must, in fact, "congratulate herself on the poets she already possesses ..." They had made a distinct and important contribution to her self-knowledge. "A nation's best benefactors," concluded the critic on a note of transcendental ecstasy, "are its poets, for it is their office to refine and exalt material progress by evolving from it that divine life and thought without which it is but a body without a soul."[38]

Science, like education and literature, was conscientiously promoted as a nationalist tool. It would, its partisans claimed, at once heighten self-consciousness and enhance national strength. Where history deepened a people's sense of themselves in time, science broadened it through space. By isolating a country's geographical, climatic, and geological attributes, the scientists made it better known and so expanded the frame of reference within which their fellow citizens operated. And by locating its riches they helped provide it with the sinews of national strength.

Anxious to know the face of the land on which they came to live, Upper Canadians early sought to explore and catalogue its features. In 1806 the Upper Canadian assembly appropriated a small sum of money for the purchase of scientific equipment.[39] By 1830 the conviction that the British North American provinces had unique and special features deserving of systematic scientific description had grown strong enough for Charles Fothergill to propose a three-year scientific expedition to the Pacific coast. It would, he hoped, include a geologist, botanist, mineralogist, and astronomer and have as its double object an examination of the natural resources of the west and an assessment of the possibilities for settlement there.[40]

Increasing interest in the province's geological character and natural history led the York Literary and Philosophical Society to request a grant from the legislature in 1832. Seeking, it informed the legislature, to do everything necessary to promote acquaintance with the character of the country, it proposed to use any funds received for the purpose of investigating the geology, mineralogy, and natural history of the province "thoroughly and scientifically."[41] Four years later William Lyon Mackenzie proposed the appointment of a select committee of the legislature to prepare a "plan for the Geological Survey or examination" of this province.[42] Finally, in 1841, the legislature of the newly formed Province of Canada appropriated £1500 for a geological survey.[43] Canadians were brought into contact with the knowledge yielded by the survey's activities in a number of ways. Reports of its work were published annually by the middle-1850s. The college museums of Canada West – Victoria College in Cobourg, Queen's College in Kingston, and Trinity College, Toronto – contained samples of Canadian minerals, while the museum of the Canadian Institute in Toronto displayed geological and other specimens from both Canada and the Maritimes.[44]

That this activity was to serve an embryonic nationalist purpose is plain from the motives of those who engaged in it. Fothergill made it clear in the 1830s that his proposal to encourage natural history was founded on the proposition that a large part of the "power" and "high character" of nations depends upon their pursuit of science and especially their having accurate knowledge of their own natural resources.[45] The *Canadian Literary Magazine*, drawing attention to the fact that scientific activity augmented the wealth of nations, pointed in 1833 to the richness of the harvest awaiting the scientific investigator. "The subterranean riches of this favored continent," it noted, "are, as yet, but very imperfectly developed: the depths of the lakes, and the recesses of the forests, are teeming with treasurers ... which no pen has yet accounted for."[46] In 1855 William E. Logan, head of the Geological Survey since 1842, made explicit the link between science, development, and his "country's" future. The purpose of the Survey, he pointed out, "is to ascertain the mineral resources of the Country, and this is kept steadily in view. What new scientific facts have resulted from it, have come out in the course of what I conceive to be economic researches carried out in a scientific way ... Economics leads to science and science to economics."[47] Canadian periodicals interested in science were especially concerned with its national relevance. Upper Canada's leading scientific magazine was conscious in the extreme of its community obligations. "A form of local pride," a student of it has noted, "incipient source of national aspirations, colours the scientific pursuits of the *Canadian Journal*."[48]

The sense that British North America was a unified society possessing characteristics binding it together and capable of being analyzed in a systematic and ordered way was heightened by the appearance in 1863 of a summary treatment of the work done by the Geological Survey over the previous twenty years. A large volume of over 900 pages, it was accompanied by an atlas containing a geological map of British North America embracing Canada, the Maritimes, and adjacent parts of the United States.[49] The next year E.J. Chapman, professor of mineralogy at the University of Toronto, wrote the first Canadian textbook on geology. Entitled *A Popular and Practical Exposition of the Minerals and Geology of Canada*, it was designed to have more than a narrowly educational utility.[50] The national relevance of this kind of work, suggested the *Canadian Illustrated News*, gave it its greatest value. That journal itself proposed to publish articles on the geology of Canada in order to "give Canadians a better idea of the land they live in." It discerned a close connection between geology, self-knowledge, and the nation's future, for the study of the country's land and resources involved its future character "in all the phases of industrial, social and national development."[51]

That old Ontario was coming to see itself as a society with its own character, needs, and identity was, perhaps, made most clear by its concern to have government participate in the process by which that sense of identity could be clarified and communicated to an ever wider audience. Government, it was argued, had a responsibility to help the community know itself. And the playing of a central role in establishing an educational system was but one way in which it might fulfil this responsibility: there were other steps that might be taken to promote the idea that the society over whose affairs it presided possessed a character and experience of its own. Only in an atmosphere of cultural vitality could a Canadian culture bloom effectively. Priority might therefore be given to the general encouragement of cultural activity. In 1824, accordingly, the government of Upper Canada voted to spend £124 annually for the purchase of books and texts to be distributed throughout the province.[52] By the early 1830s the first attempts at passing copyright legislation for the purpose of protecting Upper Canadian authors were being made.[53] By the 1850s public authorities could claim much of the credit for the fact that parts of the province enjoyed access to at least some of the masterworks of western culture. Many of the books available throughout the province, noted a government official, would have been unknown "had they not been introduced by the agency of a public department."[54]

The government's particular concern with fostering cultural activities which would amplify the sense that Upper Canada was a unique and special community soon became manifest. Major John

Richardson's request for government aid, originally put to the governor general in 1841 and later, in revised form, to the legislature, saw him seek government support on the ground that he was "generally known and acknowledged as the only Author this country has produced, or who has attempted to infuse into it a spirit of literature."[55] The request was met in 1842 with a grant of £250 to assist in the publication of his work on the War of 1812.[56]

The failure of Richardson's project did not prevent the government from coming to the assistance of others. In 1851 the committee charged with responsibility for implementing the legislature's policy of encouraging literary activity announced that "In furtherance of the encouragement usually extended by the Provincial Legislature to literary enterprise in *Canada*, the Committee have entertained several applications which have been made to them by parties engaged in various literary undertakings for assistance on behalf of their several publications."[57] In its operations the committee tried carefully to maintain standards and at the same time insure that no worthwhile Canadian project went without some form of an agreement to purchase a specified number of the books produced in order to insure, at the least, that costs of publication would be recovered. In 1852 some requests were refused on the ground that "no proof has been adduced of their special merit or value ... it is not thought advisable to encourage indiscriminate applications of this nature, or to make applications on their behalf, unless in the case of works of special excellence or utility."[58] But once the committee was satisfied that work before it did meet these standards, its "desire to foster native talent"[59] might come into play.

In time, it was easy enough for Upper Canadians to distinguish their society from those on the other side of the Atlantic. A part of the New World, it differed elementally from the Old. In its midst all might be remade and lifted to a new and unprecedented eminence. Even an anglophile such as Henry Scadding could write in the early 1830s that

> Glory belongs, I ween, fair West, to thee –
> Westward was aye her cause, and still shall be:
> When one great empire fell, in river hurl'd,
> Still westward rose another on the world.[60]

The *Colonial Advocate* informed its readers in 1830 that they had been cast by Providence "in a highly favoured land," whose natural splendours – "luxuriant harvests" and a "healthful climate" – allowed them to contrast their situation most favorably with that of Europe. Free from the class tensions of that "opulent" continent, theirs was not a society riven by the "unbounded" wealth of one class and the "degrading" poverty of another.[61] For Samuel Strickland Upper Canada was, quite simply, a "Garden of Eden."[62]

Having placed their community firmly in a New World context, many Canadians then took it as their task to indicate in what ways it differed from those other countries who could claim this distinction. There was in particular a marked interested in delineating its character in a manner which would show that for all it shared with the United States it was, in the end, a better and more perfect society.

Two things allowed this distinction: its British heritage and its location in the hemisphere's northern latitudes. Institutions and climate acted in combination to insure that the New World genius would produce in Canada the best of all possible communities. Canada participated in the character of the New World, wrote Susanna Moodie, and could therefore alter fundamentally the status and even the nature of those who crossed its borders. The immigrant, released into the beneficent atmosphere of the New World, was to be likened to "one awaken'd from the dead." It was in the West, "beyond the wave," where freedom made its home. But in Canada the New World's magic had a kind of material to work with not present elsewhere. The Canadian, heir to British liberty and freedom, along with the principal institutions in which they were contained, was "no child of bondage" but one who had inherited "all thy British mother's spirit."[63] The prospects for the realization of the perfect community were thus brighter in her society than elsewhere.

William Kirby's *The UE*, composed in 1846 but unpublished until 1859, similarly drew attention to the fact that Canada was endowed with the values, traditions, and at least some of the institutions of the homeland. Established in the north by the Loyalists, their presence insured that Canadians would not be victimized by republican excess.[64]

The Loyalists themselves began to attract much interest in the 1850s precisely because they had introduced a specific set of ideas, principles, and institutions to Canada. The passing of the Loyalist generation in the 1840s and 1850s combined with the growing self-consciousness of the Canadians to heighten interest in the men and women increasingly to be regarded as the initiators of a national tradition. It was the death of his father in 1854, noted Egerton

Ryerson, that had set him thinking about writing the history of the Loyalists. He wished "to vindicate their character as a body, [and] to exhibit their principles and patriotism."[65]

If Canadians were heir to a tradition which, by conferring upon them a particular set of institutions, ensured that in their land the elixir of the New World would not turn brackish and impure, the existence of slavery in the United States could be used to make the point with telling effect. Here, clearly, was an institution which perverted all that the New World stood for. And – this, for many Canadians, was the real point – it was an institution from which Canada was mercifully free. The argument that Canada was the true home of liberty could thus be powerfully reinforced with the assertion that

> The clank of chains, the sighs, and slavery's tears
> Shall never pain Canadians' loyal ears –[66]

To Canadians, regularly reminded of the great controversy pulling at the vitals of their southern neighbour, this thought must have been the source of convincing proof indeed that they and their society were especially blessed. For Evan McColl, "The Lake of the Thousand Isles" was infinitely preferable to the Missouri or the Ohio rivers. No matter how majestic their flow or bountiful the land through which they passed, they were irreversibly tainted with the curse of slavery.[67] Canada then, was envisioned as a society in which, paradoxically, the presence of British attitudes toward liberty and freedom insured that the egalitarianism of the New World was not qualified in any way. Its air was rent by "no heavy clank of servile chains." On its soil any man,

> ... no matter what his skin may be,
> Can stand erect, and proudly say, I'm FREE.[68]

To many observers Canada's happy mixture of the old and the new was its chief distinction. In 1824 William Lyon Mackenzie suggested that their New World location gave Canadians a rich soil and favourable climate which, in conjunction with their tie to the "land of intellectual grandeur," conferred upon them a uniquely favoured position.[69] Many travellers appraised Canadian society in similar terms. As G.M. Craig points out, they often found Canadians to have "the best of both worlds: British stability and tradition, without the encrustations of outworn institutions and the terrible problem of surplus population, from which Britain suffered; and the illimitable resources and opportunities of the New World, without the curses of mob rule and slavery which made life in the United States so unattractive."[70]

If Canada's institutional heritage helped it maintain a purer form of New World civilization, its climate was held to reinforce the manner in which those institutions operated. The clear, bright, invigorating air of the north stimulated what was best in people and so encouraged the emergence of those qualities essential if a life of freedom were to be sustained. It was, therefore, in the north that true liberty was to be found. Slaves who would enjoy it must, accordingly, direct their footsteps there. Until they could so do it was their unfortunate lot to "envy every little bird that takes its northward flight." Canada, in fact, served those slaves awaiting freedom in the same manner the North Star served mariners:

As to the Polar Star they turn
  Who brave a pathless sea, –
So the oppressed in secret yearn,
  Dear native land for thee![71]

Typical of this style of appreciating the country were the contents of the 1848 *Maple Leaf Annual.* A selection of poems – "The Trapper," "A Canadian Christmas Carol," "The Indian on Revisiting an Old Encampment," and stories – "A First Day in the Bush," and "A Chapter on Canadian Scenery," were included with the object of making Canadians generally more familiar with their country. But the volume also offered its readers poems such as "The Emigrants' Bride," containing references to "the North Countrie" and "our romantic North," or "A Canadian Winter Night," heavily laden with extravagant imagery concerning the travels of the "Queen of Night" through snow-covered, ice-encased Canada.[72]

Some observers saw the whole of British North America in possession of characteristics which, while clearly in evidence at the time of writing, were, hopefully, transitory phenomena soon to be replaced by others more true and lasting. William Lyon Mackenzie had no doubt that British America in the 1820s was characterized by a kind of cultural pluralism. But to him this engendered not so much mutual tolerance as unpleasant division. Just as the people of Britain had overcome their national differences and joined to form one great people, so must those of the New World. As it was in Britain "So let it be with British America – let every national Distinction cease among us – let not the native Canadian look upon his Irish or Scottish neighbour as an intruder, nor the native of the

British Isles taunt the other about stupidity and incapacity: Rather let them become as one race, and may the only strife among us be a praiseworthy emulation as to who shall attain the honour of conferring the greatest Benefits on the country of our birth – or the land of our choice."[73] J.R. Godley, a traveller from England, found pluralism to be a fact of Upper Canadian life. Its population, he noted, was "exceedingly heterogeneous and exotic, [a characteristic] much more remarkable here than in the United States."[74] This circumstance, he thought, was attributable to the small size of the native-born population coupled with its failure to develop a definite character to which immigrants might be assimilated. Taken together, these things made it difficult to "absorb and remodel ... the newcomers." All of this stood in marked contrast to the United Sates, where immigrants did "amalgamate to a certain extent with the native-born population, or at least are swallowed up in it." Nonetheless, Godley thought, there was "a national character in process of formation ..."[75] though he scrupulously refrained from detailing the elements which composed it.

By 1860, contended one Upper Canadian, it was possible to isolate a Canadian type and Canadian interests with which immigrants must identify. "Every person," wrote the Reverend Wellington Jeffers, "expecting to stay in Canada and expecting his children to have their inheritance here, whether he was born in England, Ireland or Scotland, ought to feel himself to be a Canadian; he ought to feel for the character and glory of Canada, and to be devoted to its interests."[76]

Although Jeffers thus saw his idea of the nation as a device that might be used to integrate its different parts into a unified and self-conscious whole (and so gave evidence of his belief that Canada could not be conceived of merely as an extension of another society, however strong the formal ties that bound the two together), he was no more capable than his predecessors of giving that idea an exact formulation. So difficult was this problem, found some Upper Canadians, that it could best be met by avoiding it altogether. Their solution, accordingly, lay not in exposition but in symbol. To comprehend their society's attributes in a single striking image would be to show that it possessed the most compact and tangible of identities. Functioning as a tool for the integration of the collective experience, the symbol would overcome any tendency towards incoherence and division and obviate the need for an elaborate and detailed description of the national character.

The maple leaf, a product of Canadian soil which knew neither Europe, nor (save for its northernmost parts) the United States, was singled out by the 1840s as an especially appropriate symbolic device. It became the title of a new literary magazine published in the last year of that decade, whose editors, having decided that "no flowers, however lovely, should be twined with 'the maple leaf,' but those that had blossomed amidst her forests,"[77] sought to give point to their determination that the magazine be unreservedly Canadian. Its peculiar association with Canada and the fact that it came out of the liberty-giving Canadian forest allowed Alexander McLachlan to suggest in 1858 that it was in "the maple dells where freedom dwells."[78] Another Canadian poet found in its fresh, green, unspoiled beauty a suitable representation of his country's hopes for the future:

> In her fair and budding beauty,
>   A fitting emblem she
> Of this land of promise,
>   Of hope, of liberty.[79]

By the 1860s the tendency to epitomize the Canadian experience in symbolic terms was sufficiently widespread to arouse concern on the part of those who felt that it inspired a mode of thinking at once simplistic and overzealous. Symbol, argued some critics, had degenerated into stereotype. A truly sensitive and feeling reaction to the land ought to inform the best writing about Canada. Instead, noted the *Saturday Reader* in 1865, many authors had failed to be "national in the true sense of the word" and attempted "to satisfy our mental cravings with a dish of beaver, stewed in maple leaves."[80]

Interest in the elucidation of Canadian themes came in time to be accompanied by a concern to articulate those themes in a manner and style appropriate to them. To be concerned with content remained vital; but form now seemed no less important. It too might locate art in, and help express, a national tradition.

The Canadian environment, it was argued, imposed an obligation on the architect to design buildings in a way that not only allowed them to function in, but also harmonized with the difficult Canadian winter. "Though we can scarcely hope to see," wrote William Hay, a Toronto architect, in 1853, "... a distinct style of pure architecture formed on the primitive log hut, something may be done to lead the taste of the Province into a direction which may tend to give a local character to our Canadian edifices."[81] Such a style might rest upon the old English architecture with its use of wood and its steeply pitched roofs, thereby drawing on an abundant Canadian resource and meeting the difficulties posed by the heavy Canadian snowfall.

Canadian critics and writers were especially preoccupied with the problem of style. The belief that Canadian subjects should be explored remained essential and the mark of a national poet; but increasingly it was argued that those subjects could not be handled adequately by employing the diction and imagery developed by another society in the course of giving expression to its special character. Charles Sangster was, accordingly, brought under critical fire by Daniel Wilson in 1858 for his tendency, even in the course of exploring Canadian themes, to repeat "old-world music and song." In much of what he wrote there was "nothing that would betray its new world parentage." The Canadian poet must be mindful of language and style: "However much taste and refinement may be displayed in such echoes [as Sangster's] of the old thought and fancy of Europe, the path to success lies not in this direction for the poet of the new world."[82] Sangster was especially lax in his stylistic treatment of that quintessential North American figure, the Indian. "At best, "wrote Wilson, "it is not true Indian, but only the white man dressed up in his attire; strip him of his paint and feathers, and it is our-world acquaintance."[83]

As the century unfolded Upper Canadians came increasingly to encompass all of British North America in their vision of the national future. By the 1860s the entire region might be comprehended in the vision of change and development witnessed by those for whom the most accurate index to a country's state and nature remained the degree to which its progress could be measured. The record, though largely written in Canada West, must embrace all of the provinces. In 1863 H.Y. Hind and his collaborators therefore proposed to lay before their readers the *Eighty Years Progress of British North America*. Progress, they pointed out, was a fact of the industrial age; nowhere was its triumph more marked than in North America; and in North America the British provinces were proving themselves at least as capable of it as the United States. Enough, in fact, had been accomplished to suggest a rate of progress that "shall place the provinces, within the day of many now living, on a level with Great Britain herself, in population, in wealth, and in power."[84]

Other Upper Canadians, sharing this frame of reference, argued that since the provinces possessed a unity of spirit, character, and interests, they should come together in a formal way. John Beverly Robinson and John Strachan were only the first among a long line of Upper Canadians to propose a British North American union.

Their concern to advance alternatives to the union of the two Canadas projected in the early 1820s led each of them to prepare a lengthy document arguing the case for a more comprehensive undertaking. Such a scheme was practicable, Robinson thought, because it would involve the uniting of a people bound together by their common loyalty to the crown and their shared antipathy to republican institutions. The sense of community was, of course, not yet strong. One of his scheme's objects, accordingly, was to strengthen it by bringing British North Americans together within a common political framework. This would, he hoped, cause them to develop a greater sense of "community of interest and feeling among themselves."[85]

Strachan thought a general union no more difficult to effect than a union of the two Canadas, while its fruits would be far greater. Its formation would, in particular, do much to insure that no "rival power" took possession of the provinces. "What glory," he wrote, "may be expected to redound to the statesman who gives a free constitution to all the British North American colonies and by consolidating them into one territory or kingdom exalts them to a nation acting in unity and under the protection of the British Empire."[86]

By 1846 the Toronto *Globe* could point to the Hudson's Bay Territories to the west as the proper legacy of Canadians. Consciousness of that vast unopened region was heightened by the tours of Paul Kane with their harvest of dramatic paintings. Expeditions such as that undertaken by Henry Youle Hind in the 1850s furthered the work of making the west known to central Canada. George Brown's ambitions for the territory grew through the 1850s, with the *Globe* providing a powerful instrument for the promotion of the cause in whose direction those ambitions led. And this generation of Upper Canadians not only looked west; their frame of reference, like Robinson's and Strachan's, embraced the lands to the east as well. Those territories too could be comprehended in the same expansive vision. Thus might George Washington Johnson write in the early 1860s that British North America, possessing the same quality of freedom throughout its length and breadth, was free from the blight of slavery "from Erie's shore to Old Atlantic's waves."[87] The Maritime provinces, no less than Canada itself, participated in the same essential character.

Considered as a nationalist phenomenon, the frame of mind which had emerged in Canada West by the 1860s was as remarkable for its deficiencies as for the fact that it had taken shape at all. Far from involving a highly articulated vision of British North American independence and sovereignty, it supposed a Canadian future within the imperial system. British North American union, insisted its partisans, was to be supported precisely because it offered the only means by which such a future could be guaranteed. "Our connection with the Mother Country," Alexander Campbell of Cataraqui told the Legislative Council, "cannot be maintained for any great length of time without such a union."[88] The ambiguity produced by a commitment on the part of those who would make a nation to continuing subordination within the empire was dissolved by the fact that British power was held essential to the maintenance of British North America, while a unified British North America might use its imperial situation to make a place for itself in the world at large. The essential harmony between this nationalism and the brand of imperial sentiment which was its partner did not, however, always appear clearly, a fact that would produce confusion in the years to come.[89]

Nor was this pattern of thought conceptually adequate. Often tentative and the result of half-formed convictions, its most serious flaw was its failure to contain a systematized and comprehensive idea of the national character. Whatever kind of British North American nationality the politicians may have found it practically necessary to build, at the level of conceptualization the national future envisioned by many of the poets, writers, educators, and scientists of Upper Canada was an English-speaking one in which the French-speaking inhabitants of British North America had hardly a place. A truncated and incomplete vision of the new nationality might command the allegiance of those whose sensibilities it did embrace but it could hardly win the enthusiasm of those whose character and ideals it neglected. Framing a conceptualization that would overcome this considerable difficulty became the most taxing and complex problem facing the theoreticians of the new nationality.[90]

Finally, how deeply the national idea penetrated into the life of Upper Canadian society cannot with assurance be known. It was, of course, the possession of people who had the talent, the interest, and the opportunity to promote its diffusion among their fellows. They controlled the agencies through which opinion in their society was formulated and broadcast. Yet, in the last analysis, how widespread or influential these ideas were can be no more than the subject of an informed speculation.

Granting the problematical nature of this phenomenon is not, however, the equivalent of saying that it was without significance. It had, in fact, a great significance, amply demonstrated during the Confederation Debates. Because of it Macdonald could invite, and even assume, the consent of his audience to the proposition that British North America already formed, in some important sense, a union. In this way he was to get past a difficult stage in the argument by treating it as something that did not have to be argued at all. Thus might he tell the chamber, and through it the province beyond, how appropriate and unexceptionable it was that British North Americans, "belonging, as they do, to the same nation," and having "a like feeling of ardent attachment for this, our common country," should come together in a clear and formal way.[91]

The Upper Canadian Fathers, indeed, were able to finesse much of the debate by proceeding on the assumption that their audience possessed a common vision of a collective British North American future even then in process of realization. George Brown contended that the achievement of a great national destiny, far from being a project that must begin from nothing, would rest from the outset on substantial foundations. The British North American provinces, more populous and wealthy than the United States at the moment of their birth, might already be compared to the great states of Europe. How, then, could it be doubted that the child of their union would be a "future empire" of truly remarkable proportions?[92] Walter McCrea, elected to the Legislative Council for the Western District, pronounced the scheme's opponents guilty of a kind of disloyalty, no less real for the fact that its object as yet existed only in imagination. "Had a union of all these provinces existed in fact as it has existed in the minds of statesmen since the commencement of the present century," he suggested, "the man who, in the face of our present critical position ... [proposed] to dissolve that union and scatter us again into disjointed fragments, would be looked upon as an enemy to his Queen and a traitor to his country."[93]

The House, it was regularly told, could in conscience act with despatch. There had been ample opportunity to consider what was proposed. The confederation scheme, far from injecting a new element into the life and politics of British North America, found its place in an old and familiar tradition. "The question," said McCrea, "has been propounded by eminent statesmen both in the old country and on this side of the Atlantic time and again since the commencement of the present century, and has been in the minds of the people ever since."[94] Brown recalled at length that the idea of a general union had been before Upper Canadians for years.[95] A plain-speaking Macdonald reminded his audience simply that "this subject ... is not a new one."[96]

Neither the idea that British North America formed a country nor the proposition that it become a state were, then, the Fathers continually emphasized, new. What was novel and unprecedented was the rightness of the time. The conjunction of circumstance created by deadlock in Canada, civil war in the United Sates, and a changing view of empire in Britain gave the project a special urgency. It provided, in fact, an opportunity that must not be missed. Confederation, said McCrea, owed its sudden eminence to the fact that "no opportunity has ever presented itself like the present. [In these circumstances it] had but to be mentioned to take complete possession of the minds of the people."[97] The "ripeness of public opinion" thus created must, Brown argued, settle the matter, for who knew when the circumstances producing it would come again?[98] Macdonald similarly stressed the matter of timing. If this great and long-standing objective was to be accomplished, it was imperative that the "happy concurrence of circumstances" urging the provinces towards it be properly met. "If we do not embrace this opportunity, the present favourable time will pass away and we may never have it again."[99]

Old Ontario's national sense, these arguments reveal, at once allowed the creation of, and itself became, an ideology which rationalized that province's thrust towards dominance in British North America. By producing a group of nationally-minded Upper Canadians inclined to see British North America as a unity, it helped to insure that confederation would be viewed, in their province at least, not simply as an expedient for the resolution of important and pressing problems, but as the means of realizing a national destiny. Invested with this weighty significance, it could not help but finds its passage easier.[100]

Succeeding generations of Ontarians, building upon this foundation, played a leading role in defining the national idea and constructing the agencies required to sustain and amplify it. Their vision of the national character, like its parent fired in the crucible of the Ontario experience, similarly reflected that province's perspective and interest. By turns centralizing and provincialist, it was carried, thanks to the strength of its sustaining apparatus, to all parts of the country. Those who challenged it with their own sense of the manner in which the country should be understood very often found themselves on the defensive. Thus sure that its influence in defining the terms of debate concerning the national future would be primary, Ontario acquired a powerful instrument for the maintenance of its central position in the nation's affairs. In this way its early sense of the nation at once augmented its power and retained its utility.[101]

NOTES

1 Cited in H.Y. Hind, T.C. Keefer, et al., *Eighty Years Progress of British North America* (Toronto, 1863), 387.

2 Alexander Davidson, *The Canada Spelling Book* (Toronto, 1848), "Preface."

3 Egerton Ryerson, 1841 Address, Ryerson Letters, 1840–6, Victoria College Archives. Cited in J. Donald Wilson, Robert M. Stamp, and Louis-Philippe Audet, *Canadian Education: A History* (Scarborough, 1970), 218.

4 Province of Canada, Assembly, *Journals* 1846, Appendix P: "Annual Report of the Assistant Superintendent of Education, on the State of Common Schools Throughout Canada West for the year 1844," submitted by Alexander Macnab, Cobourg, 1 August 1845.

5 Ibid., 1850, Appendix 20, "Annual Report of the Normal, Model, and Common Schools in Upper Canada for the year 1849," part 1, section 12, extracts from the reports of district superintendents, Thomas Higginson, superintendent of common schools for the Ottawa District.

6 Cited in W.R. Riddell, "The First Copyrighted Book in the Province of Canada," Ontario Historical Society, *Papers and Records*, 25, 1928, 409.

7 Province of Canada, Assembly, *Journals*, 1852–53, Appendix JJ, "Annual Report of the Normal, Model, and Common Schools, in Upper Canada, for the year 1851: with appendices," by the chief superintendent of schools, E. Ryerson, 27 April 1852, sub-appendix D, Documents Relating to the Normal School, Toronto.

8 J.E. Middleton, *The Municipality of Toronto: A History*, 3 vols. (Toronto, 1923), vol. 1, 542.

9 Toronto Public Library, Campbell's British American Series of School Books, *Modern School Geography and Atlas Prepared for the Use of Schools in the British Provinces – Specimen* (Montreal and Toronto, 1865), Preface. Bound with *Canadian Booksellers' Catalogues*, vol. 2, 1856–74.

10 E.J. Barker, "Editor's Table," *Barker's Canadian Magazine*, 1(2), 1846, 112.

11 A.R.M. Lower, *Canadians in the Making* (Toronto, 1958), 233.

12 *Canadian Illustrated News*, 2(19), 26 September 1863, 218.

13 "Northwest British America," *British American Magazine*, 1, May 1863, 1–11; 1, June 1863, 167–78; 1, July 1863, 268–72.

14 "The St. Lawrence Route – A Tour to the Lower Provinces," ibid., 2, March 1864, 505–10; 2, April 1864, 598–605.

15 "Personal Sketches; or, Reminiscences of Public Men in Canada," ibid., 2, January 1864, 225–38.

16 Daniel Wilson, "Family Herald," *Canadian Journal*, ns, 5, 1860, 57. Cited in Carl Ballstadt, "The Quest for Canadian Identity in Pre-Confederation English-Canadian Literary Criticism," (MA diss., University of Western Ontario, 1959), 141–2.

17 J.B. Brown, *Views of Canada and the Colonists* (Edinburgh, 1851), 161–2, cited in S.D. Clark, *The Social Development of Canada: An Introductory Study with Select Documents* (Toronto, 1942), 283.

18 Henry J. Morgan, *Bibliotheca Canadensis* (Ottawa, 1867), 18, cited in Ballstadt, "Quest for Canadian Identity," 142.

19 A.H. Colquhoun, "The Canadian Press Association," in *A History of Canadian Journalism in the several Portions of the Dominion with a sketch of the Canadian Press Association 1850–1908*, edited by a committee of the association (Toronto, 1908), 1–4.

20 Ibid., 48.

21 Ibid., 56.

22 D'Arcy McGee, "The Mental Outfit of the New Dominion," *Montreal Gazette*, 5 November 1867.

23 J.L. Baillie, Jr, "Charles Fothergill," *Canadian Historical Review*, 25, 4, December 1944, 383–4.

24 *Literary Garland*, 4(10), 1842, 484.

25 *Anglo-American Magazine*, 1, 6 December 1852, 553–4.

26 H.J. Morgan, *Sketches of Celebrated Canadians and Persons Connected with Canada* (Quebec, 1862), vii–viii.

27 *Canadian Literary Magazine*, 1(1), 1833, 1–2.

28 Ibid., 2.

29 *The Roseharp*, 1, January 1835, 1.

30 *Literary Garland*, ns, 6(5), 1848, 246.

31 Province of Canada, Assembly, *Journals*, 1850, Appendix N, "Correspondence Relating to Education in Upper Canada, part 8: "Remarks and Recommendations with a view to the Introduction of School Libraries into Upper Canada," E. Ryerson to James Leslie, secretary of the province, 16 July 1849.

32 "Preliminary Address," *Canadian Journal*, 1(1), 1856, 3.

33 Cited in Lower, *Canadians in the Making*, 285.

34 *Canadian Illustrated News*, 2(26) 14 November 1863, 330.

35 George Washington Johnson, "Manitoulin," *Maple Leaves* (Hamilton, 1864), cited in Ballstadt, "Quest for Canadian Identity," 167.

36 Edward Hartley Dewart, *Selections from Canadian Poets* (Montreal, 1864), ix.

37 "Canadian Poetry and Poets," *British American Magazine*, 1, August 1863, 418.

38 Ibid.

39 Upper Canada, Assembly, *Journals*, 1806, 28 February.

40 Baillie, "Charles Fothergill," 386.

41 Upper Canada, Assembly, *Journals*, 1832–33, 7, 10 December.

42 Ibid., 1836, 3 February.

43 F.J. Alcock, "Geology," in W.S. Wallace, ed., *The Royal Canadian Institute Centennial Volume, 1849–1949* (Toronto, 1949), 63.

44 Hind, Keefer, et al., *Eighty Years' Progress*, 474.

45 Upper Canada, Assembly, *Journals*, 1836–7, Appendix, vol. 1, no. 30, "Report of the Select Committee on the Petition of Charles Fothergill, Esquire, 20 January 1837.

46 *Canadian Literary Magazine*, 1(1), 1833, 2.

47 Province of Canada, Assembly, *Report of the Select Committee on the Geological Survey* (Quebec, 1855), 38–9. Cited in L.S. Fallis, Jr, "The Idea of Progress in the Province of Canada 1841–1867, PH.D. diss., University of Michigan, 1966, 109.

48 Robert L. McDougall, "A Study of Canadian Periodical Literature of the Nineteenth Century," PH.D. diss., University of Toronto, 1950, 101.

49 Frank Dawson Adams, "The History of Geology in Canada," in H.M. Tory, ed., *A History of Science in Canada* (Toronto, 1939), 12.

50 Ibid., 18.

51 "Sir William Logan," *Canadian Illustrated News*, 2(12), 1 August 1863, 133.

52 A provision of the Common School Act of 1824 (4 Geo. IV, c.8).

53 Upper Canada, Assembly, *Journals*, 1833–34, 10 December.

54 "Reply to Objections Which Have Been Made to the Introduction of Libraries in Upper Canada by the Educational Department" (extract from the annual report of the chief superintendent for 1854, 9–13). Cited in *A General Catalogue of Books in Every Department of Literature, for Public School Libraries in Upper Canada* (Toronto, 1857), 246.

55 Public Archives of Canada, MG 20, vol. 4, no. 415, Major John Richardson to Lord Sydenham, 20 July 1841. Cited in D. Pacey, "A Colonial Romantic: Major John Richardson, Soldier and Novelist, part 2, 'Return to America,'" *Canadian Literature*, no. 3, winter 1960, 49.

56 Province of Canada, Assembly, *Journals*, 1842, 8 October, 117.

57 Ibid., 1851, 18 August, 292–4.

58 Ibid., 1852–53, 13 April, 714.

59 Ibid., 13 June, 1077.

60 Henry Scadding, "Emigration," *Canadian Literary Magazine*, 1, 1832. Cited in Ballstadt, "Quest for Canadian Identity," 56–7.

61 *Colonial Advocate*, 9 September 1830. Cited in Margaret Fairley, ed., *The Selected Writings of William Lyon Mackenzie, 1824–1837* (Toronto, 1960), 183.

62 Samuel Strickland, *27 Years in Canada West* (London, 1833), 1, 65. Cited in Fallis, "The Idea of Progress," 8.

63 Susanna Moodie, "Canada," *Victoria Magazine*, 1, 1847–48, 3. Cited in Ballstadt, "Quest for Canadian Identity," 97–8.

64 William Kirby, *The UE: A Tale of Upper Canada in XII Cantos* (Niagara, 1859). See also Carl Berger, *The Sense of Power: Studies in the Ideas of Canadian Imperialism 1867–1914* (Toronto, 1970), 92–3.

65 Egerton Ryerson, *The Loyalists of America and their Times*, 2 vols. (Toronto, 1880), vol. 2, 191. Cited in Berger, *The Sense of Power*, 92.

66 George Washington Johnson, "No Despot – No Slave," *Maple Leaves* (Hamilton, 1864). Cited in Ballstadt, "Quest for Canadian Identity," 169.

67 Evan McColl, "The Lake of the Thousand Isles," in Dewart, *Selections from Canadian Poets*, 118.

68 Pamela S. Vining, "Canada," in ibid., 105.

69 *Colonial Advocate*, 18 May 1824. Cited in Fairley, *William Lyon Mackenzie*, 109.

70 G.M. Craig., ed., *Early Travellers in the Canadas, 1791–1867* (Toronto, 1955), xxxv.

71 Helen M. Johnson, "Our Native Land," in Dewart, *Selections from Canadian Poets*, 82.

72 *The Maple Leaf or Canadian Annual*, 1848.

73 *Colonial Advocate*, 30 March 1826. Cited in Fairly, *William Lyon Mackenzie*, 112.

74 J.R. Godley, *Letters from America*, 2 vols. (London, 1844), vol. 1, 200. Cited in Craig, *Early Travellers in the Canadas*, 143.

75 Craig, 144.

76 *Christian Guardian*, 29 August 1860. Cited in Lower, *Canadians in the Making*, 184.

77 *The Maple Leaf or Canadian Annual*, 1847, Preface.

78 Alexander McLachlan, "The Genius of Canada," in his *Lyrics* (Toronto, 1858).

79 Rev. H.F. Darnell, "The Maple," in Dewart, *Selections from Canadian Poets*, 114.

80 "Canadian Literature. On What Has Been Done in it," *Saturday Reader*, 1(2), 16 September 1865, 20.

81 William Hay, "Architecture for the Meridian of Canada," *Anglo-American Magazine*, 2, March 1853, 253.

82 D.W., "Reviews," *Canadian Journal*, ns, 3, January 1858, 13, 18, 19, 20.

83 Ibid., 19–20.

84 Hind, Keefer, et al., *Eighty Years' Progress*, 4.

85 *General Union of All the British Provinces of North America* (London, 1824), 40. Cited in Craig, ed., *Early Travellers*, 104.

86 John Strachan, "Observations on a Bill for Uniting the Legislative Councils and Assemblies," 25 May 1824. Cited in J.L.H. Henderson, ed., *John Strachan: Documents and Opinions* (Toronto, 1969), 170.

87 Johnson, "No Despot – No Slave."

88 *Parliamentary Debates on the Confederation of the British North American Provinces* ([Quebec City]: Queen's Printer, 1865), 295.

89 For the thought of the imperialists, see Berger, *The Sense of Power*.

90 For some of the difficulties see Allan Smith, "Metaphor and Nationality in North America," this volume.

91 *Parliamentary Debates on Confederation*, 27–8.

92 Ibid., 86, 84.

93 Ibid., 173.

94 Ibid., 169.

95 Ibid., 110–15.

96 Ibid., 25.

97 Ibid., 169.

98 Ibid., 114.

99 Ibid., 45, 31–2.

100 For an introductory statement on the nature of ideology and persuasive belief, see John Plamenatz, "Ideology as Persuasive Belief and Theory," in his *Ideology* (London and Toronto, 1970), 72–92.

101 In a celebrated 1946 article, W.L. Morton underscored the role centralizing versions of the national experience might play in helping the region whose influence they emphasized maintain its hegemony in the nation's affairs. That the centre's concern to enhance its position did not, however, limit its inhabitants to the promotion of an understanding of the national experience framed in these terms is illustrated by the vision of their country offered the people of Canada by two of Ontario's most prominent premiers. Oliver Mowat rested his case against Ottawa on a vision of the country at once decentralist and explicitly rooted in Ontario's interest. His province, he explained in 1884, had every right to resist attempts to weaken

280 Canadian Frame of Mind

and confine its authority. Indeed, a strong Ontario, acting through its government to limit the power of the Dominion and augment its own, was functioning in a manner entirely consistent with the nation's character and needs. "It is," he argued, "in the interest of the Dominion, as well as of the provinces composing the Dominion, that the limits of Ontario should not be restricted. Ontario is, in fact, the 'back-bone' of the Dominion; and we desire that it should continue to be the position of our province." The provinces at large, mindful of their pressing needs and not yet aware of the implications a decentralized federal system containing no agency capable of checking the power of the large provinces would have for them, responded with enthusiasm to Mowat's doctrine. By the 1930s some of them were prepared to question an understanding of the nation and its politics which, in the changed circumstances of that decade, seemed all too clearly to serve the interests of Ontario and the wealthier provinces alone. Their support for a new kind of centralism was, however, complicated by the fact that for so long they had built their case for a more equitable union on its opposite. It was, therefore, almost too easy for Mitchell Hepburn to place those who opposed his criticism of the Rowell-Sirois Report at a tactical disadvantage by founding that criticism on a conception of the national character which for decades they had taken as orthodoxy. Having thus disarmed his opponents at the level of argument, he found his victory the more assured. Again Ontario's interest was rationalized by a non-centralist vision of the national character. See W.L. Morton, "Clio in Canada: The Interpretation of Canadian History," *University of Toronto Quarterly*, 15(3), 1946, 227–34. Mowat's remarks are quoted in C.R.W. Biggar, *Sir Oliver Mowat: A Biographical Sketch*, 2 vols. (Toronto, 1905), vol. 1, 428. For Hepburn's case against the Rowell-Sirois Report, see Neil McKenty, *Mitch Hepburn* (Toronto, 1967), 228–30.

10 Defining British Columbia

Few collections of historical literature demonstrate more clearly than the works produced by British Columbia's historians the truth of the proposition that historians' visions of the past result from a complex process of interaction involving their own intelligence, the changing character of the reality they contemplate and the conceptual lens through which they view it. Each of the three main divisions into which historical writing about British Columbia falls must, in consequence, be defined not only in terms of the structure given it by the varying phenomena of which the historians producing it found it necessary to take account but also by the manner in which their sense of what formed an appropriate subject of investigation was shaped by the changing framework of assumption, hypothesis and value within whose confines they operated. What follows, then, at once records the shifting picture of the British Columbia past painted by its historians and attempts to explain how that picture acquired the balance and composition that set it apart. In so doing – the point should be made clear at the outset – it makes no attempt to examine exhaustively the body of historical writing dealing with British Columbia but concentrates instead on work which seeks to make a comprehensive statement about its subject or contributes importantly to the articulation of a significant point of view about that subject.[1]

BC Studies, no. 45, Spring 1980, 73–102.

The first generation of British Columbia's historians approached their task through the agency of conceptual tools drawn directly from the values and experience of bourgeois Victorians. Human activity, they believed, was to be judged in terms of the extent to which it released the wealth of the world, created moral communities and illustrated the truth that the individual was the master of his fate. In British societies, moreover, such activity had also to stand up under the scrutiny of those who sought to satisfy themselves that the interests of an entity of worldwide scope were being served.

On all of these counts the shape and content of the British Columbia experience did more than meet the test, for nothing seemed clearer than that the province was a place of wealth and splendour whose inhabitants were daily advancing themselves and their community down the road to development, the fulfilment of its imperial responsibilities, and moral perfection.

It helped, of course, that the province's inhabitants had been given much with which to work. The generation of British Columbia's historians active from the 1880s to World War I was, in fact, struck more forcibly by the abundance of its material resources than by any other single factor in its character. Extravagantly endowed with land and fisheries,[2] in possession of vast mineral and timber reserves,[3] it seemed truly a land of plenty.[4] One could, indeed, hardly exaggerate its potential. It comprised, noted two early students of its past, "an empire equal in area to a third of Europe, and, though still in a state of savage nature, rich beyond measure in political and industrial possibilities."[5] Even reference to the immense difficulties geography had placed in the way of realizing that potential – the work, noted provincial librarian and archivist E.O.S. Scholefield, was "herculean" in its proportions[6] – served only to magnify the already considerable scope of what was being accomplished. As Scholefield himself insisted, the province's "progress within the fifty years succeeding the fur-trading era is the most remarkable in history."[7] Taking their cue from this stupendous fact, moving forward to consider what lay in front of them, the province's historians advanced as one to follow the lead given by Ontario immigrant and popular historian Alexander Begg in his efforts "to place on record ... the rise and progress of British Columbia from its earliest discovery to the present."[8]

There was, inevitably, disagreement concerning which events in the province's history were to be assigned special status in its march towards greatness. Some thought it had all begun with the discovery of gold;[9] others took the view that the land-based fur trade precipitated the development of the colony;[10] all, however, agreed that whatever the significance of these early events, the coming of the CPR had been decisive. More than any other that event had opened the way for unimagined growth and even the assumption by the province of a role of truly global significance.[11]

If the province's material progress had been extraordinary, there was, its historians insisted, equally compelling evidence that what it had experienced in the field of moral improvement was no less worthy of note. The action of Douglas in dealing with the American miners of the gold rush period offered one clear indication that standards of morality and order prevailed, but those wishing to prove how civilized life in British Columbia was found no need to stop short after having cited that familiar example. Few commentators, in fact, hesitated to speak in sweeping and all-inclusive terms of the striking contrast they saw between peaceful and law-abiding British Columbia and the settlements to be found on the American frontier. "In British Columbia," reported R.E. Gosnell, the province's first provincial librarian and archivist, "towns of the coast society were leavened with an especially religious and moral element,"[12] while, emphasized Scholefield, "even when Barkerville reached its high water mark of prosperity, the population was generally distinguished for its sobriety and orderliness."[13]

Commentators, in fact, found a number of indications that life in British Columbia had attained a quality and perfection unmatched elsewhere. Schooling, noted Scholefield, "with all its softening and cultural influences"[14] had early been introduced into the life of the province, a point that the American historian H.H. Bancroft emphasized in closing his volume with a lengthy chapter on "Settlements, Missions, and Education 1861–1866."[15] Technology, too, had been instrumental in improving the quality of life. "Victoria city," noted Gosnell, "was one of the first cities in America to be lighted by electric lights," and the existence of its people had also been eased by trolley systems and hydroelectric power.[16] Even coal mining in British Columbia had a purer and less debilitating character than was the case elsewhere. "Beautifully situated with bright skies [and] pure air ... [Nanaimo]," Bancroft claimed, "presents little of that sooty, opaque appearance, either physical or moral, so common to the colliery villages of England."[17] How, enthused Begg, could one doubt that in British Columbia there was much indeed to "delight the gaze of the enraptured visitor."[18]

This model society, insisted its historians, at once owed much to, and offered a nearly perfect environment for, the activities of the individual. While few commentators linked the themes of individualism and progress so explicitly as Gosnell and Scholefield – they entitled the sections of their history which contained biographical sketches of the province's great men "Sixty Years of Progress" – most were quite as concerned to make the point that the good society could have no real existence apart from the individuals who had shaped it. Captain Vancouver and Alexander Mackenzie, the voyageurs of fur trading days and the prospectors of the gold rush, the officials of the HBC and the businessmen at the end of the nineteenth century were alike portrayed as men embodying the classic virtues of will, initiative, character, and pluck. Some, like Vancouver[19] and Douglas,[20] were celebrated for having lifted themselves far above the common level; others, such as the voyageurs[21] and the gold prospectors,[22] exemplified an anonymous populist virtue; still others – the words are Gosnell's, describing Judge Matthew Begbie – were seen as "men who left strong finger marks on the history of British Columbia in the plastic day of its first growth."[23] In each case, the message was the same: much of what was valuable and important in the history of the province had been created by self-reliant and enterprising individuals. The British Columbia experience, as Gosnell put it, was "illustrative of a phase of Canadian individual enterprise that in recent years has evolved so many men of large affairs out of the rugged elements of Canadian life and produced so much wealth from the resources of a country rich in opportunity and rapid in development."[24]

Important as it was, this emphasis on the individualist theme did not wholly supplant other ways of assessing the elements of provincial growth. Given the province's geography and early dependence on external markets and transportation links, it was, indeed, hardly possible to ignore the fact that what happened to the province and its people had much to do with circumstances beyond the control of any one individual. "Success," as Gosnell put it, "was in a general way dependent upon railway construction and communication with the outside world." In making possible the development of the interior, allowing commercial contacts with the rest of the Dominion, and opening direct trade with the Orient and Australasia, this mode of development had done much to make possible the great work of the province's citizens.[25] Even as they wrote of individuals' power, commentators thus devoted no small degree of attention to at least one part of the context within which they and their community were working out their destiny.

The American Bancroft was, paradoxically, one of the most determined of this group of historians to insist on the reality and importance of British Columbia's association with Canada. The province's imperial orientation did not escape his notice, but he was equally anxious to stress the fact that "we must ... consider [B.C.] as linked with her sister colonies, with Vancouver Island as one with herself, and with the Dominion of Canada."[26] Begg, very much concerned to introduce British Columbia to eastern Canadians, was similarly anxious to locate it in a Canadian context. The CPR, he conceded, might have an imperial dimension, but its construction had also made possible the "Union of East and West," a fact the meaning of which had been underscored by the visits of the Governor-General to British Columbia, all of which Begg chronicled in detail.[27]

Other commentators were, however, less sure that the Canadian link was to be given pride of place. Mindful of the province's maritime origins, aware of the role played by the HBC in the formative years of its history, and much impressed by the fact of Britain's imperial power in their own day, it seemed to these observers that the province's relationship to Canada was to be conceived largely in terms of its provincial and imperial relevance. This did not mean that British Columbia's links with the Dominion were held to be of no importance: Gosnell and his collaborator in writing the life of James Douglas, for example, took the effective development of British Columbia to have begun with the commencement of Northwest Company activities on the Pacific Coast. They pointed out that Douglas had considered after 1859 that the province's population would be built up by settlement from Canada rather than Britain, and they reminded their readers that the westernmost part of the continent had played an important part in the development of North America as a whole.[28] What received consistent emphasis was, nonetheless, British Columbia's isolation from what lay to the east. In terms both of its population and its external links, Scholefield insisted, mid-nineteenth century British Columbia was an imperial community completely lacking "any relations whatever with any other portion of British North America."[29] Even after the eastern provinces joined together, the west coast remained isolated. "Geographically," noted Gosnell, "[it] was far removed from the seat of [Federal] Government. An almost insuperable barrier of mountains cut it off from the rest of the British possessions ... The country ... was in every sense foreign to Canada."[30] What was more, suggested one-time journalist and Speaker of the BC Legislature D.W. Higgins, the feeling was mutual: the British Columbia delegates sent to Ottawa to negotiate terms were regarded "as visitors from one of the heavenly planets, who, having ventured too near the edge of their world, had missed their footing and, falling into

space, had landed at the federal capital."[31] This meant, insisted
Gosnell, that union with Canada was in no sense a foregone conclusion. What produced it was, in fact, a quite rational calculation of
provincial interest coupled with a strong sense that such a move
had an important imperial relevance. It was, indeed, unlikely that
in the absence of such a relevance, matters would have proceeded,
for "throughout the length and breadth of the Empire there is no
part where the people as a whole are so wholly and unreservedly
devoted to the idea of imperial unity and to British institutions as
in British Columbia."[32] This meant that matters affecting the
province were to be assessed in terms of their impact on it as part
of the empire. The CPR, certainly, was very much to be viewed as
having an imperial rather than a merely national role to play. The
driving of the last spike, asserted Coats and Gosnell "was a grave
moment in the history of Canada and the British Empire ... The
gateway to the Orient had been opened at last by land."[33] Even the
Panama Canal was to be judged in terms of its capacity to allow
British Columbia to move towards the assumption of a British-like
status in world affairs. That remarkable engineering feat, predicted
Gosnell, "will inevitably build up an industrial and mercantile
Britain on the British Columbia coast, corresponding in all material
respects to the Great Britain of many centuries old."[34] British
Columbia, its historians insisted, was thus very much an imperial
rather than a Canadian province, firmly rooted in a larger world.
Having, as Gosnell put it, "interests which are *sui generis* in a degree
greater perhaps than is true of any other province of Canada," it
had perforce to deepen its sense of its destiny, enlarge its understanding of the direction in which the unfolding of the historical
process was taking it, and so avoid the dismal and pedestrian fate of
becoming content with provincial status in a mere agglomeration
of other and lesser jurisdictions.[35]

For all that they were concerned with painting the history of British
Columbia in the brightest and most flattering colours, the early
historians of the province were not entirely unaware that by the
end of the nineteenth century the study of history had become a
disciplined and critical undertaking. Begg, to be sure, was largely a
compiler of others' work, but Bancroft displayed a Rankean enthusiasm for original sources and the kind of truth that flowed from
them,[36] Gosnell was familiar with the germ theory of historical
development and had some awareness of the relativity of historical
judgment,[37] and both he and Scholefield were fully alive to the

importance of documentary evidence.[38] It was, nonetheless, only after the Great War that historians of British Columbia developed an approach to their subject which, in moving them away from the special pleading on behalf of development, empire, and self-made men which had characterized so much of the early work, showed that they were prepared to take matters of perspective, analysis and objectivity with due seriousness. What they wrote could hardly lose all trace of its ideological cast – as time passed it in fact more and more assumed the informal duty of rationalizing the claims of the regional interest groups that became steadily more prominent in both the economy and the government – but overall it acquired a noticeably more rigorous, disciplined, and methodologically sophisticated quality.[39]

The fact that growth and development were still basic realities in the province's life insured, of course, that they would continue to receive attention, a guarantee also offered by the prevailing conceptual wisdom, which, in emphasizing geographical determinants, made it virtually impossible to ignore the important role played in the shaping of the province's history by exploitation of its resources. None of this was, however, incompatible with the taking of a more rounded and analytical view of the province's economic history. On the contrary, the application of environmentalist concepts to the study of British Columbia's evolution reinforced the moves in the direction of adopting a more critical perspective which had been encouraged by society's maturing and the emergence of history as a university-based discipline.[40] These developments, moreover, were in their turn powerfully reinforced by the growth of a reformist critique of big business which in conjunction with the onset of the Great Depression stimulated the impulse to observe the province's growth from something other than a blandly approving point of view.[41]

Even, in consequence, as commentators continued to place emphasis on the ruggedness of the environment and the difficulties it put in the way of road and railway builders[42] they focused attention on such technical details as the difficulties created for the timber industry by the immense size of British Columbia logs[43] and began the process of re-examining the province's early economic history, paying particular attention to the relative importance of the land-based and maritime fur trades.[44] Notwithstanding the persistence of familiar lines of argument – the University of British Columbia's W.N. Sage, for example, never really abandoned his judgment that "it was the production of gold in British Columbia which in the end determined the future of both colonies"[45] – other elements in the province's economic life thus began to receive systematic consideration.

The single most important conceptual innovation in these years was undoubtedly that derived from the work of the staple theorists. Economist W.A. Carrothers' early work on the timber industry clearly betrayed the influence of the idea that BC development was best understood through the technique of relating it to the evolution of resource based industries,[46] an approach he pursued in his examination of the fishing industry.[47] The leading national exponents of staple theory also interested themselves in the structure of the BC economy. A.R.M. Lower included Carrothers' work on the BC forest industry in his *North American Assault on the Canadian Forest*, while H.A. Innis examined mining in the Kootenays,[48] emphasized the links between the forest industry and the autonomist outlook of British Columbia,[49] and noted the particular character which its land-oriented, inshore nature had given the province's fishing industry.[50]

In all of this work there was a clear concern not simply to emphasize the importance of staple production but also to provide a more fully articulated view of economic development than had previously been made available. At the same time that investigators provided gross accounts of production and growth, they also, therefore, tried to characterize the activity with which they were dealing. Carrothers, certainly, emphasized the peculiar technology terrain and size made it necessary for the forest industry to develop,[51] while Margaret Ormsby's reminder that agricultural activity was firmly rooted in the province's economic history drew particular attention to the role played by both technological and institutional innovation in that field.[52]

The more careful look at the province's economic life inspired by the economic and intellectual history of the interwar period not only resulted in a body of work that presented the province's history as the consequence of the exploitation of a series of staples; it also stimulated an attempt – never, regrettably, carried to fruition – to view the province's social and political life as a function of these activities. Innis himself, of course, played a key role in this process. His classic *Fur Trade in Canada* (Toronto, 1930) outlined the case for viewing geography and economics as the vital determinants of the political framework within which BC had come to operate, while in later work he drew attention to the manner in which the production of new staples had enhanced the strength of centrifugal forces in Canadian federalism, thereby strengthening autonomist tendencies in British Columbia as elsewhere.[53] Historians closer to home also made contributions in this area. In

1937 Sage suggested the existence of linkages between mining activity in the province and its peculiar outlook,[54] while by 1942 Judge F.W. Howay could emphasize the fur trade's preparation of the ground not only for settlement but for political division as well.[55]

More far-reaching in its impact on the writing of the province's historians – in fact a fundamental component of it – was the attention paid to the matter of situating the province in its appropriate context. Concern with this issue was not, it need hardly be said, new, but where the first generation of historians had been led by its emphasis on steam technology and its sentiment for empire to emphasize the province's imperial orientation, the decline of the Empire coupled with the new investigators' concern with staples and markets led them to pay close attention to its regional character and its continental connections.[56] They had, indeed, already been pointed in this direction by their adoption of the frontierist modes of thought still fashionable in North American scholarly circles in the 1920s. Much influenced by H.E. Bolton and F.J. Turner, Sage noted in 1928 that "Canadians have not as a rule regarded their history from the North American point of view, still less from the standpoint of an historian of the Americas who sketches the evolution of the twin continents from the North Pole to Cape Horn."[57] When, he continued, they did look at it from this vantage point they would discover that their history could not be separated from that of the continent as a whole. Particularly concerned to insist on the existence of a single North American frontier,[58] Sage found his belief in its reality leading him to support André Siegfried's view that the natural divisions of the continent ran north and south and that, in consequence, "each of the settled regions of Canada is more closely in touch with the adjoining portion of the United States than with the next region of Canada."[59] The lesson to be extracted from this was clear – "If Canadian historians are to present in the future a more balanced picture it is essential that they should keep the whole development of the nation and of the five cultural regions more constantly before them"[60] – and Sage did not hesitate to apply it. In doing so he did not deny the importance of the orientation to the nation, to the Empire and to the Pacific, that history had given BC,[61] but he was even more anxious to underscore the fact that geography had made a contribution of its own: "The isolation of the province from the rest of Canada," he informed his readers, "is an essential fact. British Columbians are Canadians with a difference."[62]

Utilizing this perspective, and harkening back to the role markets and the structure of the economy played in the orientation of societies, political scientist H.F. Angus was led in 1942 to conclude that the province was, in fact, part of no single geographical or economic system. There had, it was true, been much economic involvement with the US, but the emergence of political boundaries had created rival economies and so made it "quite wrong to consider the Pacific slope as constituting a single economic area."[63] Equally, however, no integrated national economy had developed, for the 1920s had seen the province's export markets oriented increasingly towards foreign buyers. "British Columbia's economic interests had," in consequence, "become independent of those of Canada."[64] That the province had links in several quarters but was pointed clearly in none seemed clear to Canadian-born historian James T. Shotwell: "Although still separate from the East by over a thousand miles of prairie and a wilderness untamed except by the national railway system, British Columbia found in federal union with the provinces farther east, a safeguard for the essentially British character of its traditions and institutions. At the same time its contacts with the western states increased."[65]

The uncertainty to which adoption of the regional-continental perspective had led was unwarranted to some – Innis had little patience with it[66] – but the difficulty of locating BC in the proper context remained. Even Margaret Ormsby's work demonstrated a degree of ambivalence on the matter. Very much committed to a fixed and unchanging view of the character of the province's internal life – she placed much emphasis on coast-interior rivalries, on the character of the valley communities, and on the shaping influence of Anglo-Irish and Canadian elements[67] – she resolved the larger problem of BC's place in the world only with the passage of time. Preoccupied with purely regional concerns in the 1930s, wartime centralism, her sojourn in Ontario, and the influence of the Rowell-Sirois approach to national issues moved her for a period in the direction of a centralist view of the nation's history and British Columbia's relation to it.[68] Once back in British Columbia, however, she returned to a more fully province-centred view of the region's relationship to the country at large.

Central to her later work – and in this her essential regionalism plainly revealed itself – was the conviction that functions vital to the life of the province were rooted in the province itself. "From this time on," suggests John Norris, "there is observable in her writings a growing emphasis on the importance of the province as the true centre of cultural and social function. The Canadian union was increasingly viewed as a permissive entity, allowing variation – ideally, a loose federation permitting unity in emergencies."[69] As Ormsby herself put it in her 1966 Presidential Address to the

Canadian Historical Association, "the fact of the matter was that in nation-building the nation would have to take much of its energy from tension. It would be desperately difficult to secure the articulation of regional economies and disparate cultural traditions."[70]

This Sage-like emphasis on the fundamental importance of regionalism in Canada did not, however, imply a Sage-like continentalism. Where Sage sought to work against the victory of a narrow provincialism by emphasizing the province's continental situation, Ormsby moved towards the same end by drawing attention to its British and imperial character. As she argued as late as 1960, only if the region were viewed in this context could its nature be fully understood. "Above all," as she put it, "we need to put the colonies on the Pacific seaboard into the setting of empire, since, forgetting that they were merely part of a greater whole, we are still too much inclined to think of them as isolated political units."[71] The province, to quote John Norris once more, was thus to be seen as "a British community whose provincialism is rooted in the large cosmopolitan civilization of a world-wide empire."[72]

While, then, the middle period had seen historians of British Columbia move away from the earlier emphasis on progress, development, and individualism, it also – as Ormsby's call to remember the imperial dimension in the province's past made clear – witnessed an important degree of continuity. Ormsby's own work laid undiminishing emphasis on the British and imperial background, and economic development – albeit viewed through different spectacles than in the earlier period – remained very much in the forefront as well. Overall, however, the fact of change was in the air. The impact of environmentalist modes of thought had been considerable, and as Ormsby's work – synthesized in her 1958 *British Columbia: A History* – itself made clear, much new light had been shed on the province's character and development by considering its internal geography, its location in space, and the rivalries of its people. It would, a double set of events in the life of the province insured, be this thrust in the direction of change which would be carried forward in the future.

Just as the changing conceptual framework of British Columbia's historians after World War I had combined with alterations in the nature of the world in which they lived to displace the early emphasis on empire, progress and individualism in favour of a concern with geographical and economic determinants, so by the 1960s another conceptual shift and further changes in the nature

292 Canadian Frame of Mind

of reality were moving the focus of investigation in yet another direction. The complex process, to speak concretely, by which North American historians discovered that society, possessed of its own structure and dynamic, could not be understood solely in terms of the impact on it of the primary environment, stimulated an unprecedented interest on the part of British Columbia historians in the British Columbia variant of that phenomenon.[73] At the same time the changed position of Indians and orientals in British Columbia society, the arrival of significant numbers of European immigrants and the clear emergence of a class-based politics created conditions which, in attracting attention to phenomena which could only be understood as components of society, invited the deployment of modes of analysis appropriate to their study.

Moves in the direction of dealing with themes in the history of society in British Columbia did not, of course, involve an absolute break with what had gone before. Even work which continued to concern itself with the familiar themes of development, growth, and external links came, however, to possess a new cast. Not only did it offer a more nuanced look at such matters as investment patterns and the orientation of the economy – making the point that American involvement had not been so clearly dominant as had earlier been thought[74] – it also drew on the concepts of urban historians such as Lampard and Warner to begin the process of anatomizing the British Columbia city, providing a picture of urban growth, and specifying the role in it played by the various groups involved.[75]

For all, however, that changes in approach and emphasis could be discerned in these areas, it remained true that the most dramatic evidence that new developments were occurring came in other fields. One of them had, indeed, long profited from the attention paid it by the social scientists. In making their extraordinarily fruitful investigations into the lives and culture of the Northwest Coast Indians the anthropologists had not, however, produced much that historians found worthwhile. Those commentators, sharing the perspective of the worthies whose exploits in civilizing the province they were recounting, were prevented by the world view in terms of which they operated from seeing the native population as anything other than a pitiful obstacle to progress and development, doomed to eclipse by the movement of history. When, therefore, the first generation of the province's historians did not ignore Indians altogether it dealt with them in the accents – disgust, superiority, paternalist condescension – of the civilization whose accomplishments it was recounting.[76]

As the movement of time made clear the magnitude of the European triumph over the native population and so diminished any sense that it was to be seen as a barrier on the path to progress, historians began to moderate their judgments. It became possible to view the native Indians first as an object of sympathy[77] and then, the passage of still more time having removed them yet further from the sight of the society from which historians took their cue, to see them as an irrelevance which, having in relative terms hardly figured in the province's past, need scarcely be mentioned at all. [78] At length the wheel came full circle. The very fact that Indians had almost disappeared from sight underscored the circumstance that their conquerors lived in a society founded on their displacement. The emerging realization that this was so – in part stimulated, be it said, by a new militance on the part of the Indians themselves – led to a developing interest in the process which had produced so devastating a result. It was at this juncture that the relevance of work done in the social sciences finally commended itself to historians, disciplining their inquiry and suggesting – as the emergence of the field of ethnohistory had already made clear – that they need not seek to make amends for past neglect by indulging in a naive and guilt-ridden romanticization of the Indians' experience. Students of the British Columbia past, like students of North American history in general, thus found themselves taking a wholly new view of the Indian component of it.

This shift in perspective was simple but decisive. Once Indian societies began to be viewed as entities possessing societal integrity and coherence, the character of their relationship with the incoming Europeans assumed a much different aspect than it had been earlier thought to have. The components of Indian society were now seen to have formed a tough and cohesive whole which had been far from passive in its contacts with the Europeans. This was, to be sure, a point the burden of making which was still largely assumed by the anthropologists,[79] but by the 1960s there was clear evidence that historians had begun to take up the task. One of the most remarkable incidents in the history of contact in British Columbia could, in fact, be viewed by an historian of the Victorian world with quite remarkable results. William Duncan's success in building his model village at Metlakatla had, Jean Usher could insist, as much to do with the Tshimshians' own powers of adaptation and with Duncan's willingness to adjust his plans to meet their needs as it did with his determination and the power of the civilization he represented.[80] That the native population had been anything but supine during much of the contact period was demonstrated with particular force by Robin Fisher. The Indians' response to the arrival of the whites was, Fisher argued, in no small measure to be understood "in terms of the priorities of their own culture." Before 1858, the year the fur trade ceased to be the dominant element in the province's economy and society, "Indians and Europeans shared a mutually beneficial economic system"[81] in which the integrity of Indian civilization was not seriously affected; only after that year, with the advent of settlement, did Indians lose their capacity to control in some measure what was happening to them.

If Indians' changing relationship to white society played a part in preparing the way for a new view to be taken of them, broadly similar alterations in the oriental's position led to much the same result. So long as Asian immigrants remained a largely alien presence in a society still very much in process of formation – a presence linked, moreover, to exotic civilizations with whom neither British Columbia nor Canada at large had significant contact – discussion of them aroused intense feelings. Most of those who commented on their lives in British Columbia in fact found it impossible to avoid participating in the controversy to which those lives had given rise. This was true of the early historians whose anxiety to support the building of a British society led them to approve the racial exclusivism they regularly noted,[82] it was true of Chinese historian Tienfang Cheng's plea for fair treatment for his compatriots,[83] it was true of Lower and Woodsworth's concern over the relationship a Japanese presence on Canada's west coast might bear to Japanese expansion,[84] and it was true, thanks to their approval of restrictions on oriental immigration and their advocacy of a quota system, of the work of the first sociologists to investigate the problem.[85]

With, however, the defeat of Japan, the fact of war-time cooperation with China, and the ongoing acculturation of the Japanese in Canada, the revulsion against racism produced by Nazi excesses could act with the continuing work of the social scientists to produce conditions in which it was possible to take a less heated view of the Asian minorities in British Columbia. The results the adoption of such a perspective might yield had indeed been anticipated before the war in the fact that the 1933 study undertaken by sociologists Charles H. Young and Helen R.Y. Reid did not simply implicate its authors in the controversy by virtue of the policy recommendations it made, but actively sought to locate the roots of racism itself by drawing on conceptual tools – especially those dealing with the effects in multicultural societies of competition for status and subsistence – developed by Robert E. Park and others.

The key developments, however, came after 1945. Writing in the immediate post-war period, sociologist Forrest LaViolette showed how observers might begin to view white-oriental relations by the expedient of attempting at least for purposes of analysis to distance themselves from direct involvement in them. Conceding that "race prejudice most certainly does have an economic component," he nonetheless argued that "more than mere economic competition and its associated processes" were involved in the generation of anti-oriental feeling in British Columbia.[86] A fuller explanation, he suggested, lay in the peculiar circumstances of the British Columbia community itself. There the problems of community building and integration always present in new societies were compounded by geographical isolation, concern about American expansionism, and a desire to remain British. These factors, joined to the relative absence of a creed which, in emphasizing individualism and citizenship, would have facilitated integration into the community of peoples of diverse backgrounds, ensured that highly visible and culturally distinct elements in the population would be perceived as posing a particularly sharp threat to the building of a unified community and so would become objects of discriminatory behaviour and policy.

By the 1970s a new generation of historians, contemplating the changed nature of the white-oriental relationship, inhabiting a climate of opinion which did not involve them in the old controversies about racism, and sensitized to the perspectives of the social scientists, were developing a genuine sympathy towards the idea that white-oriental relations could be best comprehended by employing a way of viewing behaviour which insisted that all facets of it – however strong the feelings of sympathy or revulsion they might arouse – were, in Durkheim's famous formulation, social facts, rooted in, and intelligible in terms of, a complex social whole to the comprehension of which a rigorously objective viewpoint was essential.[87] To be sure, Ken Adachi's account of the Japanese-Canadian experience,[88] for all that it provided a valuable insight into the factors inducing the Japanese-Canadians to accept their fate, remained essentially an indictment of white attitudes and policies, and in that sense did no more than Barry Broadfoot's popular account to grapple with the causes of racism.[89] Patricia Roy's sympathy with the more disciplined and critical approach of the social scientist was, however, clearly evident in her impatience with those who, preferring to see prejudice as the property of the perverse and wrong-headed, showed little disposition to understand its roots. She insisted, too, on the necessity of getting a sense of the time in which the events under study took place, and, no less importantly, on the need to go beyond simple economic explanations for anti-oriental feeling in favour of an insistence on the central role of the irrational.[90]

Carrying forward LaViolette's emphasis on the role a concern to consolidate and integrate the community in support of a specific set of values and modes of behaviour had played in creating anti-oriental feeling, and insisting, like Roy, on the centrality of the irrational, historian W.P. Ward made effective use of the concepts of social psychologist Gordon W. Allport in pointing to the tensions engendered between whites and orientals by British Columbia's existence as a pluralist society. The province's whites – thanks, Ward argued, to the important role stereotypical thinking played in such circumstances – could do no other than perceive the orientals as a threat to their values and a serious obstacle to the building of a homogeneous society. "Cultural pluralism," he argued, "was unacceptable to the white community ... [for] the plural condition generated profound, irrational racial fears [and] stirred a deep longing for the social cohesion which could only be achieved, it seemed, by attaining racial homogeneity."[91]

The experience of Indians and orientals notwithstanding, acquisition over time of a lower profile was only one way in which different elements of the community might find themselves being viewed in a new way. The assumption by certain groups of a more obvious role in the life of the province could, it soon became clear, have precisely the same result. Where, accordingly, the relative absence of continental European stock in the province's population had allowed the first two generations of historians to indulge their British bias freely – as late as 1937 Sage could identify the province as "distinctly British"[92] – by 1970 historian Norbert MacDonald found it necessary carefully to underscore the role European immigration had played in the growth of its largest urban centre.[93] The interest in articulating the multicultural character of British Columbia to the growth of which MacDonald's work pointed was, of course, in part a manifestation of the concern – widespread in the decades after World War II – to build a strong and integrated community by making all its members feel that they had a place in it. One of the first attempts to focus systematic and organized attention on the province's ethnic groups was made in connection with the 1958 centennial,[94] while John Norris' 1971 account of the ethnic presence in British Columbia took form as part of the one-hundredth anniversary celebration of the province's entry into Confederation.[95] Even, however, in devoting itself to the task of redefining the character of the province's life in a way that legitimized the presence in it of many ethnic and racial groups, this work exposed to view many of the factors – prejudice in the host society, the immigrants' pre-migration background, their expected roles and statuses in their new country – governing the ethnic experience in British Columbia as elsewhere. Attention was not, however, focused only on those adjustments which had been made relatively painlessly; in some instances the character of the immigrant experience made it necessary for historians to draw particular attention to the kind of conflict which the clash of cultures produced by that experience could create. In their study of one of the most difficult of these cases, George Woodcock and Ivan Avakumovic sought to explore the tension which resulted when an intensely self-conscious minority – the Doukhobours – determined to maintain its identity collided with a majority no less firmly committed to enforcing what it viewed as minimum standards of conformity.[96]

The rise to prominence of the ethnic fact in British Columbia's life was not the only new reality demanding attention in these years. The social, economic, and political division which seemed to acquire the status of permanent and central features in the province's life after 1945 also did their share in producing an altered picture of the province's character. There was, of course, nothing novel about the fact of conflict itself, for union activity, strikes, and a radical politics had been features of British Columbia's life sine the late nineteenth century. The general shape of the province's history and, more especially, the peculiar configuration of its political life had, however, conspired to shift attention to other matters and so allowed these to sink into a general and all encompassing oblivion. Where, that is to say, in other British North American and Canadian communities the clash of rival groups soon became institutionalized in clearly comprehensible political formations, conflict in British Columbia manifested itself in a less coherent rivalry between island and mainland, in faction forming based on attitudes towards the federal tie, and in a politics of personal attachment and ascendancy of a distinctly eighteenth-century sort, a circumstance which led to a clear tendency to characterize the province's politics as without form and substance. As Coats and Gosnell, reflecting this tendency, put it, "a lack of leadership and even of constructive party organization ... has been a feature of the politics of British Columbia ... to make the obvious comparison with the eastern colonies, there was here no feud of ruling races to allay, no Family Compact to uproot, no Clergy Reserve to divide, no complicated fiscal policy to arrange."[97] Even when party lines did emerge in 1903 they appeared to delineate divisions among the members of the province's leading groups which seemed, if anything, more random and indeterminate than those to be found between Liberals and Conservatives in other parts of the country. "An examination of party platforms, resolutions of local and provincial Associations, speeches from the Throne, [and] debates in the legislature," Edith Dobie's 1936 survey of the first three decades of party history in British Columbia noted, "reveal[s] almost complete agreement between Liberals and Conservatives both in theory and in politics."[98]

Where, then, the clearly demarcated struggles between Reformers and Tories in Upper Canada or the clash of rival interests on the prairies invited the writing of a history that focused on the activities of distinct political alternatives definable at least to a point in terms of real differences in outlook, the apparently vague and indeterminate character of conflict in British Columbia elicited only cursory and uncomprehending looks from those hurrying by to consider what seemed the manifestly more important, and certainly more readily understood, matters of growth and development. Even so astute an observer as Gosnell could make little sense of what he saw,[99] while later observers were content to repeat D.W. Higgins' attempts to introduce the categories of whig history into their discussion of the province's politics[100] or deal with such major events as the introduction of party politics in terms of its character as a stabilizing measure in a chaotic and volatile situation.[101]

The clear emergence in the 1930s of socialism as a key element in the province's political system forced a reconsideration of the character of that system which, thanks to the Beardian categories employed by its creator,[102] stressed both conflict and the existence of a relationship between economic interest and political behaviour, but by 1948 Sage, returning to a discussion of politics before 1903, abandoned this line of analysis in favour of one cast largely in terms of the conviction that "provincial politics in British Columbia was largely a game of the In's and Out's and a struggle between the Mainland and the Island."[103] Neither John Saywell's 1951 discussion of the relationship between economic interest and political organization in the early history of socialism in British Columbia[104] nor Margaret Ormsby's account of the difficulties economic geography and sociological background placed in the way of effective political organization by British Columbia's farmers[105] committed the same oversight, but what resulted from their work was, nonetheless, only a partial account of the manner in which division and conflict had manifested itself in the province's life.

If this absence of any sustained and comprehensive discussion of conflict in British Columbia society had meant only that students of the province's history were being spared what Donald Creighton once referred to as the "colossal tedium" of dealing with it in terms of the pseudo-struggles of party,[106] it might have been no bad thing; but it meant also that British Columbia's historians – with the exceptions above – maintained a peculiar blind spot when it came to social and economic conflict in general. The result was to reinforce the tendency to eschew discussion of the structure of the province's society in favour of situating it spatially, celebrating its growth and development, and concentrating attention on the great individuals who had contributed so much to its making. Captives of the obvious, enmeshed in the surface of events, British Columbia's historians not only failed to generate anything approaching the work of a Morton, a Lipset, or a Macpherson; they did not even duplicate L.G. Thomas' achievement in writing the history of an established party.[107]

That this was an unsatisfactory state of affairs seemed more than clear by the 1960s. The presence of division and conflict in the province's life has been made obvious both by the character of its politics and by the strength of its labour movement, facts which almost literally cried out for discussion and analysis. It was, appropriately enough in view of the view of the awareness she had earlier shown of the relationship between politics, interest group membership, and the character of the economy, Margaret Ormsby who in 1960 made it clear that understanding of a whole dimension of the province's life was lacking. "We are ignorant," she wrote, "of the mainsprings of our political development. We can name our premiers, describe their career, and recount their legislative enactments; but, as yet, we have not probed deeply enough to explain the basis of our early non-party tradition or the basis of the schisms and the realignments which have occurred since parties were first established."[108]

The convergence of a clear need to deal with these matters with the realization by Canadian scholars that the concept of class could be a useful one in the analysis of the historical process did much to ensure that the task would be carried out largely through the agency of that analytical tool. Where class and the conflict flowing from it could once have been dismissed as a kind of infantile disorder bound to disappear with the passage of time – "Nowhere in Canada," observed Coats and Gosnell in 1909, "have industrial disputes been waged with greater bitterness and violence than in British Columbia. This, however, is but to say that the province ... is still in its infancy as an industrial community, and that the impulse which it obeys is western"[109] – the new circumstances did not allow it to be set aside so easily, for even the most casual observer could see that the province's political and industrial life had come to be affected in what seemed a fundamental way by a species of class activity. The peculiar militance of the British Columbia working class now, indeed, became a subject of discussion in its own right. Labour economist Stuart Jamieson, seeking in 1962 to locate its sources, found them in factors – the province's frontier character, its strike-prone type of industry, the influence of conditions in the United States, the structure of the province's labour legislation – specific to British Columbia,[110] while Paul Phillips, preferring to explain its existence in terms of more general factors, emphasized the role played in the rise of a militant labour movement by the unstable character of the market for labour in an economy dependent on primary products for export, the impact of technology, and the effect of social and economic dislocation.[111] This, it should be noted, did not mean that Philips rejected out of hand the idea that class-based organizations in British Columbia had a particular character. For him, however, that special character was to be seen not so much in the circumstances which had given rise to those organizations as in the fact that their members had become more politically active than their counterparts in other sections of the country. In seeking anti-oriental legislation, protection for workers against exploitation by employers, and economic planning that would reduce the instability inherent in a resource-based export-oriented economy, British Columbia workers, Phillips suggested, had early learned the value of political action and so were more fully influenced than other Canadian workers by the socialist ideology which was "in the air" at the turn of the century and after.[112]

That the British Columbia political system as a whole was class based became the governing assumption of the most ambitious examination of the linkages between the province's politics, society, and economy so far undertaken. Arguing that the "non-partisan" character of British Columbia's politics, the nature of its radicalism and the ascendancy of Social Credit were all linked to the character of the province's social and economic life, political sociologist Martin Robin's semi-popular account of the province's political growth sought to show that the presence of large enterprises in the timber and mining industry, the growth of a wage-earning class, the emergence of a petit-bourgeoisie oriented mainly towards the service sector and the absence of a significant number of independent commodity producers had produced a political system characterized by a succession of groupings, parties, and coalitions through the agency of which the large interests could maintain their influence, by an anti-capitalist rather than an anti-eastern protest tradition, and ultimately by a brand of populism whose petit bourgeois base made it first the enemy and then the ally of the large concentrations of power that dominated the economic life of the province.[113]

What Robin's work demonstrated – that the British Columbia political experience was, like other departments of the province's life, susceptible of analysis in terms of perspectives drawn from the social sciences – dramatically underscored the fact that discussion of the province's character and history had come to occupy ground far different than that on which it had earlier stood. How long scholars would continue to find the components – ethnic, racial, and class – of which society consisted an appropriate object of investigation would depend, as always, on what resulted from the interplay between the data historical reality presented for consideration and the conceptual tools by means of which those data were perceived and assessed; at the end of the 1970s there was, however, little evidence that this critical process was altering the framework within the confines of which those concerned with the British Columbian past had been working for much of the preceding two decades. The focus of study, it seemed likely, would remain firmly fixed on society and its nature.

For all that the perspective on the province's past employed by British Columbia's historians altered through time, one element in the changing picture they painted remained fixed and constant. Whether they placed emphasis on the province's imperial and national linkages, on its geography, on its orientation towards eternal markets or on its intelligibility in terms of concepts based on the experience of society at large, they demonstrated a strong and consistent commitment to the idea that British Columbia could not be understood without taking full account of its relationship to the world around it. Even as the regional focus of their activities anticipated Canada's national historians in underscoring the legitimacy of the regional approach, they thus voided falling victim to a narrow provincialism.[114]

This did not mean that they knew at all times to what larger entity – nation, continent, or empire – the province was linked; it certainly did not mean that they had a clear sense of the major realities – the individual, class – animating its internal life; least of all did it mean that they were able to produce a fully realized vision of the province's character and history. What, however, it did signify was that the province's most able and representative historians – no matter in what period they wrote – never fell victim to the illusion that the community of which they spoke could be understood in terms of anything other than its place in a larger world. The result was a body of writing which in its attempts to grapple with problems of context, orientation, and social dynamic at all times showed its authors anxious – within the conceptual limits specified above – to situate British Columbia in an appropriately comprehensive framework of analysis and discussion. At the same time that it demonstrated the complex nature of the relationship between historians' circumstances, the reality they contemplate and the work which results, that writing thus also made plain the cosmopolitan thrust of those who concerned themselves with the past and the character of Canada's westernmost province.[115]

NOTES

1 For a good general bibliography of BC history, see H.K. Ralston, "Select Bibliography on the History of British Columbia," in J. Friesen and H.K. Ralston, eds., *Historical Essays on British Columbia* (Toronto: McClelland and Stewart, 1976), 281–93. For an excellent discussion of the work of some of the province's leading historians, see J. Friesen, "Introduction," in ibid., vii–xxv.

2 Hubert Howe Bancroft, *History of British Columbia, 1872–1887* (San Francisco, 1887), 743–8.

3 R.E. Gosnell, *A History of British Columbia* ([Vancouver?], 1906), 273, 289.

4 The maker of these remarks was D.W. Higgins, one-time editor of the Victoria *Colonist* and a former speaker of the BC Legislature, who contributed 110–45 to R.E. Gosnell, *A History of British Columbia*. For the comments referred to here, see 122.

5 Robert Hamilton Coats and R.E. Gosnell, *Sir James Douglas* (Toronto, 1909), 94.

6 E.O.S. Scholefield, "Part One," in E.O.S. Scholefield and R.E. Gosnell, *A History of British Columbia* (Vancouver and Victoria, 1913), 156. "No other part of Canada," Scholefield emphasized, "had so much to contend with in this particular as had the Colony of British Columbia," 187.

7 Ibid., 67.

8 Alexander Begg, *History of British Columbia From its Earliest Discovery to the Present Time* (Toronto, 1894), 7.

9 Bancroft, *History ... 1872–1887*, 758; Scholefield, *History of British Columbia*, 153.

10 "The sailor," wrote Coats and Gosnell, "showed the way, but it was the overland traveller who entered and took possession," Coats and Gosnell, *Sir James Douglas*, 49–50; see also ibid., 79, 310–11.

11 "The period from 1886 to 1892," noted D.W. Higgins, "was one of unexampled prosperity ... throughout the province." Coats and Gosnell claimed that "the completion of the Canadian Pacific Railway marks from many points of view the beginning of a new era in the development of British Columbia" and Gosnell himself argued in 1913 that "progress ... since the CPR has been completed, has been rapid and during the last decade phenomenal." See Higgins in Gosnell, *A History of British Columbia*, 141, Coats and Gosnell, *Sir James Douglas*, 328, and E.R. Gosnell, "Part Two," in E.O.S. Scholefield and R.E. Gosnell, *A History of British Columbia* (Vancouver and Victoria, 1913), 3.

12 Gosnell, *History of British Columbia*, 7.

13 Scholefield, "Part One," in Scholefield and Gosnell, *History of British Columbia*, 174.

14 Ibid., 180.

15 Bancroft, *History ... 1872–1887*, 707–39.

16 Gosnell, "Part Two," in Scholefield and Gosnell, *History of British Columbia*, 178.

17 Bancroft, *History ... 1872–1887*, 574.

18 Begg, *History ... to the Present Time*, 7.

19 Ibid., 50–1.

20 Coats and Gosnell, *Sir James Douglas*, 353.

21 Gosnell, *History of British Columbia*, 39.

22 Bancroft, *History ... 1872–1887*, 758; Gosnell, *History of British Columbia*, 100–1; Scholefield, "Part One," in Scholefield and Gosnell, *History of British Columbia*, 178.

23 Gosnell, *History of British Columbia*, 94.

24 Gosnell, "Part Two," in Scholefield and Gosnell, *History of British Columbia*, 186, n.

25 Ibid., 13, 4.

26 Bancroft, *History ... 1872–1887*, viii–ix.

27 Begg, *History ... to the Present Time*, 457, 434–40, 509–45.

28 Coats and Gosnell, *Sir James Douglas*, 56–7, 253–4, 2.

29 Scholefield, "Part One," in Scholefield and Gosnell, *History of British Columbia*, 179.

30 Gosnell, *History of British Columbia*, 200–1.

31 Higgins, in Gosnell, *A History of British Columbia*, 123.

32 Gosnell, "Part Two," in Scholefield and Gosnell, *History of British Columbia,* 5.

33 Coats and Gosnell, *Sir James Douglas,* 326. See also Gosnell, "Part Two," in Scholefield and Gosnell, *History of British Columbia,* 114.

34 Gosnell, "Part Two," in Scholefield and Gosnell, *History of British Columbia,* 196–7. See also Gosnell, *History of British Columbia,* 195–6.

35 Gosnell, "British Columbia and British International Relations," *Annals of the American Academy of Political and Social Science,* 45, 1913, 2.

36 "The simple truth in plain language was all," he once wrote, "I aimed at, and if any doubted my judgment or questioned my inferences, there before the reader should be the sources of my information from which he might draw his own conclusions." Hubert Howe Bancroft, *Retrospection: Political and Personal* (New York, 1912), 324.

37 Gosnell, "A Greater Britain on the Pacific," *Westward Ho! Magazine,* 2(1), 1908, 8; Gosnell, "Prefatory," in Scholefield and Gosnell, *History of British Columbia.*

38 "Many hundreds, "reported their editor, "indeed thousands, of authorities and original sources of information – represented in individual recollections, old manuscripts, diaries, official documents and state papers, magazines, newspapers, pamphlets, and books – were consulted." See "Editor's Foreword," Scholefield and Gosnell, *History of British Columbia.*

39 This shift was not equally clear in all quarters. F.W. Howay, one of the middle period's most prolific historians, continued to trade very largely in the intellectual commodities of the pre-war era. The Victorian certitudes which informed his major work, written in collaboration with Scholefield and published in 1914, were equally in evidence in what he produced in later years. He was particularly captivated by the myth of the self-made man. Cook, he would assert in 1928, was "the son of a day labourer ... [who] by sheer industry and merit ... rose rapidly," while David Thompson was also "a wonderful example of a self-made man." He continued, too, to believe that the province's history could best be written around the theme of progress, a fact underscored by the title of his 1930 contribution to the *Cambridge History of the British Empire.* Even University of British Columbia historian W.N. Sage, very much alive to new currents of thinking, did not wholly escape the influence of the old. His 1930 biography of Sir James Douglas showed him to be still very much impressed by the role the individual could play in the historical process – Douglas, he wrote, was "a great man, the greatest in the history of British Columbia" and had done much to shape its future – and as late as 1946 he was prepared to advance the proposition

that the history of the province's largest city could be usefully approached in terms of the concept of progress. See E.O.S. Scholefield and F.H. Howay, *British Columbia from the Earliest Times to the Present,* 4 vols. (Vancouver, 1914); F.H. Howay, *British Columbia: The Making of a Province* (Toronto, 1928), 15, 60; F.H. Howay, "The Settlement and Progress of British Columbia, 1871–1914," *Cambridge History of the British Empire,* vol. 6 (Cambridge, 1930); Walter N. Sage, *Sir James Douglas and British Columbia* (Toronto, 1930), 347; and Walter N. Sage, "Vancouver – 60 Years of Progress," *British Columbia Journal of Commerce Yearbook, 1946* (Vancouver, 1946).

40 What H.F. Angus had in mind when he suggested in 1929 that the time had come for historians and social scientists to consider in a close and detailed way the province's social and economic history, focusing, in particular, on the experience of representatives communities in order to get a sense of the manner in which the community as a whole had developed. See H.F. Angus, "A Survey of Economic Problems Awaiting Investigation in British Columbia," *Contributions to Canadian Economics,* 2, 1929, 47.

41 By the early 1940s Angus could dismiss the overweening concern with development which had been characteristic of British Columbia's businessmen at the turn of the century as the outcome of a "predatory psychology," while ten years after that Margaret Ormsby balanced what John Norris called her "hinterlander's" approval of development as something that brought "comfort, leisure, education, and civilization" against the fact that such development was often uneven in its impact, and, in consequence, productive of serious social and economic inequities. See F.W. Howay, W.N. Sage, and H.F. Angus, *British Columbia and the United States* (Toronto and New Haven, 1942), 379, and John Norris, "Margaret Ormsby," in John Norris and Margaret Prang, eds., *Personality and History in British Columbia: Essays in Honour of Margaret Ormsby* (Victoria, 1977), 17.

42 Especially noticeable in such works as Noel Robinson, "Mining, Roads, and Development," in F.W. Howay, *Builders of the West: A Book of Heroes* (Toronto: The Ryerson Press, 1929), 218–31, but also to be seen in Howay, Sage, and Angus, *British Columbia and the United States,* 228.

43 A theme developed by W.A. Carrothers, "Forest Industries of British Columbia," in A.R.M. Lower, *The North American Assault on the Canadian Forest* (Toronto and New Haven, 1938), 246, reference to which is also made in Howay, Sage, and Angus, *British Columbia and the United States,* 302.

44 In which work Howay took great interest. For a summary of his views, see F.W. Howay, *British Columbia: The Making of a Province* (Toronto, 1928), 90.

45 Sage, *Sir James Douglas and British Columbia* (Toronto, 1930), 237.
46 Carrothers, "Forest Industries."
47 W.A. Carrothers, *The British Columbia Fisheries* (Toronto, 1941). With a foreword by H.A. Innis. University of Toronto Political Economy Series No. 10.
48 H.A. Innis, *Settlement and the Mining Frontier* (Toronto, 1936). Published in one volume with A.R.M. Lower, *Settlement and the Forest Frontier in Eastern Canada* (Toronto, 1936).
49 H.A. Innis, "Editor's Preface," A.R.M. Lower, *The North American Assault on the Canadian Forest* (Toronto and New Haven, 1938), vii–xviii.
50 H.A. Innis, "Foreword," Carrothers, *The British Columbia Fisheries*, v–xii.
51 Carrothers, "Forest Industries," 246.
52 "It was," she wrote, "in the field of specialized agriculture and experimentation in controlled marketing that British Columbia was to make its unique contribution to Canadian agriculture." See her "Agricultural Development in British Columbia," *Agricultural History*, 19(1), January 1945,11, and her "The History of Agriculture in British Columbia," *Scientific Agriculture*, 20(1), September 1939, 61–72, where these points are first outlined. For another commentator's view of the importance of agriculture in the province's development, see G. Neil Perry, "The Significance of Agricultural Development and Trade in the Economic Development of British Columbia," 73–86.
53 Innis, "Editor's Preface," vii–xviii.
54 W.N. Sage, "Geographical and Cultural Aspects of the Five Canadas," Canadian Historical Association *Annual Report*, 1937, 34.
55 Howay, Sage, and Angus, *British Columbia and the United States*, 41.
56 Their preoccupation with its imperial situation had not, of course, completely blinded the first generation of historians to the fact that the province had a continental dimension to its experience. Bancroft had seen it as part of the civilization of the Pacific slope, Okanagan historian J.A. MacKelvie had emphasized the manner in which its interior geography had linked it to the United States – "stretching from the Peace River to the Gulf of Mexico," he noted, "is a general succession of valleys and plains lying in a continental depression behind the coast range of mountains, and of this chain the Okanagan forms an important link" – and even Gosnell made it clear that he found geography to have tied BC closely to the continent as a whole. In the main, however, the realities of the age in which these figures lived combined with the conceptual tools in terms of which they operated to ensure that their attention would be focused elsewhere. See Bancroft, *History ... 1872–1887*, MacKelvie, "The Devel-

opment of the Okanagan," in Scholefield and Gosnell, *History of British Columbia*, 211, and Gosnell, "British Columbia and the British International Relations," 3.

57 W.N. Sage, "Some Aspects of the Frontier in Canadian History," *Canadian Historical Association Annual Report*, 1928, 62.

58 Ibid., 63. In a 1940 reprint of this article, Sage stressed the interconnectedness of the two societies even more strongly. "*This interlacing of the frontier*," he wrote, italicizing his words for emphasis, "*is most important.*" See W.N. Sage, *Canada From Sea to Sea* (Toronto, 1940), 32.

59 Sage, "Five Canadas," 28.

60 Ibid., 34.

61 There were, he freely conceded in 1932, forces within British Columbia itself which had impelled the colony in the direction of union with the rest of British North America, and by 1945 he could advance the argument that the early years of the twentieth century had seen British Columbia – thanks largely to changes in the character of its population and the links provided by the CPR – integrated into the Dominion. The CPR, he wrote elsewhere – and here his emphasis on the imperial tie was clear – had in fact been not only "the iron link of Confederation" but also "of great strategic importance to the British Empire," while the Pacific, he continued, "is at [British Columbia's] door and the orient just beyond." See Walter N. Sage, "The Critical Period of British Columbia History, 1866–1871," *Pacific Historical Review*, 1(4), 1932, 424–43; Walter N. Sage, "British Columbia Becomes Canadian 1871–1901," *Queen's Quarterly*, 52(2), 1945, 168–83; Walter N. Sage, "Five Canadas," 34. See also Walter N. Sage, "British Columbia," in George M. Wrong, Chester Martin, and Walter N. Sage, *The Story of Canada* (Toronto, 1929), 347, 351.

62 Sage, "Five Canadas," 33.

63 Howay, Sage and Angus, *British Columbia and the United States*, 380.

64 Ibid., 388.

65 Shotwell, "Introduction," in ibid., vi.

66 See his review in *Canadian Historical Review*, 35(3), 1943, 311–12.

67 Ormsby's emphasis on the heterogeneous character of British Columbia society had been anticipated by Sage's remark that "Geographically there are six or seven British Columbias ... The centres of population are on the coast and many portions of the vast interior are exceedingly sparsely settled. The division of the province into coast and interior is vital. The older division of island versus mainland still exists." Assessments of this kind were in fact common enough even in the writing of the first generation of historians, but Ormsby's special feeling for the interior communities allowed her to elaborate the point in a wholly unprecedented way. Her general his-

tory made frequent reference to the valleys and their people, and part of the strength of her Presidential Address to the Canadian Historical Association derived from the attention it gave the British Columbia character as a phenomenon rooted in the small communities of the province. Even her discussion of Susan Allison's life in British Columbia focused on the nature of life in the hinterland communities rather than the experience of pioneer women; here, too, as John Norris suggests, Ormsby was concerned to portray the Similkameen and Okanagan settlements Allison inhabited as "examples of the warm, intimate communities which provide the basic strength of a society in any era." Sage, "Five Canadas," 33–4; Ormsby, *British Columbia: A History* (Toronto, 1958), 440; Ormsby, "A Horizontal View," Canadian Historical Association *Historical Papers*, 1966, 11; Ormsby, *British Columbia: A History* (Toronto, 1958), 440; Ormsby, "A Horizontal View," Canadian Historical Association *Historical Papers*, 1966, 11; Ormsby, *A Pioneer Gentlewoman in British Columbia: The Recollections of Susan Allison* (Vancouver, 1976); John Norris, "Margaret Ormsby," in John Norris and Margaret Prang, eds., *Personality and History in British Columbia: Essays in Honour of Margaret Ormsby* (Victoria, 1977), 26.

68 "Prime Minister Mackenzie, the Liberal Party, and the Bargain with British Columbia," *Canadian Historical Review*, 26(2), June 1945, 148–73; "Canada and the New British Columbia," Canadian Historical Association *Annual Report*, 1948, 74–85.

69 Norris, "Margaret Ormsby," 24–5.

70 Ormsby, "A Horizontal View," 8.

71 Ormsby, "Neglected Aspects of British Columbia's History," *British Columbia Library Quarterly*, 23(4), 1960, 10.

72 Norris, "Margaret Ormsby," 15.

73 The conviction that society is a phenomenon possessing its own structure and dynamic and can usefully be approached carrying the tools of the social scientist did not, of course, impress itself on all North American historians with equal force. For a comment on its failure, in the early stages of its development in the US, to do so there, see A.S. Eisenstadt, "American History and Social Science," *The Centennial Review*, 7, Summer 1963, 255–72. In the next year, however, a group of American historians could co-operate in the writing of a volume intended to acquaint their colleagues in the field with the utility of this approach; by the early 1970s interest in it had grown to the point where, in Samuel P. Hays' view, there was as much of a need to insist on discipline and rigour in the field as there was to urge historians to enter it; and by 1977 the body of work in the history of American society, especially that of the colonial

period, had begun to generate a critical literature of its own. See Edward N. Saveth, ed., *American History and the Social Sciences* (New York, 1964); Samuel P. Hays, "A Systematic Social History," in G. Grob and G. Bilias, eds., *American History: Retrospect and Prospect* (New York, 1971), 315–66, and Richard Beeman, "The New Social History and the Search for 'Community' in Colonial America," *American Quarterly*, 29(4), 1977, 422–43. Canadian historians, urged in 1965 to give attention to the history of society and more especially the class component in it, took up the task with a steadily growing enthusiasm. For S.R. Mealing's suggestions that this approach would be a profitable one, see his "The Concept of Social Class and the Interpretation of Canadian History," *Canadian Historical Review*, 46(3), September 1965, 201–18. For a survey of the word produced, see Carl Berger,"Social and Intellectual History," in J.L. Granatstein and Paul Stevens, eds., *Canada Since 1867: A Bibliographic Guide* (Toronto, 1974), 75–86; Michael Cross, "Canadian History," in C.F. Klinck, Alfred G. Bailey, et al., eds., *Literary History of Canada*, 2nd ed. (Toronto, 1976), vol. 3, 63–83; and H.J. Hanham, "Canadian History in the 1970s," *Canadian Historical Review*, 58(1), March 1977, 2–22.

74 H.K. Ralston, "Patterns of Trade and Investment on the Pacific Coast, 1867–1892: The Case of the British Columbia Salmon Canning Industry," *BC Studies*, 1, Winter 1968–1969, 37–45; Patricia E. Roy, "Direct Management from Abroad: The Formative Years of the British Columbia Electric Railway," in Glen Porter and Robert D. Cuff, eds., *Enterprise and National Development: Essays in Canadian Business and Economic History* (Toronto, 1973), 101–21.

75 J.M.S. Careless, "The Lowe Brothers, 1852–1870: A Study in Business Relations on the North Pacific Coast," *BC Studies*, 2, Summer 1969,1–18; the same author's "The Business Community in the Early Development of Victoria, British Columbia," in David S. Macmillan, ed., *Canadian Business History: Selected Studies, 1497–1971* (Toronto, 1972), 104–23; Norbert MacDonald, "Seattle, Vancouver, and the Klondike," *Canadian Historical Review*, 49(3), 1968, 234–46; and the same author's "Population Growth and Change in Seattle and Vancouver, 1880–1960," *Pacific Historical Review*, 39(3), 1970, 297–321.

76 Begg, for example, saw the triumph of white civilization, however unfortunate for the Indians themselves, as at once inevitable and a sign of progress; Scholefield thought them "lawless savages" kept in hand by the "paternal solicitude" of the Hudson's Bay Company; and Coats and Gosnell found them an "inferior" and "docile" people who had lived no more than a "barren existence." See Begg, "The Native Tribes and Civilization," 115–19; Scholefield, "Part One," in Schole-

field and Gosnell, *History of British Columbia*, 57, 85; and Coats and Gosnell, *Sir James Douglas*, 80. The one important exception to this general rule was the treatment given the Indians by Father A.G. Morice, whose anthropological interests coupled with his sojourn among the Indians allowed him to develop a degree of sympathy with their culture, values, and institutions. See A.G. Morice, *The History of the Northern Interior of British Columbia, 1660–1880* (Toronto, 1904).

77 By 1928 Howay could concede that "the Indian had his own standards of morality," and by 1942 he found it possible to note "the finely balanced economic and social fabric" of tribal life. See Howay, *British Columbia: The Making of a Province*, 9; Howay, Sage, and Angus, *British Columbia and the United States*, 13.

78 Ormsby's general history gave them scant attention, and her 1960 appeal for new work made no reference to them at all. Ormsby, *British Columbia*, and the same authors's "Neglected Aspects."

79 See, for example, Forrest LaViolette's *The Struggle for Survival: Indian Cultures and the Protestant Elite in British Columbia* (Toronto, 1961, 1973), which makes the point that Indian concern to preserve the potlatch did not grow out of heathenish perversity but was the consequence of a desire to preserve a key element in a functioning social system, and Wilson Duff's *The Indian History of British Columbia*, vol. 1: *The Impact of the White Man* (Victoria, 1965), which argues that Indian culture was capacious and elastic enough to absorb, at least for a time, innovations in technology, social organization, and culture introduced by the whites.

80 Jean Usher, "Duncan of Metlakatla: The Victorian Origins of a Model Indian Community," in W.L. Morton, ed., *The Shield of Achilles: Aspects of Canada in the Victorian Age* (Toronto, 1968), 286–310; *William Duncan of Metlakatla: A Victorian Missionary in British Columbia* (Ottawa, 1974).

81 Robin Fisher, *Contact and Conflict: Indian-European Relations in British Columbia 1774–1890* (Vancouver, 1977), xi, xiv.

82 Coats and Gosnell dealt with them in unflattering terms with a clear emphasis on steps taken to restrict Asian entry, while as late as 1928 Howay could refer to the Japanese as "wily little yellow men." See Coats and Gosnell, *Sir James Douglas*, 336"7; Howay, British Columbia, 265.

83 "All intelligent people," he wrote, "are willing to admit that Canada, the United States, Australia, and New Zealand have a perfect right to keep their country [*sic*] as white as possible; but it is highly desirable that they should always consider the honour and dignity of the Oriental nations, so that in excluding the orientals they will not

create racial hatred and racial conflict in the future." Tien-fang Cheng, *Oriental Immigration in Canada* (Shanghai, 1931), 267.

84 A.R.M. Lower, *Canada and the Far East* (New York, 1940); Charles J. Woodsworth, *Canada and the Orient: A Study in International Relations* (Toronto, 1941).

85 "Conclusion," in Charles H. Young and Helen R.Y. Reid, *The Japanese Canadians* (Toronto, 1938), 171–93.

86 Forrest LaViolette, *The Canadian Japanese and World War II: A Sociological and Psychological Account* (Toronto, 1948), 283.

87 Durkheim wrote in *The Rules of Sociological Method,* trans. Sarah A. Solovay and John H. Mueller (Chicago, 1938), 141: "All that [sociology] asks is that the principle of causality be applied to social phenomena." Cited in H. Stuart Hughes, *Consciousness and Society: The Reconstruction of European Social Thought 1890–1930* (New York, 1958), 281.

88 Ken Adachi, *The Enemy That Never Was: A History of the Japanese Canadians* (Toronto, 1976).

89 Barry Broadfoot, *Years of Sorrow, Years of Shame: The Story of the Japanese Canadians in World War Two* (Toronto, 1977).

90 See, on the first point, her review of Adachi's book in *The Canadian Historical Review,* 59(2), 1978, 255–7. Her own understanding of the issue can be found in Patricia E. Roy, "The Oriental 'Menace' in British Columbia," in S.M. Trofimenkoff, ed., *The Twenties in Western Canada* (Ottawa, 1972), 243–58; "Introduction," Hilda Glynn-Ward, *The Writing on the Wall* (Toronto, 1974), vi–xxxi; and "The Soldiers Canada Didn't Want: Her Chinese and Japanese Citizens," *Canadian Historical Review,* 59(3), 1978, 41–57.

91 W.P. Ward, *White Canada Forever: Popular Attitudes and Public Policy Towards Orientals in British Columbia* (Montreal, 1978), 92–3.

92 Sage, "Five Canadas," 34.

93 "The distinctly new feature in Vancouver's make-up [in the post-war period]," he insisted, "was the great increase in persons of European origin." MacDonald, "Population Growth and Change in Seattle and Vancouver, 1880–1960,"316.

94 Dorothy Blakey Smith, *Ethnic Groups in British Columbia: A Selected Bibliography* (Victoria, 1957).

95 John Norris, *Strangers Entertained: A History of the Ethnic Groups of British Columbia* (Vancouver, 1971).

96 George Woodcock and Ivan Avakumovic, *The Doukhobors* (Toronto and New York, 1968).

97 Coats and Gosnell, *Sir James Douglas,* 338, 342.

98 Edith Dobie, "Party History in British Columbia 1903–1933," *Pacific Northwest Quarterly,* 27(2), 1936, 154.

99 What he wrote of the period 1897 to 1904, indeed, summarized his sense of the politics of the preceding thirty years: "... the [political] events referred to appear highly kaleidoscopic in their rapidity of succession and changing complexities and combinations ... Conditions were in a state of ferment, of unrest,and the process of clarification which ensued [the formation of parties] might be compared to a casual admixture of highly reactive chemical elements." Gosnell, "Part Two," in Scholefield and Gosnell, *History of British Columbia*, 149.

100 Neil Robinson, "The Struggle for Responsible Government," in F.W. Howay, ed., *Builders of the West: A Book of Heroes* (Toronto, 1928), 232–6.

101 F.W. Howay, *British Columbia: The Making of a Province* (Toronto, 1928), 241; W.N. Sage, "British Columbia," in George M. Wrong, Chester Martin, and Walter N. Sage, *The Story of Canada* (Toronto, 1929), 348.

102 The introduction of party lines in 1903, suggested Edith Dobie, had been made partly as the result of a desire on the part of the province's elites to avoid political division based solely on opposition between socialists and non-socialists, since, in their view, such a division could only augment the strength of the socialists, and partly to ensure much-needed stability in the interest of getting particular programs approved. Edith Dobie, "Some Aspects of Party History in British Columbia, 1871–1903," *Pacific Historical Review*, 1(2), 1932, 247, 250. The major change introduced into the province's political life by the CCF's assumption of the status of official opposition, she wrote in a second article, produced "what seems a new and genuine party alignment on the question of the fundamental structure of society" and so pointed to the existence of a clear relationship between economic interest and political behaviour. Edith Dobie, "Party History in British Columbia 1903–1933, *Pacific Northwest Quarterly*, 27(2), 1936, 165.

103 W.N. Sage, "Federal Parties and Provincial Political Groups in British Columbia, 1871–1903,"*British Columbia Historical Quarterly*, 12(2), 1948, 152.

104 John Tupper Saywell, "Labour and Socialism in British Columbia: A Survey of Historical Development Before 1903," *British Columbia Historical Quarterly*, 15(3–4), 1951, 129–50.

105 Margaret A. Ormsby, "The United Farmers of British Columbia: An Abortive Third-Party Movement, *British Columbia Historical Quarterly*, 17(1–2), 1953, 53–73.

106 Donald Creighton, "Sir John Macdonald and Canadian Historians," *Canadian Historical Review*, 29(1), 1948, 7.

107 In undertaking to investigate a regionally or provincially based political formation in terms of the social, economic, and geographical factors that brought it into being, each of these scholars demonstrated a far surer grasp of the nature and complexity of the links between these two sets of phenomena than anything which had up to that time been produced by students of the British Columbia experience. See W.L. Morton, *The Progressive Party in Canada* (Toronto, 1950); Seymour Martin Lipset, *Agrarian Socialism: The cooperative Commonwealth Federation in Saskatchewan. A Study in Political Sociology* (Berkeley, 1950); C.B. Macpherson, *Democracy in Alberta: Social Credit and the Party System* (Toronto, 1953); L.G. Thomas, *The Liberal Party in Alberta: A History of Politics in the Province of Alberta 1905–1921* (Toronto, 1959).

108 Margaret Ormsby, "Neglected Aspects of British Columbia's History," *British Columbia Library Quarterly*, 23(4), 1960, 10.

109 Coats and Gosnell, *Sir James Douglas*, 335.

110 Stuart Jamieson, "Regional Factors in Industrial Conflict: The Case of British Columbia," *Canadian Journal of Economics and Political Science*, 28(3), 1962, 405–16.

111 Paul Phillips, *No Power Greater: A Century of Labour in British Columbia* (Vancouver, 1967), 160–2.

112 Ibid., 162–4.

113 See Martin Robin, "The Social Bases of Party Politics in British Columbia," *Queen's Quarterly*, 74(4), 1965–66, 675–90; his "British Columbia: The Politics of Class Conflict," in Martin Robin, ed., *Canadian Provincial Politics: The Party Systems of the Ten Provinces* (Toronto, 1972), 27–68; his *The Rush for Spoils: The Company Province 1871–1933* (Toronto, 1972), and his *Pillars of Profit: The Company Province 1934–1972* (Toronto, 1973). For a sharply critical comment on Robin's work, see Alan C. Cairns, "The Study of the Provinces: A Review Article," *BC Studies*, 14, Summer 1972, 73–82; for Robin's reply and a further comment by Cairns, see *BC Studies*, 16, Winter 1972–73, 77–82.

114 Sage's insistence, in opposition to the Laurentianism that was emerging in the 1930s as an important organizing principle in the study of Canadian history, that the regions of Canada should provide the main focus of the historian's study found a parallel on the prairies in the form of W.L. Morton's 1946 plea for a Canadian history that would take due account of the experience, and point of view, of the parts which composed it. Not, however, until the late 1960s, when shifts in the distribution of national power had persuaded some eastern-based historians that a centralist view of the country's history was no longer tenable, did the regional approach find a following in

their part of the country. See Sage, "Five Canadas"; W.L. Morton, "Clio in Canada: The Interpretation of Canadian History," *University of Toronto Quarterly*, 15(3), 1946, 227–34; J.M.S. Careless, " 'Limited Identities' in Canada," *Canadian Historical Review*, 50(1), March 1969, 1–10; Paul G. Cornell, Jean Hamelin, et al., *Canada: Unity in Diversity* (Toronto, 1967); Mason Wade, ed., *Regionalism in the Canadian Community, 1867–1967: Canadian Historical Association Centennial Seminars* (Toronto, 1969).

115 For a recent example of this kind of cosmopolitan regionalism, see A.D. Scott, "Introduction: Notes on a Western Viewpoint," *BC Studies*, 13, Spring 1972, 3–15.

11 The Ideology of Regionalism: The West against Ottawa in the 1970s

For decades one set of interest groups – that based largely in populous, wealthy Ontario – has been able to exercise a profound influence on the way Canada has been run. In the absence of serious rivals in other parts of the country, these centre-based business people, politicians, and bureaucrats were able to shape an economic and constitutional system clearly reflecting their understanding of how the nation should operate. What was more – and this was no small factor in their success – they were able to place their opposite numbers in the different regions and provinces very much on the defensive. The largely centralist principles of government and policy which they and their ideologues supported took on a validity which meant that those who opposed these principles could be dismissed as hopeless provincials, altogether lacking in any true understanding of their society's greatness and the means necessary to sustain it. In the last few years this long-standing pattern has begun to dissolve. Regional discontent cannot now be viewed as the slightly disreputable effusion of disgruntled farmers, second rate politicians, and backward French Canadians, a phenomenon all the less deserving of serious consideration because it so clearly conflicts with the sensible and broad interest which local elites – the regional figures who *really* count – have in maintaining their regions' links with the country's central institutions. The emergence of new interest groups, tied closely to regional econom-

Canadian Forum, 58(681), June–July 1978, 12–15.

ies and regional institutions which are themselves changing, has made this old view obsolete. Demands for change now come, very clearly, from able and aggressive groups of business people, politicians, and civil servants whose perspective has been shaped by their participation in the increasingly complicated economic, political, and bureaucratic lives of the provinces. The consequence is a new and more substantial kind of opposition to Ottawa's rule – a turn of events which signals difficulty ahead for those who want to defend the continued existence of a strong central government.

To say this is to do more than refer again to the familiar story of Quebec's evolution since the Second World War. Changes have occurred in the west as well, and these, too, have created new groups who do not perceive their interests to be served by existing arrangements. As in Quebec, economic alterations have been fundamental. The decline in the relative importance of the old, renewable staples (wheat, timber) exploited by a small population, and the rise of new, non-renewable resources (oil, gas, potash) exploited by a large and growing population has produced extraordinary results. Simultaneously bringing the west a new measure of economic power, new technological, bureaucratic, and business elites, and a new concern for its economic future, the shift has lead to a fresh emphasis on planning and development which, in its turn, has inspired an unprecedented series of western challenges to the kind of federalism championed by Ottawa and its supporters.

Even the old staples play a role in reinforcing this new regional discontent. The impact of the dollar's decline on exports – particularly on forest and agricultural products – has stimulated the western conviction that, since the western provinces are net earners on their export trade, they do more than their share in the struggle to balance the nation's payments – and, in fact, earn no small part of the money that pays for Ontario's costly and extensive range of imports. Western farmers, mine owners, and lumberers have enlarged their claim to a voice in the formation of the country's trade policy, a claim which they say is already long overdue, given the manner in which the west has for decades subsidized the central Canadian economy.

All of this, however, merely puts a gloss on the much more fundamental impatience with the west's position in Confederation which has developed as a consequence of the region's preoccupation with its new range of economic activities. The full significance of what is occurring here cannot be gauged simply by re-stating the facts, important though these are, that Alberta produces eighty per cent of the country's oil and gas, stands to enjoy even more substantial revenues from those resources than it has already gained, and is resentful of what it views as Ottawa's moves to interfere with getting them. One cannot even obtain a wholly accurate reading of the western frame of mind by taking note of Premier Blakeney's public annoyance with Ontario backers of Ottawa's oil export duty who, in his view, hardly hesitated to use a startlingly unambiguous and clearly anti-western double standard – my resources are mine, yours are the nation's – in framing their case for federal action. No one can hope to understand feeling in the west without taking these realities into account. Plumbing the depths of western concern nonetheless means recognizing a much more important fact. Thanks to its exploitation of the new resources, its growing population base, its increasing economic diversification, and its development of new foreign and domestic markets, the west believes itself to be acquiring something it never had before: a real prospect of moving away at last from exclusive reliance on primary production. What gives current feeling in the west its particularly sharp edge is the conviction – widely held by the new elites – that the region is about to turn a vitally important economic corner, but that it is being prevented from doing so by the continuing insistence of the east that it should operate within an institutional framework shaped by eastern interests. This is especially galling to western leaders since – as they believe their own high profile testifies – a combination of hard work, good fortune, and minimal help from the east has now provided the west with much of the infrastructure it needs to release it from its historic dependence on eastern institutions. What it lacks now (and thanks to the present constitution, is having trouble getting) is an opportunity to flex its newly acquired muscle.

It is hard to deny the reality of a new kind of western economy. If the more aggressive role played in recent years by the Winnipeg Commodities Exchange (the successor to the old Grain Exchange) has not allowed that particular institution to get much beyond its traditional business of handling agricultural products, other areas of the western economy have a quite startling new look. Steel fabrication, farm implement manufacture, the design and production of logging machinery, construction and engineering, a burgeoning service sector, and most dramatically, the technological and product innovations made by Alberta's petrochemicals industry mark a genuine new orientation for the western economy. In much of this activity (again, the analogy with Quebec is striking) public policymakers have taken a leading role. During the last fifteen years governments have organized, expanded, or acquired ownership of giant utilities (British Columbia Hydro), transportation systems (Pacific Western Airlines, British Columbia Railways) and basic resource industries (potash in Saskatchewan). With the establishment of such financial institutions as the Bank of British Columbia, Alberta's huge Heritage Fund, and the recently established Northland Bank, with headquarters in Winnipeg, the west is also acquiring a greatly enlarged capacity to finance its own growth. To be sure, massive projects such as the Alaska pipeline will require a substantial measure of outside financing; and there can be no doubt that the old national banks will continue to do the bulk of the west's business for the foreseeable future. But Westerners will now have an opportunity to get the financial services they require without necessarily dealing with extra-regional institutions – an opportunity which increasing numbers of them are seizing.

The effects of these changes on the west's economic growth have been phenomenal. In the last decade the economic output of the four western provinces has climbed from sixty per cent to eighty per cent of Ontario's. As population continues to shift westward, and as the percentage of the national income earned by the industrial sector declines further, there can be little doubt that the manufacturing component of the west's economy will continue to enjoy a rate of growth proportionately higher than that of manufacturing in the country at large. Indeed, as western industry becomes more efficient, it should cut more deeply into the volume of business done in the west by manufacturers from beyond its borders. Some commentators suggest that the economies of scale eventually to be attained by western manufacturers through the growth of local markets should make possible the development of a range of internationally competitive products beyond those already marketed by some sectors of the petro-chemicals and forest products industries.

In these heady circumstances, it is hardly surprising that the west's elites are determined that their region should not remain vulnerable to economic, transportation, and financial arrangements over which they have little control. In their view, it is imperative that present opportunities not be lost. Their sensitivity to federal policy thus grows out of circumstances quite different from those which produced the old arguments, at their peak in the protest politics of the 1920s and 1930s, over the tariff, freight rates, natural resources, and the marketing of wheat. Then the west's impotence was the critical factor. Now what is fundamental is what westerners believe to be their region's growing institutional and economic maturity. At last, western politicians and businessmen argue, the region is in a position to shape its own future. Its governments must therefore be secured against federal encroachments which erode their capacity to manage and direct economic development. This is why the Supreme Court's 1977 decision invalidating Saskatchewan's oil taxation legislation has had such serious repercussions here. In restricting that province's right to revenues from one of its resources, the decision also deprived it of the funds it needs to expand its activities in potash exploitation and management – a double blow against the province's attempt to break through to a new plateau of economic activity, which would move it away from its historic reliance on the wheat economy.

Even the westerners' continuing concern with the tariff has, thanks to the evolution of the western economy, acquired a different character. One still hears of the hardship the tariff works on primary producers, especially farmers, by compelling them to buy at artificially maintained prices at the same time that they must sell their products for what they can get on the world market. Increasingly, however, it is western business people who are dissatisfied. What disturbs them is the fact that the Canadian tariff on textiles, shoes, wood products, wide-flanged steel, and steel rods discriminates against the goods of the west's trading partners and so discourages them from importing what that region has to sell – semi-finished and finished goods as well as unprocessed ones. At the same time the tariff compounds the difficulties of western manufacturers in getting the cheap materials they need to produce a competitive product. Western industry, oriented towards external markets and, in some cases, external sources of supply, thus finds that it, like western farmers, has a grievance against a policy designed ostensibly to encourage national industrial growth which in fact tends to concentrate it regionally.

These realities, important enough in their economic phase, display a significant psychological dimension (and here too there is a parallel with Quebec). Long used to viewing their region as a hinterland, feeling themselves destined to operate within an economic and political framework shaped elsewhere, those who objected to these arrangements were formerly relegated to a politics of protest which was itself a measure of their subordination. Western elites have now begun to acquire a measure of confidence and authority which distinguishes them noticeably from their predecessors. Western discontent can still manifest itself in shrill demands for more power, in a singular impatience with Quebec, and, especially in the far west, in a peculiar disinclination to comprehend the terms of national political debate. It is now, however, more typically expressed in the disposition to organize agencies like the Prairie Economic Council (formed in 1965), in the move to define mutually acceptable positions which has taken place as a consequence of the Western Premiers' Conferences (held annually since 1973), and in such documents as the *Report* of the Western Premiers' Task Force on Constitutional trends, released in May 1977, which lists almost sixty cases of recent or impending federal incursions into provincial fields of jurisdiction. All of this reflects a conviction that, because the west controls resources and a hinterland of its own, because it is now building a more diversified economy on this foundation, and because its parts are now able to unite in support of regional interests transcending purely provincial concerns, it has acquired leverage in the national political system of a kind that it never possessed before. Western politicians no longer consider themselves to be posturing bit players on the national scene.

It would be misleading to leave the impression that western discontent with present power-sharing arrangements implies fundamental opposition to the Canadian union. Apart from the activities of fringe groups, nothing warrants such an assessment. The western provinces continue to make use of a complex web of transportation, financing, and marketing arrangements which, despite their decreasing importance, still bind them to each other and to the larger Canadian whole. The federal government's role in equalization makes its presence significant not only to Manitoba and Saskatchewan but to parts of British Columbia and even Alberta. But if east-west linkages continue to be sustained by powerful economic interests, they must now coexist with new realities, underpinned by new economic circumstances, whose evolution makes the need for new constitutional arrangements more and more difficult to resist.

The seriousness of the western premiers manifested in the obvious contrast between William Benett and his predecessors, in the single-minded intensity of Peter Lougheed, in the intelligently argued regionalism of Allan Blakeney, and in the stolid determination of Sterling Lyon, thus reflects something more substantial than individual temperament. Each of them heads a political and administrative apparatus which feels the weight of a new kind of responsibility, and each wants the authority to discharge that responsibility effectively. In marked contrast to the indifference to constitutional questions which they displayed only a few years ago, western political leaders have now joined journalists and academics in advancing a case for an altered Canadian federalism. They are beginning to insist that policy formation in the fields of resource exploitation, taxation, external trade, industrial development, transportation and communication must be carried out to allow the provinces an adequate role. At the least, it should take full account of what the provinces themselves believe should be done. Second, western politicians are concerned with the constitution's role as a largely symbolic representation of what the nation and its parts are. Even if one admits the frequently made argument that the present constitution is not only infinitely malleable but can in practice be ignored (as the numerous *ad hoc* arrangements for the transaction of federal-provincial business now demonstrate) one is left with the document as a description of a reality that no longer exists. The provinces, say western politicians, are simply not the junior jurisdictions that the BNA Act supposes them to be. They are now major entities, and they want to be seen that way. As Premier Bennett's claims for a British Columbia veto on constitutional amendments suggests, they hanker after a kind of status which the present constitution does not, in principle, allow them. They do not want to be seen seeking permission or entering into negotiations to secure what is theirs – even if, in the end, they will probably get it.

In the view of those westerners – including journalists, academics, politicians, and advisers to government – who have most closely considered the matter, there are three solutions to the constitutional problem which are compatible with the maintenance of a federal union. Maximizing provincial power at the centre has appeal for those who insist that a vital centre, capable of sustaining the support of the periphery, can be kept in being only by allowing that periphery some control over what it does. The centralist bias which these critics believe to be exhibited by the present federally-appointed Supreme Court is, then, to be overcome by allowing the provinces a share in its composition, or, as Premier Lougheed has suggested, by creating a constitutional court to which the provinces as well as Ottawa would make appointments. Advocates of this approach have not, however, explained how a winner-take-all process of adjudication, in conjunction with a system of appointments that would make the court even more of a political instrument than it now is, would operate to reverse the existing trend away from use of the courts as a means of settling constitutional disputes. Premier Bennett's suggestion that a second chamber patterned on the West German *Bundesrat* be considered presents difficulties of its own. Quite apart from the serious implications that the existence of such an institution would have for the practice of responsible cabinet government, its introduction would certainly involve growth in the power of the federal centre. The participation of the West German *länder* in federal decision-making ought not to obscure the fact that such participation is, indeed, a measure of the extent to which power in the Federal Republic is exercised, not by the states as such, but by them as agencies influencing federal legislation – a quite different thing. Their input is, moreover, made possible by the fact that there is a substantial measure of agreement on fundamentals between the two levels of government, both of which represent a society which, unlike Canada's, is linguistically and culturally homogeneous and geographically compact. Even if these realities could be ignored, such an institution would be exotic in the Canadian constitutional landscape, and unlikely to flower without significant changes in attitude towards both the theory and practice of government. Regionally representative federal agencies and commissions (such as the CRTC and the CTC) are even less likely to be introduced successfully. Members of Ottawa-based organizations, no matter what their principle of appointment, are likely over time to lose sight of the regional interests they would be there to serve – a point made forcefully and often by those westerners who have seen their agents compromised again and again by the need to conform to "national" interests and priorities. None of these proposals, finally, is likely to satisfy any government holding power in Quebec. (Westerners realize in increasing numbers that proposals for reform will have to meet that criterion if they are to have any hope of success.)

If institutional change in the direction of intrastate federalism and the provincialization of national institutions would meet with only limited success, the second kind of solution – a redistribution of powers devolving more authority on those provinces – is also open to criticism. Unless the provinces desiring enlarged jurisdiction wish totally to emasculate the central power – and it is by no means clear that, even in Quebec, this is the case – they must face the fact that no redistribution of responsibilities, however rationally conceived, will ever eliminate conflict between the two levels of government. There is the equally compelling circumstance that, once the decision to maintain two levels of government is taken, policymakers will (as experience over the last several years has made clear) be faced with a number of matters in which effective action can only occur after consultation. Some western observers have been suggesting that the only approach likely to resolve these awkward realities is one that would at once reduce the potential for conflict and allow for a wide measure of cooperation between the two levels of government.

The third solution, in addressing itself to this problem, proposes not simply a redistribution of power between the federal and provincial governments, but the addition of a *third* main schedule of responsibilities, these to be held jointly, action on which would be taken after agreement by the leaders of the country's governments meeting in regular session, supported by a permanent federal-provincial secretariat in place of the *ad hoc* one that now exists. Such a schedule of powers would, its proponents suggest, almost certainly have to include transportation, economic development, social policy, and equalization. It might even involve, as Premier Lyon has been suggesting, federal-provincial management of the money supply. Policy decisions in these areas would not be easy; but who pretends that they are so now? More positively, this arrangement would have the double advantage of providing for a more sustained and organized input by the provinces, as such, into federal policy through the executive branch of government, where it would be the most immediately effective, without necessitating a departure from the arrangements which have evolved on an *ad hoc* basis with the increasing prominence of federal-provincial consultation since 1960. This kind of executive federalism, in Donald Smiley's phrase, would simply give formal recognition to the power-sharing that already enjoys extra-constitutional status. With this recognition of the provinces' power would come an equally explicit placing of responsibility on them for the maintenance of national standards in incomes and services. Equalization would not, in other words, have to depend on the maintenance by the federal government of its extensive taxing and spending capability. The more prosperous provinces would act in the future, as federal governments have in the past, to maintain income levels in the poorer provinces, and for much the same reasons: they too would be responsive to the fact that the manufacturers in their jurisdictions depend for their economic health on the maintenance of minimum levels of income and consumption across the country. Inter-provincial aid programs of another sort – Alberta's loan to Newfoundland is an example – might also be developed. While it would be idle to pretend that there would be no dislocation as a result of federal withdrawal from these areas, alternatives to federal action do exist.

Influential groups of westerners may be developing a clear enough view of the desirability of getting more power for their governments. They are, however, less certain what their attitude towards the province of Quebec ought to be. That province is still widely thought of as the spoiled child of Confederation, which, having got more than anybody else, should now be made either to take its substantial number of marbles and keep quiet or to pack up and get out. Two things, however, suggest that these groups may be in the process of altering their approach to Quebec. First, as the shock of the PQ victory dissipates, there is a growing realization that opinion in Quebec, and even in the PQ, is not united in some absolute and unchanging way behind the separatist option. Second, as the west comes to a fuller appreciation of the extent to which its own concern with federal power grows out of the development of its economy, it is gaining an appreciation of what its situation gives it in common with Quebec. A sense that Quebec and the west share some of the same concerns is thus emerging at the same time that events in Quebec itself are making it possible to argue that cooperation with that province does not necessarily mean underwriting moves to dissolve the nation. The likelihood that a Quebec-western alliance in support of a renewed federalism will emerge is hardly, of course, an immediate prospect; yet there are indications that this is not wholly inconceivable. Ex-Premier Barrett of British Columbia has held talks with René Lévesque, Premier Lougheed of Alberta has made it clear (in terms of at least some of its constitutional demands) that Quebec will never find itself isolated, and the west's heightened interest in constitutional reform is, as I have said, accompanied by a growing recognition that such reform cannot be achieved without the support of Quebec. Western politicians, in what looks remarkably like a response to PQ diplomacy, are even beginning to demonstrate a real measure of sympathy for the educational claims of their French-speaking minorities.

The west, in sum, is undergoing it own kind of Quiet Revolution. Neither so fundamental in its impact nor so tightly focused in its demands as that of Quebec, it nonetheless imposes strains of its own on the Canadian federal system. Once all the groups concerned – in the west as well as the east – appreciate the full significance of that fact, movement towards a new federalism is likely to begin in earnest, with the western provinces engaged in the process as they have never been before. In these circumstances Quebec may find itself, not opposed by, but acting in concert with, a group of western provinces with a fresh sense of the future.

12 The Myth of the Self-made Man in English Canada, 1850–1914

Recent scholarship concerning society and values in English Canada has placed much emphasis on the extent to which their evolution demonstrates a continuing Canadian attachment to conservative principle. Strongly concerned to establish the ways in which the Canadian nation may be distinguished from the American, scholars have drawn particular attention to the role played in its growth by deference, a belief in the rights of the community over those of the individual, and a sense that the collective experience of those who compose it gives society its substance and texture. The Canadian mind, they argue, has been characterized not so much by faith in the potency of the individual as by a conviction that actors in society must accept the authority of those who preside over their affairs. Living in a community which has been shaped by metropolitan institutions – the church, the fur trade, government, corporations – has, they suggest, made Canadians inclined to value behaviour that allows an harmonious existence within a framework of organization, discipline, and order. Canadians, they continue, have doubted the wisdom of experimenting with new modes of political organization, preferring to cast their lot with institutions whose capacity to allow people to live together in peace, order, and good government has been clearly proved. It was, indeed, the Canadians' lack of enthusiasm for doctrines espousing the primacy of the individual that led them to

Canadian Historical Review, 59(2), 1978, 189–219.

structure a transcontinental nation dedicated to the furtherance of essentially conservative aims. In time their adherence to a value system in which a strong reverence for individualist modes of behaviour was displaced by a belief in class and community prepared the way for a measured but explicit commitment to social democracy. Even business people, contends a recent study, seriously qualified their individualism. In the midst of this welter of collectivist and quasi-collectivist belief, little room was left, scholars have concluded, for a Canadian assertion of faith in the power of the individual. In S.M. Lipset's formulation, "Horatio Alger has never been a Canadian hero."[1]

While there can be no doubt that the makers of this argument have contributed fundamentally to our understanding of Canadian society and the values, attitudes, and ideas of those who formed it, perhaps it is now time to look at the other side of the coin. Is there evidence to suggest that Canadians thought in individualist terms? Did they adopt individualist heroes? Were they, in short, men and women of their age? There can be little doubt that the answer to these questions is Yes. From the middle of the nineteenth century, when they first began to offer their compatriots sustained and regular instruction in what modes of behaviour were worthy of emulation, until the Great War, after which the emergence of new social and economic realities pushed discussion of these matters into a wholly new phase, English Canadians made it very clear indeed that the myth of the self-made man informed no small part of their thinking about society and its nature.

Many Canadians, certainly, did not hesitate to portray their society as one which at once allowed unlimited scope for, and had been shaped by, individual activity. Anxious to encourage the hard work which seemed so essential to the country's development, and convinced that the pain and struggle involved in doing that work would be more palatable if their results were seen to have special significance, these observers emphasized the degree to which individual effort was historically important, productive of great personal satisfaction, and likely to bring dramatic rewards. A deep-seated impulse to self-reliance, some of them insisted, was, in fact, to be found at the very core of the national experience. It was, they suggested, a matter of record that such figures as James Wolfe,[2] Sir Frederick Haldimand,[3] Sir William Phipps,[4] Lord Selkirk,[5] John Strachan,[6] and Tecumseh[7] had made their mark thanks in large part to the qualities of character, determination, and ingenuity which they so conspicuously displayed.

The commonly expressed contention – at its most grandiose and explicit in the multi-volume *Makers of Canada*, published early in the twentieth century[8] – that individualist modes of behaviour had been exemplified by the founders of the nation, legitimized by the historical process itself, was accompanied by the equally widespread claim that the life of the present no less than the experience of the past was given shape and body by the latitude it allowed the creative, self-determining individual. There could be no doubt, insisted the popular historian C.R. Tuttle, that life in contemporary Canada provided anyone willing to work with ample opportunity to better himself. Incontrovertible proof of this proposition, Tuttle continued, was available to anyone who scrutinized the careers of the most eminent Canadians. One had only to consider the achievements of such men as Tupper, Mackenzie, and Macdonald to see that, in Canada, talent and ability could overcome the humblest of origins.[9]

What was demonstrated by the lives of Canada's leaders, claimed another chronicler of the Canadian experience, had been quite as clearly evidenced by those of its people. As historian John McMullen put it in 1855, what they were able to accomplish demonstrated beyond doubt that Canada was a society in which "enterprize, economy, and prudence ... are the avenues to wealth ... everyday experience presents to our notice mechanics who, as the architects of their own fortunes, have won their way to positions alike well merited and honorable."[10] As the figure who had been most intimately associated with one of the central features of Canada's existence – the clearing of the land – the pioneer farmer received particularly close attention from Canadian acolytes of the self-made man. By his hard work he at once advanced himself and gave content to his country's development. He was, claimed his literary friends, in the fullest sense his own master, free of all constraint and interference, quite literally able to shape his world as he wished, the heir to an abundant and fulfilling future. And what allowed him to attain these heights – the moral was driven home with unmistakable clarity by poet Isabella Valancy Crawford – was no more nor less than his own capability: "... all men," insisted Crawford, "may have the same/That owns an axe! an' has a strong right arm!"[11]

By the early years of the twentieth century the conviction that in Canada past and present combined to authenticate the individualist principle had become deeply rooted. As the University of Toronto's Pelham Edgar put it in 1909, the belief that Canada was "the land of limitless possibilities ... where old age may [never] lament ... as in countries less rich in rewards, the life-long absence of opportunity ..." was so firmly entrenched that, he continued, it was past time to remind Canadians of Matthew Arnold's contention that an overweening concern with material advancement signified not progress but barbarism.[12] But if some of his compatriots heeded this and similar arguments, others continued to revere the man of success and accomplishment. Even Sir William Van Horne's none too scrupulous tactics in building the first Cuban railway justified his identification in the pages of the *Canadian Magazine* as a pre-eminent man of achievement whose industry, determination, and ingenuity had overcome all obstacles.[13]

If, in sum, the Canada of these years contained no scarcity of figures who could be shown to have shaped their careers in the finest traditions of the self-made man, it also contained no shortage of writers who thought it important that this fact be brought to the public's attention. Canadians, like the Americans and British, must be taught the virtues of self-help. What better way to do it than by showing them that what was best in their own society was the product of, gave ample encouragement to, and found its perfect expression in, individual effort?

For all its appeal, the uncomplicated picture painted by these partisans of the self-made man had serious shortcomings. The society in which their heroes functioned did not long remain – it had never really been – a place where unadorned virtue and simple hard work automatically brought fulfilment beyond measure. It was, some observers had noted early on, a labyrinthine structure the mastery of whose byways depended on more than strength, fortitude, and determination. As early as the 1840s the transformation of Upper Canadian society into a more complex and differentiated entity had produced changes in the way it was viewed. It was no longer, some observers argued, to be seen as raw and unfinished, waiting for the hand of man who, in transforming it, would make his own career. It was instead a complicated and ever changing mechanism. Success in coping with it involved more than will and initiative. Special training was required. In these circumstances, as the *Kingston Chronicle* put it in 1842, education was "the young man's capital." A tool in the struggle for self-sufficiency, it was "the best assurance of further competency and happiness."[14]

Six years later, educator Egerton Ryerson pointed to the existence of a dynamic quality in society with which individuals must be trained to cope. This, he noted, was a time of "sharp and skilful competition" and "sleepless activity." It was all, moreover, just beginning. "The rising generation should, therefore, be educated not for Canada as it has been, or even now is, but for Canada as it is likely to be half a generation hence."[15] Education's virtue thus lay in the fact that in a universe of flux and change it equipped one to make his own way: with schooling Canadians might, in the words of one of Ryerson's contemporaries, "be prepared, at least, to make some near approach to that place in the social scale, which their more intelligent, because better educated, [American] neighbours, now threaten to monopolize."[16]

Within twenty years this line of argument had become a familiar one. As one Canadian, recalling his early experiences, put it: "I had heard that knowledge was power – and I looked upon Algebra and Euclid and the whole academic course as the rudimentary steam-engine with which I should sometime run a train of first-class cars, freighted full of hope and worldly success into some great depot of happiness. I looked upon education as a toolchest – as something to work with ..."[17] The 1869 death of the American banker-philanthropist George Peabody provided the occasion for another observer to underscore the connection between success and education. Where Peabody's lack of schooling might once have been linked with his life of achievement to establish the fact that it was only by overcoming obstacles and relying upon oneself that one made his way, the connection was now made for quite a different reason. Peabody, readers of the *New Dominion Monthly* were assured, had always seen his failure to get an education as a handicap. His mature interest in it, therefore, "probably arose in part from the fact that he was taken from school at eleven years, and thus himself felt the need of the advantage he so liberally supplied for others."[18]

What possession of those advantages might lead to was made clear to Canadians in a five-volume work published in 1891. Setting out to show what hard work, perseverance, and preparation could accomplish in almost any field, the title alone of the Reverend William Cochrane's *The Canadian Album, Men of Canada: or Success by Example, in Religion, Patriotism, Business, Law, Medicine, Education, and Agriculture* ... clearly indicated that success was to be associated with special training – often professional – in a defined field of activity. Some commentators chose to add emphasis to the point by introducing fictional heroes who displayed a marked appetite for study and eventually became successful doctors or lawyers.[19] The living of a happy and fulfilling domestic life was in its turn shown to depend on the acquisition of certain skills.[20] The power of education to equip individuals with what was necessary to a successful career was, it seemed, unlimited. Even deficiencies of character which individuals could do nothing to ameliorate on their own might, claimed one educator, be overcome by training and example. That was why, argued John M. Sangster in 1892, teachers must exhibit no tendency towards laziness. Their deportment no less than the substance of their lessons had a role to play in fitting their pupils for life's struggle.[21]

Emphasis on learning as an adjunct to success was occasionally accompanied by a vigorous anti-intellectualism. It was necessary, some commentators insisted, to distinguish between learning that was useful and learning that was not. The training which had most to do with one's struggle to advance oneself did not, they claimed, come from the schools at all. "Great men," noted an 1868 observer, "learn very little of what the world admires them for knowing, during what is called their "educational" course. They are men who are constantly observing little things and great things passing around them ... it is this knowledge obtained among men and from men that is the most useful in any walk of life, literary or commercial."[22] Whatever its source, agreed another commentator, knowledge must be practical in its application. Schooling must produce "a well-educated, properly finished man, ready to grapple with the numerous many-sided questions sure to present themselves in his day and generation."[23] He who would be successful must also strive to broaden his practical experience. "The young businessman who spends his whole life in the study of business in his own town or city has," insisted a 1901 observer, "far less chance of success than the man who has seen business done in a dozen cities."[24]

One way of mastering the tasks of the workaday world within the context of a system of formal training was provided by the commercial and business schools of post-Confederation Canada. Their activities, in turn, were complemented by manuals offering systematic instruction in the steps necessary to achieve success in the world of commerce and practical affairs. Those who aspired to rise in that world might read John Macdonald's *Business Success*,[25] or, perhaps, listen to a series of lectures Macdonald gave to the students of Toronto's British American Commercial College. Published under the title *Business Character* in 1886, their statement of the relevance "the old principles of truth and honesty and industry and patience ..." bore to the new situation earned them an enthusiastic response from *The Week*: the little book, it said, "cannot fail to benefit every young man who is wise enough to make its precepts his."[26]

Learning, whether formal or not, continued to be associated with mobility. One commentator drew the required lesson from Franklin's career. That luminary, he reminded his readers, had "educated himself while fulfilling his labours as printer, editor, and booksellers ..." This considerable accomplishment, moreover, was directly responsible for his success in later life. It had been "by dint of his persevering struggle after improvement [that he became] an author, a philosopher, and a statesman."[27] Another observer, more inclined to emphasize the value of schooling, insisted on its continuing relevance to those who wished to move in step with a changing world. "The world," she noted, "is progressing, and he who would be successful in any calling must keep pace with the rapid onward march."[28]

By the turn of the century the relevance of a university education to the plans of those who wished to advance themselves was being adumbrated. "People are beginning to realize," argued a supporter of post-secondary institutions in 1904, "that the old orthodox way of making a fortune – to come into London or Montreal with fifty cents in your pocket and all the rest of it, is not the only way." University training, and the mental discipline acquired in getting it, were, he continued, becoming more and more necessary, and those who have them will be the ones who will achieve success.[29] As another writer put it, the businessman who went to college would, other things being equal, be more successful than the one who did not.[30] More importantly, insisted a third observer, providing businessmen with a university education was likely to make them less bumptious and more humane. The self-made man, unadorned by anything save his money-making powers, was "the pest of modern life." Transformed by a liberal education, he would be an altogether different being. When its civilizing capability was set alongside its relevance to income and status, the case for higher education in fact established itself.[31]

Some commentators, even more concerned to emphasize the fact that education must stimulate and develop the higher side of human nature if one's powers as a free and responsible individual were to be fully engaged, claimed that the educational enterprise itself was being perverted by emphasis on the acquisition of marketable skills and practical knowledge. "The true aim of education," contended an 1894 critic, "is being lost sight of ... The instruction that will fit for making money is considered of primal importance; the education that develops character, manliness, patriotism is considered of secondary importance."[32] The moral education of the young, agreed journalist J.A. Cooper, must not be neglected. Here the family had a special responsibility. It must not, Cooper argued in 1899, abandon it. This was, indeed, vital, for only the sort of sensitivity to the moral dimension of existence that would come from a proper family upbringing could create a truly self-directed and creative human being. Nowhere but in the midst of the family could young people be taught that "education may come from within as well as without, that every individual is the architect and builder of his own life-building."[33]

Other commentators were similarly persuaded that the development of character and a sense of responsibility could not be ignored. They insisted, however, that the relationship this sort of moral improvement bore to self-reliance made it, like self-reliance, dependent on the acquisition of values, attitudes, and even skills that – in some circumstances at least – only schooling could provide. The arrival of the great wave of European immigrants in the early years of the twentieth century allowed this proposition to be illustrated in a particularly striking way. In their case, it was argued, schooling would provide not only needed skills – language, for example – but also the orientation towards society the newcomers required if they were to advance themselves. By inculcating the principles of self-reliance and initiative, it would overcome the bovine stolidity that so many observers found characteristic of the immigrants. This would at once lay the groundwork for their assimilation into Canadian society and make it possible for them to realize the opportunities – moral and material – open to them in their new situation.

Saskatchewan educator J.T.M. Anderson, anxious to show what a failure to equip themselves with knowledge of the language and *mores* of their new country had meant for many immigrants, advanced countless examples of men whose continuing attachment to the old ways had held them back. A young Polish immigrant who had got an education therefore emerged as one of his principal heroes. After overcoming a variety of obstacles, the Pole had become fluent in English, completed high school, and won his way through to a university education. That accomplishment, in equal measure the reward for past efforts and the means of future advancement, won him high marks from Anderson: "What a splendid record of obstacles encountered and overcome, of worthy ambition, of loyal self-sacrifice, and youthful devotion to duty in the pursuance of a grand ideal!"[34] His feat, were it to be duplicated in immigrant communities across the prairies, would assure the advancement of the immigrant population in general. Schooling allied to character and initiative would help the new Canadians as it had the old to find their way to success and fulfilment.

The realization that Canadian society was complex did more than underscore the argument that individuals' chances of success would be seriously diminished if they did not equip themselves with special skills; it also compelled some observers to admit that even if they had received schooling, and no matter how hard they worked, they might not alter their position in any appreciable way. Nor, some of them continued, was it necessarily desirable that they should. Canada, they argued, needed nothing so much as a disciplined and productive work force. Getting one meant, in part, breeding up a race content in the knowledge that its fate was to be hewers of wood and drawers of water. These points could not, however, be made without reservation. To cast them in categorical and unambiguous terms would be to take a dangerous step in the direction of denying mobility and affirming the existence of class. That, in its turn, would be to grant a major part of the case being framed by the critics of the individualist idea. Partisans of individualism, thus faced with the task of conceding what it seemed impossible to deny without, at the same time, doing violence to the essentials of their doctrine, sought to resolve their problem in the only way open to them. They would seek to persuade individuals frustrated by lack of success that there was no real conflict between their situation and the idea that the social universe offered absolute scope for all to live a happy and fulfilled life thanks to their own efforts alone. If the resources available for use and pleasure sometimes seemed limited, that, they were assured, in no sense called the individualist idea into question. On the contrary, one's modest stock of goods was a function of the fact that there existed a generally egalitarian system of apportioning society's bounty which was a necessary condition of individual fulfilment. By ensuring a more or less equitable distribution of what society had to offer, that system, argued its apologists, guaranteed everyone what was required to sustain freedom and independence; limited means, quite simply, signified equality of condition, and equality of condition was to be viewed as the *sine qua non* of individual happiness and achievement. And if, continued some observers, there were occasions when opportunities leading in the direction in which one wished to move seemed few in number, that meant only that one should learn to find satisfaction in work in some field of activity where they were more abundant – and where, it was sometimes added, one was likely to be of more use. In neither of these cases, commentators insisted, was there reason to conclude that the individualist idea had lost its relevance. All remained in charge of their fate. What they had to do to shape its contours perhaps involved paying more attention to circumstance than had once been thought necessary, but there could be no question that it remained within their power to make a full and satisfying life for themselves.

The Toronto *Globe*, particularly concerned with influencing the wage earner's assessment of his position, played its readers a variation on the first of these themes in the early part of 1872. Far from being an impoverished exception in a community of the fabulously wealthy, the salaried worker was, that journal suggested, on a level with all Canadians. Canadian society was not to be thought of as a place whose representative figures were men of spectacular achievement. It remained open, to be sure, a place in which all created their own destiny. "We all work," the newspaper insisted. "We all began with nothing, We have all got by hard work all we own ..." Set alongside these familiar propositions, however, were others whose burden was that while hard work and self-reliance remained important, what should be expected to result from them were achievements of a modest and restrained sort. Activity on one's own behalf was, the *Globe* explained, attended not by dramatic and unlimited success, but by "an ample independence." Extravagant examples of good fortune were, in fact, specifically eschewed. "We have," it continued, "no such class as those styled capitalists in other countries. The whole people are the capitalists in Canada." The principal fact about the country, readers were assured, was that its people were "frugal" and "industrious," the creators of a society in which "the richest among us work still and like to do it."[35] The moral to be extracted from all this was, then, clear: all must work hard, look after themselves, not expect great material success, and take satisfaction from the knowledge that their society was composed of people whose position and aspirations were the same.

There was, suggested a contributor to *Rose-Belford's Canadian Monthly*, another way in which individuals' limited share of the world's goods was compatible with the claim that they were autonomous and self-directed beings. By throwing them back on their own resources their limited means called into play – indeed made mandatory the exercise of – the very qualities that allowed them to be defined in these terms. Far from rendering them impotent, the most straitened of circumstances thus had a special role to play in emphasizing the fact that they shaped their own fate. What became of them remained nothing more than a measure of the extent to which, thanks to their attributes of initiative and self-reliance, they turned to account whatever they had been given to work with. They must of course learn, explained *Rose-Belford's* correspondent, not to scorn what lay at hand. Even the finite and the trivial, the most unprepossessing of means, had its uses. "The great lesson" – here was the article's central message –"is not to despise the day of small things."[36] Once, however, they had taken that injunction to heart, they would know that no matter how unpropitious the situation seemed, their lives, still and as always, would be what they made of them.

The suggestion that their modest circumstances merely put individuals on their mettle, like the contention that they were proof of nothing more sinister than the fact that they lived in a society of equals, allowed the character of those circumstances to be conceded without making necessary a parallel concession that their existence deprived individuals of control over their fate. If, however, this careful avoidance of any suggestion that people no longer mastered their destiny played an important part in arguments designed to make society's members content with a limited share of the world's goods, it occupied a less prominent position in the case of those anxious that people who laboured for a living learn to derive pleasure and satisfaction from what they actually did rather than continually searching for some other livelihood the finding of which, as they seemed to think, would bring them happiness and enjoyment beyond measure. One commentator, single-mindedly striving to make ordinary workers content with their lot, came in fact perilously close to arguing that they should learn to be satisfied with their daily round because they were likely to be involved with it for the rest of their working lives. It was, argued L.R. O'Brien of the Ontario Society of Artists, imperative that society – and especially those of its members destined to be workingmen – understand that there was simply no room for everyone to advance. Only if this fact were grasped, O'Brien asserted, could those whose prospects were limited reach an accommodation with themselves and their situation that would enable them to live contented lives. That this should happen was in the interest of all of society, for only a real measure of satisfaction on the part of the worker with what he did would overcome the indifferent workmanship and – equally important for those anxious to curb labour agitation – the discontent with one's job that seemed characteristic of the age.

O'Brien's residual individualism moved him back, in the end, from fully embracing the claim that the workingman had lost the ability to move himself upwards in the social scale. His refusal to go so far had, however, the effect of reinforcing rather than qualifying his argument's principal theme: opportunity for advancement might indeed exist, but before the worker could take advantage of it he had to demonstrate his suitability for a more lucrative and responsible position by the exemplary performance of the duties now occupying his attention. Advancement in the future was thus tied to a willing acceptance of one's position and the tasks associated with it in the present. It was, as O'Brien put it, imperative that the wage earner see that he would "rise by the excellence of his work, rather than by shirking it to seek for some easier mode of living or advancement."[37]

Other observers agreed that workers must keep their eyes fixed firmly on what lay before them. To be sure, they, like O'Brien, avoided unambiguously suggesting that workers be told that the social universe was a place of closed options and no hope. Equally, however, their concern that workers be disabused of the idea that unlimited success and advancement automatically attended hard work led them to make an even stronger statement condemning what had become in their view a wholly spurious notion. The situation, argued the 1889 report of the federal commission investigating industrialism in Canada, was, in fact, urgent. Far too many children, their parents caught up in the belief that education was the highroad to success, were being enroled in programmes meaningful only as preparation for professional and business careers. There were, however, few openings in these areas. At the same time the need – much more pressing in an industrializing society like Canada – for people trained to work with their hands was going largely unfilled. In these circumstances, the report suggested, those who gave the average child his picture of the society in which he must function had a duty to represent its character accurately. They must not continue the encouragement of extravagant expectations. Their task was to see to it that the child's training and, indeed, the whole of the socialization process to which he was exposed, contrive to make him content with a limited future. "An effort should be made," the report concluded, "to instill in the minds of the young a preference for industrial avocations rather than the overstocked professional and commercial callings."[38]

As much of the foregoing implies, an important part of the complicated business involved in conceding the reality of circumstance without denying the proposition that individuals were responsible for what befell them depended on getting those individuals to accept an altered idea of what constituted success. Explaining what in many cases they already knew – that they did not operate in a wholly free and open universe – could not, by itself, do what was necessary. So long as they continued to covet wealth and power, their encounter with the limitations imposed by circumstance was, as O'Brien had suggested, likely to disillusion and embitter them, and so interfere with their interest in doing society's work. Equally disturbing, in the view of one observer, were the consequences that encounter entailed for society's moral tone. Some individuals, having recognized that circumstance was not to be overcome by hard work alone, were being led by their unmodified ambition to seek other means of dealing with it. The result, claimed J.A. Cooper in 1900, was a craven and undignified opportunism. Principled adherence to honourable behaviour was becoming a rarity. The ambitious were stooping to any level in their efforts to confound circumstance. "The surest way to success," as Cooper put it, was now "by bending. Notice," he continued, "the politicians; they bend almost double. Notice the acrobatic actions of the successful businessman; they are the result of a long course of physical culture. Start out by accepting things as they are and proceed from that point."[39]

Moving people away from an understanding of success that led in these directions required a sure and delicate touch. What replaced such an understanding must leave intact the idea that what one made of life was a product of one's own efforts. The result of those efforts had, moreover, to be attractive or one would have no incentive for doing the work necessary to achieve it. In their search for a goal that would be at once attainable and worth pursuing, philosophers of success found it difficult to do other than restate the idea that the proper end of human activity was a morally sound existence, one characterized by hard work, charity, and discipline. They who were successful were they who had shaped a moral life. In thus defining the goal in terms of the behaviour necessary to achieve it, commentators at once powerfully reinforced that behaviour and allowed wealth to be dispensed with as the object with which it would be rewarded.

This move, certainly, was consistent with Cooper's view of what was required. Only the person in whom means and ends were fused in one moral whole could, he thought, earn recognition as "one of the world's truly great."[40] It was, as well, a tactic that stood to have vitally important consequences so far as workers were concerned. Winning their assent to this definition of success would play a central part in the difficult process of persuading them to accept the continuing validity of individualist assumptions even as their circumstances were compelling the conclusion that a life guided by them did not, in its externals at least, undergo significant change. Emphasis was, accordingly, laid on the notion that self-reliance, character, and discipline were to be their own rewards. Habits of thrift and industry were to be adopted by workers, not primarily as a means of moving themselves upward in the social scale, but as a way of ensuring a full, satisfying life for themselves where they were. Workers must identify with these values and attitudes, not so much because a life lived in accordance with them would ensure one's rise, but because it would lead to the kind of satisfaction that could only come from the responsible and conscientious performance of one's task viewed as an end in itself. "Let the workingmen of Canada learn," as nine-hour day opponent C. Henry Stephens expressed the matter in 1872, "... to live frugally, temperately, and with a high and proper sense of the power and responsibility with which they are entrusted, and they will do more to ameliorate their position than by any reduction of their hours of labour, or by any fictitious appearance of material gain."[41]

Material gain – at this juncture the influence of the Protestant tradition plainly revealed itself – could now in fact be pronounced incompatible with a truly successful life. In leading, as in its detractors' view it inevitably did, to self-indulgence and a weakening of moral fibre, it imposed a burden too great for anyone to carry. As one writer, extracting the lesson from his story of a hickory tree felled in a storm, had put it in 1864: "... he had carried too large a top. Too great a wealth and growth of greenness had proved his ruin. Prosperity had been his bane. And many a one who walks the earth today, and many who do not, have thus, too, fallen!"[42] The awful inexorability with which this process worked itself out was dramatically illustrated for readers of the *New Dominion Monthly* a few years later. Storyteller J.R. Ramsay, chronicling the history of a fictional Canadian family, made a special point of the fact that one of its branches had undergone moral collapse owing to the failure of its members to cope with their success. A distillery started by one of them had prospered, but "... with wealth came luxury; with luxury temptation; with temptation, disgrace."[43]

Stephens was, of course, not alone in amplifying this theme. To be sure, those who joined him in embellishing it did not always take precisely the same tack. If writer-historian W.D. Le Sueur's 1875 statement – "To live worthily we must set before us an ideal, and that ideal must be something more than mere worldly success"[44] – was quite categorical in its refusal to equate wealth and achievement, some observers declared themselves willing to countenance at least a measure of material prosperity. The fundamental concern in each case remained, however, the same. The moral content of one's life, commentators insisted, provided the true means of measuring its worth. Wealth in itself had no value. Achievement did not bestow the right to behave irresponsibly. It certainly conferred no right to demean oneself. The successful must, in the words of Canniff Haight, "guard against the enervating influences which are too apt to follow increase in wealth ... Wealth can give much, but cannot make a man, in the proper and higher sense ..."[45] The Reverend W.R.G. Mellen thought it imperative that wealth, once acquired, be put to proper use. Wealthy citizens must emulate the Peabodys, Vassars, Hopkins, and Cornells, and make their money available for the public good. It was delivered into their hands as a trust, and it must be used as such.[46] Personal deportment was also of great importance. Far from indulging themselves, persons of wealth must adopt a style of life in which restraint, even unworldiness, figured prominently. They should, indeed, practice a kind of secular asceticism. The comment of British railway contractor Thomas Brassey's wife, that her husband "was a most unworldly man," was, then, suggested a Canadian commentator, worthy of special attention: "This may," he noted, "seem a strange thing to say of a great contractor and a millionaire. Yet, in the highest sense, it was true. Mr. Brassey was not a monk; his life was passed in the world, and in the world's most engrossing, and, as it proves in too many cases, most contaminating business. Yet, if the picture of him presented to us be true, he kept himself 'unspotted from the world.' "[47]

By the early years of the new century, those who worked in the environment created by cities, industry, and commerce had been equipped with a definition of success in which material achievement played a relatively unimportant part. Although Toronto's Casa Loma was hardly the project of a man "unspotted from the world," its builder Sir Henry Pellatt won favourable mention in the pages of the *Canadian Magazine* because of his charitable activities. It was they, the journal implied, which had put the capstone on a successful career.[48] That journal could also proclaim railway magnate Sir William Whyte a truly successful man not simply because of his talents as a businessman, but also thanks to his adherence to Christian principle: "It was what Mr. Whyte possessed in addition to business qualities," journalist R.G. MacBeth assured his readers, "that made him too great a human to be swallowed up by commercial concerns."[49] Businessmen themselves fostered this understanding of what conferred worth and reputation. In their view, argues

Michael Bliss, "real success was not necessarily the achievement of wealth ... In its ultimate implications the [businessman's] success ethic had little or nothing to do with making money, everything to do with the cultivation of moral character."[50]

The realities of life in urban, industrial Canada had, in sum, made necessary a restatement of what composed a successful life. The promise of an abundant future might still inspire activity in less developed parts of the country, but in the cities the holding out of such a hope could only give rise to disillusionment and cynicism. The result would be, at the least, a recalcitrant and unco-operative work force, and, at the most, one likely to be driven into the arms of agitators animated by quite a different set of assumptions about the nature of man in society. If the myth of the self-made man was to retain its credibility, a new understanding of the kind of self he made had to be developed. Wealth, in consequence, ceased to be the yardstick of success and became its enemy. By thus falling back upon a restatement of the principles of the Protestant ethic, these commentators neatly squared a difficult circle. They were able to give up the untenable idea that wealth and position attended hard work without having to concede that individuals had no control over the shaping of their lives. With the definition of success deprived of its materialist content, the way was open – in principle – for workers to be adjusted to the fact that mobility did not exist. At the same time, they as individuals were left the master of their fate. If something which had to be defined as failure did occur, there could be no reason to attach blame to anything other than their own shortcomings. The ideologists of individualism were thus able to redefine their creed in a way that encouraged forma-tion of a stable workforce, contributed to the adjusting of that force to the fact that social mobility was not a prominent feature of life in industrial Canada, and by retaining the credibility of the indi-vidualist idea, helped to deny the legitimacy of opposing views of society and the individual.

By the end of the century theorists of individualism found them-selves confronting another fact about life in society which seemed to raise questions about the accuracy with which their ideas repre-sented it. Practice consistent with the principles of individualism was, it seemed clear, steadily receding from view. Collective action was assuming more and more importance in the shaping of the so-cial and economic order. Labour, business, and government alike were yielding to the thrust towards bureaucracy and organization.

The principles of *laissez-faire* might, as one observer put it in 1907, still constitute "a good sermon, but it is to be feared that most of the congregation are away worshipping in other tabernacles."[51]

These circumstances plainly required some response from those who wished to maintain the claim that the individualist view of the world continued to describe its dynamic. Removing the lack of congruence between their principles and the practice that now seemed so central a part of life in society was not, however, an easy task. To concede in principle that collectively organized behaviour was an integral part of life in society would be to modify in significant ways the individualist idea of reality as it had been expressed through much of the nineteenth century. To deny, on the other hand, that the new collectivism had implications for the individualist world view would be tantamount to rejecting the evidence of one's senses.

Those who were prepared to accommodate the new collectivism sought to reconcile this step with their continuing attachment to the individualist idea by suggesting that certain forms of collective behaviour were quite compatible with, and in some cases had become an indispensable condition of, individual fulfilment. To be sure, the doctrinaire assertions of the socialists were unacceptable. As Nova Scotia's attorney-general J.W. Longley put it in 1896, implementing their proposals would "destroy the great stimulating influence of competitive exertion" and so deprive society's engine of its fuel. But, as he was equally concerned to make clear, once socialist orthodoxy was set aside one was left with a set of propositions whose acceptance depended only on a pragmatic recognition of the fact that a more subtle understanding of the individual's relation to society and the forces at work in it had become necessary. And once one grasped that, one would also see that "socialist" principles – especially in relation to such matters as education, public health, and communications – had informed public policy for decades. All of this made it clear, Longley continued, that the individualism of liberals like himself was not threatened by the new approaches. Socialism, properly understood, was in fact the ally of self-reliance. The two were alike "consistent with true liberalism." Viewed in this light, the new collectivism was quite compatible with the terms of individualist theory.[52]

The distinction Longley made between the dogmatic collectivism of the socialists and the more flexible kind validated by common sense allowed other partisans of the individualist idea to concede the existence of a collective dimension in society without requiring them to jettison their attachment to the individualist creed. Queen's University political economist Adam Shortt was thus able to pair a statement recognizing the importance of society's role in the shaping of individuals – it was "our character ... as a community" which determined their nature – with one reminding his readers that "... the dominance of men of exceptional capacity, force, and power [is essential] ... the world never has got on, and never will get on without the one man power, that is, without leadership in every department of life ... It all depends on the one man ..."[53] O.D. Skelton, Shortt's successor as Sir John A. Macdonald Professor of Political and Economic Science at Queen's, similarly dealt with society in collectivist terms without abandoning his essential individualism. State intervention, he argued, might be welcomed in some circumstances as that which would accomplish what experience indicated individuals were not capable of doing on their own: it would introduce a measure of principled behaviour into their relations with one another. The state, functioning as a "referee," would ensure that the interests of the "weak and helpless" did not suffer. They might be unable to look after themselves, but that did not mean that they should fall by the wayside. Yet, Skelton insisted, competition remained the fundamental fact of social life. Its "ethical level" might be raised by state intervention, but society was still to be conceived of as an agglomeration of contending, self-interested individuals whose relations were to be characterized, in the classical metaphor of the Social Darwinists, as "the struggle."[54]

Other commentators took up the theme that a selective and limited collectivism might be the means to the realization of traditional individualist ends. Mackenzie King, as deputy minister in the newly-formed Department of Labour, was careful to argue that mechanisms which restrained individual action in one place might foster it in another. Unionism was therefore to be defended on the ground that in restricting the rights of irresponsible employers it made it possible for the workingman, as King put it, "to preserve his independence of character." Collective action of this sort had, in fact, allowed the worker to resist what, in the view of the individualists, was the most demeaning of fates: "he is now able," King observed, "to drive a bargain and does not have to accept a dole."[55]

The discussion of old-age pensions which was sustained in these years provided a particularly illuminating example of the manner in which a careful distinction between means and ends allowed individualist thinkers to reconcile collectivist procedures with individualist principles. Generally upholding the view that the state should play a role in helping the worker prepare for old age, they nonetheless insisted that it act only in ways that involved encouraging him to put aside money on his own behalf. Otherwise the effect would be to make him a charitable case, with the predictable result that his self-respect and moral fibre would be eroded. European plans were, therefore, to be favourably contrasted with those of other parts of the British Empire precisely because they sought to maintain the individual's responsibility for his own well-being. France's programme, argued one commentator, offered a good example of what should be done: it "encourages thrift and a spirit of independence among the people, which would be entirely lacking in any government [financed] scheme ..."[56] Bismarck's pioneering measure, said another, was a triumph just because it had so perfectly reconciled individualism and the general good: "no man saw more clearly how the basic principle of self-help could be made to contribute to national and social stability and at the same time further the profoundest policy of the statesman."[57] The Canadian government's 1909 annuity scheme, insisted a third observer, was to be praised on the ground that it, too, used the mechanisms of the state to assist individuals to help themselves. By demanding contributions from those who would benefit by it ... "it supplies a strong motive to thrift, and by the call which it makes on the personal responsibility of the annuitant, it tends to develop the valuable qualities of independence and self-reliance ..."[58]

If these manoeuvres tended to deflect the full force of the collectivist onslaught by suggesting that some kinds of collectivist procedures were reducible to a description of them framed in terms compatible with individualist theory, those attempted by other commentators were more audacious. Their stratagem was to close the gap between the new realities and their idea of what worked best in society by denying that gap's existence. The new practice, they insisted, was perverse and wrongheaded. The social universe remained comprehensible exclusively in terms of individualist theory. Those who claimed otherwise were dogmatic and irresponsible theorists whose ideas, if embodied in policy, would ruin society. "The best of all governments," insisted Goldwin Smith in 1893, "is that which has least occasion to govern."One could, in fact, scarcely imagine a more doubtful proposition than "that society can be metamorphosed by the action of the State ..." Instead of speaking of unionism and strikes, labour spokesmen should be reminding the artisan of "the improvement which [he] might make in his own condition by thrift, temperance, and husbandry of his means." Even schooling was properly a private matter. It was the individual's responsibility to clothe and feed his children: so he ought to educate them.[59]

Clergyman John Hay, writing in the *Queen's Quarterly* three years later, was quite as firm in his belief that an unyielding statement of first principles was the most effective way of dealing with claims that the new realities made necessary a revolution in one's view of the way society worked. What was worthwhile in the socialist case, Hay insisted, amounted to a statement of the obvious: there were abuses in society and the state was the agency best equipped to deal with some of them. Conceding that truth, however, hardly represented an abandonment of principle. The traditional individualist view of society remained as vital as ever. And not only socialism, Hay continued, was built on "false premises." Every doctrine which failed to take account of the truths upon which individualism rested was equally doomed to fail. "Any scheme," as Hay put it, "that tries to place all men on an equality, or that would abolish private property, contends against the law of man's being. In order that man may make progress he must indeed be free, and have access to those natural opportunities without which he can do nothing."[60]

Smith and Hay were reacting to phenomena of whose existence they were merely observers; other turn-of-the-century partisans of self-reliance bore, however, a more complicated relation to the new realities. As actors deeply involved in the world of practical affairs, they made extensive use of the collectivist procedures now available in it. Their claim that the individualist idea continued to describe reality thus involved them in denying the implications of their own behaviour. It appears, on this account, an even bolder step than that taken by those who occupied the manse or the study.

Some of those who followed this route seemed, indeed, scarcely to hesitate in offering a description of the way society worked which even a casual observer might have been expected to find seriously at odds with what the nature of their own actions signified. British Columbia's Sir Richard McBride, committed in practice to business collectivism, believing in the closest relationship between government and business, and persuaded that the power of the state must be used to create favourable conditions for economic growth, thus maintained a public and quite unequivocal enthusiasm for the individualist creed. "All of his speeches," writes Martin Robin, "revealed a fervent belief in the mythology of the free enterprise system and the philosophy of Social Darwinism ... He denied the significance of class differences, asserted a common interest in economic development spearheaded by private enterprise, and believed that British Columbia was an open system where the coal miner of today became the coal baron of tomorrow."[61]

Language inconsistent with the nature of the reality it claimed to be describing was, in fact, used frequently on the frontier. Developments there which were primarily the result of carefully co-ordinated corporate activity were regularly offered as proof of what strong men acting individually could accomplish. McBride himself, having brought the power of government to bear on the development of British Columbia, continued to profess a belief in "the ideology of frontier conquest through private enterprise."[62] The opening of the farming frontier in the Ontario north, part of a concerted plan to promote economic development in that region, was similarly depicted in terms which suggested that it was to be understood in much the same way as the opening of the old agricultural frontier had been: as a project undertaken by self-reliant individuals bent on self-improvement. "There is no means," trumpeted on Ontario government publication in 1903, "whereby the man without other capital than the power and will to labour can so readily attain a competence and a substantial position in the community as by taking up a bush farm."[63] The myth of the self-sufficient pioneer, clearly at variance with the reality of the situation, survived for decades. "Pioneer agricultural self-sufficiency ..." wrote V.C. Fowke as late as 1962, "has been and remains a persistently fostered Canadian myth."[64]

Plainly in evidence in the developing parts of the country, this espousal of a faith only marginally consistent with the actions it was meant to describe can also be discerned in other sections of it. To be sure, businessmen and manufacturers chastened by their proximity to the bewildering array of forces associated with Polanyi's "great transformation" might, as Michael Bliss suggests, not only qualify their individualist practice; they also muted their expression of the individualist creed. They were, however, far from abandoning that creed altogether. Remaining, as Bliss puts it, "deeply individualistic," their ideas about others "moulded in the categories of individualism," they inevitably joined their progress towards "self-interested collectivism" to a profession of faith hardly less inconsistent with it than McBride's ideology was at variance with the action he undertook.[65]

Large and substantial in retrospect, this gap between what the quasi-collectivist partisans of individualism said and what they did was not, however, particularly evident to their contemporaries. What helped hide it from view was, paradoxically, the very element which now points so clearly to its existence: the quasi-collectivists' continuing attachment to the individualist idea. Whether they were consciously engaged in a game of bluff and deception, whether they simply failed to perceive the contradiction between what they were saying and what they were doing, or whether they thought their recourse to collectivism a temporary and regrettable expedient which in no way invalidated basic principle, their insistence on the individualist faith played its part in sustaining a structure of belief and idea whose character did much to ensure that thought framed within its confines would remain oriented along individualist lines. The nature of what Quentin Skinner calls the "formally crucial" process involved here is, of course, familiar enough, even if it remains "empirically very elusive ... The models and preconceptions in terms of which we unavoidably organize and adjust our perceptions and thoughts ...themselves tend to act as determinants of what we think or perceive."[66] Merely by dealing in the currency of the individualist idea, the quasi-collectivists were helping to ensure that the individualist system of "models and preconceptions" did not languish and decay and so lose its capacity to shape the thought of those exposed to it.

This was an important development. Having come, like Dorothy in the Land of Oz, to view what lay before them through spectacles tinted with a particular hue, commentators framing their thoughts in terms of individualist categories would continue to consider the partial and imperfect picture so gotten as an accurate representation of reality only so long as they had no reason to doubt the integrity of the medium through whose agency it was made available. Rhetoric, the effect of which was to insist on that medium's undiminished relevance and utility, would thus play a critical role in ensuring that these observers continued to view the behaviour of the quasi-collectivists under its auspices – an operation that would, *pace* Skinner, throw individualist elements in that behaviour into high relief while simultaneously casting collectivist ones into the shadows. They would, in consequence, see, not the trusts or government-supported ventures that were actually in front of them, but the enterprising and self-reliant individuals the architects of this important element in their society's ideological system told them were there.

This triumph of appearance over reality had profound effects. It left the quasi-collectivists at liberty to insist that the actions of others – labour organizers, reformers, anyone who sought collectivist action of a sort they judge incompatible with their own interests – be assessed in terms of an individualist standard from which, when circumstances demanded, they were in practice prepared to exempt themselves. The onus would be on those others to demonstrate why they should be permitted to use methods not sanctioned by the conventional individualist wisdom. By an exasperating irony they would be denied easy access to the collectivist procedures which were the logical consequence of their theory, while their opponents – still professing the individualist creed – were able to employ those procedures as they saw fit. The anxiety of socialists and reformers to escape this conundrum explains why they were so concerned to show that business and government had, as Canadian Socialist League member George Wrigley pointed out in 1900, collaborated on such undertakings as the Intercolonial Railway.[67] Only if the individualist idea could be shown to offer a fundamentally inadequate description of what even its staunchest defenders were doing could the way be opened for its rejection. The very fact that the point had to be argued demonstrates, however, how successfully the nature of the activities undertaken by practitioners of self-interested collectivism had been obscured. So potent did this expression of faith in the free and responsible individual remain that it affected the terms in which some of the enemies of the business-government alliance cast their own argument. Even after the pure milk of the individualist idea had gone noticeably sour, veteran socialist J.S. Woodsworth himself could be drawn onto the ground of his opponents. A moderate socialism was not, he would suggest to the founding convention of the CCF in 1933, merely a matter of tactics; the Canadian left must in fact qualify its attachment to collectivism in order to reflect the realities of the environment in which it found itself – an environment which, he continued, was in important ways susceptible of explanation only in terms of the individualist idea. He himself, he insisted, embodied the kind of individualism of whose existence the new creed must take account, "I am," he informed the assembled delegates, "a Canadian of several generations, and have inherited the individualism common to all born on the American continent.[68]

If, then, as H.V. Nelles has suggested, one part of Canada's ideological system – its "much discussed" tory component – served in these years to rationalize and legitimate power concentrations, stratification, and class by stressing the harmony and interdependence of an ordered arrangement of groups and the idea of a community interest served by an activist state,[69] another element of it – the individualist idea – continued to mask the existence of these phenomena by insisting on the reality of competition, self-reliance, mobility, and the atomic individual. It thus played an important role in the process by which those who held power were able to control and manipulate the new forces in social and economic life. Particularly effective in containing the pretensions of the left, it managed either to limit the application of doctrines from that end of the political spectrum or to discredit them altogether. What, in short, might have signalled the beginning of the end for the individualist idea gave it a new lease on life. The range of ideological weaponry available to those whose activities shaped and defined their society remained very nearly as broad and ample as it had ever been.

All of this suggests that it is easy to paint an imperfect picture of the way English Canadians viewed their society if the individualist idea is ignored. Emphasis on the conservative principle, for all its utility in explaining what is uniquely Canadian, cannot tell us everything that we need to know about the character and function of the ideas English Canadians used to guide and shape their behaviour. Whatever may have been the objective circumstances of their collective existence – and evidence suggesting that society was organized along class lines with a minimum of social mobility and a high degree of government intervention, much of it on behalf of special interests, continues to mount[70] – there seems good reason to believe that many of those English Canadians who were able to articulate and promote a view of society wished, like other people in other nineteenth-century societies, their world to be viewed within the framework of a belief in the free and responsible individual. With its insistence on the capacity of individuals to master fate, such a world view could legitimate both success and failure without reference to forces beyond their direct control. It would thus operate to deny the legitimacy of social theories which drew attention to such forces and so undermine the credibility and influence of those who put them forth. In this way the position of those who wished to organize their affairs unconstrained by anything other than their own sense of what was just, possible, and in their interest would be materially strengthened, for what they did would appear to be action undertaken in a manner consistent with the way the social universe actually worked.[71]

This creed in fact operated in a number of ways to induce satisfaction with existing forms of social organization and economic activity. By celebrating the work of the farmers, it strove to make those beings happy with their lot and so encouraged activity essential to the development of an important sector of the national economy; by stressing the value of education, it played its part in producing a skilled and semi-skilled workforce; by talking of success and fulfilment in terms of intangibles it reconciled workers to the fact of class; and by obscuring the nature of the new collectivism, it masked the fact that society's thrust toward bureaucracy and rationalization was making it steadily more difficult to sustain the proposition that individuals controlled their destiny.

The individualist idea in Canada did not, to be sure, evolve neatly through a series of stages. Its different manifestations largely co-existed in time as functions of the varying social and economic circumstances which, in the view of the several commentators considered here, predominated in different parts of the country through the same several decades. English Canadians were not, then, confronted in their daily lives with a set of rigid and schematic variations on a theme; what, with cause, frequently appeared to them to be a confusion of proposals about the individual's prospects and capabilities served, in fact, to make the task of individualist theorists, striving to close the gap between theory and practice, more difficult. Equally, however, these patterns of belief exist as something more than analytical abstractions, having their being only, as it were, in the mind's eye of the historian. Linked in an intelligible way to social and economic circumstance, they were working ideas. Their role in investing a certain type of behaviour with normative significance and so encouraging activity consistent with it made their presence in the lives of nineteenth-century English Canadians no less real and immediate than that of those more tangible instruments – schools, factories, asylums, prisons – similarly operating to shape thought and action. And if their undeniably variegated character was sometimes a cause of difficulties, it also pointed to a uniquely important source of strength. In signalling the presence within them of a suppleness and elasticity quite lacking in the structures set in place by the social engineers, it testified to the existence of a remarkable capacity to adapt to changing circumstance. The presence of this attribute, in the language of T.S. Kuhn,[72] gave the individualist paradigm an extraordinary facility in the assimilating or ignoring of anomalies. As late as the Great War its strength and appeal had been, in consequence, only marginally diminished. The vast collective efforts necessary to the prosecution of that war would of course deal its claims on behalf of the individual's power a serious blow. A decade later, the bankruptcy of individualist nostrums would be delineated even more clearly by the advent of the Great Depression. Even in the face of these challenges the individualist idea was, however, able to maintain in the minds of many the belief that it described something fundamental in the life of society. For all that Keynesianism, social democracy, corporate planning, business conformity, and other

manifestations of the new collectivism succeeded in complicating
its existence, they did not, in the end, extinguish its appeal.

The search for a fully articulated picture of the English-Canadian value system has not, in sum, ended. In emphasizing its
collectivist attributes scholars may, indeed, have been looking in
the wrong direction. Perhaps, as students of Canadian society have
recently been suggesting, a balanced representation of this phenomenon will be available only when an image of it framed in terms
of what distinguished it in North America is set beside one derived
from an examination of the attributes it shares with other systems,
North American as well as European. Certainly such a construct will
be more comprehensive in scope than its predecessors; it will also
probably be more accurate in detail. By shedding additional light
on the character and function of ideas in Canadian life, it may even
make clear how those ideas have helped give texture and shape to
concrete historical circumstances at the same time that they themselves were being moulded by those circumstances. And if it does
this, it will have succeeded in focusing attention on the manner in
which society and thought in Canada were joined to each other in
accordance with the same general principles that governed their
relationship elsewhere – an accomplishment which will in its turn
move the history of ideas in Canada onto a new plane of discussion
and analysis.

NOTES

1 These themes have been explored by a number of historians and
social scientists. See, in particular, Donald Creighton, *Canada's First
Century* (Toronto, 1970); W.L. Morton, *The Canadian Identity* (Toronto, 1961); S.F. Wise,"Conservatism and Political Development: The
Canadian Case," *South Atlantic Quarterly*, 69(2), 1970, 226–43; Gad
Horowitz, *Canadian Labour in Politics* (Toronto, 1968), 3–57; S.D.
Clark, "The Canadian Community and the American Continental
System," in his *The Developing Canadian Community* (Toronto, 1962),
185–98; the same author's "Canada and the American Value System," in *La dualité canadienne à l'heure des États-Unis* (Québec, 1965),
93–192; J.M. Bliss, *A Living Profit: Studies in the Social History of Canadian Business 1883–1911* (Toronto, 1974); and Seymour Martin
Lipset, *The First New Nation: The United States in Historical and Comparative Perspective* (Garden City, NY, 1967), 284–312. The Alger
quote is on pages 287–8.

2 John Mercier McMullen, *The History of Canada from its First Discovery to the Present Time* (Brockville, 1855), 158, 132, 159.

3 H.J.Morgan, *Sketches of Celebrated Canadians and Persons Connected with Canada, from the Earliest Period in the History of the Province down to the Present Time* (Quebec, 1862), 102.

4 Elsie Trevor, "Clarice: An Old Story of the New World." *Canadian Monthly and National Review*, 6(1), 1874, 26.

5 W.H. Withrow, *A History of Canada for the Use of Schools and General Readers* (Toronto, 1876), 273.

6 W.H. Withrow, *A Popular History of the Dominion of Canada from the Discovery of America to the Present Time* (Boston, 1978), 355.

7 Lynn Hethrington, "Tecumseh," *University Magazine*, 8(1), 1909, 137.

8 See, in particular, Duncan Campbell Scott, *John Graves Simcoe* (Toronto, 1909), 232–3; John Lewis, *George Brown* (Toronto, 1909), 265; Robert Hamilton Coates and R.E. Gosnell, *Sir James Douglas* (Toronto, 1910), 353; and N.E. Dionne, *Champlain* (Toronto, 1909), xiii. Local and regional histories also celebrated the individuals whose talent had allowed them to shape a civilization out of the void. See R.E. Gosnell, *A History of British Columbia* (Vancouver, [1906]); G.M. Adam, *Toronto, Old and New ... with some sketches of the men who have made or are making the provincial capital* (Toronto, 1891); Alexander Fraser, *A History of Ontario, its Resources, and Development*, 2 vols. (Toronto and Montreal, 1907); Archibald Oswald MacRae, *History of the Province of Alberta*, 2 vols. ([Calgary?], 1912); and *The Story of Manitoba: Biographical – Illustrated*, 3 vols. (Winnipeg, Vancouver, Montreal, 1913). Three-quarters of the MacRae study consisted of biographical sketches, while two-thirds of the Fraser and Gosnell books were composed in the same way. As well as insisting on the role of individual effort in creating new societies, these volumes also made much of the scope those societies offered men who wished to advance themselves. The remarks made in the Manitoba history on the career of railwayman J.R. Turnbull were typical: "The history of J.R. Turnbull is that of a man who worked his way upward by reason of the persistency of his purpose, the force of his character and the utilization of his opportunities. While he entered the employ of the Canadian Pacific Railroad in a minor capacity, the recognition of his merit won him advancement," vol. 2, 6. Similarly compiled on the assumption that Canada had been built by enterprising individuals whose virtue and accomplishments must be exhibited to the public, the biographical dictionaries which appeared in this period also fed and sustained the individualist vision of Canadian society. See, for

example, *The Canadian Biographical Dictionary and Portrait Gallery of Eminent and Self-Made Men, Ontario Volume* (Toronto, Chicago, 1880); *Quebec and the Maritime Provinces Volume* (Chicago, 1881); George Maclean Rose, ed., *A Cyclopedia of Canadian Biography; being chiefly men of the time,* 2 vols. (Toronto, 1886–88); G.M. Adam, ed., *Prominent Men of Canada: a collection of persons distinguished in professional and political life, and in the commerce and industry of Canada* (Toronto, 1892); John Alexander Cooper, ed., *Men of Canada: a portrait gallery of men whose energy, ability, enterprise, and public spirit are responsible for the advancement of Canada, the premier colony of Great Britain* (Montreal and Toronto, 1901–2); and *An Encyclopedia of Canadian Biography; containing brief sketches and steel engravings of Canada's prominent men,* 2 vols. (Montreal, 1904–5).

9 C.R. Tuttle, *Tuttle's Popular History of the Dominion of Canada ...together with ... biographical sketches of the most distinguished men of the nation,* 2 vols. (Montreal, 1877).

10 McMullen, *History of Canada,* Preface.

11 Isabella Valancy Crawford, "A Hungry Day," in her *Old Spookses Pass, Malcolm's Katie, and Other Poems* (Toronto, 1884). That the farmer was the creator of the nation's wealth, the builder of his own world, and a natural aristocrat unrivalled by those whose position was owing solely to lineage and descent were frequently articulated themes. For some variations on them, see R. Cooper, "The Farming Interest," *Anglo American Magazine,* 1(5), 1852, 401; W.S. Darling, "The Emigrants: A Tale of the Backwoods," *British American Magazine,* 1(1), May 1863, 53; D.W., "Canada," *Canadian Monthly and National Review,* 4(6), 1873, 472; A. Kemp and G.M. Grant, "From Toronto to Lake Huron," in G.M. Grant, ed., *Picturesque Canada: The Country as it was and is* (Toronto, 1882), vol. 2, 584; Abraham Gesner, *New Brunswick; with Notes for Emigrants* (London, 1847), 244–7. Cited in Michael S. Cross, ed., *The Workingman in the Nineteenth Century* (Toronto, 1974), 24; *Canada Farmer,* 1, 1847, 1, cited in Laurence Sidney Fallis, Jr, "The Idea of Progress in the Province of Canada: 1841–1867" PH.D diss., University of Michigan, 1966, 145; Pamela S. Vining, "Canada," in Edward Hartley Dewart, ed., *Selections from Canadian Poets* (Montreal, 1864), 105; W.W.S., "A Settler's Own Tale," *British American Magazine,* 1(2), June 1863, 193; Charles Sangster, "Song for Canada," in Dewart, *Selections,* 107; J.G. Bourinot, "Titles in Canada," *Canadian Monthly and National Review,* 12(4), 1877, 350; Canniff Haight, "Ontario Fifty Years Ago and Now," *Rose-Belford's Canadian Monthly,* 6(5), 1884, 449; and "Buffalo Bill Abroad," *The Week,* 4(52), 24, 1887, 841.

12 Pelham Edgar, "A Confession of Faith and a Protest," *University Magazine,* 8(2), April 1909, 305.

13 C. Lintern Sibley, "Van Horne and His Cuban Railway," *Canadian Magazine,* 51(5),1913, 444–51.

14 Kingston *Chronicle,* 5 March 1842. Cited in R.D. Gidney, "Upper Canadian Public Opinion and Common School Improvements in the 1830s," *Histoire sociale/Social History,* 5(9), 1972, 56.

15 Egerton Ryerson, "The Importance of Education to a Manufacturing and a Free People, *Journal of Education of Upper Canada,* October 1848, 300. Cited in Susan E. Houston, "Politics, Schools and Social Change in Upper Canada," *Canadian Historical Review,* 53(3), 1972, 271.

16 "Report of the Colborne District Council on the Gore Memorial," in J. George Hodgins, eds., *Documentary History of Education in Upper Canada,* 8 vols. (Toronto, 1894–1910), vol. 7, 116. Cited in Houston, "Politics," 271.

17 Anonymous, "How I Made a Fortune in Wall Street," *Saturday Reader,* 2(27), 10, 1866, 11.

18 "The Late George Peabody," *New Dominion Monthly,* January 1870, 61.

19 See, for example, Jeannie Bell, "The Highway to Honor; or the Secret of Lindsay Atwood's Success," *New Dominion Monthly,* July 1871, 37–40; August 1871, 101–5; September 1871, 171–5. This was the story of an orphan who became an apprentice in a lawyer's office and by "diligence in study" advanced himself. See also Virna Sheard, "Fortune's Hill," a six-part serial which appeared in the *Canadian Magazine* from November 1902 to April 1903. It recounted the efforts of two medical students – one from a well-to-do family, the other the son of a blacksmith. Both graduate, but it was the blacksmith's son who by study and hard work became a double gold medallist.

20 "How to Succeed," *New Dominion Monthly,* June 1875, 356–7.

21 John M. Sangster, "Ontario's Schools, *Educational Journal,* 21, 15 March 1892, 679.

22 "Self-Education," *New Dominion Monthly,* February 1868, 299.

23 C. Clarkson, "A Liberal Education," ibid., October 1875, 262.

24 "People and Affairs," *Canadian Magazine,* 17(5), 1901, 483.

25 Twelve copies of which were given to the Toronto Mechanics' Institute by Belford Brothers Publishers in 1876. [Ontario Archives] Mechanics Institutes of Toronto, Papers, Case A, no. 3, Annual Reports 1838–82; Annual Report 1876, Appendix C.

26 *The Week,* 3(31), 1886, 501.

27 J.J.Y., "The Necessity of Improvement," *Educational Journal*, 5(15), 1891, 582.

28 Miss M. Robertson, "Growth," ibid., 16(1), 1892, 598.

29 John Macnaughton, "University Lecture," *McGill University Magazine*, 3(2), 1904, 33.

30 A.W. Flux, "Commercial Education," ibid., 1(2), 1902, 201–2.

31 Norman DeWitt, "The Educated Layman," *University Magazine*, 9(1), 1910, 28.

32 Alexander Steele, "Relation of Education to Our National Development," Ontario Teachers' Association, *Proceedings*, 1894, 49. Cited in J. Donald Wilson, Robert M. Stamp, and Louis-Philippe Audet, eds., *Canadian Education: A History* (Toronto, 1970), 293–4.

33 "Editorial Comment," *Canadian Magazine*, 12(4), 1899, 368.

34 J.T.M. Anderson, *The Education of the New Canadian: A Treatise on Canada's Greatest Educational Problem* (London and Toronto, 1918), 177.

35 *Daily Globe* (Toronto), 23 March 1872. Cited in Cross, ed., *Workingman*, 262.

36 Wm. C. Howells, "Superficial Learning," *Rose-Belford's Canadian Monthly*, 1(4), 1878, 430, 432.

37 L.R. O'Brien, "Art Education – A Plea for the Artizan," ibid., 2(5), 1879, 584–91. All quotes are from 585.

38 Greg Kealey, ed., *Canada Investigates Industrialism* (Toronto, 1973), 58.

39 J.A. Cooper, "People and Affairs," *Canadian Magazine*, 16(1), 1900, 88.

40 Ibid.

41 C. Henry Stephens, "The Nine Hours Movement," *Canadian Monthly and National Review*, 1(5), 1872, 430.

42 William Wye Smith, "The Woods," *British American Magazine*, 2(6), 1864, 622.

43 J.R. Ramsay, "Chronicles of a Canadian Family," *New Dominion Monthly*, June 1868, 147.

44 W.D. Le Sueur, "Old and New in Canada," *Canadian Monthly and National Review*, 7(1), 1875, 2.

45 Haight, "Ontario," 454.

46 Rev. W.R.G. Mellen, "Wealth and its Uses," *Rose-Belford's Canadian Monthly*, 2(3), 1879, 341–50.

47 "A True Captain of Industry," *Canadian Monthly and National Review*, 2(4), 1872, 223.

48 Newton McTavish, "Henry Mill Pellatt: A Study in Achievement," *Canadian Magazine*, 19(2), June 1912, 109–19.

49 R.G. MacBeth, "Sir William Whyte: A Builder of the West," ibid., 43(3), 1914, 264.

50 Bliss, *Living Profit*, 32.

51 O.D. S[kelton?], review of Goldwin Smith, *Labour and Capital* (1907), *Queen's Quarterly*, 14(4), 1907, 332.

52 J.W. Longley, "Socialism: Its Truths and Errors," *Canadian Magazine*, 6(4), 1896, 304, 301.

53 Adam Shortt, "In Defence of Millionaires," *Canadian Magazine*, 13(6), 1899, 498.

54 O.D. Skelton, *Socialism: A Critical Analysis* (Boston and New York, 1911), 47–8.

55 Canada, Department of Labour, *Report of the Royal Commission on Industrial Disputes in the Province of British Columbia* (1903), 63. Cited in R. MacGregor Dawson, *William Lyon Mackenzie King*, vol. 1 (Toronto, 1958), 141.

56 Andrew T. Drummond, "A Social Experiment," *Queen's Quarterly*, 8(1), 1900, 49.

57 M.D. Grant, "Old Age Pensions," *University Magazine*, 8(1), 1909, 152.

58 Francis Asbury Carman, "Canada's Substitute for Old Age Pensions," *University Magazine*, 60(3), 1910, 437.

59 Goldwin Smith, "Social and Industrial Revolution," in his *Essays on Questions of the Day, Political and Social* (New York and London, 1893), 38, 36, 25, 13. See also Smith's *Labour and Capital: A Letter to a Labour Friend* (New York, 1907).

60 John Hay, "A General View of Socialistic Schemes," *Queen's Quarterly*, 3(4), 1896, 292, 291.

61 Martin Robin, *The Rush for Spoils: The Company Province 1871–1933* (Toronto, 1972), 130.

62 Ibid.

63 Ontario, Crown Lands, *Land Settlement in New Ontario: A Short Account of the Advantages offered Land Seekers in Ontario* (Toronto, 1903), 21. Cited in Morris Zaslow, *The Opening of the Canadian North 1870–1914* (Toronto, 1971), 179.

64 V.C. Fowke, "The Myth of the Self-Sufficient Canadian Pioneer," Royal Society of Canada, *Transactions*, 54, ser. 3, 1962, 24.

65 Bliss, *Living Profit*, Conclusion, 134–44, especially 138, 142.

66 Quentin Skinner, "Meaning and Understanding in the History of Ideas," *History and Theory*, 8(1), 1969, 6. There is an extensive literature on the manner in which the concepts, models, values, and attitudes in terms of which intellectual operations are carried out shape the view of reality that these operations yield. For the view of a social psychologist, who describes the process as "one of being *prepared* to perceive or react in a certain way," see Floyd H. Allport, *Theories of Perception and the Concept of Structure* (New York, 1955), 239. T.S. Kuhn's

notion of the paradigm, a framework of theory, assumption, and idea which, he argues, conditions the way scientists in any field in any epoch view and organize their data has relevance for the understanding of intellectual activity in other areas – as the work of E.H. Gombrich in the history of art makes clear. See T.S. Kuhn, *The Structure of Scientific Revolutions* (Chicago, 1962) and E.H. Gombrich, *Art and Illusion* (London, 1960). Many commentators, inspired by the Marxist concept of ideology, have explained the emergence of these mediating ideas in terms of class structure and class interest. For the development of this notion, see George Lichteim, "The Concept of Ideology," *History and Theory*, 4(2), 1965, 164–95. For an application of Antonio Gramsci's Marxist-based concept of hegemony, involving the argument that the dominant ideas in any society are not merely derivative and superstructural but possess a measure of autonomy which allows them to shape values and behaviour, see Eugene D. Genovese's *Roll, Jordan, Roll: The World the Slaves Made* (New York, 1974). Some observers, unwilling to advance a categorically class-based analysis of this phenomenon, have nonetheless emphasized the manner in which ideas, values, and attitudes are related to social structure. See Peter L. Berger and Thomas Luckmann, *The Social Construction of Reality: A Treatise in the Sociology of Knowledge* (New York, 1966) and John Plamenatz, *Ideology* (London, 1970). One cannot, finally, omit mention of two classic works, one in the Marxist, the other in the non-Marxist tradition. Georg Lukacs' *History and Class Consciousness: Studies in Marxist Dialectics*, trans. Rodney Livingstone (London, 1968), framed under the influence of Lukacs' recovery of the Hegelian dimension in Marx's thought, emphasizes the dialectical relationship between ideas and circumstance, and, in particular, insists that the former simultaneously arise from, and shape, the latter. Karl Mannheim's argument, in some respects (as Louis Wirth points out) similar to that of the American pragmatists, depends on the claim that ideas condition the outlook of those exposed to them in ways that tend either to stabilize or undermine existing social arrangements. See his *Ideology and Utopia: An Introduction to the Sociology of Knowledge*, trans. Louis Wirth and Edward Shils (New York, 1936).

67 G.W. Wrigley, "Socialism in Canada," *Toronto Labour Day Sovereign*, 1900, 33. Cited in Martin Robin, *Radical Politics and Canadian Labour 1880–1930* (Kingston, 1968), 34.

68 Report of the First National Convention (1933) CCF. Cited in Walter D. Young, *The Anatomy of a Party: The National CCF* (Toronto, 1969), 45.

69 H.V. Nelles, *The Politics of Development: Forests, Mines, and Hydro-Electric Power in Ontario, 1849–1941* (Toronto, 1974), 494.

70 Historians of nineteenth-century English-Canadian society have been revealing it as a place in which social mobility was low, economic, and political decision-making monopolized by a few, and the formation of a workforce dependent for survival on the sale of its labour an ongoing process. Nor is it now very controversial to note that public institutions were used in the furtherance of "class" purposes. "It would be difficult," argues Michael Katz, "to deny that class was a fundamental fact of life in mid-nineteenth century urban Canada." See his *The People of Hamilton, Canada West: Family and Class in a Mid-Nineteenth-Century City* (Cambridge, MA, 1975), 43. See also J.T. Copp, "The Condition of the Working Class in Montreal, 1897–1920," Canadian Historical Association, *Historical Papers*, 1972, 157–80, and his volume entitled *The Anatomy of Poverty: The Condition of the Working Class in Montreal, 1897–1929* (Toronto, 1974). For the contribution Marxist scholars have made to this discussion, see especially H.C. Pentland, "The Development of a Capitalistic Labour Market in Canada," *Canadian Journal of Economics and Political Science*, 25(4), 1959, 450–61 and Gary Teeple, "Land, Labour, and Capital in Pre-Confederation Canada," in G. Teeple, eds., *Capitalism and the National Question in Canada* (Toronto, 1972), 43–66. That private groups, principally groups of businessmen, sought to use the power of government to promote their interests was noticed long ago. "Canadian businessmen," observed Elisabeth Wallace in 1950, "while protesting their devotion to the principles of laissez-faire, have never objected to state intervention in economic matters to benefit industry, and have frequently been clamorous in demanding it." See her "The Origin of the Social Welfare State in Canada, 1867–1900," *Canadian Journal of Economics and Political Science*, 16(3), 1950, 383. More recently, the work of Gabriel Kolko and others in United States history has inspired an interpretation of Canadian government action in economic affairs which suggests that even action ostensibly taken to regulate the operations of businessmen was directed by them to their own ends. See, for example, the work of H.V. Nelles cited above.

71 Some commentators, noting the Bendix-Lipset argument that rates of mobility in industrial societies – including the United States – have been more or less the same, have explained the failure of an explicitly class-related politics to establish itself in the US by pointing to the success with which the *belief* that individual effort would be rewarded with advances in status, income, and property was maintained there. Michael Katz, following Stephan Thernstrom and Peter Knights, observes: "This expectation of mobility, in one line of argument ... has kept the American working class committed to a

capitalist social system ... Has it been, then, the existence of an *ideology* of mobility that has kept American workers capitalist in contrast to their counterparts in much of the rest of the world?" See Seymour M. Lipset and Reinhard Bendix, *Social Mobility in Industrial Society* (Berkeley, 1960); Stephan Thernstrom and Peter Knights, "Men in Motion: Some Data and Speculations about Urban Population Mobility in Nineteenth Century America," in Tamara K. Hareven, ed., *Anonymous Americans: Exploration in Nineteenth Century Social History* (Englewood Cliffs, NJ, 1971), 17–47; and Katz, *People of Hamilton*, 135. While this argument emphasizes how important ideology can be, it does not take account of the fact that modifications in it become necessary in order that it retain its credibility. As this paper has tried to suggest, the manner in which the ideology of mobility and the self-made man was altered was, in the Canadian case, an important factor in its continuing success.

72 T.S. Kuhn, *The Structure of Scientific Revolutions* (Chicago, 1962).

13 Conservatism, Nationalism, and Imperialism: The Thought of George Monro Grant

George Monro Grant, clergyman, educator, patriot, and controversialist, was one of the most active of the small group of intellectuals who, in the last years of the nineteenth century, strove to give direction and content to life in the new Canadian nation.[1] The result, embodied in a steady stream of books, articles, essays, and lectures, was a vision of nationality, and the imperial future action in conformity with which, Grant firmly believed, would set Canadians on the path to greatness and salvation in the present and for generations to come. To examine the contours of that vision is, then, to consider a system of ideas which stood in dynamic relationship to a particular appreciation of what was happening in Canadian society, to a precisely defined assessment of the direction events in the world at large were taking, and to a certain understanding of the principles structuring the operations of the universe itself. Unless that point is grasped at the outset, the full meaning of what Grant tried to accomplish will remain unclear.

No small part of the precision and insistence with which Grant spelled out his views derived from his belief – rooted in his early Christian training, reinforced by his seven-year sojourn among the leading proponents of Scottish idealism,[2] and sharpened by his association with the distinguished Queen's philosopher John Watson[3] – that the nature of reality could be understood only by those who saw that the truth which really mattered lay far beyond the

Canadian Literature, no. 83, Winter 1979, 90–116.

realm of the senses. Its beholders must for that very reason report what they had seen with force and exactitude, for in an age already too much inclined to disregard phenomena for whose existence no direct and tangible proof was available such things were to be spoken of with special care. Making clear how one acquired knowledge was a matter of particularly great importance, for only if that were firmly established could the claims of the century's ever more confident empiricists be viewed in the proper perspective. In spite of all the advances made by science God's truth could not, it was crucial to see, be fully understood by those who persisted in using nothing but its method. Beyond a certain point on the road to understanding – here a distinctly Kantian element entered Grant's thought – "nature's face is veiled," and once those who sought to uncover her secrets using the technique of science had reached that point, they could do no more than speak of an "unknown and unknowable God." An altogether different approach was, in consequence, required if one wished to move into the realm of ultimate truth. Faith was a necessary element in the journey, and faith, as Grant put it, "cometh not of science. Faith is the vision of the unseen, faith assumes revelation."[4]

One could not, however, conclude from this – here was the other, equally important side of the proposition – that intellect had no role at all to play in the process by which one came to know God's truth. It was, indeed, only through a Christian ordering of one's mind and reason that the "nobler elements" of one's nature could be brought into play, an essential step if one were to comprehend the Divine order in anything like its full range and subtlety. The church, the press, the school, and the college therefore had important responsibilities, for more than any other of society's agencies, they had the power to make one free. The results to be yielded by the exercise of that power might come slowly – Grant was under no illusions on that score – but "in the end" what he called "the educational method" was, he assured Canadians, bound to "prevail."[5]

A partisan of rigour in matters of schooling – he remained convinced throughout his life that study of the classics played an important role in training the mind[6] – neither Grant's enthusiasm for traditional methods nor his belief that scholarship and science could carry one only so far down the road to understanding blinded him to the relevance new departures in the world of learning might bear to the search for truth. In thus supporting such innovations in scholarship as textual criticism[7] and in opposing the hand of authority in matters of the intellect, he made it clear that, in his view, a refusal to accept change and development would militate against attainment of the very objectives it was supposed to help achieve. "How," as he put it, "can a Church expect to produce great divines if it muzzles the thinker and scholar?"[8] Rejecting the instruments – linguistic criticism, epigraphy, archaeology – which had done so much to amplify God's truth would, indeed, be tantamount to blasphemy, for were not these things gifts of the Creator Himself?[9] Even Darwin's work earned a positive response from Grant, for he found in it a demonstration of the mystery and strange purposefulness of God's ways. In thus recognizing, as one of his contemporaries observed, "no conflict between the teachings of true religion, in its broadest sense, and the discoveries of modern science,"[10] he gave clear evidence of his belief that all forms of inquiry had a place in the grand search for truth.

If education had a signal role to play in this fundamentally important enterprise, its part in the determination of secular affairs was, thought Grant, even more central. His belief that there was no real division between spirit and matter – "the ideal divorced from the actual," he once put it, "is a mere Chimera"[11] – led him to argue that even as improving the mind brought society's members closer to knowledge of God it would lead to a practical strengthening of the community. He therefore opposed anything that looked like a tax on knowledge,[12] and made it clear that a major requirement for Canada's development was "properly-educated brains."[13] Cultivating the powers of the intellect on a broad scale was, indeed, a *sine qua non* of national survival. "Every country," he pointedly remarked, "must take its share in the common burden and give its contribution to the solution of these problems, old as the race, which appear in new forms of every age, or accept the position of a mere dependent upon others and sink into spiritual decrepitude or petrifaction."[14]

Grant's emphasis on the relevance education bore to the country's future never, of course, involved him in losing sight of its higher purposes – "universities," he wrote on one occasion, "represent the spiritual side of man"[15] – and he made it clear that education, even in the service of national development, was a serious matter which would be properly managed only if it concentrated first on those at the apex of the learning pyramid. "It is a sound maxim," he informed those who heard his inaugural address at Queen's, "that if you would improve the education of a country you must begin at the top."[16] The educational edifice had, in sum, to be shaped by those who realized that education was important, "not because of its money value, but because – if of the right kind – it develops the spirit in man, the spirit which values literature, science, art, in a word, all truth, for its own sake."[17]

Insistence upon the importance of spiritual development in its relation to national growth was, Grant thought, particularly vital, for in the absence of such development there could be no national existence worthy of the name. Only those who had grasped the fact that the foundations of reality were moral and ideal and were able to engage their compatriots at the same high level of discourse and comprehension could be trusted to give the national life the richness and form it required. "A nation to be great" – the point emerged with naturalness and inevitability from all that he wrote on the subject – "must have great thoughts; must be inspired with lofty ideals; must have men and women willing to work and wait and war 'for an idea.'"[19] The structuring of a mature and self-reliant polity thus required – it was an observation which appeared perhaps more frequently in Grant's work than any other – "not more millions either in men or money ... but more of the old spirit in the men we have; not a long list of principles, but a clear insight into those that are fundamental."[20]

As a man who considered his own list of principles short and his insight clear, Grant thought himself well-fitted to discharge the important obligation of equipping his fellow Canadians with the knowledge they needed if they were to guide their actions properly. Capable of being succinctly stated – all things in God's universe were directly linked to Him, and to each other, by the indissoluble bonds of the spirit; there was no real division between matter and mind, for one was but an aspect of the other; one could envision no genuine hierarchy of any sort among God's creatures, for each of them stood in the same relation to the Creator, and each had its own essential part to play in the shaping of His grand design[21] – the body of principle which made up that knowledge informed all of his writing. And in communicating awareness of it to his compatriots – here one gets a particularly clear view of the importance he attached to the preaching of the word – he intended far more than that they should simply assimilate its meaning; their grasp of its significance would be manifest in behaviour as well as thought, for – he believed – it was hardly possible to understand the principles in accordance with which God intended the world to be run without wishing to do one's part to insure that it would in fact be regulated by them. The faith Grant placed in his system's power to inspire right action was, then, one of his most telling characteristics. Nothing offers more eloquent testimony to his belief in the force of ideas, and nothing explains more clearly the importance he attached to specifying the proper principles of behaviour in all departments of human activity.

The insistence on the equality of God's creatures which formed a central part of Grant's system had a particular relevance for his understanding of the principles which ought to govern human relations. One should, he believed, strive to prevent those relations from coming to rest on the assumption that people were irreducibly different. What appeared at first sight to be humanity's complicating and troublesome diversity was, in fact, no more than a veil behind which reposed a collection of beings each of whom had been created by God and all of whom were engaged in the same divinely inspired enterprise.

This was, Grant thought, a lesson his compatriots, open to immigration and exposed by geography and membership in the Empire to influences of a worldwide scope, were particularly fitted to absorb. Canadians, of all peoples, should be able to see "that the life of the world is one, that all men are brothers and that the service of humanity is the most acceptable form of religion to the Common Father."[22] The truth of the proposition that the elements composing reality had within themselves the stuff of a transcendent unity was, indeed, being forced on Canadians by what was happening at their very doorstep. The different strands of the Canadian experience, it was clear to all who troubled to look, were being inexorably knit together by the Canadians' emerging realization that what they had in common was of far more consequence than the elements by which they were divided. One had only to remember that "it takes a long time build a national structure; and the greater the variety in the materials the longer the time needed, though as a compensation the more beautiful will the structure eventually be."[23]

Grant's relegation of diversity to the status of an element which would do no more than impart texture and spice to a national life whose components would otherwise be united in support of a common body of goals and principles gave him a conceptual tool of great utility. Retention of their culture by the French Canadians was not, it enabled him to assert, a threat to the nation's survival. Notwithstanding their attachment to their own ways they had in war and peace alike demonstrated a capacity to serve the higher unity.[24] The generous and accommodating principles encased in the Quebec Act thus remained the best guide to the handling of the French Canadians, for applying them insured, not division and strife, but co-operation in pursuit of the highest goals.[25] The lesson all of this taught was clear: "The supposition that national unity requires uniformity of language and race is an abstract conception scarcely worth refuting. ... The highest form of national life does not depend on identity, but rather on differences that are transcended by common political interests and sentiments."[26]

The country's experience as a whole, Grant was convinced, more than confirmed the truth of this proposition. Far from impoverishing the national life, weakening its thrust towards unity, or interfering with the emergence of a national frame of reference, the existence of regional and provincial differences had enriched the nation. In the very act of confronting their dissimilarities, Canadians were being brought to see how fundamental were the possessions they had in common. And if Grant's own experience showed this process to be a reality – "I ... have," he noted in the midst of the growing provincial rights agitation of the late 1880s, "learned to respect my fellow-countrymen and to sympathize with their Provincial life, and to see that it was not antagonistic but intended to be the handmaid to a true national life"[27] – he believed that Canadians in general were no less touched by it. Indeed, with Confederation and the opening of the West, a kind of moral transformation had taken place among them. They had developed a broader field of vision, become noticeably less provincial, and set themselves firmly on the path to nationhood. In these new and salutary circumstances, it was hardly surprising that "old religious differences shrivelled into insignificance, and old watchwords once thought sacred lost their meaning."[28]

As much of the foregoing implies, Grant's acceptance of diversity, in principle unlimited, was in practice subject to one overriding condition. Those whose attachment to their own ways was being tolerated must be in process of demonstrating that their reverence for their own culture and values was compatible with union with their fellows in support of the higher truth which bound all together. He distinguished sharply between those who held the conviction that movement towards this goal was the direction in which their destiny was carrying them and those who still laboured under the weight of their own narrow concerns. And if those in the second group could hardly be allowed to shape events, it was equally plain that this responsibility must be seized by those in the first. Grant did not, accordingly, hesitate to suggest that, in some circumstances, movement towards the higher unity could best be encouraged by a careful curtailment of the activities of certain groups. In considering the vexed question of oriental immigration, he thus opposed legislation on the California model, not on the ground that it would work an injustice on a group which, like the French Canadians, had proved its capacity to unite with the majority in support of the higher truth, but because such legislation would represent a triumph for the small and mean in the Canadians' own outlook. Those with a properly developed sense of the whole had a duty to see that its interests were fully served, and in the circumstances created by the anti-oriental agitators, that meant reminding the collectivity that its most treasured beliefs and ideals would be endangered if it allowed itself to be swayed by the arguments of the exclusionists. "We cannot live," Grant forcefully reminded his compatriots, "where men are treated as anything less than men ... the common weal is most promoted when the rights of the meanest are respected."[29]

Grant's decision to fight the battle on this piece of ground was of immense significance, for it demonstrated his willingness to intervene in the community's growth in order to be sure that it proceeded in a manner consistent with movement towards the kind of unity he favoured. Progress towards that important goal could not be left to chance. If necessary, steps must be taken to insure that those who would interfere with its achievement be prevented from having their way. Paradoxically, then, the building of the whole might involve restricting the activities of certain of its parts. In one set of circumstances such a proscription might simply mean – as it did in the case of the British Columbia exclusionists – a refusal to tolerate racist proposals. But in others – here the logic of Grant's position drew him on to quite another sort of ground – it would entail a much different result.

What that result might be emerged with particular force from the view he took of prairie settlement. Immigrants to the Canadian west must, he argued, set down their roots in soil that would grow a society of the proper sort. It was the job of those who oversaw that settlement to insure this happened. The surest way to guarantee that outcome was to import the institutional framework of the older provinces. The life of the prairies must replicate that of the East. Alien influences, in short, were to be carefully limited. "The people who go to the North-west from our older provinces," he argued, "should feel that they are going away neither from their own country nor their own Church. In the interest of patriotism and religion it is desirable that all the forces that mould the character of a people to high issues should be brought to bear upon the immigrants who are pouring into the North-west."[30] If a society of the kind he envisioned failed to emerge as a consequence of this procedure, Grant was prepared to go still further. Those whose refusal to respond to the imperatives of their new situation was complicating the thrust towards the higher unity were, quite simply, to be turned away. People of low character, whose only interest was in free land, were certainly to be viewed with suspicion – "Why," asked Grant, "should the country pay men to coax foreigners to accept from us free farms?"[31] – while the admission of those whose cultural and ethnic heritage made it doubtful that they could attune themselves to the nation's higher purposes ought surely to be curtailed. "Let our governments," he urged, "recall the agents who are paid to bring us any and every kind of immigrants. We have as many people of strange languages as we can digest. Our best settlers are own children, and those who come from the south of their own accord ... [along with] those who have suffered for conscience sake. They are sure to be good stock."[32]

For all his anxiety lest precipitate action be taken in the matter of British Columbia's Asians, Grant's overriding concern with creating conditions likely to foster the higher unity led him to reconsider his position even on that contentious issue. He remained, to be sure, unsympathetic to exclusion. It would complicate relations with China, be inconsistent with missionary work in that country, and, as always, constitute a denial of the Asians' basic humanity.[33] British Columbia's evolution as a harmonious community, and its effective integration into Canada and the Empire was, nonetheless, the primary consideration, and Grant's observation of affairs in the American south led him to believe that racial homogeneity would aid the achievement of those goals. While Canada ought not to act arbitrarily in the matter, it should seek an agreement with China by which, just as the Chinese limited the sojourn of foreigners there, so the Canadian government would be able to limit the stay of the Chinese in Canada. It was above all else imperative that the thrust towards unity be sustained and that it not lose its fundamental character. "We intend," Grant made clear, "British Columbia to be Canadian, and of the Caucasian, not the Mongolian type."[34]

The case of the French Canadians, too, came in for additional scrutiny at the end of the century. Here, however, Grant saw no need to alter his position. Even in the circumstances created by English Canada's resentment of the French Canadians' lack of enthusiasm for the imperial enterprise, he thought it enough to insist that the French speakers' loyalty and support would be kept in the future, as they had been secured in the past, by toleration of their language and culture. The French Canadians' defining peculiarities had, he insisted anew, long since been emptied of significance by their proprietors' acceptance of their duties in the Empire. Indeed, he argued, the degree to which French Canadians showed acceptance of the new imperialism was far more remarkable than the extent to which they opposed it.[35] In this situation the point, spelled out clearly enough in the past,[36] that toleration of their language and ways was not at all incompatible with the aim of insuring their assimilation to the truths that really counted could be restated with special force. No harm, he therefore insisted once more, would be done the majority by its concession of French Canadian rights, while the French Canadians, assured again of its goodwill, would move the more readily to embrace its principles. It was, in fact, only in this way that the desired result could be obtained. "There," as Grant put it, "the *habitant* was, there he had been from the first, there he intended to remain; and the more generously his rights were recognized the sooner would fusion take place."[37]

The goal towards which all must move was, then, acceptance of the proposition that they were bound together in common service to a set of transcendent truths. Those who accepted this broad vision could be left in possession of their own language, culture, and local loyalties, for they had seen that these things were not the end-all of existence. Those, on the other hand, who had not caught this vision were to be denied – so far as possible – the opportunity to trivialize and demean the world with their small and narrow vision of the particular's importance. Certainly no other approach would work for Canada, for without this emphasis on the higher unity the nation would dissolve into a claque of squabbling rivals, each consumed by its own self-interest. Only by keeping firmly fixed in their mind's eye a vision of the higher truth could Canadians avoid this fate and in so doing build a nation capable of the great work for which it had been destined.

There was, Grant held, a close relationship between awareness of one's association with other beings and one's sense of the principles which ought to govern action in the everyday world. This relationship was founded on the assumption that those principles, like the reality of association itself, derived – here Grant's idealism revealed its unmistakably Protestant character – from the fact that the spiritual dimension of one's being linked one directly with God. As he put it in 1894, the Protestant reformers had "discovered the individual and gave him his rightful place in the Church and in society ... they taught that man as man entered into union with God by a spiritual act, and that every man who did so was a king, a priest, and a prophet."[38] The individual, thus exalted, was not, of course, free to think of himself as an isolated being, at liberty to go his own way; on the contrary his relationship with God at once linked him to all other men and defined his life in terms of duties he could not properly shirk. In giving him the potential to understand something of God's nature and plans for his universe, it in fact conferred on him the obligation to act in a manner consistent with that knowledge. He must, in particular, strive to live a life worthy in its morality and discipline of a being who was simultaneously linked to the Divine and able to comprehend something of its true nature. Realizing what was best in himself thus became a personal duty and an obligation to God.

Throughout Grant's work the person who remained mindful of this sublime obligation won high praise.[39] Lives of this quality were not, of course, lived easily. Grant accordingly set much emphasis on the fact that the development of one's capacity to place oneself in harmony with the divine order was owing to constant and ceaseless effort. As he put it near the end of his own struggle, "all life is a battle, but only in overcoming these is character formed and life made complete."[40] What this life-defining contest might yield was, Grant thought, particularly evident in the case of his fellow Nova Scotian Joseph Howe, for Howe had seen clearly that he who would be a truly successful man must learn restraint, self-discipline, and the secret of work. Perhaps, observed Grant, "the great lesson that Howe's earlier years teaches is the one so hard to learn, that there is no royal road to success. When a man wakes up some morning to find himself famous, we may be sure that he has earned the success by years of previous toil ..."[41]

Grant's insistence on the centrality of these truths was in part a reflection of his belief that, notwithstanding their importance, society as a whole was far from allowing itself to be guided by them. The speculators in the east who preyed like "a brood of barnacles and vultures" on the settlers clearing the land,[42] the factory owners who denied the just claims of their workers,[43] the tariff legislators who kept the farmers in thrall,[44] and "the insane greed of corporations and their callousness to the interests of the community"[45] alike offered proof that too many individuals were prepared to follow the low road of greed, immediate gain, and self-indulgence. It was, indeed, in this fact that the origins of society's problems lay: they were ultimately to be explained by the failure of individuals to act according to their best lights. While, then, Grant was at one with reformers in denouncing certain abuses in society – and in this he was far in advance of most of his colleagues who thought it no business of a clergyman to be involved in the wages and other questions – he was equally at odds with progressive opinion when it came to specifying a cure. Since abuses in society ultimately derived from a failure of Christian leadership, it followed that, once that failure was repaired, abuses would disappear. "Honest and capable leaders,"[46] men who understood that "true leadership consists not in yielding to the cries of the people, but in persuading, inducing, and enabling them towards effort in the right direction"[47] were what was required.

In emphasizing the results which could be expected to flow from the moral regeneration of individuals, Grant made a basic distinction between the outcome of the process he envisioned and the kind of consequences the reformers and radicals of his day expected to flow from their activities. This distinction, in its turn, rested on a quite different understanding of the nature of the individual's power. Where the reformers thought one's ability to understand the world gave one the capability to intervene in its operations and change them at will in accordance with a rationally arrived at sense of how matters ought to operate, Grant considered that this same capacity would lead to the humbling realization that reality, complex and interdependent, was shaped by a host of forces of which humanity was only one. To be sure, he shared with some of the reformers the view that humanity was socially defined. "Only in society," as he put it, "is man understood, and only in society does he attain the perfection of his being."[48] This did not, however, mean that society was to be viewed as a mechanism to be endlessly rebuilt in the hope of altering its impact on the individuals it enclosed. It was instead to be seen as a complex, living organism, the production of a long history, possessed by its own spiritual character, an entity on whose being the action of a mere individual could have little impact. If they were to make effective use of what power they did have individuals must first realize this. Then they would begin to understand why the framework within which they existed could be altered only slowly, and why they should look to self-improvement rather than changes in social environment as the source of ameliorative action. While government could doubtless do some of what was necessary – Grant did not hesitate to call for legislation when he thought it appropriate – in the last analysis reform could come only from a species of inner renewal manifesting itself in a kind of *noblesse oblige* on the part of society's leadership and in a sense of individual responsibility on the part of its members. Those who advocated only institutional and social change could, then, hope to touch no more than the externals of the problem. They would, in fact, distract attention from the real issue which, in his view, had to be conceived in far subtler terms. Socialism and anarchism could thus be pronounced "anti-Christian,"[49] with anything that looked like support for the idea that they would cure the ills of society being dismissed out of hand. Even the ideas of Henry George, at first – thanks to the tones of righteousness in which they were enunciated – in receipt of a rather more careful and positive scrutiny,[50] were finally rejected.[51] In Carl Berger's words, Grant's style of improvement remained throughout his career "the kind of reform which is addressed to the reformation of character as opposed to the redistribution of property."[52]

As individuals grew by taking positive action, so, Grant believed, national character was built when a people, having discerned the nature of its collective responsibilities, moved to meet them. But if the nature of the challenge was clear – the country, like the individuals of which it was composed, must with God's help overcome selfishness and materialism in order to attain its "great future"[53] – it seemed less obvious to Grant that the battle to accomplish this end had even been joined. This was, of course, partly owing to the fact that the Dominion, adrift in an historical backwater, had had little opportunity to display the stuff of which it was made. "Our national sentiment," as Grant explained it, "has never been put to the test."[54] There was, however, evidence that this unfortunate situation was changing. The shifting world order, the evolution of Empire, and Canada's own growth were creating a new set of opportunities which seemed tailor-made for Canada. The way in which it met them would, indeed, determine whether or not it would exist as a nation worthy of the name: "we are," Grant warned his countrymen in 1887, "nearing that point in our history when we must assume the full responsibilities of nationhood, or abandon the experiment altogether."[55] By 1894, in Grant's view, that point had been reached. Of equal importance, the evolution of opinion in Canada was showing that Canadians had begun to realize that they as a people could achieve their destiny only by accepting the obligations that circumstance had placed on them. They must do their share in upholding the principles upon which their faith and civilization rested, and that, they were now seeing, meant nothing less than action, within the framework of the Empire, on the world stage. "The days of isolation," Grant enthused, "are over. Canada cannot hold aloof even if she would, and her young men are too virile to shun the needed strain and conflict if they could."[56]

What Grant viewed as Canada's increasingly prominent role in imperial affairs was, he thought, proof positive that the nation had come of age. At first inclined towards support for the Boers of South Africa in their struggle against Britain, he came to see the Laurier government's despatch of troops to their country as a step of key importance on Canada's march towards nationhood, for it demonstrated beyond doubt acceptance of the obligations and responsibilities of maturity. "The larger patriotism, which has now taken possession of Canadians, cannot," his contemplation of it led him to proclaim, "possibly vanish ... We are henceforth a nation."[57] Continuing in this track would, indeed, allow Canada to challenge the power of its New World rival itself, for "we shall be ... equals [of the Americans] only when we share the burdens and responsibilities as well as the privileges and glory of the Empire."[58]

Grant's doctrine of responsibility thus arose directly out of his understanding of the manner in which nations and individuals alike formed part of a comprehensive whole. Only by bearing their share of the burden that whole had to carry could they contribute to its strength and integrity, and only by making such a contribution could they insure that their own lives were appropriately rich and full. Personal duty, public good, and service to God were linked in a splendid and all-encompassing construct whose true purposes could be served only by those who understood the universal significance of individual action and acted in a manner consistent with the demands that understanding made upon them.

Notwithstanding the powerful emphasis he placed on its utility in the development of national character and strength, Grant's concern that Canada acknowledge its imperial obligations rested on more than his belief that there was a relationship of decisive importance between fulfilment, growth, and the acceptance of responsibility. In shouldering its share of the imperial burden Canada would, he believed, be doing nothing less than demonstrating its fitness to act out the role assigned to it by the historical process. God, it was not to be doubted, revealed his plans for mankind in the dimension of time no less than the amplitude of space. To contemplate the flow of history was, in consequence, to consider yet another set of divine lessons for the edification of mankind. "We should," he therefore informed Canadians, "study the history of the past for our guidance in the present. History is indeed that revelation which, as Carlyle says, no one in or out of bedlam can question."[59]

The nature of the truth which would be revealed by this quasi-religious scrutinizing of the historical record was, Grant believed, clear: Britain, even a casual glance at the evolution of nations made obvious, had been created the first among the world's civilizations. Nowhere had institutions and culture combined over time to produce a more perfect mixture of the elements of true freedom. All that people required to live a fulfilled and godly existence was available to them there. As Grant put it, "Let the history of liberty and progress, of the development of human character in all its rightful issues, testify where liberty and authority have been more wisely blended than in the British Constitution."[60]

As the heirs and benefactors of this triumphant resolution of the central problem in the organization of human affairs – here, for Grant, was the real lesson – Canadians were obliged to see that its integrity was maintained and its influence extended. The accomplishment of these goals must, in fact, become one of the major impulses informing their lives. They must take as their guiding sentiment "a faith that the British name and British institutions are worth making sacrifices for." Action in the future was to be governed by knowledge of what had happened in the past, and – Grant brought the point sharply into focus – "the chief glory of that past from the days of Alfred, the barons of Runnymede, Hampden, or Sydney, is the memory of ancestors who have willingly died for the good old cause of human freedom."[61] The Canadians' honouring of that memory could best be done by remaining faithful to the work these great men had sought to do, and that, it seemed clear, meant continuing their struggle. Canadians must, then, do in the present what these illustrious figures had done in the past. They must act to insure that the forces which had shaped so fruitful and glorious a tradition be allowed to work their will in the future. Any attempt to interfere with those forces was, indeed, to be vigorously resisted, for it would represent a denial of all that had gone before. Particularly to be eschewed was anything that would involve weakening the British tie. "We believe," as Grant told Canadians in the early 1870s, "that loyalty is a better guarantee of true growth than restlessness and rebellion [and] that building up is worthier work than pulling down."[62] Action consistent with maintaining the integrity of the British and imperial past was therefore the only action permissible, for any other kind threatened to disrupt the measured pace of freedom's unfolding. The web of history had been delicately woven, and "every break in the continuity of its life is injurious."[63]

If Grant's insistence on maintaining history's even flow gave him a powerful argument in support of imperial consolidation, the refusal to accept disruptive change that was its obverse provided him with a weapon he used with no little effect in his continuing campaign against those – Goldwin Smith was the leading example – who were urging some form of Canadian-American union. Such proposals were unsound, he argued, not because they sought to associate the two countries,[64] but because they proposed to do it by violating the deliberate march of historical development. Smith's suggestion that union between Canada and the United States would do nothing more than duplicate the relationship between Scotland and England was of particularly dubious validity, for it overlooked the fact that Canada, unlike Scotland, would have to sunder a pre-existing association.[65] "We too," Grant was at pains to make clear, "hope for a reunion of the English-speaking race, but we seek it along historical and not theoretical lines. It must not begin with further disunion; and a preliminary sacrifice of the Queen, the Prince of Wales, the House of Lords, the Established Churches, India, and other trifling possessions ought not to be absolutely necessary."[66]

The proper course to follow was, then, plain. Only consolidation of the empire was consistent with the movement of history. Only "imperial federation" would place "the capstone on that structure of Canadian nationality which we have been working at so long." Canadians would as a consequence of such action not only find themselves getting "full citizenship" in the Empire, and occupying ground that would make them "peers and not the dependents of their fellow citizens in the British Islands."[67] They would be attaining the sublime state towards which everything in their experience from their most cherished traditions to their internal history on the North American continent had been impelling them.[68] In doing that, moreover – for Grant, a hardly less important point – they would be giving clear proof of their understanding that the imperatives created by the historical process could not be set aside. In thus demonstrating acceptance of the proposition – again a characteristically vigorous figure of speech – that "the nation cannot be pulled up by the roots,"[69] they would be making it clear that they saw, as he did, that no other line of action would give them a chance to carry their burden in the world, do so much to fulfil their individual and collective potential, or provide them with the opportunity to maintain the continuity of the historical process. They would, in sum, be showing their final acceptance of the fact that they had no option but to follow the course all things in their experience had set before them.

If the unfolding of the historical process was impelling Canada in a clear and unmistakable direction, so too, Grant believed, were the country's geographical circumstances. To be sure, its configuration in space presented certain problems. As a nation of sections next to a powerful and seductive neighbour, it had to take firm steps to insure that it neither fragmented nor got drawn into the arms of what lay to the south. Grant's willingness to talk of military installations as part of what was necessary to meet the second of these challenges was one measure of how seriously he viewed it,[70] but in the main he relied on the railway and immigration to do what was necessary. Canadians must make good their claim on "half a continent" by populating it, while the construction of a national communications system would at once knit the country together and make possible its resistance to American expansion.[71] To Smith's argument that all of this was an artificial and foredoomed attempt to set aside the dictates of nature Grant found a ready reply in the contention that much of human history depicted delimitation of the natural world by virtue of humanity's intellect and technical prowess. "Man," he noted, "triumphs continually over geography or nature in any form."[72] Canadians, whatever Smith though of the matter, were thus doing what their species had done since time immemorial. What was more, they were succeeding at it. "We have established," Grant felt able to argue by 1896, "an unequalled system of internal navigation from the Straits of Belle Isle into the heart of the continent, and we have added to that an unparalleled railway system ... every part of our great Northern Confederacy has been linked together by steel as well as sentiment."[73]

In effectively ending any likelihood that the country would be absorbed by the United States, consolidation of its material base did not mean, Grant was anxious to point out, that Canada should insulate itself from involvement with the Republic. Its people must, of course, be watchful of their relations with that powerful state; but completely isolating themselves on the North American continent would be as much at variance with their national interest as it would be contrary to the dictates of geography.[74] The nation must, indeed, not only welcome contact with the United States, providing such contact was on the right terms; it must recognize the fact that it, too, was a community of the New World, heir to the abundance, resources, and regenerative powers of that fabulous place, and, in the end, even more likely than the United States to play a decisive role in the re-making of the world. Grant had, in fact, been struck from the moment of his first contact with "Greater Canada" by the immensity of its material wealth. Notwithstanding the contention in the pages of his *Ocean to Ocean* that "the destiny of a country depends not on its material resources ... [but] on the character of its people,"[75] that record of his journey across the new dominion made clear his belief that Canada was a country of extraordinary potential.[76] Thanks to what geography had conferred upon it, the country possessed resources sufficient to underpin limitless growth.[77]

If Grant's satisfaction in contemplating the physical endowments of the Dominion was obvious enough, he was no less struck by the opportunity the opening of a new and untouched world offered for the creation of a better human society. In a land uncontaminated by the vices of civilization, people of character, morality and determination would find it possible to create a community unparalleled in human history for its virtue and justice. Canada's settlers thus had every reason to hope that they would "found in the forests of the west a state in which there would be justice for all, fair reward for labour, a new home for freedom, freedom from grinding poverty, freedom from the galling chain of ancient feuds, mutual confidence and righteousness between man and man, flowing from trust in God."[78]

Canadians in fact occupied a uniquely privileged position in the scheme of things. Vitalized by the abundance and opportunity of the New World, yet mindful of all that their position as heirs of the British tradition could teach them, they enjoyed the best features of the Old and the New. "We have ... not," noted Grant "been obliged to sacrifice any of the inestimable treasures accumulated by our fathers, while at the same time we keep our minds and eyes open to receive new teaching from this new world where everything is possible to man."[79] Canada thus combined – in Grant's view the point could not be made strongly enough – "the self-control, reticence, and modesty begotten by conservative training ... with that freedom from routine and readiness to experiment that belongs to a new country."[80]

For all that he allowed himself to be enraptured by geography's influence in giving Canada an unmistakable new world dimension, the country's location in space, Grant made equally clear, allowed it to be defined in other terms as well. Utilizing a line of argument being developed by the British geographer H.J. Mackinder, Grant took the view that Canada was delineated not only by its position on the North American continent but by its location between the two great oceans of the world. Seen from this perspective, the nation had a relevance that was truly global. It was, indeed, nothing less than "the natural keystone between the old world of northern Europe and the older world of China and Japan ... the living link between Great Britain and the sunny lands under the Southern Cross ... the bridge between East and West, and the bond that unites the three great self-governing parts of the British Empire."[81]

What, in short, its history demanded, its geography made possible. Equipped with every conceivable material advantage, possessing a land mass that linked it to all corners of the world, Canada could do no other than take up the work every element of its being and circumstances directed it to perform.

In specifying the nature of the role Canada was foreordained to play, its geography and history did more, in Grant's view, than simply disclose what lay in the immediate future. The securing of a position of influence and power within the framework of the Empire was, of course, a vital short-term goal. Grant did not, however, consider its accomplishment an end in itself. The nation, positioned by its circumstances to serve the cause of British liberty and Christian truth, was destined for nothing less than duty on the most sublime field of action imaginable. In association with its imperial partners, it would serve as the successor of the Old Testament Hebrews, the agency which would bear witness to Gold's presence in the world. "We have," Grant accordingly told his compatriots, "a mission on earth as truly as ancient Israel had ..."[82]

What precisely that mission was, and how exactly it was to be fulfilled, could, Grant thought, be clearly specified. There was, in fact, an ineluctable logic about the whole process: the first stage – aiding in the consolidation of the Empire – was obvious enough. That accomplished, two further objectives would remain. Attaining the first of these would involve the country in exploiting its position as a community with roots on both sides of the Atlantic. It must use that position to bring Britain and the United States together. Notwithstanding the fact that it was occasionally a source of friction between the two powers, its place in their ultimate reconciliation was, in Grant's view, assured. For all that the eventual reunion of the two would owe to their common traditions and "high common ends,"[83] that momentous event would be materially aided by the intervention of Canada. His nation would, in fact, function as nothing less than "the link that shall unite the great mother and her greatest daughter, the United States of America."[84] So important was this task, and so central was the role Canada would play in accomplishing it, that there must be no mistaking the significance of either. "No greater boon" – Grant spelled the matter out in the clearest possible terms – "can be conferred on the race than the healing of [the] schism of [1776]. That is the work that Canada is appointed by its position and history to do ... We are to build up a North American Dominion, permeated with the principles of right-eousness, worthy to be the living link, the permanent bond of union, between Britain and the United States."[85]

The forging of that link – the flow of Grant's argument hardly slowed – was, in its turn, of inestimable importance, for it would make possible the gaining of the second grand objective. The union of the Anglo-Saxon race which would result from Canada's mediation between the two great nations to which it was bound would mean the creation of a force capable of establishing world hegemony. One could, in consequence, anticipate the day when the globe as a whole would be brought under the sway of Christian principle and Anglo-Saxon virtue.The solidarity of the race would, then, function as much more than a vehicle by means of which Canada and Canadians, or even Anglo-Saxons generally, could achieve their own destiny. It would be an important stage in the process by which the fragmentation of humanity would be over-come. Under the auspices of this revitalized Anglo-Saxon influence the world's people would be bound together in a complex yet perfectly integrated whole at the same time that Christianity's unfolding truth came to permeate every fibre of their being.

Grant had no doubt that this grand vision, involving all the peoples of the world, was a pluralist one. Although it would be the Canadians and the British, and – once they had seen the light – the Americans who would take the initiative "in the glorious mission of establishing freedom, righteousness, and peace upon earth,"[86] his tolerance, humanity, and respect for what was good in other traditions led him to deal circumspectly with the precise weight Anglo-Saxon influence would have in the character of the new order that would be created by this action. The result of it, he suggested on more than one occasion, would be a kind of grand synthesis in which individuals would be united in support of a common body of principle to the making of which all had contri-buted. "Our evolution," Grant told the World's Parliament of Religions in 1893, "has taught us that ideas belong to no one country, that they are the common property of mankind, and that we should borrow from every country that has found by experiment that they work well."[87] He wrote, too, of Tennyson's Parliament of

Man, that great "Federation of the World" in which its people would come together and yet retain their own character and identity.[88] When all, however, was said and done his commitment to a world order which would combine elements from different traditions in a grand pluralistic whole was more apparent than real. In the end his tolerance functioned essentially as a tactical device, the effect of whose operation would be – as in the Canadian case – to insure final admission to the inner circle only of those who were prepared to assign their own culture and values an inferior place to those he himself espoused. His rhetoric left no doubt that the truth in support of which all must ultimately unite would be a Christian truth, just as his Tennysonian frame of reference made it clear that the institutional complex in which this unity would find expression would be an Anglo-Saxon one.

Canada, "in the van of the world's battle," would thus come to play a central role in the process by which the peoples of the world, uplifted by their association with the Anglo-Saxons of the North Atlantic, would realize their potential for unity by accepting a destiny that was specifically linked to the religious experience of that Protestant civilization. Mankind's "common humanity," attaining fulfilment in "accomplishing its mission to establish the Kingdom of God upon earth," would define its being in the explicit and unambiguous language of evangelical Protestantism.[89] The vast edifice of universal peace and harmony, in whose construction Canada was to play so important a part, would finally come to rest, not on a genuinely pluralist and synthetic foundation, but on a base provided by one civilization's view of what constituted humanity's purpose and destiny on earth. All would indeed be bound together, but their unity would derive from their acceptance of a particular body of truth whose doctrines would by virtue of that acceptance vanquish all rivals.

Grant's system of ideas can best be understood as the construct of a man deeply concerned lest forces of change and innovation sweep away the values and the leadership he believed essential to a properly functioning Christian society. More, accordingly, is involved in understanding the genesis and character of that system than a simple application to its diagnosis of the proposition that ideas and interests are closely linked. Account must also be taken of the fact that concern to maintain and extend acceptance for one's world view will be particularly strong if one sees it, and the social arrangements it validates, being challenged by a rival set of conceptions. In the words of Peter L. Berger and Thomas Luckmann, "the appearance of an alternative symbolic universe poses a threat because its very existence demonstrates empirically that one's own universe is less than inevitable ... The confrontation of alternative symbolic universes implies a problem of power – which of the conflicting definitions of reality will be 'made to stick' in the society."[90] Grant, thanks to the emergence of the new and vastly more complex Canada created by industrialization, immigration, and the shrinking globe, found himself in the midst of just such a confrontation. Determined that the selfish particularisms of the new order and its representatives should not abridge the bright promise of a vital and expansive Christian community acting in fulfilment of a global mission, he sought to insure that it would be the definition of reality held by those who thought as he did that would be "made to stick" in Canadian society.

His anxiety to contain the new forces all around him never, however, – and in this one can see the full measure of his intelligence and subtlety – led him to pursue the path of blind reaction. He believed the challenge the new realities represented could best be met by effecting their absorption into the very system they threatened to displace. It is, indeed, a measure of his belief in that system's resilience and flexibility that he thought its power would be augmented by the assimilation of elements which at first sight seemed to guarantee its destruction.

Yet the decision to attempt the accommodation of the new forces was not a purely tactical one. In Grant's Hegelian-influenced view, the Christian idealism it was his aim to promote was to be defined largely in terms of its extraordinary capaciousness. Doing one's duty to it would involve an approach to all the elements of which really consisted, which, with a generosity born of the confidence that one understood the workings of the universe, would recognize the fact that each of them, no matter how fractious and contrary it seemed, had a role to play in the total scheme of things.

Fully effective assimilation of the new forces required, of course, more than a simple acceptance by Grant and those who saw the world as he did of a conceptualization of the universe which insisted that each of the elements in it belonged to the Kingdom of God and, whether they realized it or not, were contributing to that Kingdom's triumphant onward march. All of the human agents through which these forces operated had to be made conscious of this truth. Only then would a comprehensive spirit of co-operation with the acceptance of Christianity's imperatives replace the indifference and hostility to them which seemed so conspicuous as features of modern life. Here as well Grant's Christian idealism was of immense assistance. By inviting all people, no matter what character their activities possessed, to conceive of themselves as essentially moral beings linked to each other and to the divine by their common participation in a spiritual whole it in fact provided a near perfect vehicle for the attainment of this end. In insisting on the directness of individuals' links with God it simultaneously commended itself to them by exalting their importance and gave them an inducement to think in terms that transcended their immediate interests. And, in insisting that once they had accepted this larger view of themselves they act in a manner consistent with the dignity and responsibility of a being linked to the divine, it provided a powerful argument in support of the contention that behaviour should approximate the standards laid down by those who – like Grant – had caught the full vision of what this involved. Such people would thus, if all went as it should, be in a position to define the elements of good behaviour in the new circumstances as they had in the old.

Despite his appreciation of his creed's potential as an agency which, properly deployed, could blunt the force of the new realities, Grant was by no means persuaded that the values and behaviour it would serve to strengthen were in fact holding their own. The end of his life thus saw him disposed to argue that the forces against which he had fought throughout its length still maintained a global presence. "The nineteenth century," he sadly informed his readers, "is closing in moral gloom as dense as that which shrouded the closing decade of the eighteenth."[91] What was happening at home, moreover, made it clear that the enemies of Christian truth and honourable behaviour were maintaining themselves on the domestic front as well. "What threatens the life of Canada most seriously," he wrote after a lifetime's effort to root it out, "... [is] the uncleanness ... the vulgar and insolent materialism of thought and life ... [and the] aggressive commercialism which penetrates to the inner most courts of the sanctuary."[92]

Too much should not, however, be made of his disappointment at the failure of his world view to win a clear triumph over its adversaries. Far more central to an understanding of his system, its character, and its place in nineteenth-century Canadian life is a sense of the prodigious effort he made on its behalf. In articulating it with such vigour and consistency he at once provided a measure of the extent to which he felt it threatened and made himself a leading spokesman for the values it contained. If, in sum, an examination of his thought sheds light on the way in which ideas may be related to shifting patterns of status and influence in society, it also provides opportunity for contact with a particularly forceful, clear, and comprehensive expression of an important strain in late nineteenth-century Canadian thought. In thus allowing a close look at a representative expression of that strain, in directing attention to the status of its proponents, and in making possible the construction of an argument suggesting how the two were linked, it does much to refine our grasp and extend our understanding of the elements defining the English Canadian phase of the great nineteenth-century struggle between liberal and conservative modes of thought. Its relevance is ultimately more than national, as Grant himself was much more than merely a patriot.

NOTES

1 For an account of the Canadian formulation of some of the leading ideas of this period, see A.B. McKillop, "A Disciplined Intelligence: Intellectual Inquiry and the Moral Imperative in Anglo-Canadian Thought 1850–1890," PHD diss., Queen's University, 1976. For an examination of some representative Canadian intellectuals active in the generation following, see S.E.D. Shortt, *The Search for an Ideal: Six Canadian Intellectuals and their Convictions in An Age of Transition 1890–1930* (Toronto: University of Toronto Press, 1976). For the ideas of Canadian conservatism in the late nineteenth century, see Carl Berger, *The Sense of Power: Studies in the Ideas of Canadian Imperialism 1867–1914* (Toronto: University of Toronto Press, 1970). The thought of Grant's most implacable opponent is summed up in Goldwin Smith, *Canada and the Canadian Question*, introduction by Carl Berger (Toronto: University of Toronto Press, 1971).

2 "The Pulpit in Scotland As It Is, And As It Was Forty or Fifty Years Ago," *Queen's Quarterly*, 7, January 1900, 195.

3 The Scottish-born and -educated Watson was an influential figure in late nineteenth- and early twentieth-century idealist circles on both sides of the Atlantic. For an account of his life and ideas, see J.M. MacEachern, "John Watson," in R.C. Wallace, ed., *Some Great Men of Queen's* (Toronto: Ryerson, 1941), 22–50; and W.E. McNeill, "John Watson," *Proceedings and Transactions of the Royal Society of Canada*, ser. 3 (33), 1939, 159–61. McKillop considers Watson at some length. Watson's own views on the relationship between Christianity and Idealism are set out in his appropriately titled *Christianity and Idealism* (New York: Macmillan, 1896). For a general account of philosophical activity in Canada in this period, see John A. Irving, "The Devel-

opment of Philosophy in Central Canada from 1850 to 1900," *Canadian Historical Review*, 31, September 1950, 252–87. T.A. Goudge, "A Century of Philosophy in English-Speaking Canada," *Dalhousie Review*, 47, Winter 1967–68, 537–49, contains some material on Watson but is mainly concerned with the twentieth century. For a discussion of idealist modes of thinking in terms of their relevance to the thought of men like Grant, see Terry Cook, "George R. Parkin and the Concept of Britannic Idealism," *Journal of Canadian Studies*, 10, August 1975, especially 22–31.

4 Cited (no source given) in W.L. Grant and F. Hamilton, *Principal Grant* (Toronto: Morang, 1904), 74.

5 "Current Events," *Queen's Quarterly*, 5, April 1898, 332.

6 "Castell Hopkins' Life of Mr. Gladstone," *Canadian Magazine*, 6, November 1895, 87.

7 "The Pulpit in Scotland As It Is, and As It Was Forty or Fifty Years Ago," *Queen's Quarterly*, 7, January 1900, 202.

8 "Presbyterian Union and Reformation Principles," *Queen's Quarterly*, 1, January 1894, 181.

9 Grant and Hamilton, *Principal Grant*, 486.

10 Author unknown, "Distinguished Canadians. The Rev. George Munro [sic] Grant, DD," *Canadian Methodist Magazine*, 18, October 1883, 293.

11 "Hopkins' Life," 86.

12 "Anti-National Features of the National Policy," *Canadian Magazine*, 1, March 1893, 9–13.

13 "The Jason of Algoma: An Account of the Wonderful Industrial Development in New Ontario," *Canadian Magazine*, 15, October 1900, 490.

14 "The Religious Condition of Canada," *Queen's Quarterly*, 1, April 1894, 320.

15 "Current Events," *Queen's Quarterly*, 5, October 1897, 169.

16 *Principal Grant's Inaugural Address Delivered at Queen's University, Kingston, on University Day* (Toronto: Grip, 1885), 11.

17 "The University Question," *Queen's Quarterly*, 9, January 1902, 232.

18 *Ocean to Ocean* (Toronto: J. Campbell, 1873), 347–8.

19 "Thanksgiving and Retrospect," *Queen's Quarterly*, 9, January 1902, 232.

20 "Our National Objects and Aims," in *Maple Leaves: Being the Papers Read Before the National Club of Toronto at the 'National Evenings' During the Winter 1890–1891* (Toronto: National Club, 1891), 20.

21 "To [Grant]," recalled his biographers, "all the universe was God's universe; every truth was God's truth ... [spurning] the theory which cuts the world in two with a hatchet ... he believed that the universe

was an organic whole belonging to the Almighty." *Principal Grant,*
77–8.

22 "Response on Behalf of Canada to Address of Welcome, at the
World's Parliament of Religions," *Queen's Quarterly,* 1, October 1893,
160. Sometimes Grant's exposure to other currents of thought flowing in the late nineteenth century led him to cast the same point in
less mystical terms. Taking a leaf from the Spencerians' notebook, he
noted in 1900 that this diversity might simply demonstrate the capaciousness of a complex yet fully integrated life-form. "The British
Empire," as he put it, "is a ... complicated and highly developed
organism ... and can therefore include the most widely differing
stages of political life," "Current Events," *Queen's Quarterly,* 8, July
1900, 77. Occasionally, too, emphasis on the unity and coherence of
experience yielded to an unambiguous pluralism. Grant's concern to
see Queen's preserved as an independent institution led him to op-
pose the creation of a single agency of higher learning in Ontario,
while the polyglot nature of Winnipeg society in the 1880s seemed
to him an unmistakable sign of its vitality and exuberance. See
Grant's Inaugural Address, 10; "The University Question," 220; and
"The Northwest: Manitoba" in G.M. Grant, ed., *Picturesque Canada:*
The Country As It Was And Is (Toronto: Belden Bros., 1882), vol. 1,
288.

23 "Current Events," *Queen's Quarterly,* 7, January 1900, 256.

24 They might, he asserted, have "remained French in appearance and
French to the core, yet [they] fought repeatedly and are ready to
fight again side by side with the red-coats of Great Britain." "Quebec:
Historical Review," in *Picturesque Canada,* vol. 1, 2.

25 "Review of William Kingford's History," *The Week,* 9, 12 August 1892,
587.

26 "Canada and the Empire: A Rejoinder to Dr. Goldwin Smith," *Canadian Magazine,* 8, November 1896, 77.

27 "Canada First," *Canadian Leaves* (New York: Napoleon Thompson,
1887), 264.

28 "The Religious Condition of Canada," *Queen's Quarterly,* 1, April
1894, 318.

29 "British Columbia," in *Picturesque Canada,* vol. 2, 880.

30 "Churches and Schools in the North-West," in John Macoun, ed.,
Manitoba and the Great North-West (Guelph: World, 1882), 528.

31 "Current Affairs," *Queen's Quarterly,* 1, October 1893, 156.

32 "Thanksgiving and Retrospect," *Queen's Quarterly,* 9, January 1902,
227.

33 Berger, *Sense of Power,* 28.

34 "Current Events," *Queen's Quarterly,* 4, October 1896, 159, 158.

35 "Instead," Grant suggested at one point, "of wondering that French-speaking Canadians are not as enthusiastic in this [Boer] war as their English-speaking countrymen, the marvel is that their representative men have as a rule spoken so warmly on behalf of the Empire." The attitude of the French Canadians, he argued at another, has, "on the whole," been "admirable." See "Current Events," January 1900, 256, and April 1900, 333.

36 Impatience with the French Canadians and their culture would, he had argued in 1891, irritate them, heighten their self-consciousness, and delay their accommodation with their fellow Canadians – results the more unfortunate at a time when it was clear that an essentially anglo-saxon nation based on Canada's existing stock and immigrants who would assimilate to English Canadian culture was taking shape. See "Review of G. Smith, *Canada and the Canadian Question*," *The Week*, 8, 15 May 1891, 382.

37 "Thanksgiving and Retrospect," 224.

38 "Presbyterian Union and Reformation Principles," 181.

39 Sometimes the type was exemplified by the Highland Scot who, isolated at Red River, had not forgotten his God; sometimes by the pioneer farmer engaged in the shaping of a British and Christian west; sometimes by the creative entrepreneur whose energies were directed towards enlarging society's bounty rather than personal gain; sometimes by the university students who, in working their way through college, "paddle their own canoes ... [thanks to their] habits of industry, economy, and forethought," and sometimes by the ordinary Canadian who in his simple Christian life provided an example of honour and integrity as uplifting as it was modest. See "Churches and Schools in the Northwest," 524; "The North-West: Manitoba," 293; "The Jason of Algoma: An Account of the Wonderful Industrial Development in New Ontario," *Canadian Magazine*, 15, October 1900, 483–94; "Anti-National Features," 12; and "Thanksgiving and Retrospect," 220.

40 "Thanksgiving and Retrospect," 225.

41 *Joseph Howe* (Halifax: A. & W. MacKinlay, 1904), 37. Grant's account of Howe's life was first published as a series of articles bearing the title "The Late Hon. Joseph Howe," in the *Canadian Monthly and National Review*, 7, May 1875, 377–87; 7, June 1875, 497–508; 8, July 1875, 20–5; 8, August 1875, 115–22.

42 "The North-West," 293.

43 "Current Events," *Queen's Quarterly*, 1, July 1893, 67.

44 "Current Events," *Queen's Quarterly*, 4, April 1897, 318.

45 "Current Events," *Queen's Quarterly*, 5, January 1898, 252.

46 "Current Events," *Queen's Quarterly*, 2, October 1894, 182.

47 "The Jason of Algoma," 491.

48 "Presbyterian Union and Reformation Principles," *177.*

49 "Religious Condition of Canada," 319.

50 *Sense of Power,* 183–4.

51 Ramsay Cook, "Henry George and the Poverty of Canadian Progress," Canadian Historical Association *Historical Papers,* 1977, 150–1.

52 *Sense of Power,* 185.

53 *Ocean to Ocean,* 358.

54 "Canada First," 252.

55 Ibid., 251.

56 "The Religious Condition of Canada," 320.

57 "Introductory Chapter," in T.G. Marquis, *Canada's Sons on Kopje and Veldt: An Historical Account of the Canadian Contingents* (Toronto: Canadian Son's Pub. Co., 1900), 6.

58 "Thanksgiving and Retrospect," 225.

59 "Review of William Kingsford's History," 586.

60 *Ocean to Ocean,* 368.

61 "British Columbia," 880.

62 *Ocean to Ocean,* 358.

63 "Review of William Kingsford's History," 586. Grant's views on the nature of the historical process were sometimes cast in language which argued the existence of a parallel between human activities through time and the character of growth and development in the natural world. "No living organism," he once wrote in support of his argument that Canada must move steadily towards national maturity within the framework of the British Empire, "can continue long in a state of arrested development ... it must grow to its full stature or petrify." Such imagery was particularly useful in stressing the evolutionary and cumulative character he thought human affairs must have. "I do not look," it allowed him to note at one point,"for any startling Constitutional change or any paper scheme for re-organizing the Empire. That is not the way of the British. They build after the fashion of the insects that construct coral reefs, atolls, and fair islands in the Southern seas. They do the duty of today, and that becomes precedent, and so 'freedom slowly broadens down,' based not on theories but on necessities." See *Imperial Federation: A Lecture Delivered in Victoria Hall, Winnipeg, on September 13th, 1889* (Winnipeg: Manitoba Free Press, 1890), and "Introductory Chapter," in Marquis, 6.

64 Grant did not share the extreme and negative views of the United States voiced by some of his compatriots. For an account of his feelings on the subject, see *Sense of Power,* 171. For the opinions of others see *Sense of Power,* 153–76; and S.F. Wise and Robert Craig

Brown, *Canada Views the United States: Nineteenth Century Political Attitudes* (Toronto: Macmillan, 1967).

65 "Review of G. Smith," 381.

66 "Current Events," *Queen's Quarterly*, 1, July 1893, 79.

67 *Imperial Federation*, 5, 4.

68 Confederation itself, thought Grant, was to be viewed as part of the process. "Canada," he noted in 1895, "took a long step politically, in the direction of Imperial unity, when Confederation was affected." "Current Events," *Queen's Quarterly*, 2, October 1895, 157.

69 *Ocean to Ocean*, 366.

70 "Quebec: Historical Review," *Picturesque Canada*, vol. 1, 31.

71 "Quebec," 31.

72 "Review of G. Smith," 832.

73 "Canada and the Empire," 76.

74 Grant did not hesitate to identify the United States as Canada's "natural market," to suggest that "we desire to trade with everyone, and most of all with our neighbours," and to celebrate the fact that while "on this continent there are barbarous alien labour laws and hostile tariffs between kindred peoples ... so far these do not extend to free interchanges of brain, heart, and capital." See "Canada First,"13; and "The Jason of Algoma," 494.

75 Ibid., 366.

76 One reviewer, struck by just this feature of it, called it "a graphic account ... of the magnificent material resources of the country." See the *Canadian Methodist Magazine*, 5, May 1877, 477.

77 Virtually all parts of the country, Grant argued, shared in this bounty. If what lay between Lake Huron and Red River was endowed with minerals "beyond conception," he was equally anxious to make it clear that "our western islands are rich in coal ... and almost every variety of mineral wealth, in lumber, fish, and soil, and blessed with one of the most delightful climates in the world." His view of the prairies' potential was expressed in particularly forceful terms. There, he wrote, was to be found "an immense tract of the finest land in the world." The fields of Red River, he noted in 1882, "have raised wheat continuously ever since" their first cultivation. Indeed, he announced the same year, the "vast region" of the west was "the true habitat of the wheat plant. Here it attains perfection." One could, in view of these circumstances, hardly doubt that the North-west "bids fair to be the future granary of the world." See *Ocean to Ocean*, 352–3; "Churches and Schools," 527; and "The North-West: Manitoba," 298.

78 "Our National Objects and Aims," 34.

79 "Response on Behalf of Canada," 159.

80 "The Religious Condition of Canada," 321.
81 "Responses on Behalf of Canada," 159–60.
82 "Current Events," *Queen's Quarterly,* 5, July 1897, 85.
83 "Current Events," *Queen's Quarterly,* 7, July 1899, 80.
84 "Canada First," 249.
85 "Our National Objects and Aims," 22, 26.
86 "Current Events," *Queen's Quarterly,* 5, July 1897, 85.
87 "Response on Behalf of Canada," 159–60.
88 "Current Events," *Queen's Quarterly,* 1, July 1893, 73.
89 "Thanksgiving and Retrospect," 232–3.
90 *The Social Construction of Reality: A Treatise in the Sociology of Knowledge*
   (New York: Anchor, 1967), 109. This confrontation, at base one
   between the groups or classes that hold these ideas, may take a
   variety of forms. At its most obvious in the conflict between major
   systems of thought – conservatism, liberalism, socialism – in clearly
   class-conscious societies, it can also manifest itself in the ideological
   devices used by threatened groups in the course of their efforts to
   maintain their status and influence. The distinction drawn between
   landed wealth and wealth earned in trade by the defenders of a
   British aristocracy very much concerned to resist displacement by a
   class whose ascendancy was based on commerce and manufacturing
   is a well-known case in point. That distinction, and the special landed virtue to whose existence it was supposed to point, represented
   the making of a very clear set of claims on behalf of the aristocracy,
   "claims which," as F.M.L. Thompson points out, "it was scarcely
   necessary to formulate explicitly until the paramountcy of landed
   property became the subject of dispute." Even societies not normally
   thought of as characterized by a high degree of social conflict may
   exhibit tendencies of this kind. Historians of the United States,
   certainly, have uncovered a number of instances in which ideas
   professed by members of certain groups have been intimately related
   to the fact that those who hold those ideas felt their status, prestige,
   and power threatened by changes in the nature of their society and
   so sought to enforce dominance of their beliefs and values as a
   means of limiting the influence of those identified as the agents of
   this change. John Higham has, for example, suggested that the
   patterns of thought associated with American nativism may be best
   understood as phenomena arising out of the reality of "status rivalries" in American society. The importance of preserving "traditional"
   ideals and behaviour was emphasized not only by those of Protestant
   Anglo-Saxon stock who saw these values, and their own dominance,
   being threatened by European and Catholic immigrants but also by
   members of some immigrant groups, who, having begun to acquire

status and position largely through their acceptance of these values, saw their position hardly less endangered by the newcomers than that occupied by those who had been in the country for generations. Historians of "genteel" culture in post-Civil War America have similarly suggested that the intensity with which its partisans held to their faith was a function of their concern to resist displacement by the new mass culture rooted in the vulgar civilization of the urban, industrial America they saw growing up all around them. "In the real world of cultural conflict," reports Stow Persons, "the status of the high culture of which the gentry were always the patrons and practitioners has been found by many observers to [have been] precarious in the extreme." Finding themselves being shouldered aside, they sought to maintain their influence by a vigorous, if cultivated, insistence on the continuing relevance of their values. "The genteel authors," argues another historian of their thought and writing, "were significant because they were the architects of a culture that embodied conservatism in a threatening age." Partisans of reform, too, have been identified as no less status-conscious than their explicitly conservative compatriots. Support for abolitionism, argues David Donald, can be linked to the declining status of its advocates: "Descended from old and socially prominent Northeastern families, reared in a faith of aggressive piety and moral endeavor, educated for conservative leadership, these young men and women who reached maturity in the 1830s faced a strange and hostile world. Social and economic leadership was being transferred from the country to the city, from the farmer to the manufacturer, from the preacher to the corporation attorney ... Expecting to lead, these young people found no followers. They were an elite without a function, a displaced class in American society ... their appeal for reform was a strident call for their own class to re-exert its former social dominance." Perhaps the most familiar attempt to use this construct in the clarification of an historical situation has been made in relation to the American Progressives. Their concern to contain, direct, and regulate the forces of big business, argues Richard Hofstadter in *The Age of Reform*, was a function of the fact that they as clergymen, academics, journalists, and lawyers felt that their position in American society was being undermined by the elites created by America's emergence as a business civilization. Progressive opposition to those elites was thus rooted in a strong desire to limit the growth and influence of the new groups and to preserve that of the old. "Progressivism," contends Hofstadter, "was to a very considerable extent led by men who suffered from the events of their time not through a shrinkage in their means but through the changed pattern in the distribution of deference and power. The group of educators, clergymen, journalists, and intellectuals with whom Grant can be most closely associated had much in common with the men and women described by these commentators. Their rural or small town backgrounds, their Christian upbringing, their humane education, and their own involvement in the life of the mind left them badly equipped to respond in positive terms to the new urban and industrial society growing up around them. Their ideology was not, to be sure, the effete conflict-avoiding construct of the genteel tradition, nor did it always – as the case of Grant himself makes clear – manifest itself in an uncomplicated equivalent of American nativism. But if its content frequently differed, it was nonetheless shaped by a similar concern that old values be asserted in the face of change. Like other Canadians of his type and generation – George Denison, George Parkin, Stephen Leacock, Andrew MacPhail, J.A. Cooper, James Cappon, Archibald MacMechan, Maurice Hutton – Grant, deeply disturbed by what the emergence of the new civilization implied for the future of people like him and ideas like his, sought to maintain the influence of both by linking the survival of the good and the true to the dominance of leaders and principles cut from the same cloth as he was. See F.M.L. Thompson, *English Landed Society in the Nineteenth Century* (London: Routledge and Kegan Paul, 1963), 4; John Higham, *Strangers in the Land: Patterns of American Nativism 1860–1925* (New Brunswick, NJ: Rutgers University Press, 1955); John Higham, "Another Look at Nativism," *The Catholic Historical Review*, 44, July 1958, 147–58; Stow Persons, *The Decline of American Gentility* (New York: Columbia University Press, 1973), vii; John Tomsich, *A Genteel Endeavor: American Culture and Politics in the Gilded Age* (Stanford: Stanford University Press, 1971), 195; David Donald, *Lincoln Reconsidered: Essays on the Civil War Era* (New York: Knopf, 1956), 33–4; Richard Hofstadter, "The Status Revolution and Progressive Leaders," in his *The Age of Reform* (New York: Vintage, 1961), 135; and, for a discussion of the lives and thought of some of Grant's associates and contemporaries, *The Sense of Power* and *The Search for an Ideal.*

91 "Current Events," *Queen's Quarterly*, 8, January 1901, 234–5.
92 "Thanksgiving and Retrospect," 231.

Index